BARAKAMON

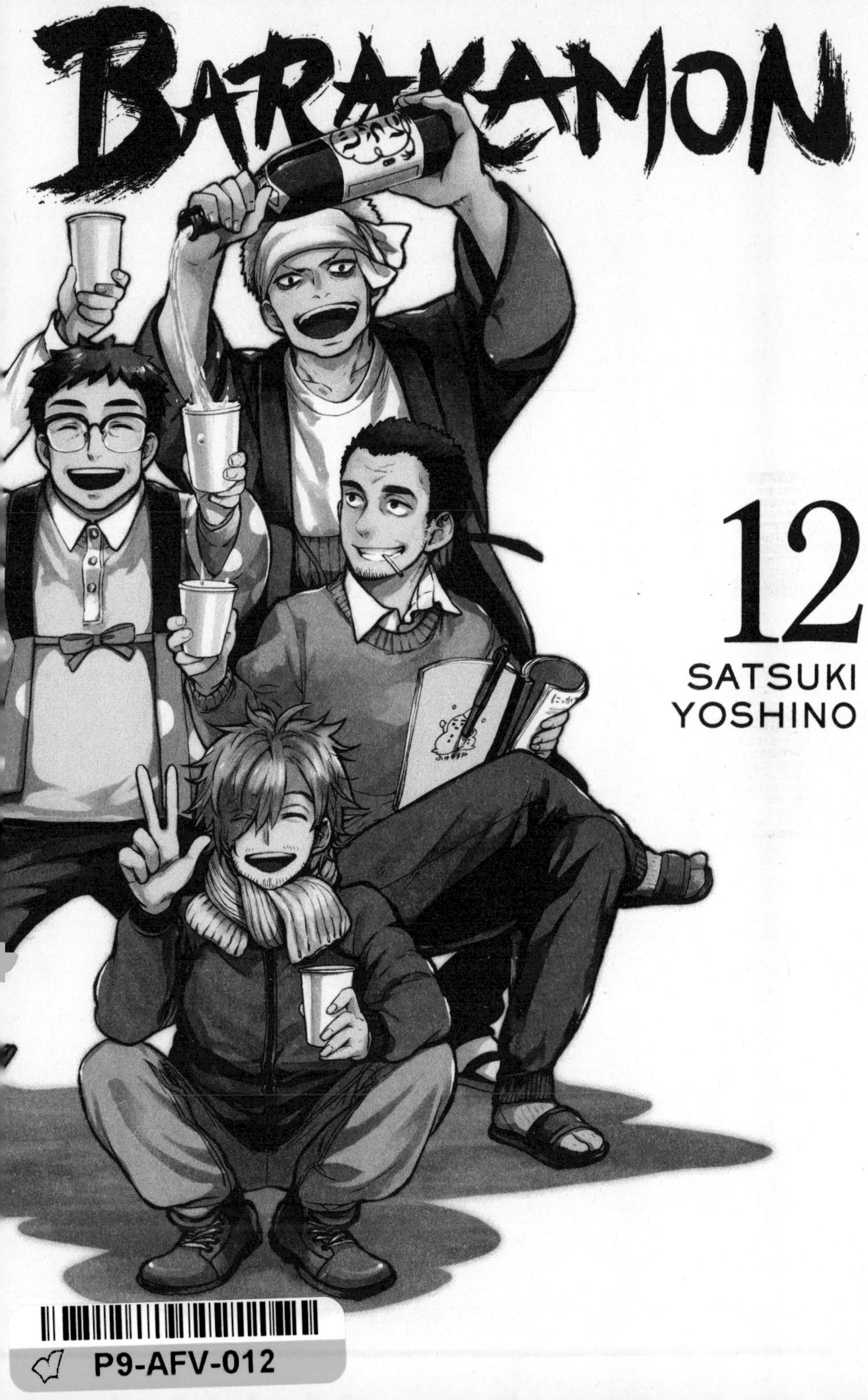

12

SATSUKI YOSHINO

Contents

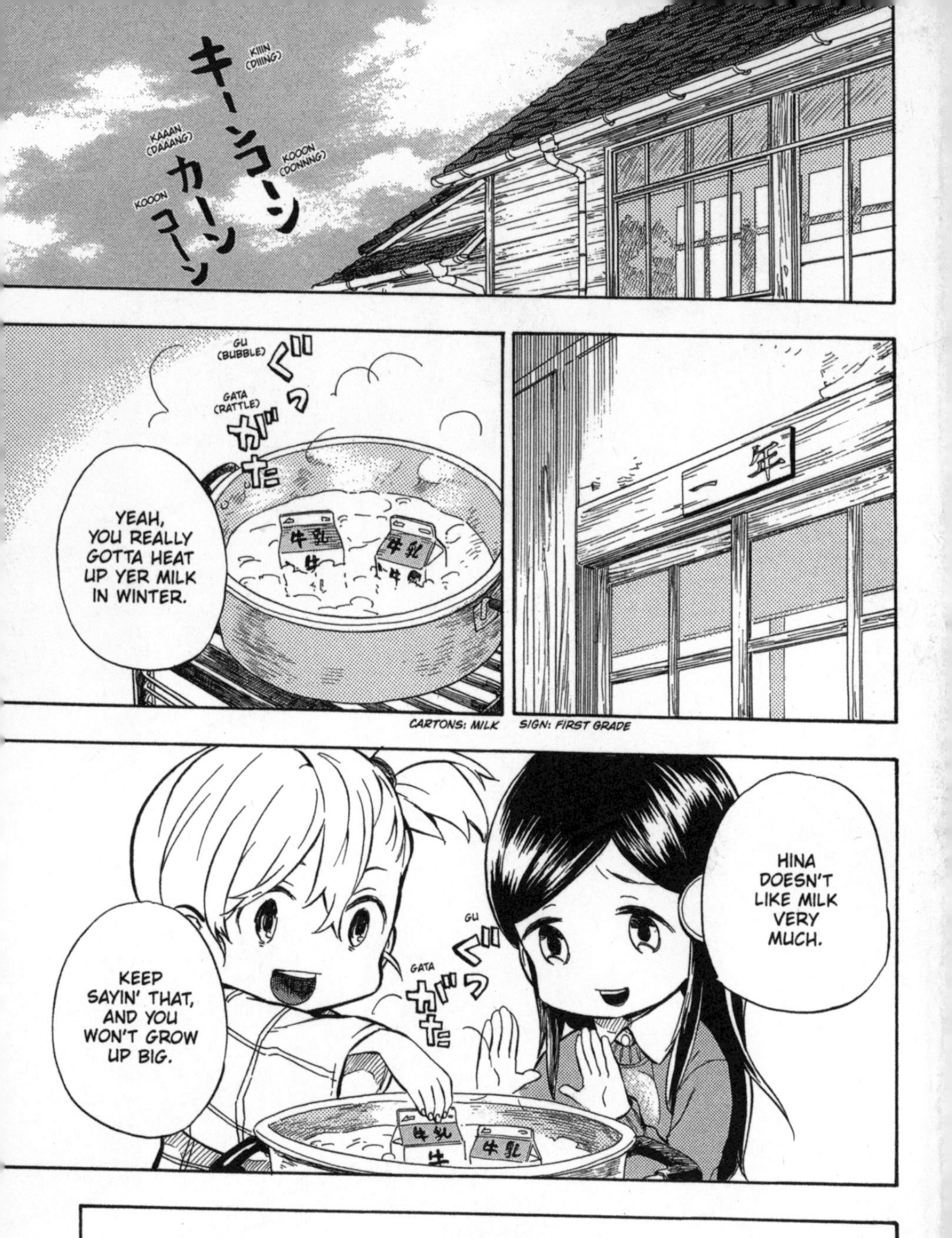
KIIN (DIIING)
KOOON (DONNNG)
KAAAN (DAAANG)
KOOON
GU (BUBBLE)
GATA (RATTLE)
YEAH, YOU REALLY GOTTA HEAT UP YER MILK IN WINTER.
CARTONS: MILK SIGN: FIRST GRADE
HINA DOESN'T LIKE MILK VERY MUCH.
GU
GATA
KEEP SAYIN' THAT, AND YOU WON'T GROW UP BIG.

Act.88

FUTO NARE YO

(Translation: Grow Up Big)

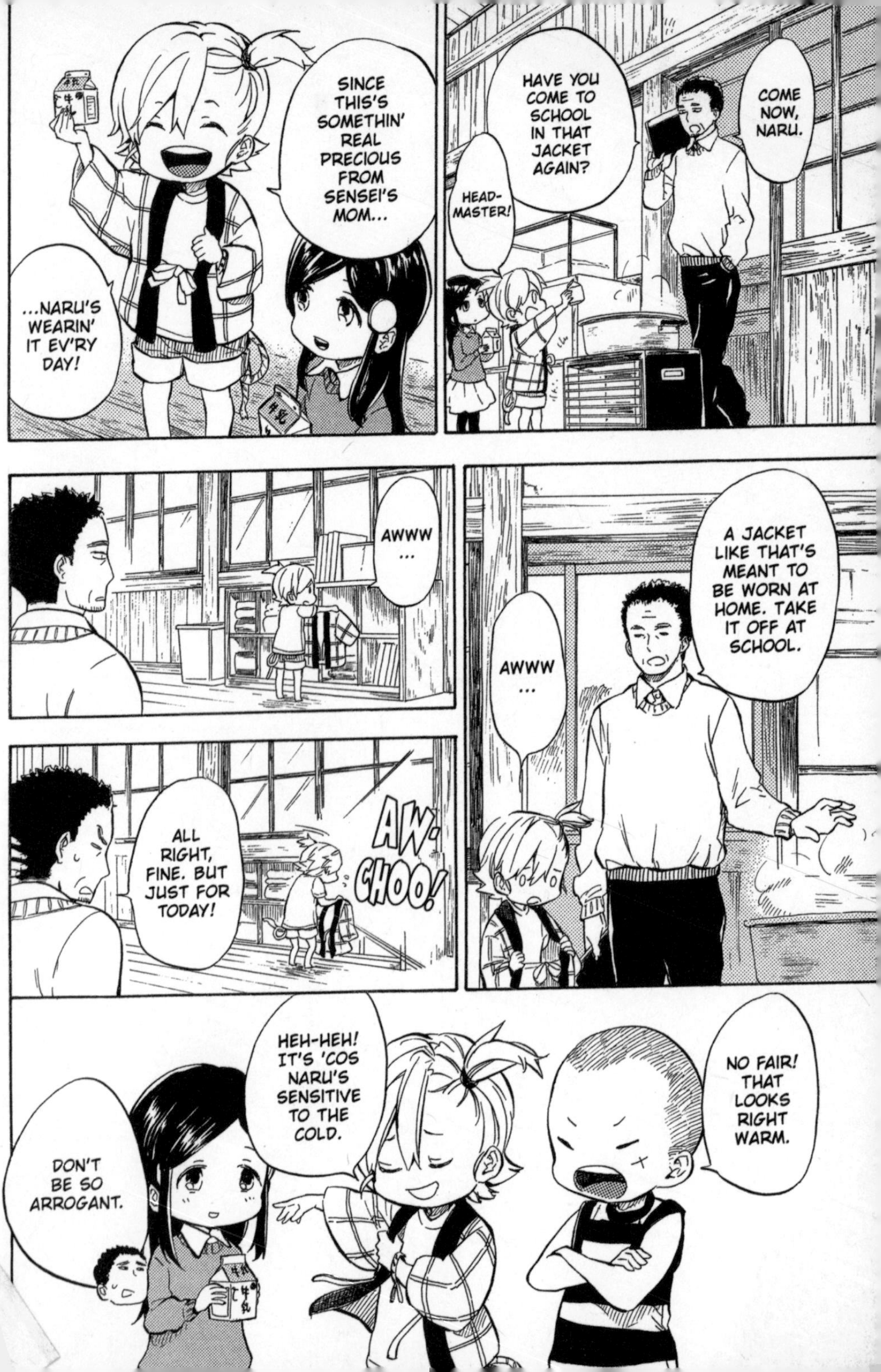
COME NOW, NARU.
HAVE YOU COME TO SCHOOL IN THAT JACKET AGAIN?
HEAD-MASTER!
SINCE THIS'S SOMETHIN' REAL PRECIOUS FROM SENSEI'S MOM...
...NARU'S WEARIN' IT EV'RY DAY!
A JACKET LIKE THAT'S MEANT TO BE WORN AT HOME. TAKE IT OFF AT SCHOOL.
AWWW...
AWWW...
AW-CHOO!
ALL RIGHT, FINE. BUT JUST FOR TODAY!
NO FAIR! THAT LOOKS RIGHT WARM.
HEH-HEH! IT'S 'COS NARU'S SENSITIVE TO THE COLD.
DON'T BE SO ARROGANT.

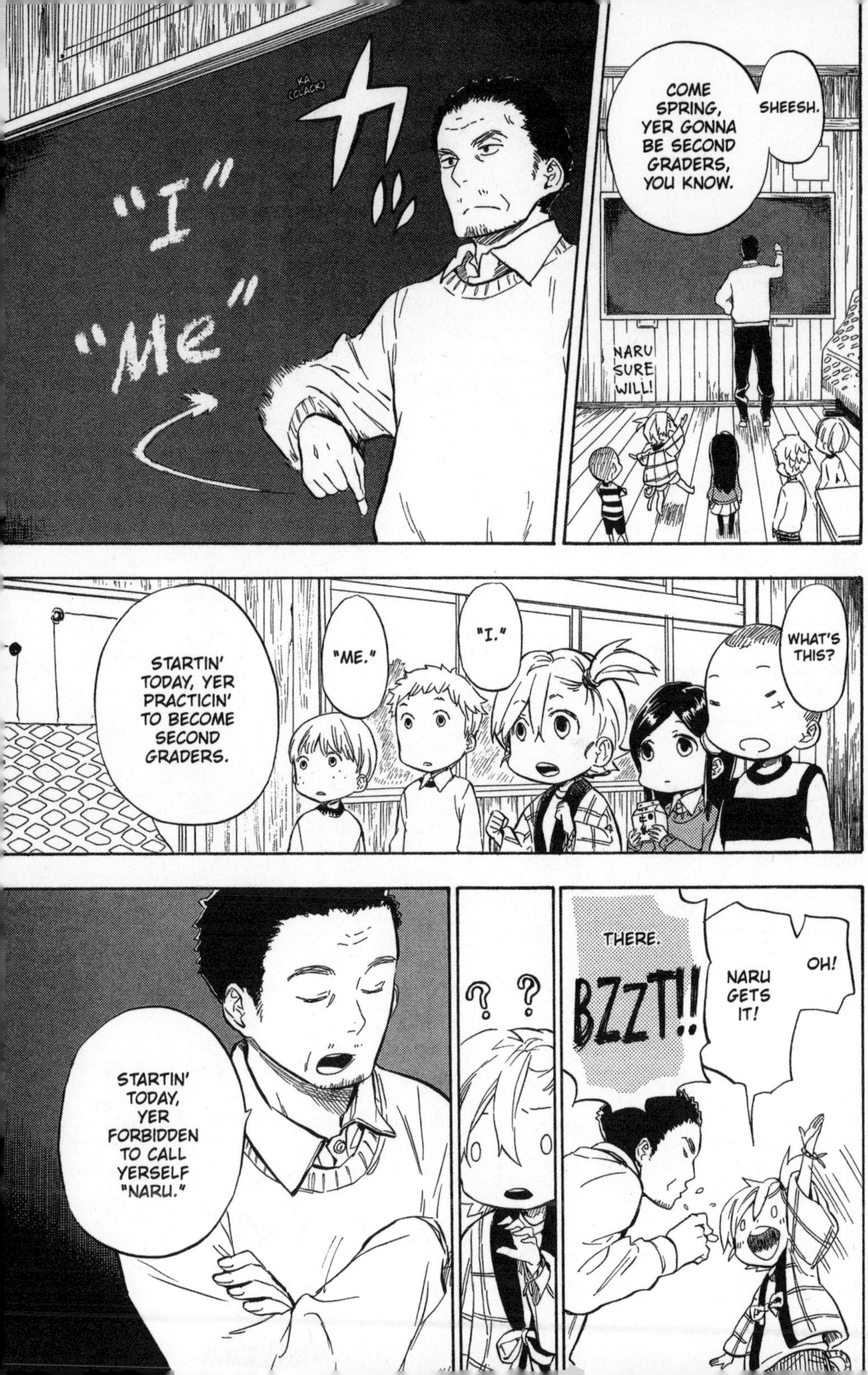
SHEESH.
COME SPRING, YER GONNA BE SECOND GRADERS, YOU KNOW.
NARU SURE WILL!
KA (CLACK)
"I"
"Me"
WHAT'S THIS?
"I."
"ME."
STARTIN' TODAY, YER PRACTICIN' TO BECOME SECOND GRADERS.
OH!
NARU GETS IT!
THERE.
BZZT!!
? ?
STARTIN' TODAY, YER FORBIDDEN TO CALL YERSELF "NARU."

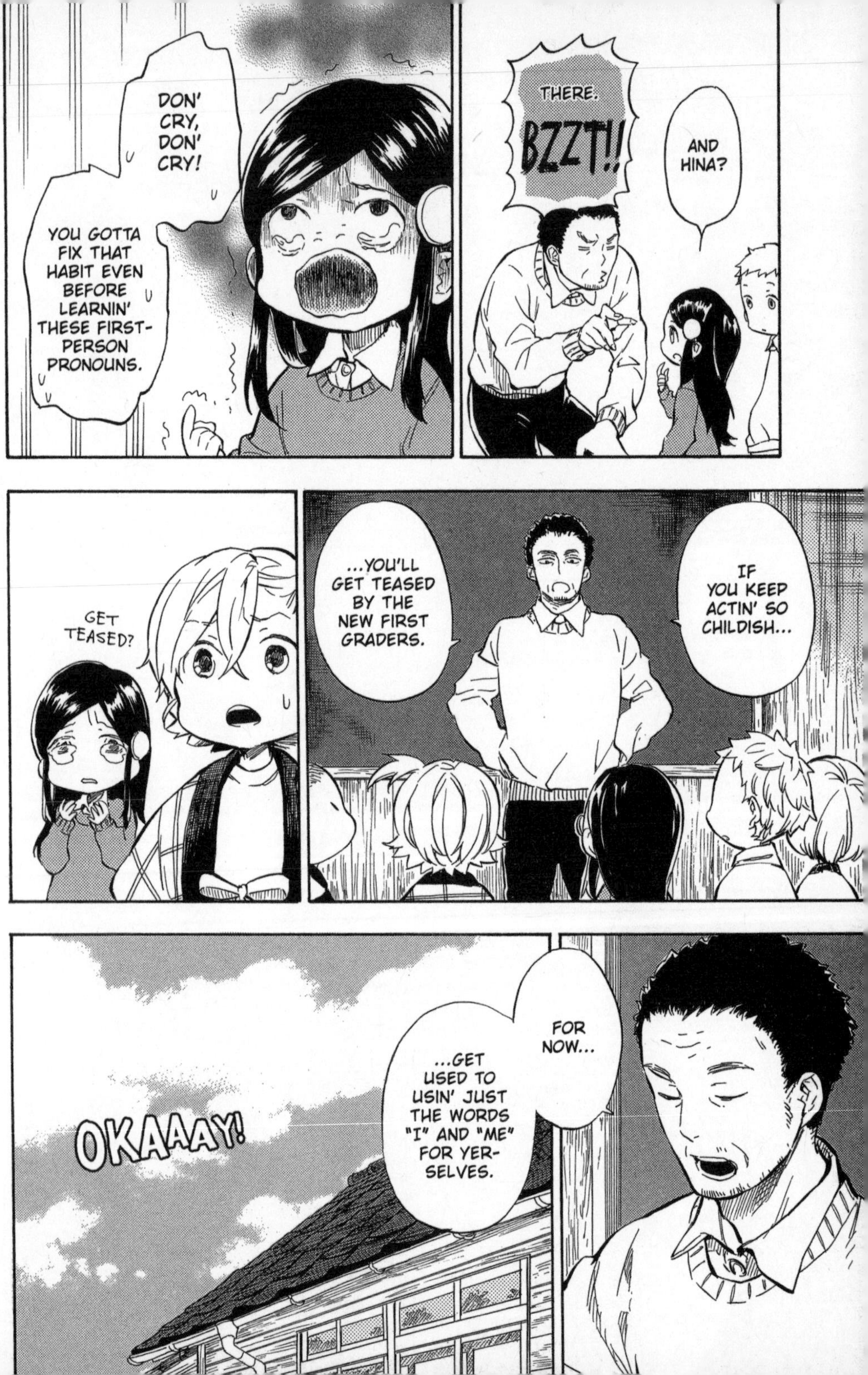
AND HINA?
THERE. BZZT!!
DON' CRY, DON' CRY!
YOU GOTTA FIX THAT HABIT EVEN BEFORE LEARNIN' THESE FIRST-PERSON PRONOUNS.
IF YOU KEEP ACTIN' SO CHILDISH...
...YOU'LL GET TEASED BY THE NEW FIRST GRADERS.
GET TEASED?
FOR NOW...
...GET USED TO USIN' JUST THE WORDS "I" AND "ME" FOR YER-SELVES.
OKAAAY!

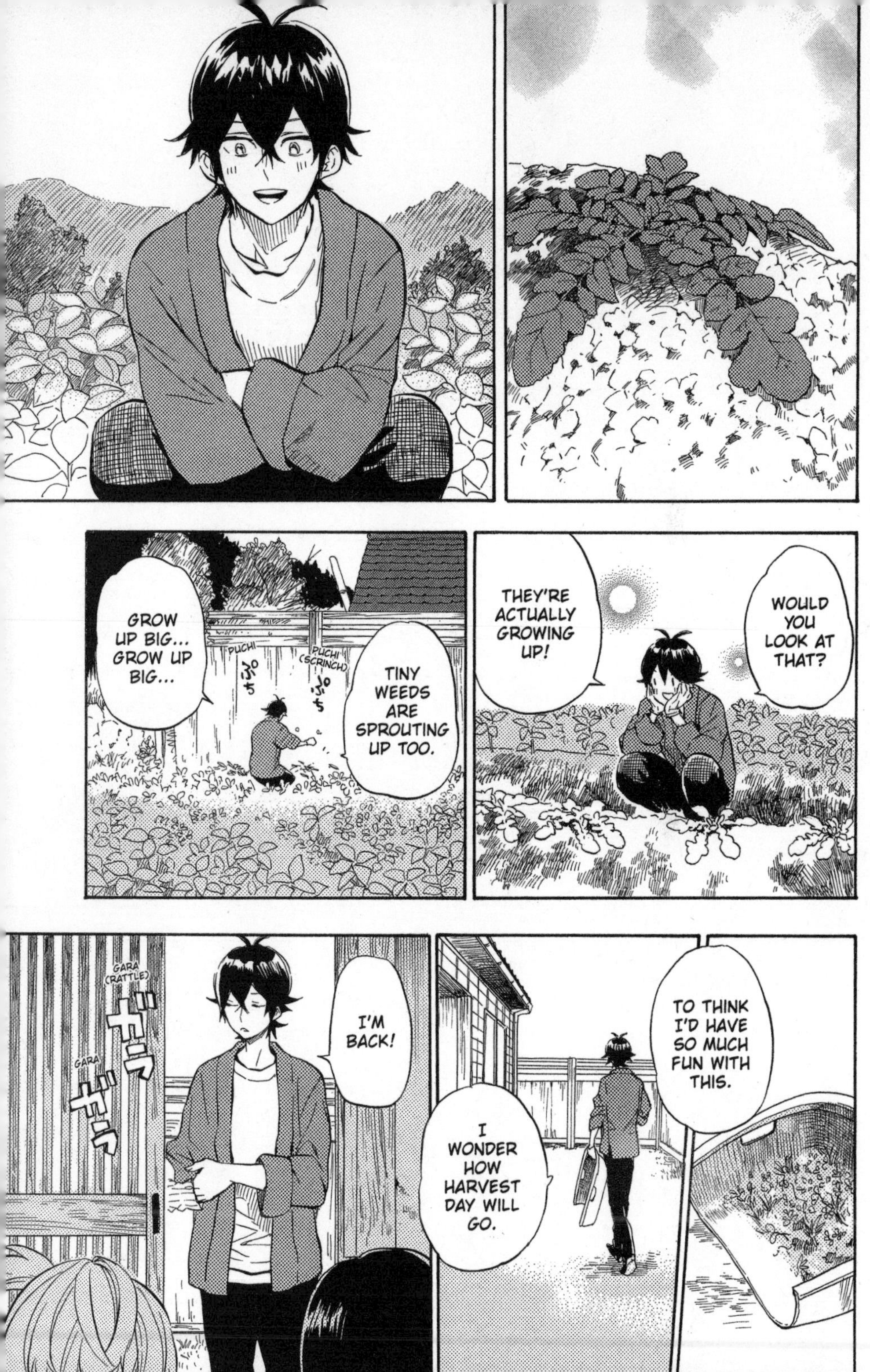
WOULD YOU LOOK AT THAT?
THEY'RE ACTUALLY GROWING UP!
TINY WEEDS ARE SPROUTING UP TOO.
PUCHI (SCRINCH) ぷち
PUCHI ぷち
GROW UP BIG... GROW UP BIG...
TO THINK I'D HAVE SO MUCH FUN WITH THIS.
I WONDER HOW HARVEST DAY WILL GO.
I'M BACK!
GARA (RATTLE) ガラ
GARA ガラ

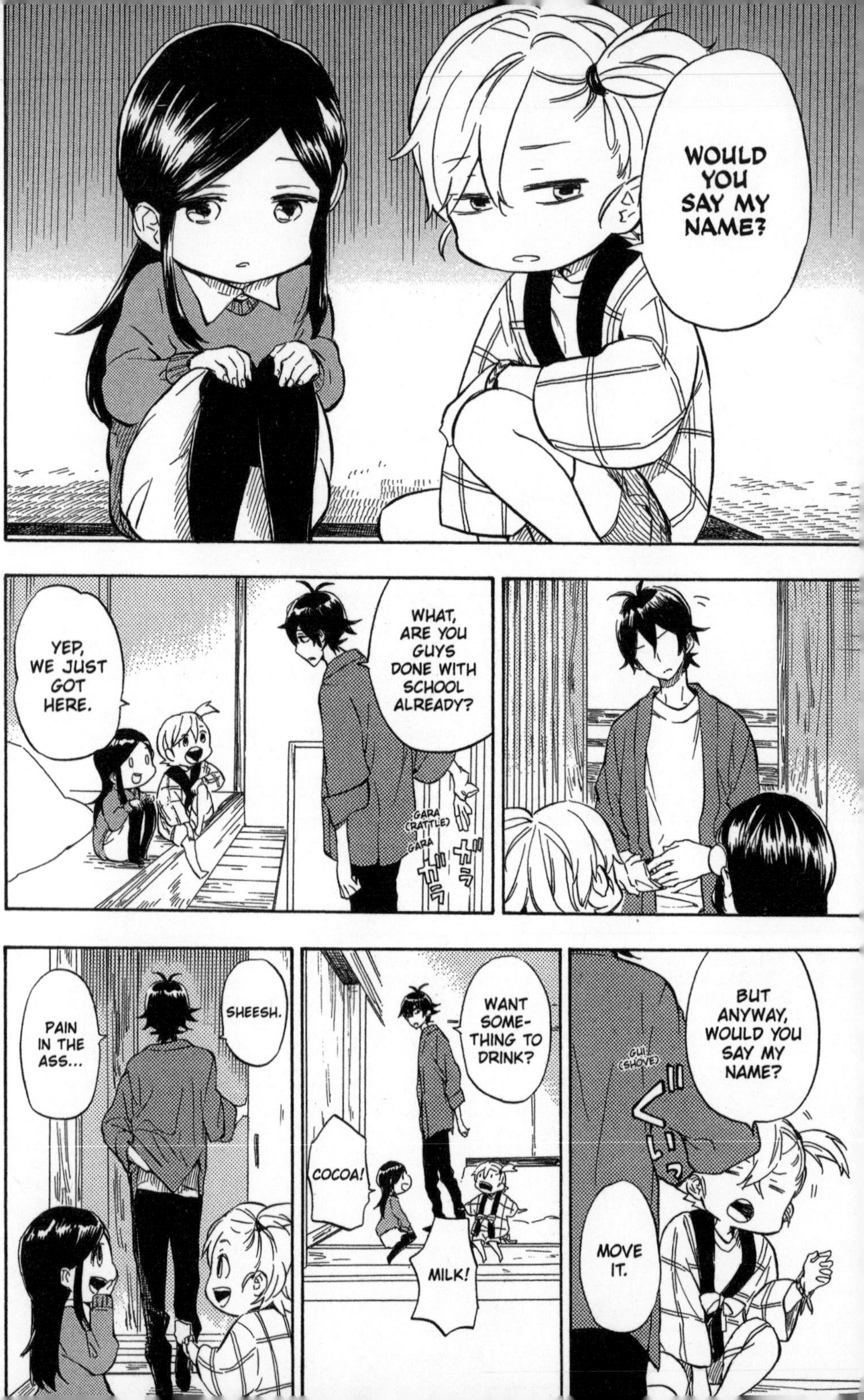
WOULD YOU SAY MY NAME?
WHAT, ARE YOU GUYS DONE WITH SCHOOL ALREADY?
GARA (RATTLE) GARA
YEP, WE JUST GOT HERE.
BUT ANYWAY, WOULD YOU SAY MY NAME?
GUI (SHOVE)
MOVE IT.
WANT SOME-THING TO DRINK?
COCOA!
MILK!
SHEESH.
PAIN IN THE ASS...

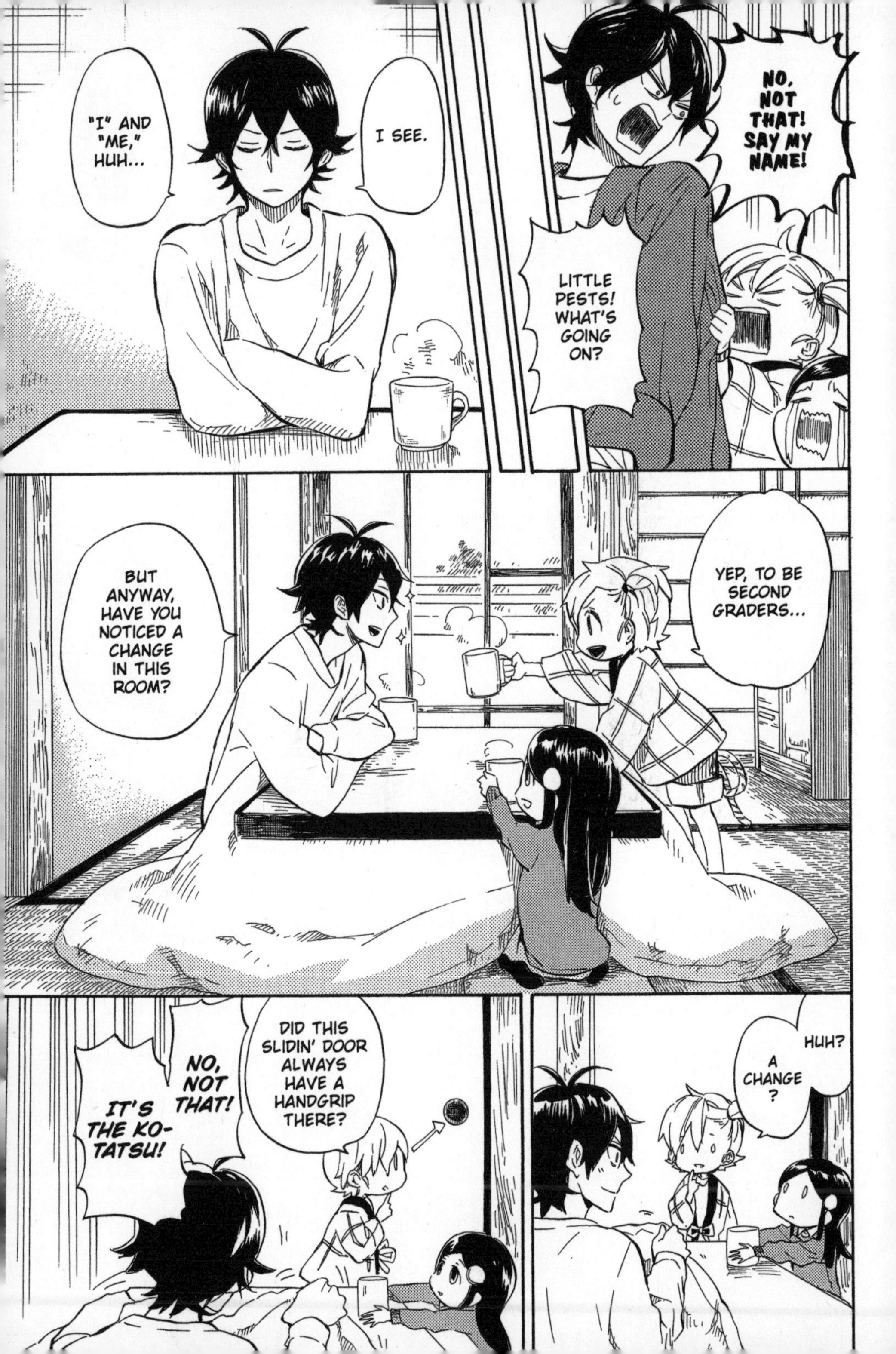
NO, NOT THAT! SAY MY NAME!
LITTLE PESTS! WHAT'S GOING ON?
I SEE.
"I" AND "ME," HUH...
YEP, TO BE SECOND GRADERS...
BUT ANYWAY, HAVE YOU NOTICED A CHANGE IN THIS ROOM?
HUH?
A CHANGE?
DID THIS SLIDIN' DOOR ALWAYS HAVE A HANDGRIP THERE?
NO, NOT THAT!
IT'S THE KO-TATSU!

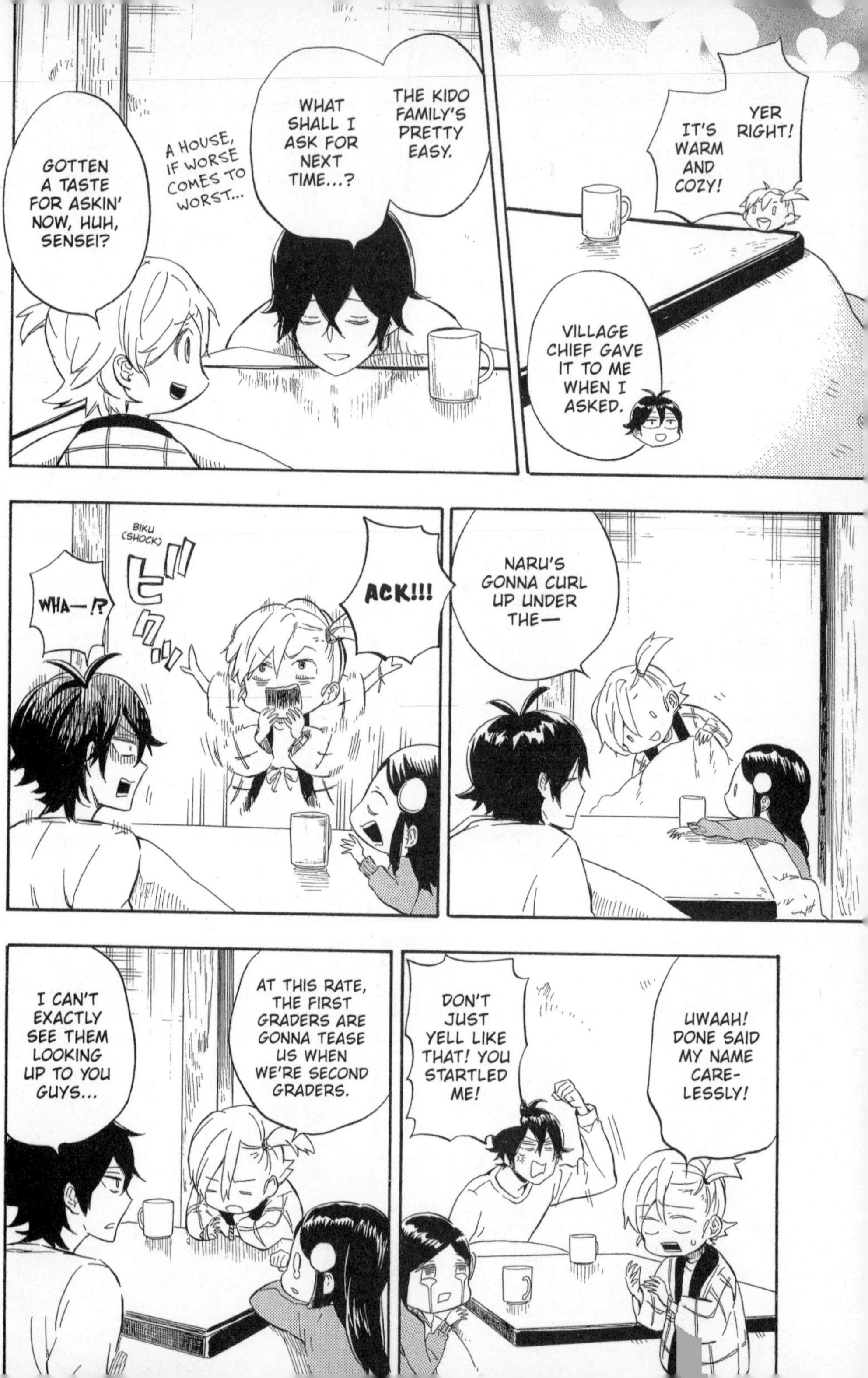
YER RIGHT!
IT'S WARM AND COZY!
VILLAGE CHIEF GAVE IT TO ME WHEN I ASKED.
THE KIDO FAMILY'S PRETTY EASY.
WHAT SHALL I ASK FOR NEXT TIME...?
A HOUSE, IF WORSE COMES TO WORST...
GOTTEN A TASTE FOR ASKIN' NOW, HUH, SENSEI?
NARU'S GONNA CURL UP UNDER THE—
ACK!!!
BIKU (SHOCK)
ビクッ
WHA—!?
UWAAH! DONE SAID MY NAME CARE-LESSLY!
DON'T JUST YELL LIKE THAT! YOU STARTLED ME!
AT THIS RATE, THE FIRST GRADERS ARE GONNA TEASE US WHEN WE'RE SECOND GRADERS.
I CAN'T EXACTLY SEE THEM LOOKING UP TO YOU GUYS...

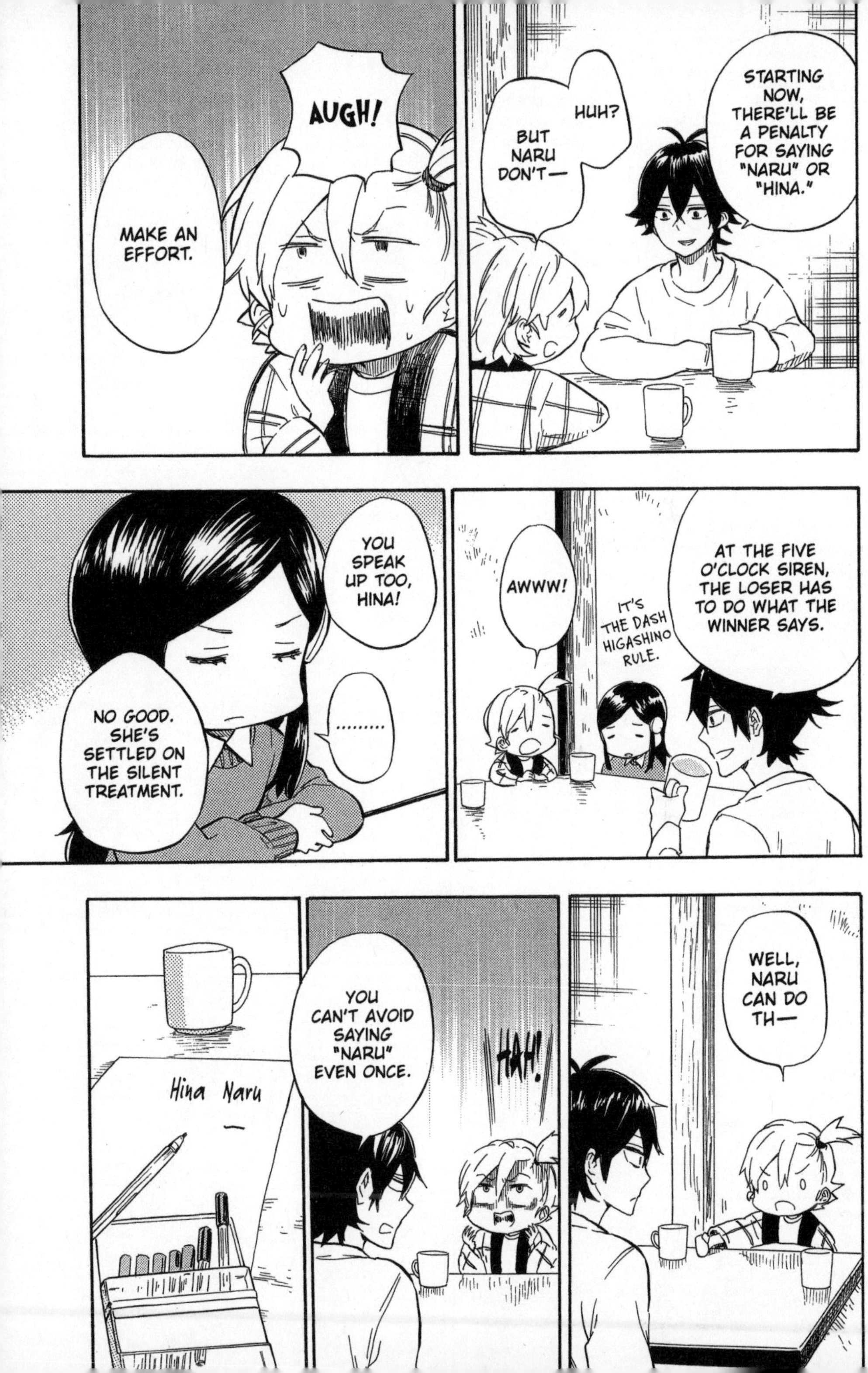
STARTING NOW, THERE'LL BE A PENALTY FOR SAYING "NARU" OR "HINA."
HUH?
BUT NARU DON'T—
AUGH!
MAKE AN EFFORT.
AT THE FIVE O'CLOCK SIREN, THE LOSER HAS TO DO WHAT THE WINNER SAYS.
AWWW!
IT'S THE DASH HIGASHINO RULE.
YOU SPEAK UP TOO, HINA!
....
NO GOOD. SHE'S SETTLED ON THE SILENT TREATMENT.
WELL, NARU CAN DO TH—
HAH!
YOU CAN'T AVOID SAYING "NARU" EVEN ONCE.
Hina Naru

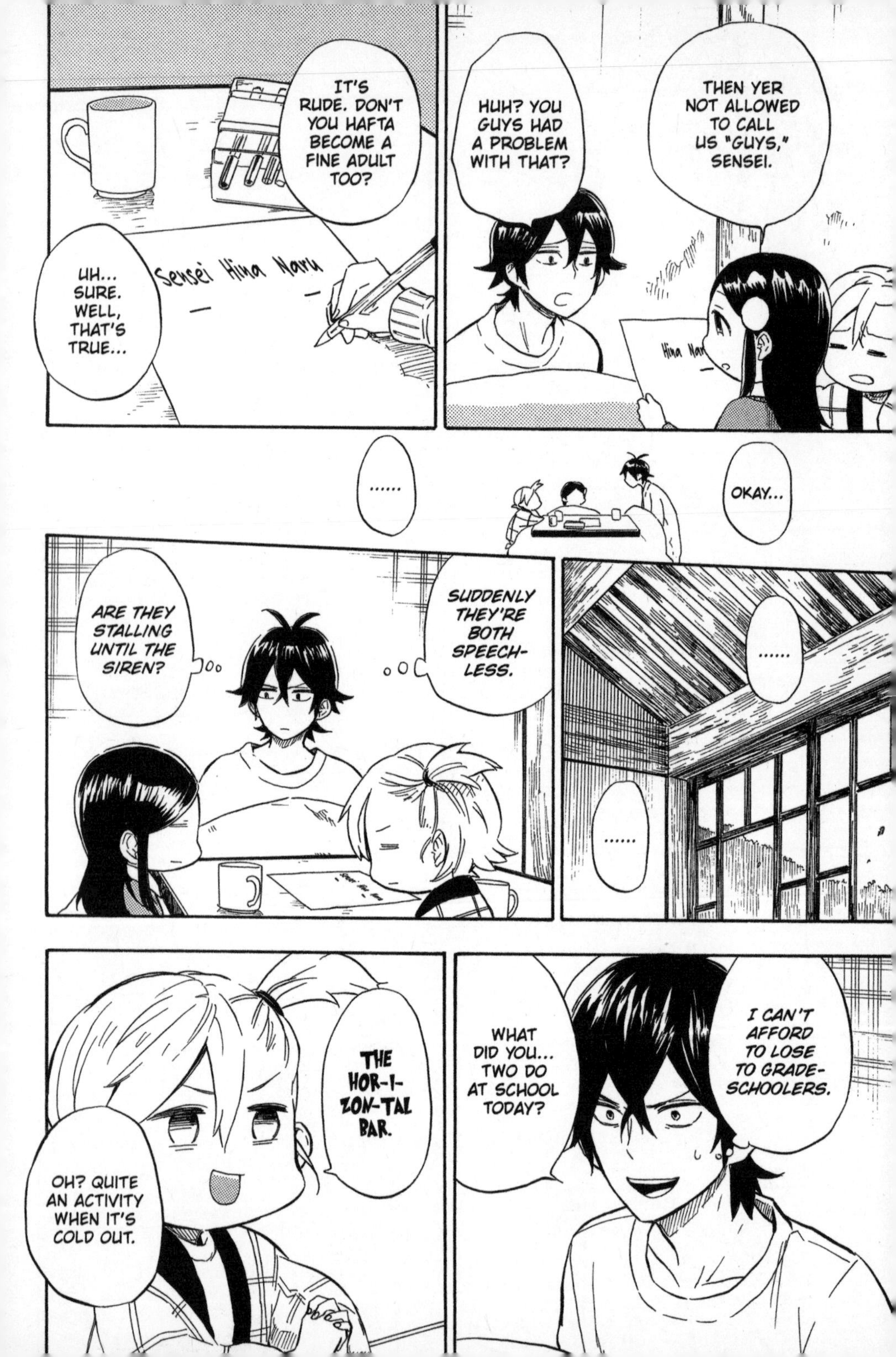
THEN YER NOT ALLOWED TO CALL US "GUYS," SENSEI.
HUH? YOU GUYS HAD A PROBLEM WITH THAT?
IT'S RUDE. DON'T YOU HAFTA BECOME A FINE ADULT TOO?
Sensei Hina Naru
UH... SURE. WELL, THAT'S TRUE...
OKAY...
......
......
......
SUDDENLY THEY'RE BOTH SPEECHLESS.
ARE THEY STALLING UNTIL THE SIREN?
I CAN'T AFFORD TO LOSE TO GRADE-SCHOOLERS.
WHAT DID YOU... TWO DO AT SCHOOL TODAY?
THE HOR-I-ZON-TAL BAR.
OH? QUITE AN ACTIVITY WHEN IT'S COLD OUT.

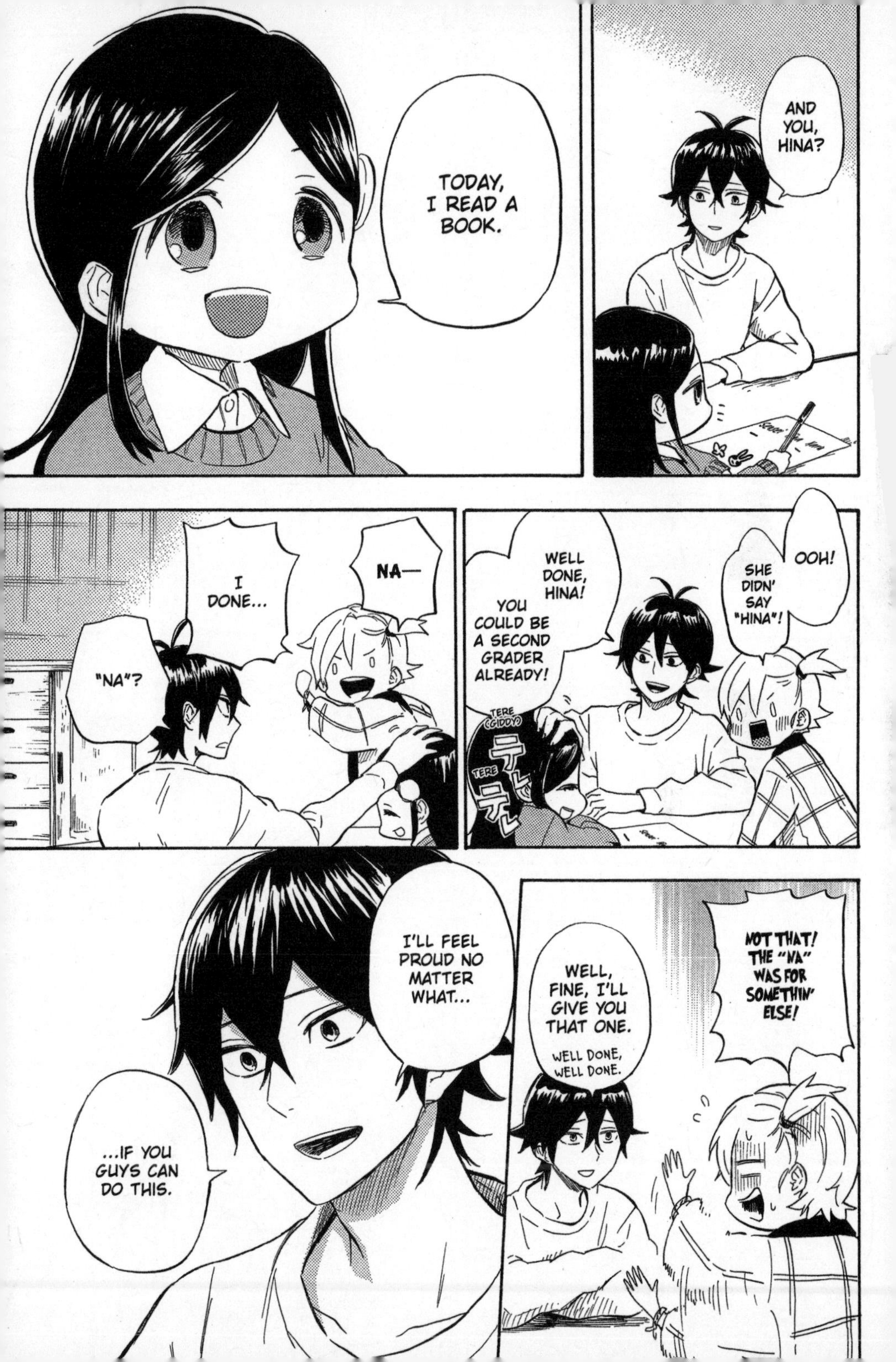
AND YOU, HINA?
TODAY, I READ A BOOK.
OOH!
SHE DIDN' SAY "HINA"!
WELL DONE, HINA!
YOU COULD BE A SECOND GRADER ALREADY!
TERE (GIDDY) TERE
NA—
I DONE...
"NA"?
NOT THAT! THE "NA" WAS FOR SOMETHIN' ELSE!
WELL, FINE, I'LL GIVE YOU THAT ONE.
WELL DONE, WELL DONE.
I'LL FEEL PROUD NO MATTER WHAT...
...IF YOU GUYS CAN DO THIS.

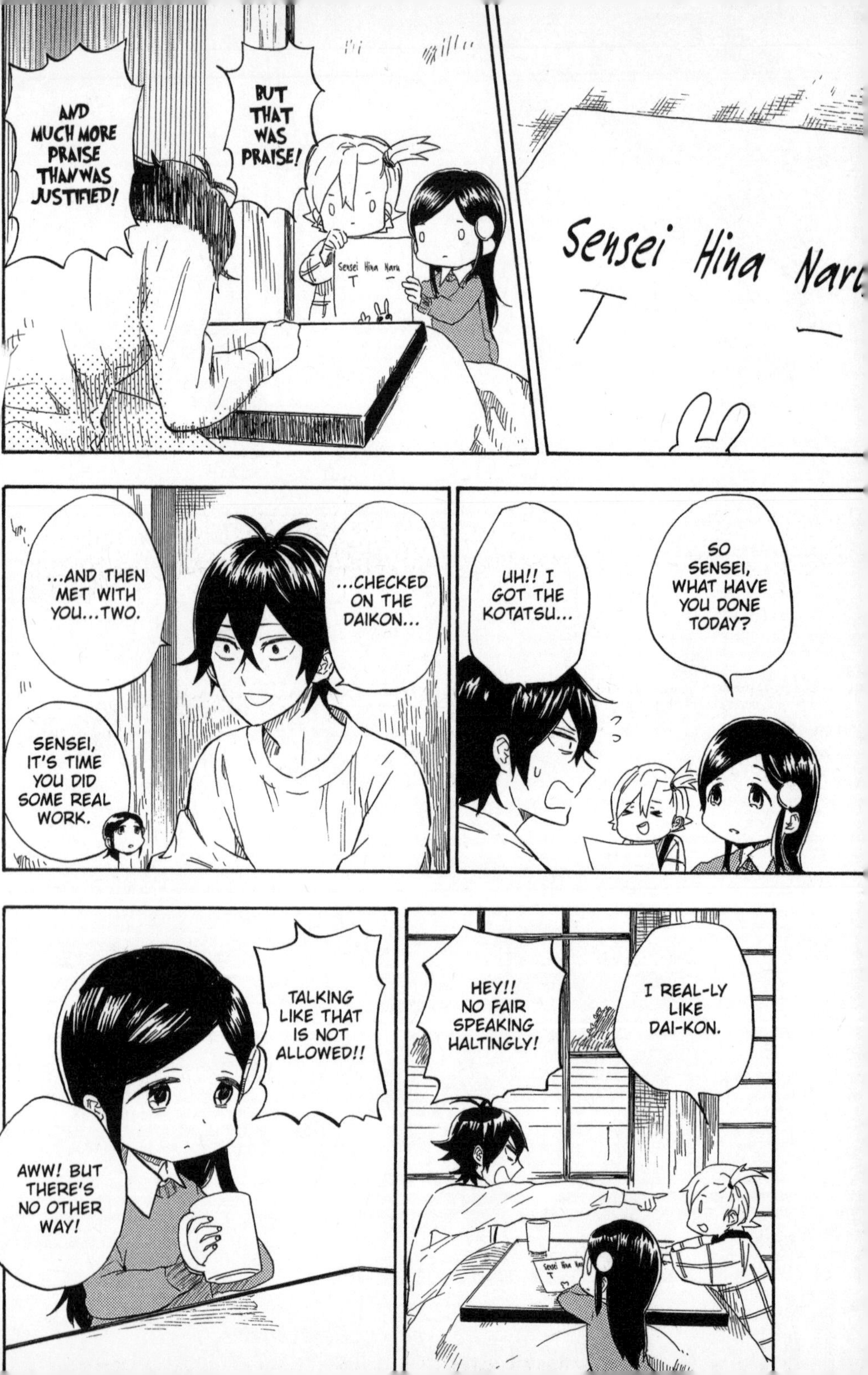
Sensei Hina Naru
BUT THAT WAS PRAISE!
AND MUCH MORE PRAISE THAN WAS JUSTIFIED!
SO SENSEI, WHAT HAVE YOU DONE TODAY?
UH!! I GOT THE KOTATSU...
...CHECKED ON THE DAIKON...
...AND THEN MET WITH YOU...TWO.
SENSEI, IT'S TIME YOU DID SOME REAL WORK.
I REAL-LY LIKE DAI-KON.
HEY!! NO FAIR SPEAKING HALTINGLY!
TALKING LIKE THAT IS NOT ALLOWED!!
AWW! BUT THERE'S NO OTHER WAY!

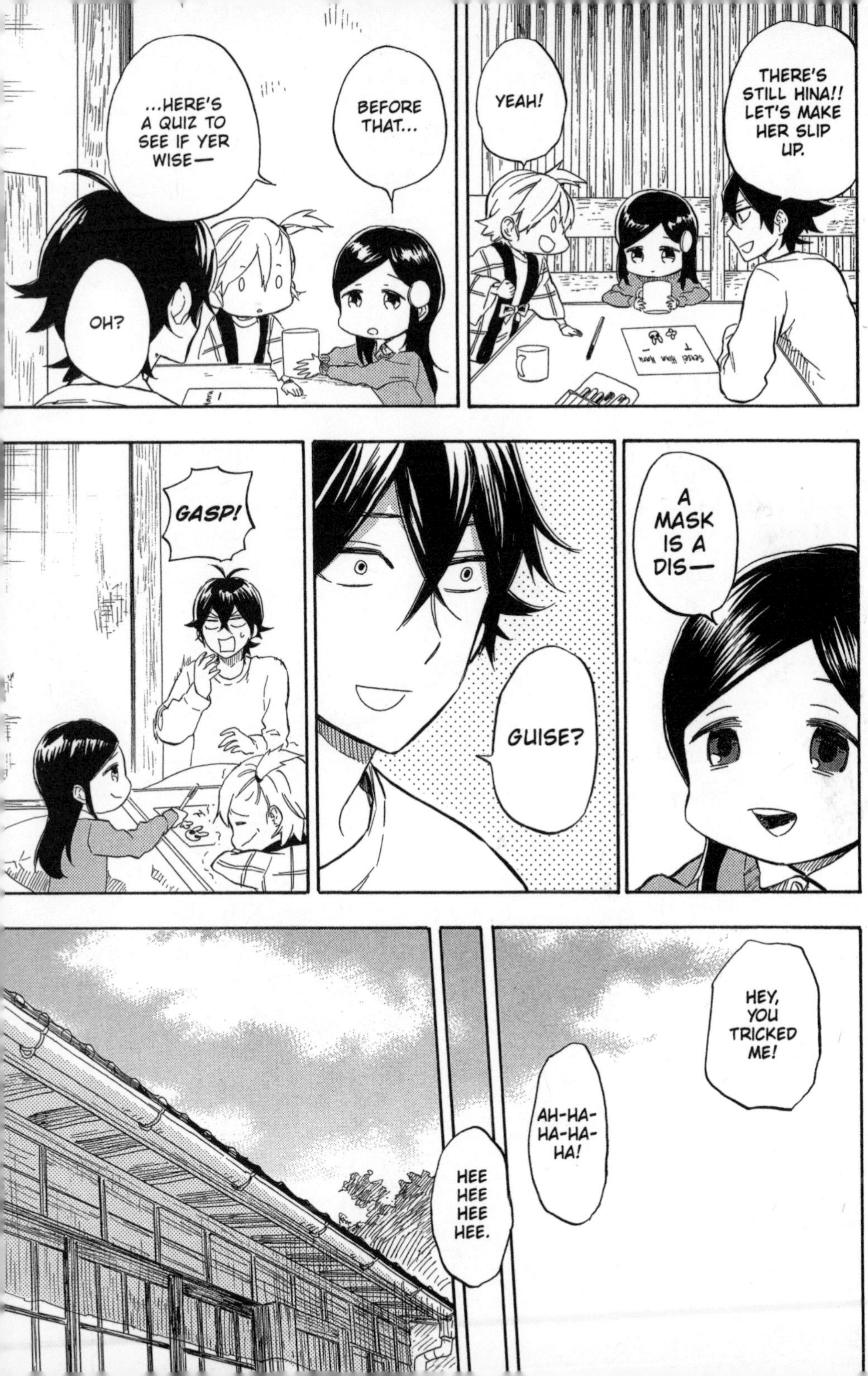
THERE'S STILL HINA!! LET'S MAKE HER SLIP UP.
YEAH!
BEFORE THAT...
...HERE'S A QUIZ TO SEE IF YER WISE—
OH?
A MASK IS A DIS—
GUISE?
GASP!
HEY, YOU TRICKED ME!
AH-HA-HA-HA-HA!
HEE HEE HEE HEE.

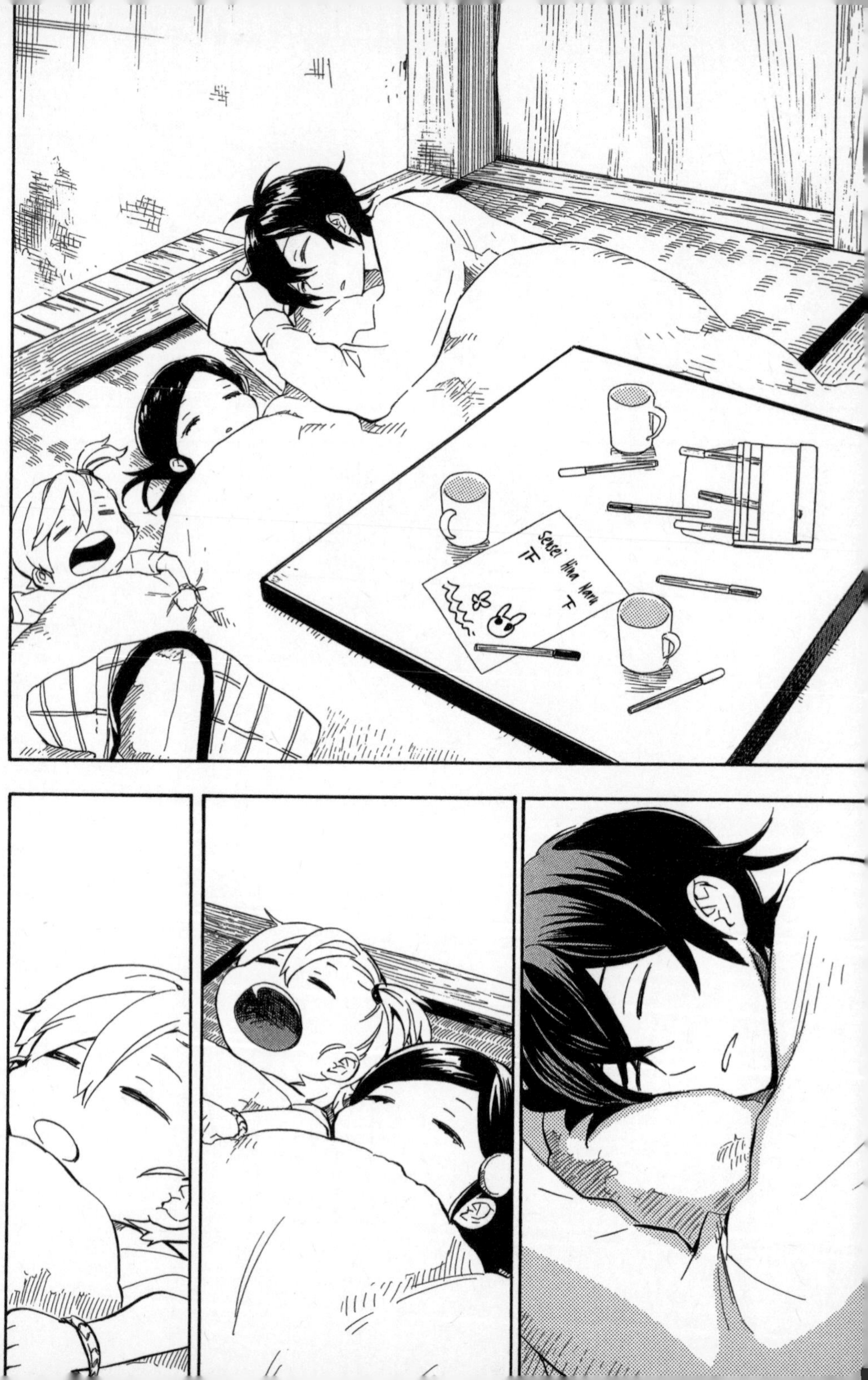
Sensei Hina Naru

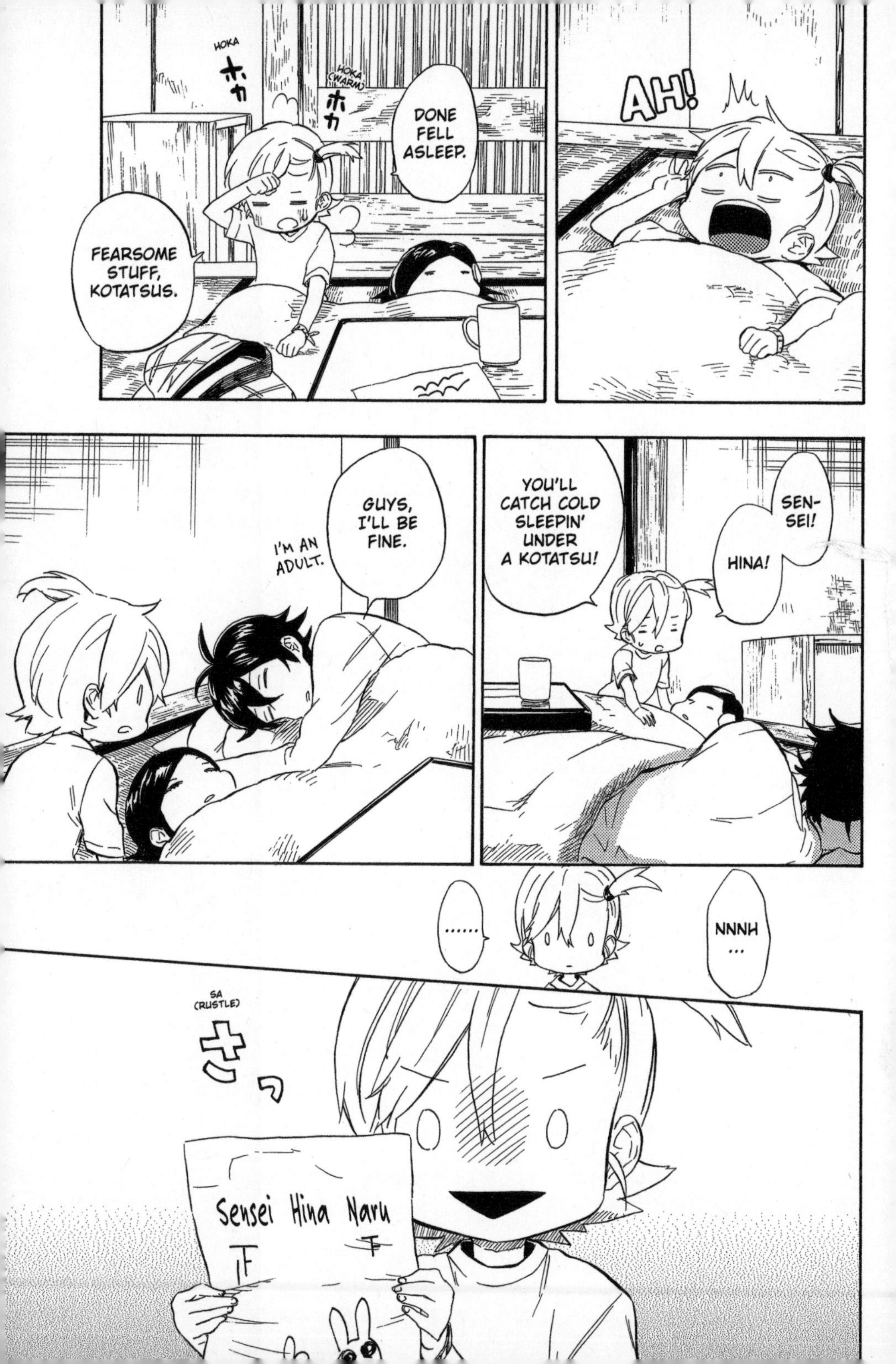
AH!
HOKA
ホカ
HOKA (WARM)
ホカ
DONE FELL ASLEEP.
FEARSOME STUFF, KOTATSUS.
SEN- SEI!
HINA!
YOU'LL CATCH COLD SLEEPIN' UNDER A KOTATSU!
GUYS, I'LL BE FINE.
I'M AN ADULT.
NNNH ...
....
SA (RUSTLE)
さっ
Sensei Hina Naru

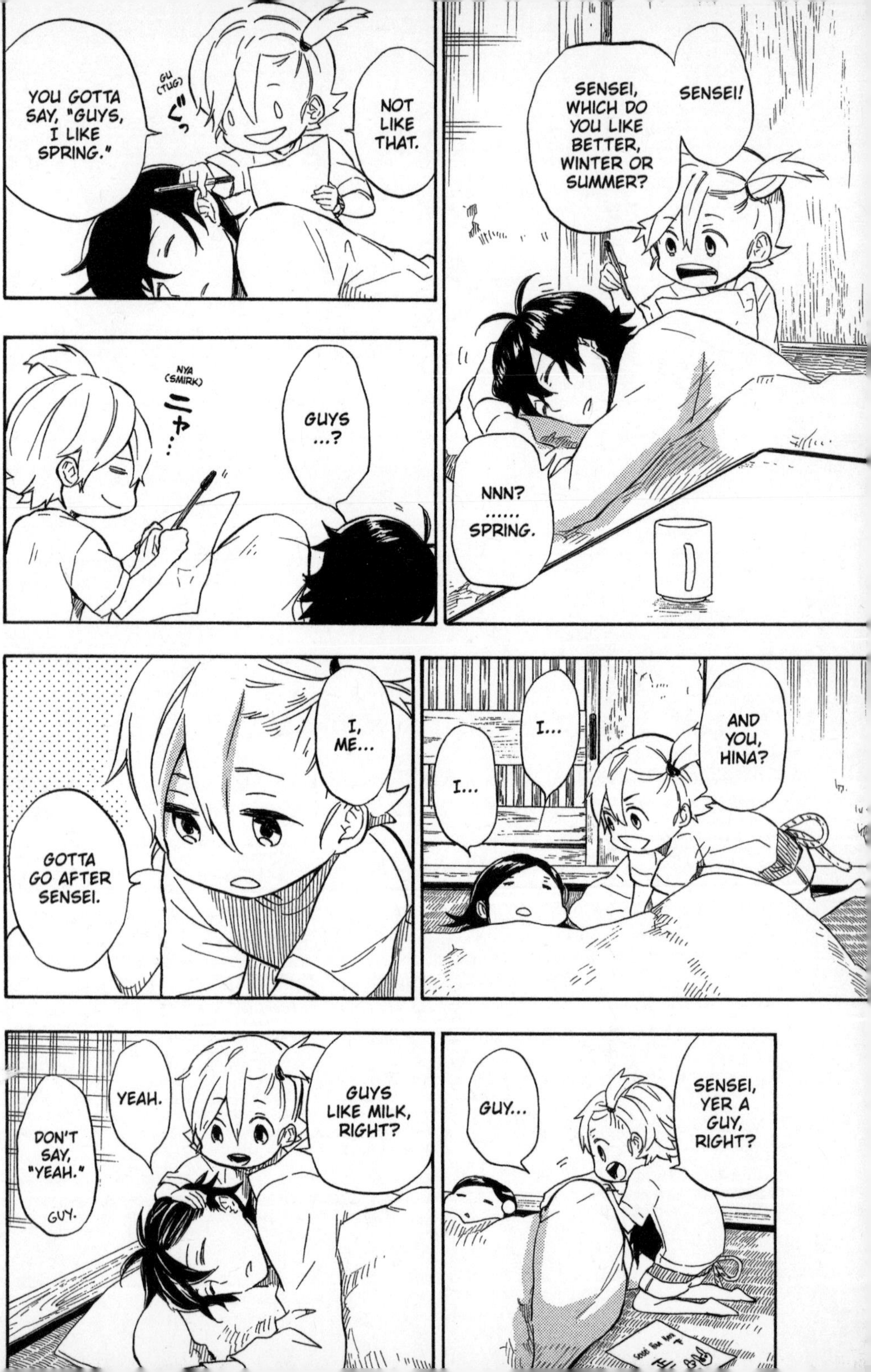
SENSEI!
SENSEI, WHICH DO YOU LIKE BETTER, WINTER OR SUMMER?
NNN? ...... SPRING.
NOT LIKE THAT.
GU (TUG)
ぐっ
YOU GOTTA SAY, "GUYS, I LIKE SPRING."
GUYS ...?
NYA (SMIRK)
ニャ...
AND YOU, HINA?
I...
I...
I, ME...
GOTTA GO AFTER SENSEI.
SENSEI, YER A GUY, RIGHT?
GUY...
GUYS LIKE MILK, RIGHT?
YEAH.
DON'T SAY, "YEAH."
GUY.

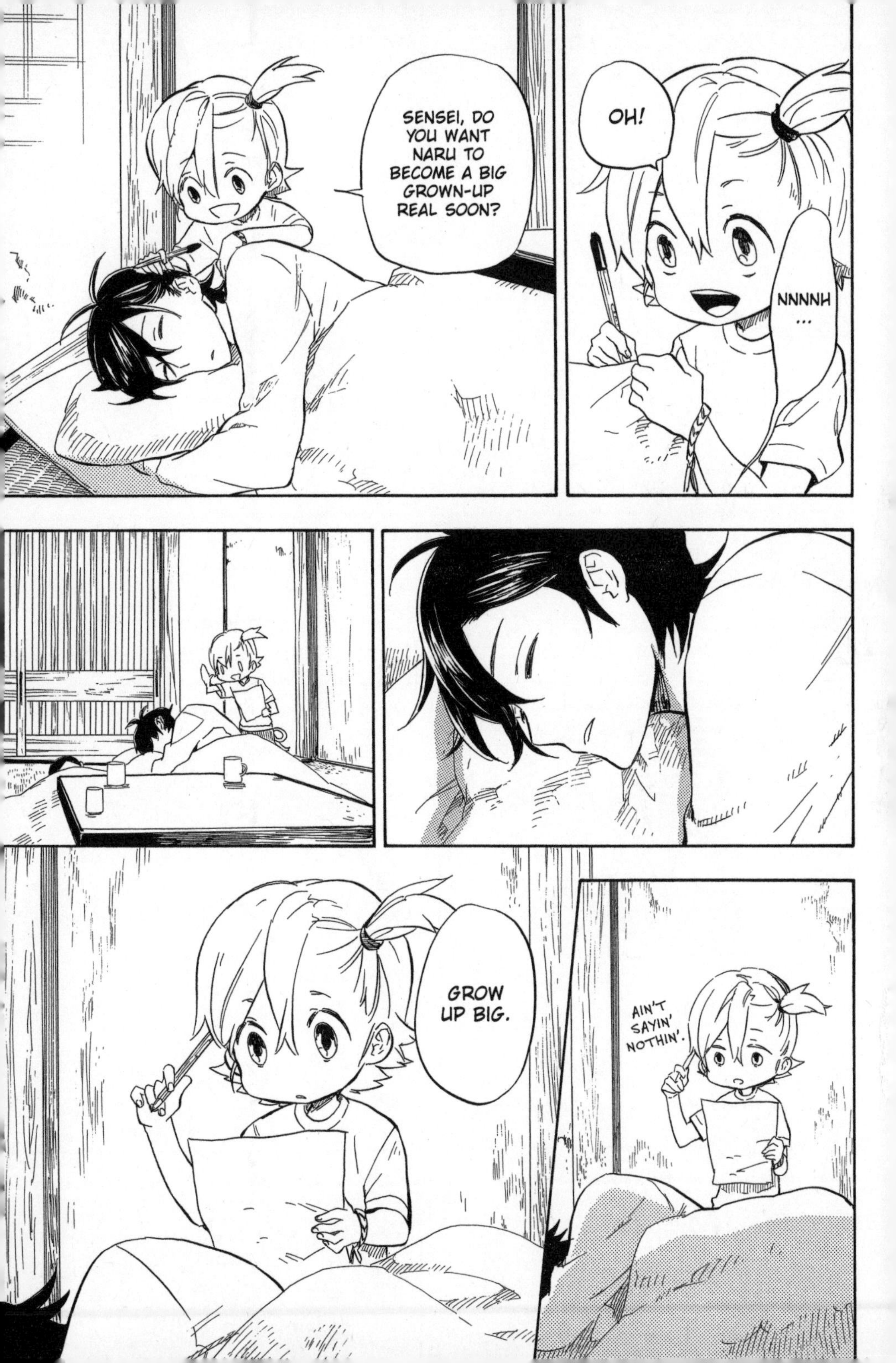
OH!
NNNNH...
SENSEI, DO YOU WANT NARU TO BECOME A BIG GROWN-UP REAL SOON?
AIN'T SAYIN' NOTHIN'.
GROW UP BIG.

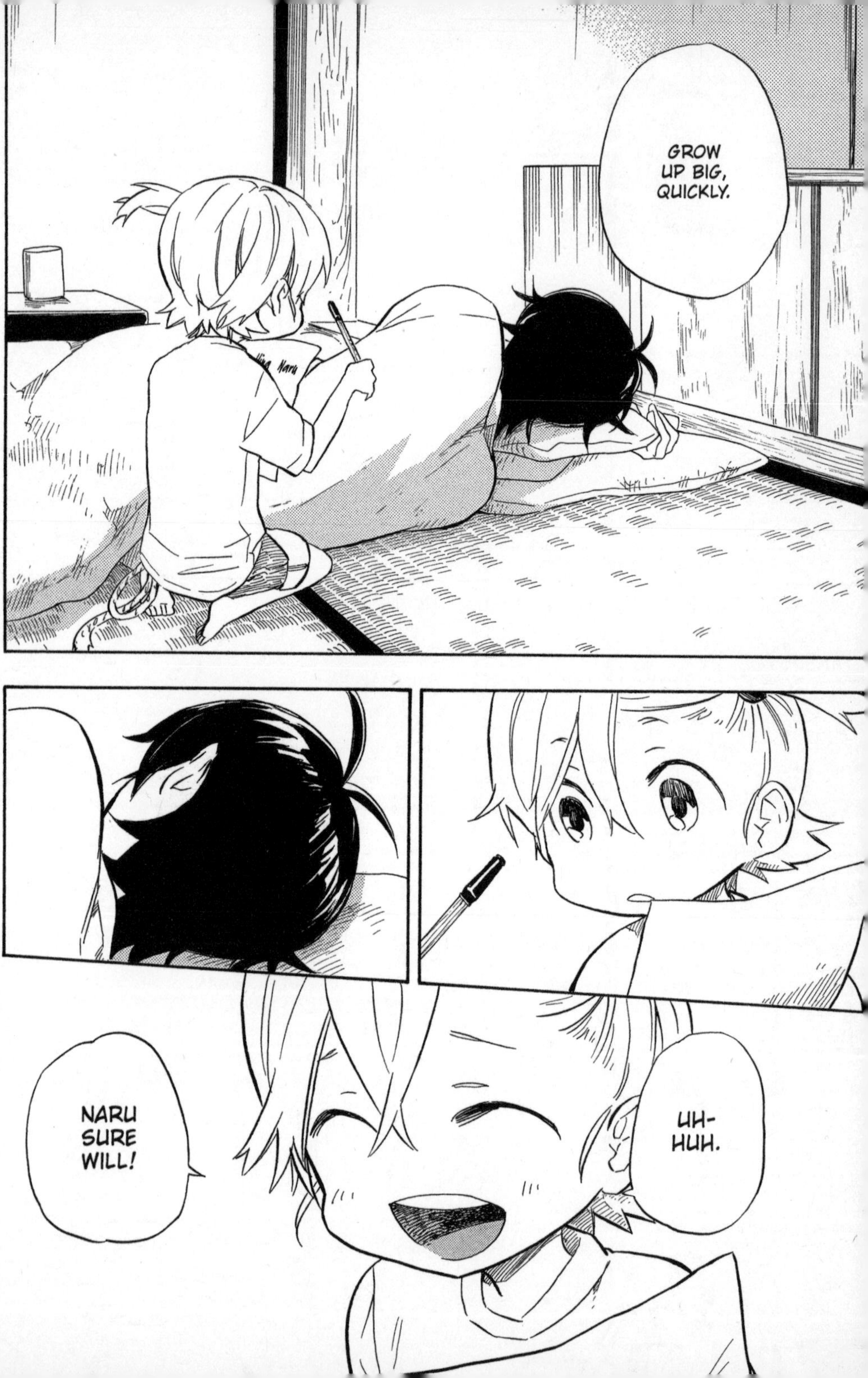
GROW UP BIG, QUICKLY.
UH-HUH.
NARU SURE WILL!

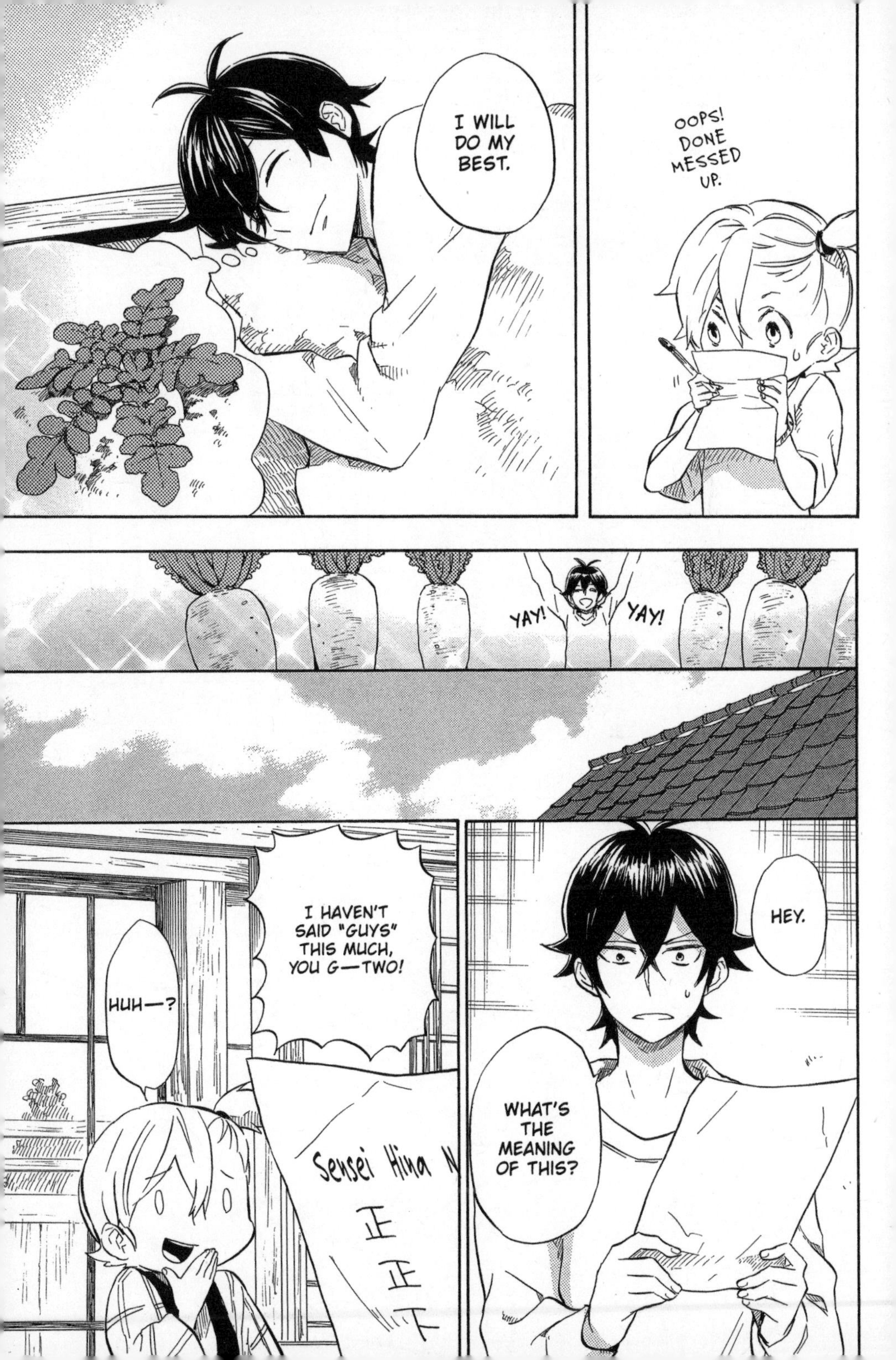
OOPS! DONE MESSED UP.
I WILL DO MY BEST.
YAY!
YAY!
HEY.
WHAT'S THE MEANING OF THIS?
I HAVEN'T SAID "GUYS" THIS MUCH, YOU G—TWO!
HUH—?
Sensei Hina N
正正下

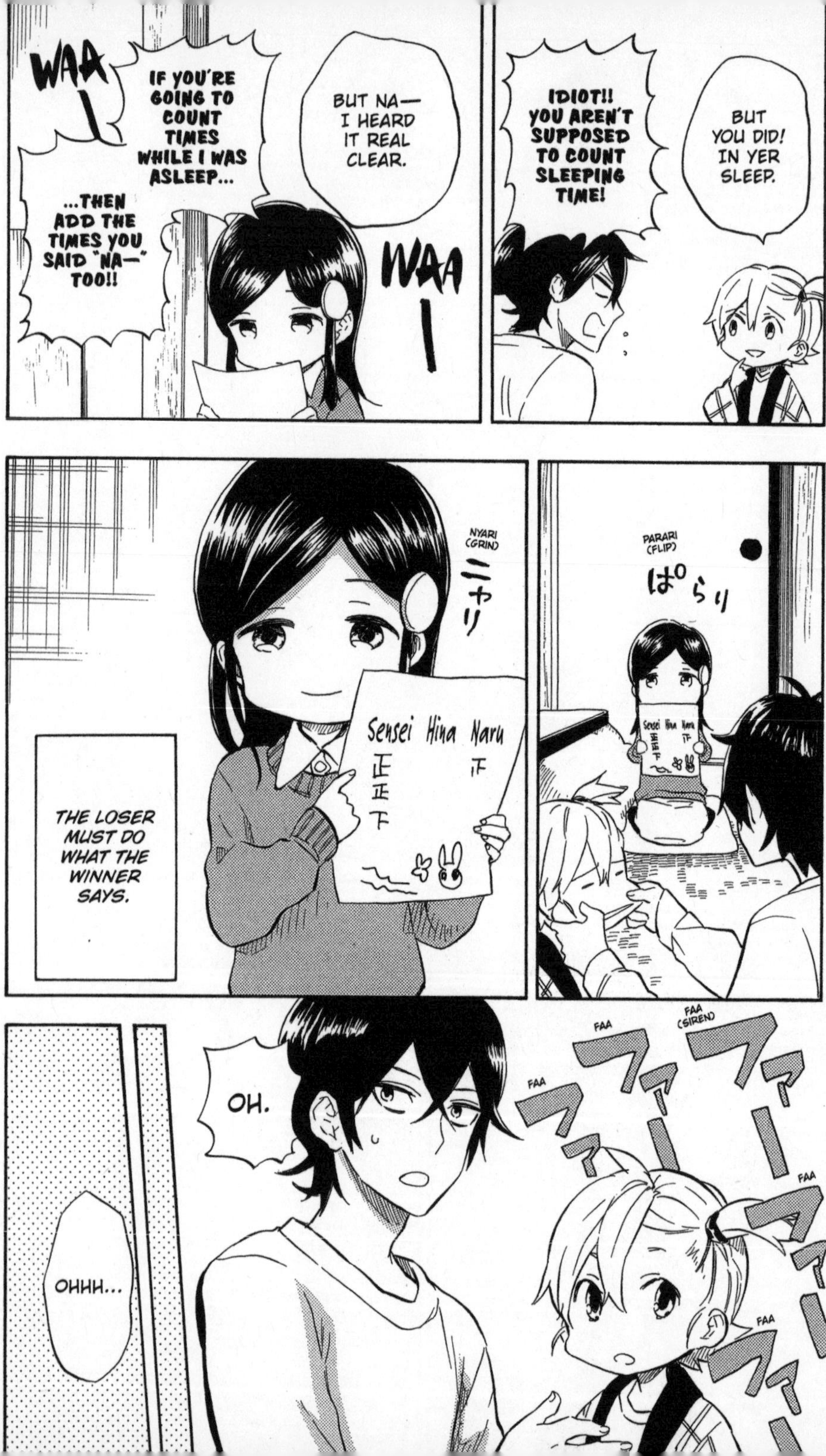
BUT YOU DID! IN YER SLEEP.
IDIOT!! YOU AREN'T SUPPOSED TO COUNT SLEEPING TIME!
BUT NA— I HEARD IT REAL CLEAR.
WAA
IF YOU'RE GOING TO COUNT TIMES WHILE I WAS ASLEEP...
...THEN ADD THE TIMES YOU SAID "NA—" TOO!!
WAA
PARARI (FLIP)
ぱらり
Sensei Hina Naru
NYARI (GRIN)
ニヤリ
Sensei Hina Naru
THE LOSER MUST DO WHAT THE WINNER SAYS.
FAA (SIREN)
ファー
FAA
ファー
FAA
ファー
FAA
ファー
FAA
ファー
OH.
OHHH...

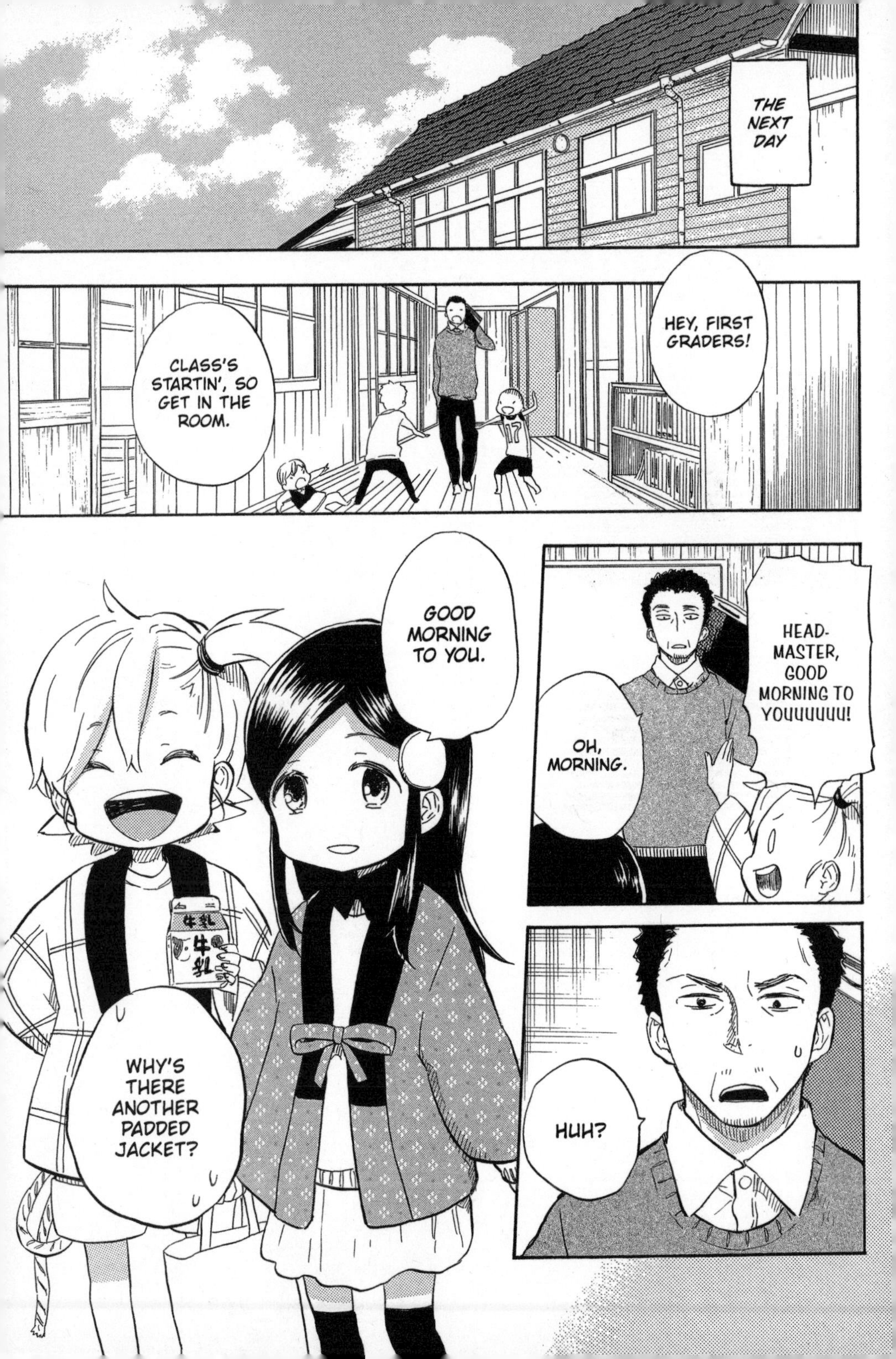
THE NEXT DAY
HEY, FIRST GRADERS!
CLASS'S STARTIN', SO GET IN THE ROOM.
HEAD-MASTER, GOOD MORNING TO YOUUUUUU!
OH, MORNING.
HUH?
GOOD MORNING TO YOU.
WHY'S THERE ANOTHER PADDED JACKET?
牛乳

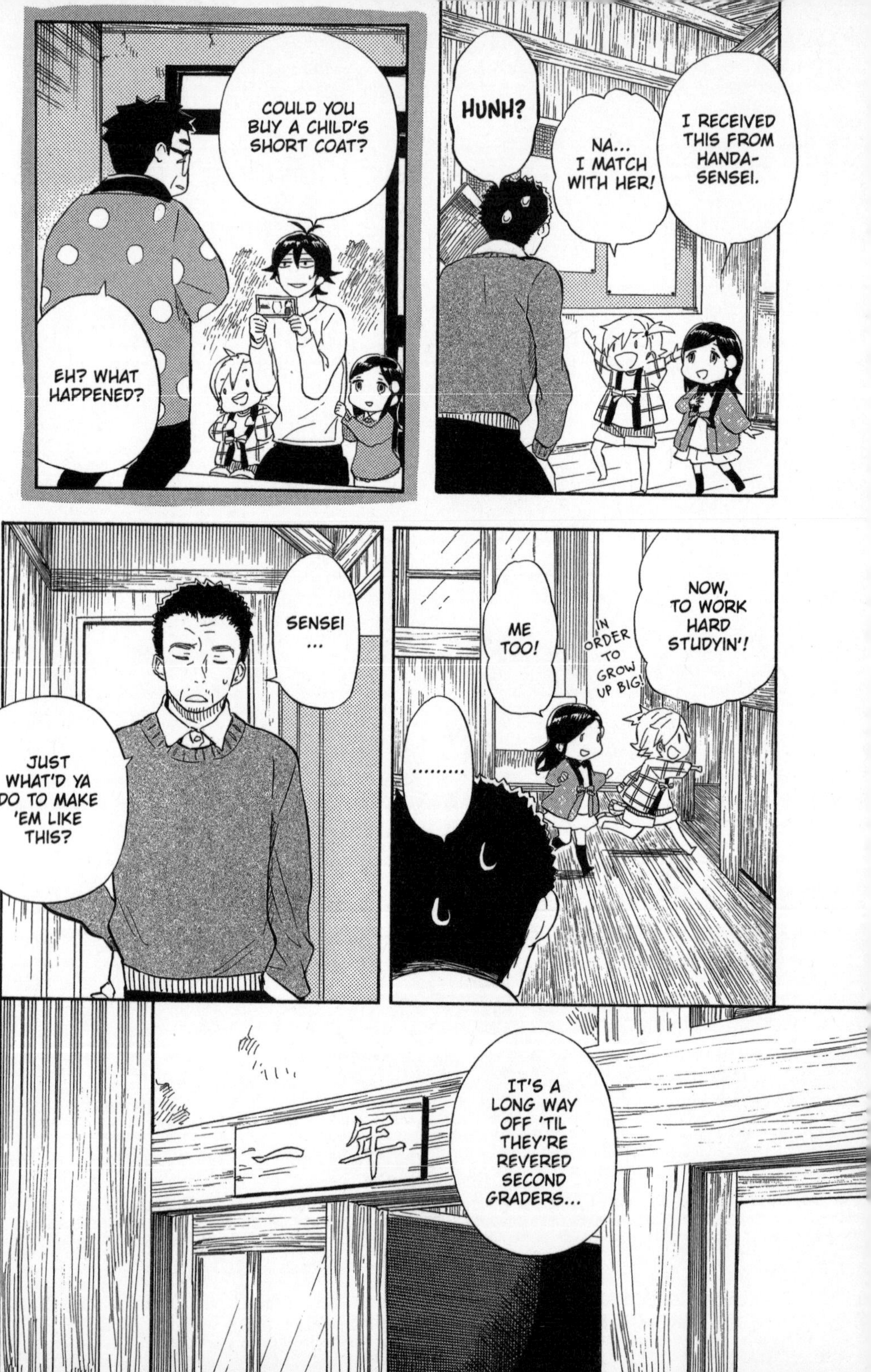
I RECEIVED THIS FROM HANDA-SENSEI.
NA... I MATCH WITH HER!
HUNH?
COULD YOU BUY A CHILD'S SHORT COAT?
EH? WHAT HAPPENED?
NOW, TO WORK HARD STUDYIN'!
IN ORDER TO GROW UP BIG!
ME TOO!
....
SENSEI ...
JUST WHAT'D YA DO TO MAKE 'EM LIKE THIS?
IT'S A LONG WAY OFF 'TIL THEY'RE REVERED SECOND GRADERS...
一年

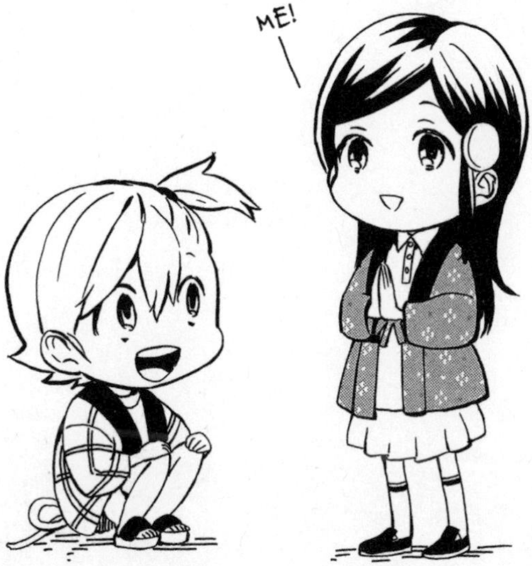
ME!

BARAKAMON

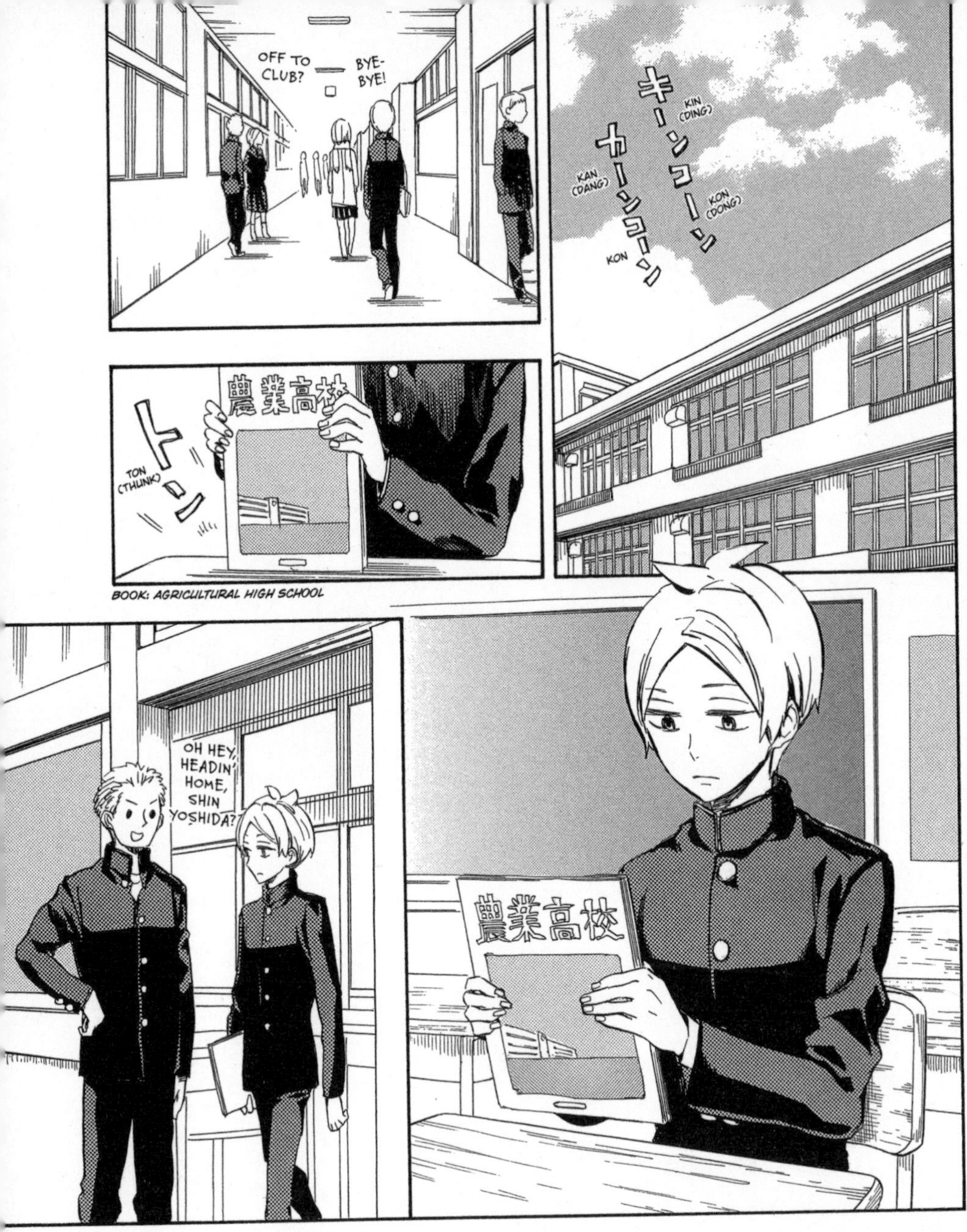
キーンコーン
カーンコーン
KIN (DING)
KAN (DANG)
KON (DONG)
KON
OFF TO CLUB?
BYE-BYE!
トン
TON (THUNK)
農業高校
BOOK: AGRICULTURAL HIGH SCHOOL
農業高校
OH HEY, HEADIN' HOME, SHIN YOSHIDA?

Act. 89
KUBBAI
(Translation: May Be Coming)

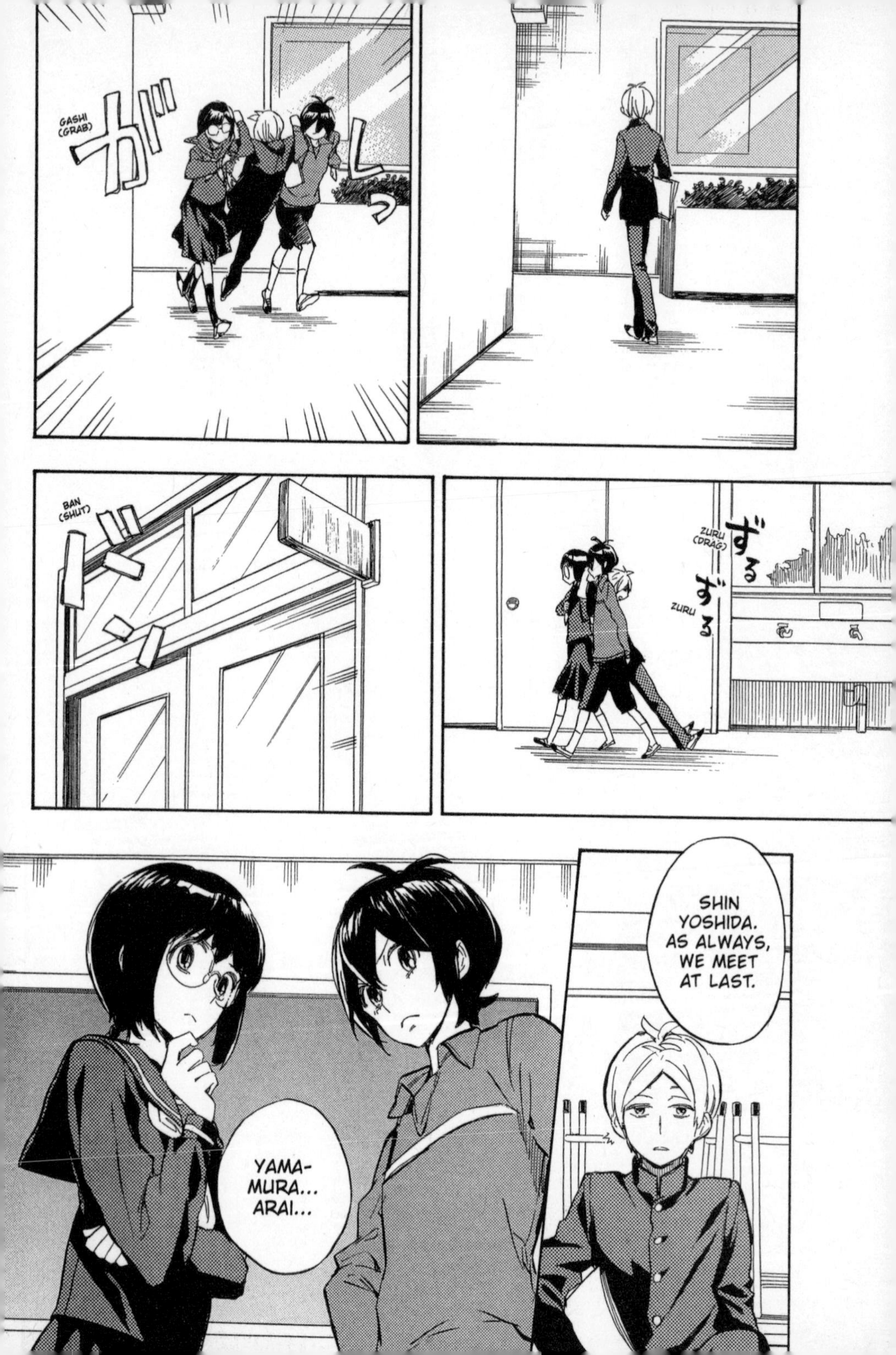

GASHI (GRAB)
がしっ
ZURU (DRAG)
ずる
ZURU
ずる
BAN (SHUT)
SHIN YOSHIDA. AS ALWAYS, WE MEET AT LAST.
YAMA-MURA... ARAI...

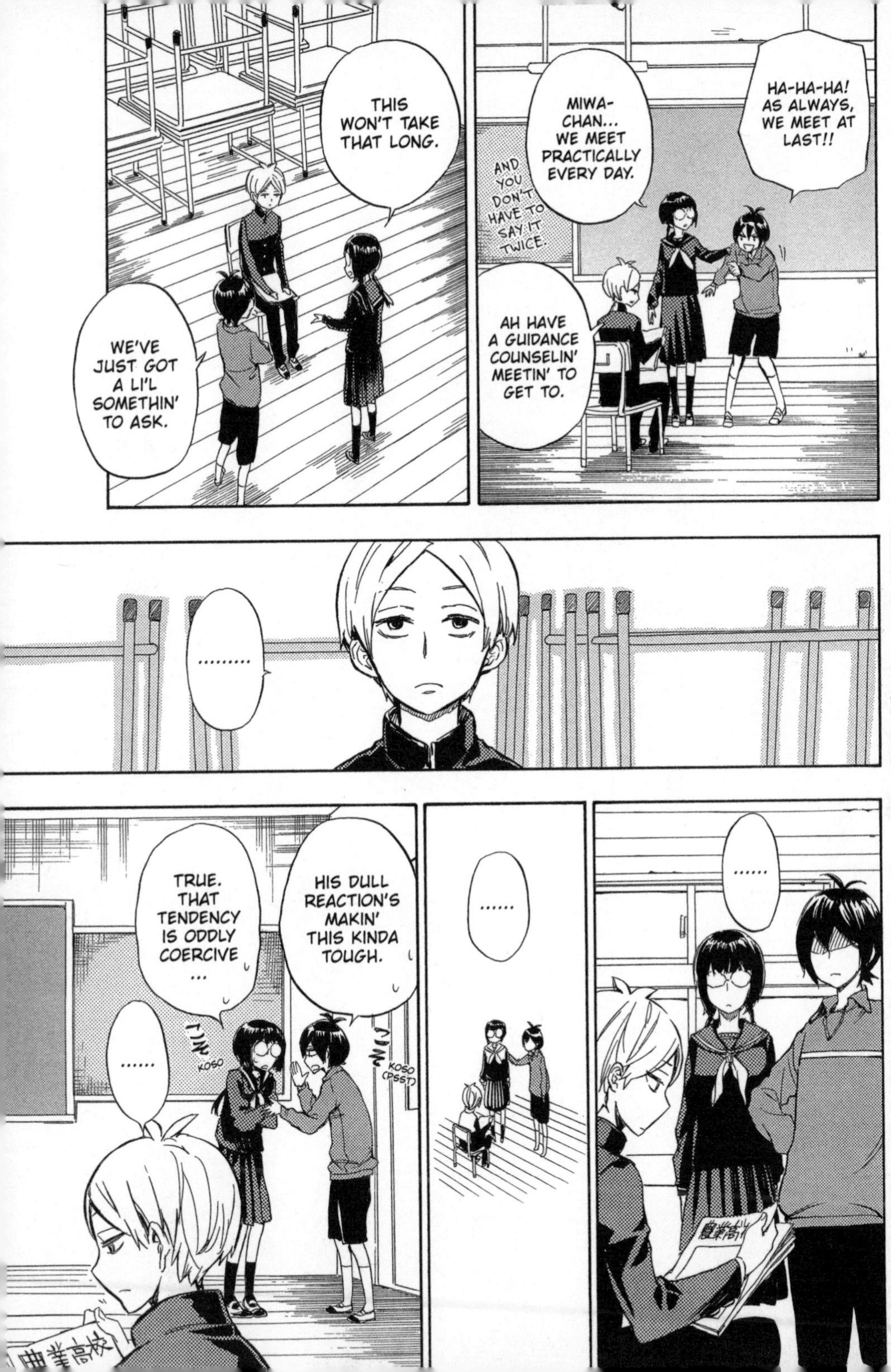
HA-HA-HA! AS ALWAYS, WE MEET AT LAST!!
MIWA-CHAN... WE MEET PRACTICALLY EVERY DAY.
AND YOU DON'T HAVE TO SAY IT TWICE.
AH HAVE A GUIDANCE COUNSELIN' MEETIN' TO GET TO.
THIS WON'T TAKE THAT LONG.
WE'VE JUST GOT A LI'L SOMETHIN' TO ASK.
....
......
......
HIS DULL REACTION'S MAKIN' THIS KINDA TOUGH.
KOSO (PSST)
TRUE. THAT TENDENCY IS ODDLY COERCIVE ...
KOSO
......

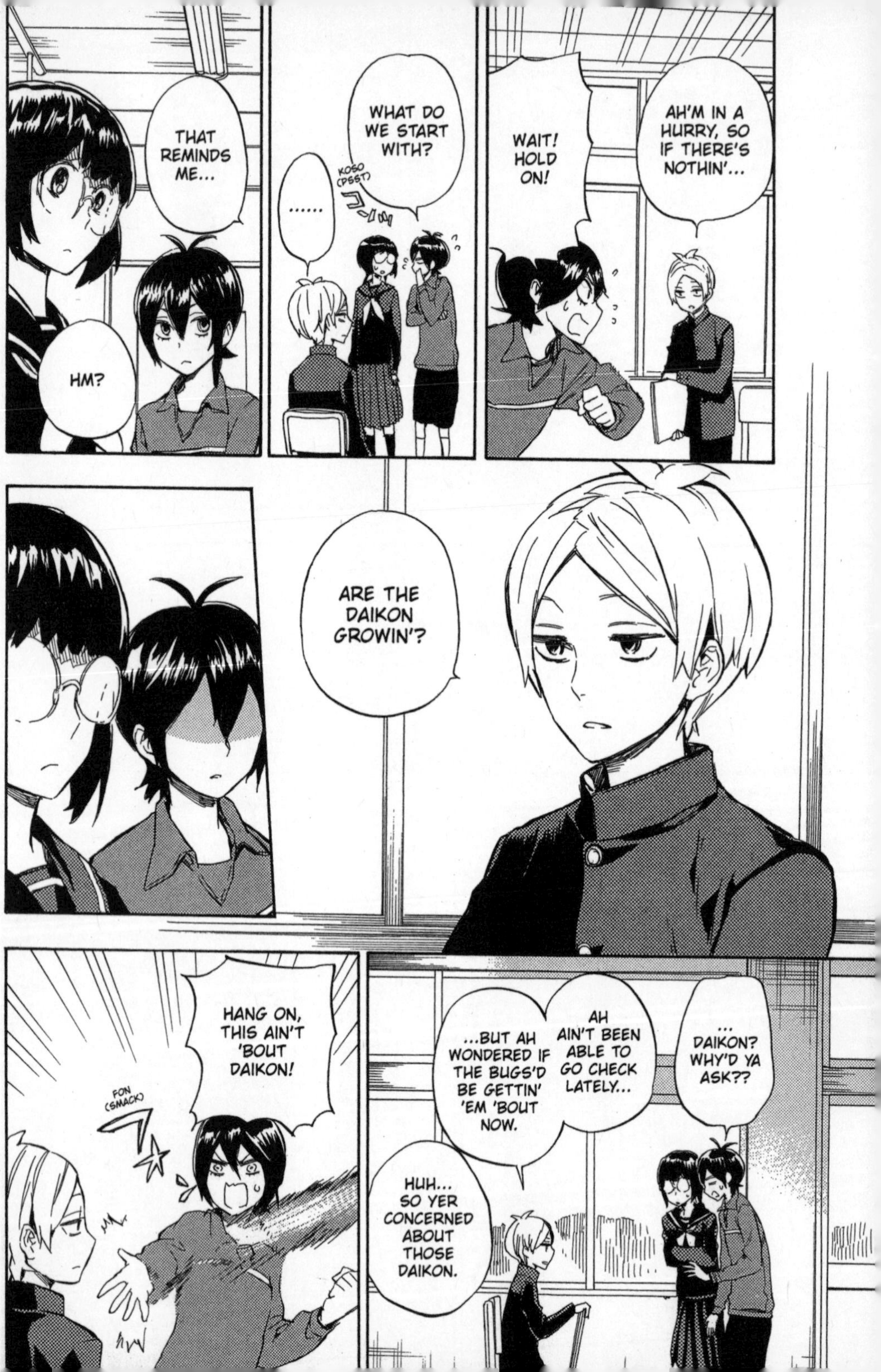

AH'M IN A HURRY, SO IF THERE'S NOTHIN'...
WAIT! HOLD ON!
WHAT DO WE START WITH?
KOSO (PSST)
......
THAT REMINDS ME...
HM?
ARE THE DAIKON GROWIN'?
... DAIKON? WHY'D YA ASK??
AH AIN'T BEEN ABLE TO GO CHECK LATELY...
...BUT AH WONDERED IF THE BUGS'D BE GETTIN' 'EM 'BOUT NOW.
HUH... SO YER CONCERNED ABOUT THOSE DAIKON.
HANG ON, THIS AIN'T 'BOUT DAIKON!
FON (SMACK)

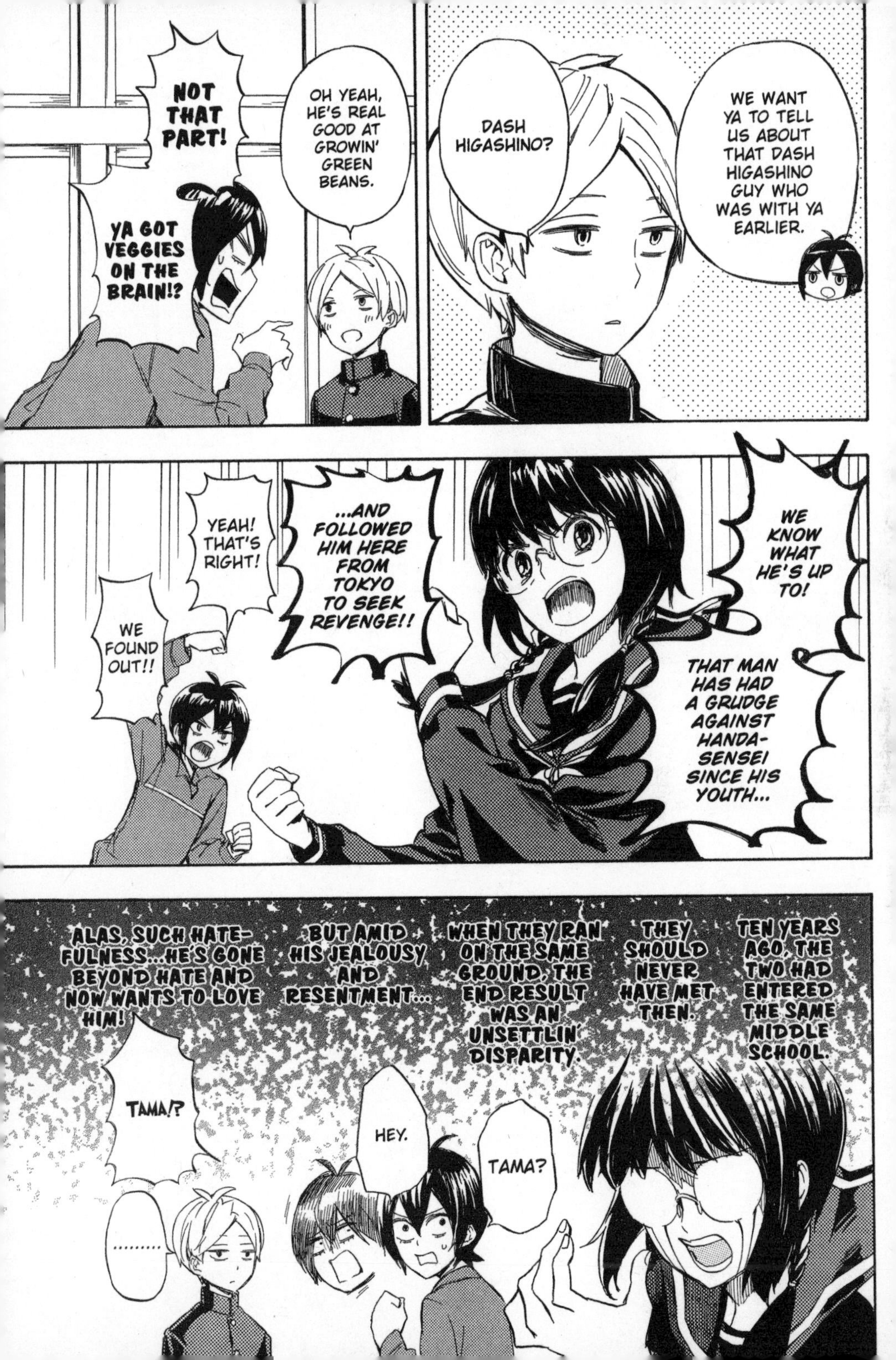
WE WANT YA TO TELL US ABOUT THAT DASH HIGASHINO GUY WHO WAS WITH YA EARLIER.
DASH HIGASHINO?
OH YEAH, HE'S REAL GOOD AT GROWIN' GREEN BEANS.
NOT THAT PART!
YA GOT VEGGIES ON THE BRAIN!?
WE KNOW WHAT HE'S UP TO!
THAT MAN HAS HAD A GRUDGE AGAINST HANDA-SENSEI SINCE HIS YOUTH...
...AND FOLLOWED HIM HERE FROM TOKYO TO SEEK REVENGE!!
YEAH! THAT'S RIGHT!
WE FOUND OUT!!
TEN YEARS AGO, THE TWO HAD ENTERED THE SAME MIDDLE SCHOOL.
THEY SHOULD NEVER HAVE MET THEN.
WHEN THEY RAN ON THE SAME GROUND, THE END RESULT WAS AN UNSETTLIN' DISPARITY.
BUT AMID HIS JEALOUSY AND RESENTMENT...
ALAS, SUCH HATE-FULNESS...HE'S GONE BEYOND HATE AND NOW WANTS TO LOVE HIM!
TAMA?
HEY.
TAMA!?
....

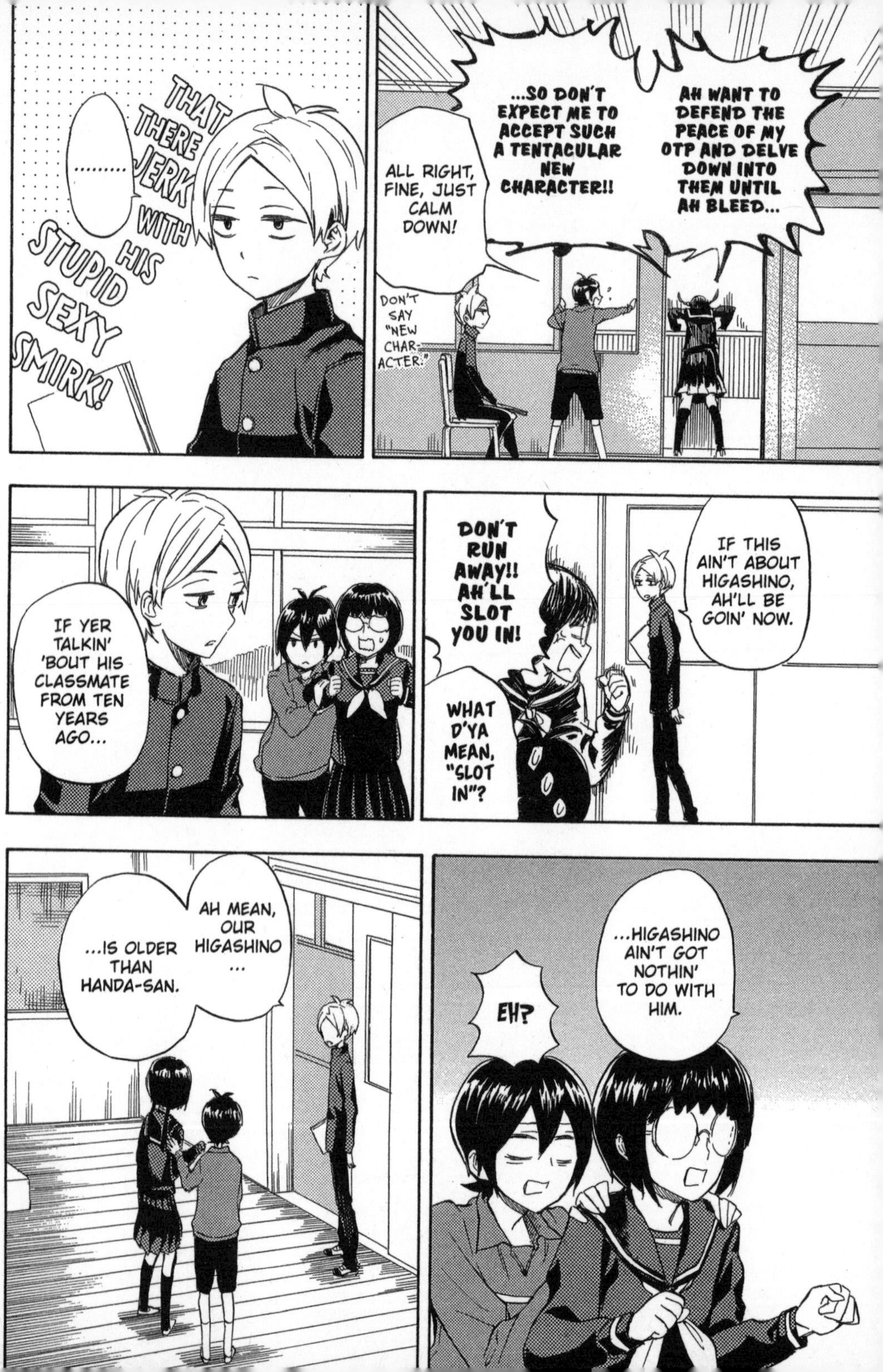
AH WANT TO DEFEND THE PEACE OF MY OTP AND DELVE DOWN INTO THEM UNTIL AH BLEED...
...SO DON'T EXPECT ME TO ACCEPT SUCH A TENTACULAR NEW CHARACTER!!
ALL RIGHT, FINE, JUST CALM DOWN!
DON'T SAY "NEW CHARACTER."
THAT THERE JERK WITH HIS STUPID SEXY SMIRK!
....
IF THIS AIN'T ABOUT HIGASHINO, AH'LL BE GOIN' NOW.
DON'T RUN AWAY!! AH'LL SLOT YOU IN!
WHAT D'YA MEAN, "SLOT IN"?
IF YER TALKIN' 'BOUT HIS CLASSMATE FROM TEN YEARS AGO...
...HIGASHINO AIN'T GOT NOTHIN' TO DO WITH HIM.
EH?
AH MEAN, OUR HIGASHINO ...
...IS OLDER THAN HANDA-SAN.

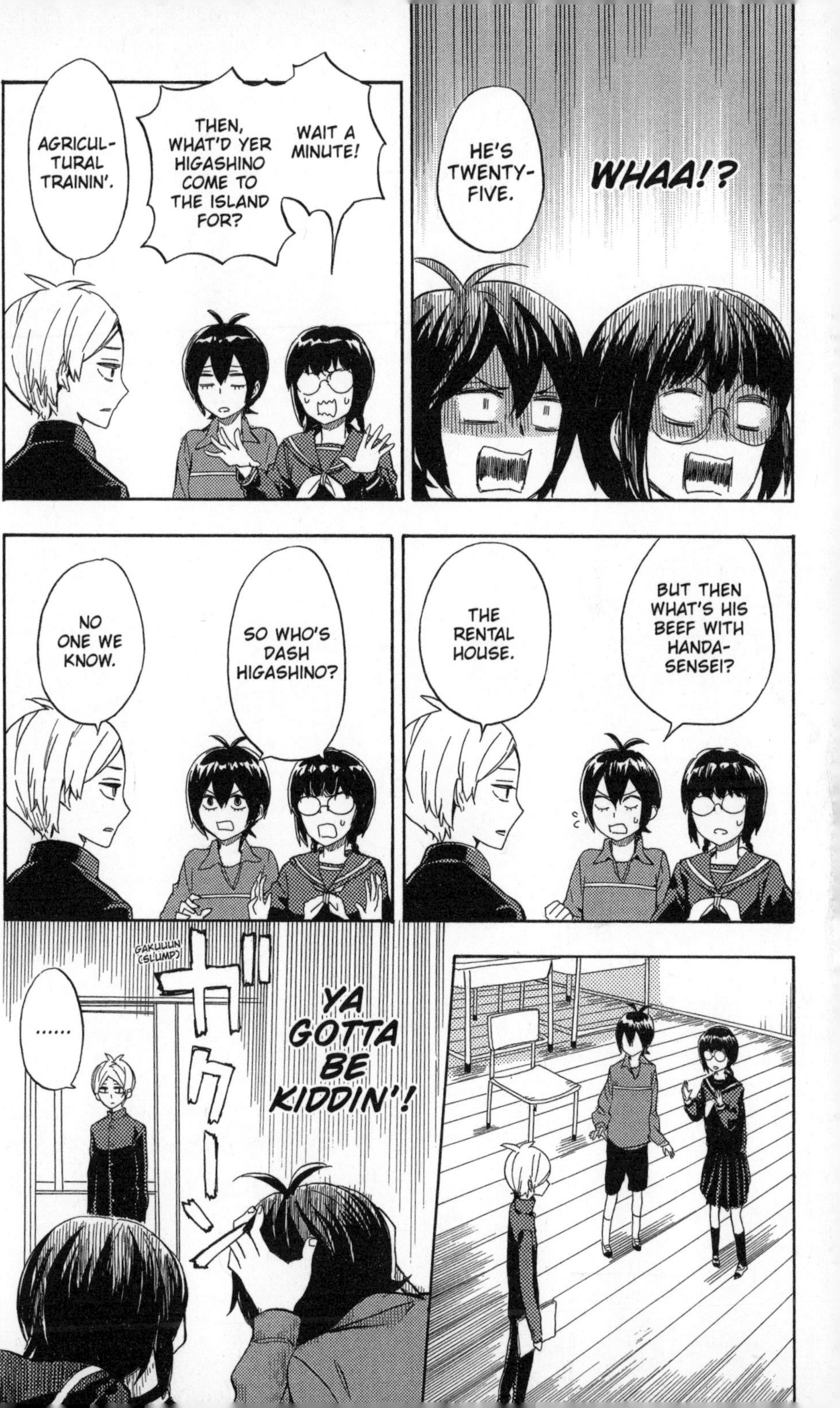
HE'S TWENTY-FIVE.
WHAA!?
WAIT A MINUTE!
THEN, WHAT'D YER HIGASHINO COME TO THE ISLAND FOR?
AGRICUL-TURAL TRAININ'.
BUT THEN WHAT'S HIS BEEF WITH HANDA-SENSEI?
THE RENTAL HOUSE.
SO WHO'S DASH HIGASHINO?
NO ONE WE KNOW.
YA GOTTA BE KIDDIN'!
GAKUUUN (SLUMP)
......

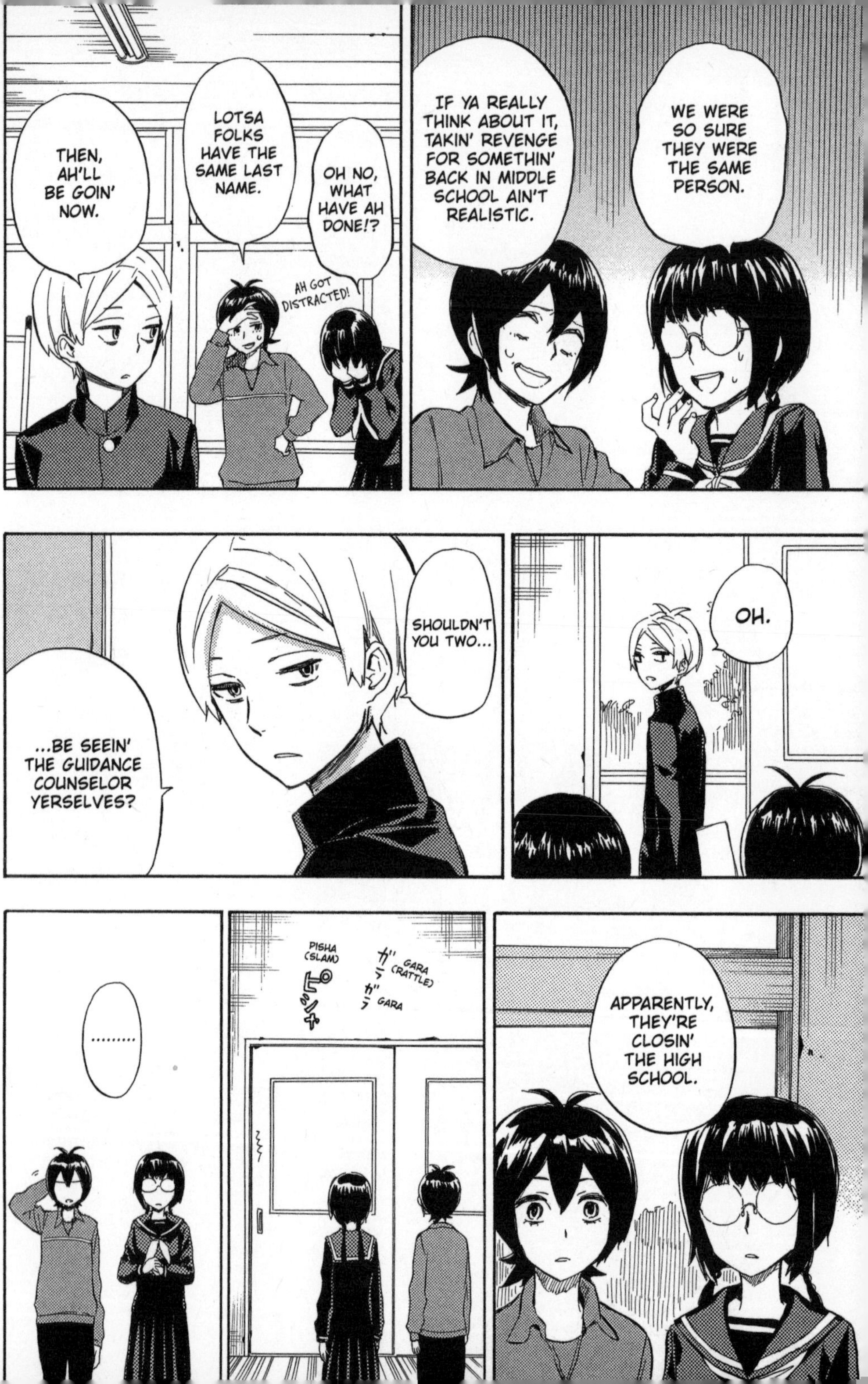

WE WERE SO SURE THEY WERE THE SAME PERSON.
IF YA REALLY THINK ABOUT IT, TAKIN' REVENGE FOR SOMETHIN' BACK IN MIDDLE SCHOOL AIN'T REALISTIC.
OH NO, WHAT HAVE AH DONE!?
AH GOT DISTRACTED!
LOTSA FOLKS HAVE THE SAME LAST NAME.
THEN, AH'LL BE GOIN' NOW.
OH.
SHOULDN'T YOU TWO...
...BE SEEIN' THE GUIDANCE COUNSELOR YERSELVES?
APPARENTLY, THEY'RE CLOSIN' THE HIGH SCHOOL.
ガラ GARA (RATTLE)
ガラ GARA
ピシャ PISHA (SLAM)
....

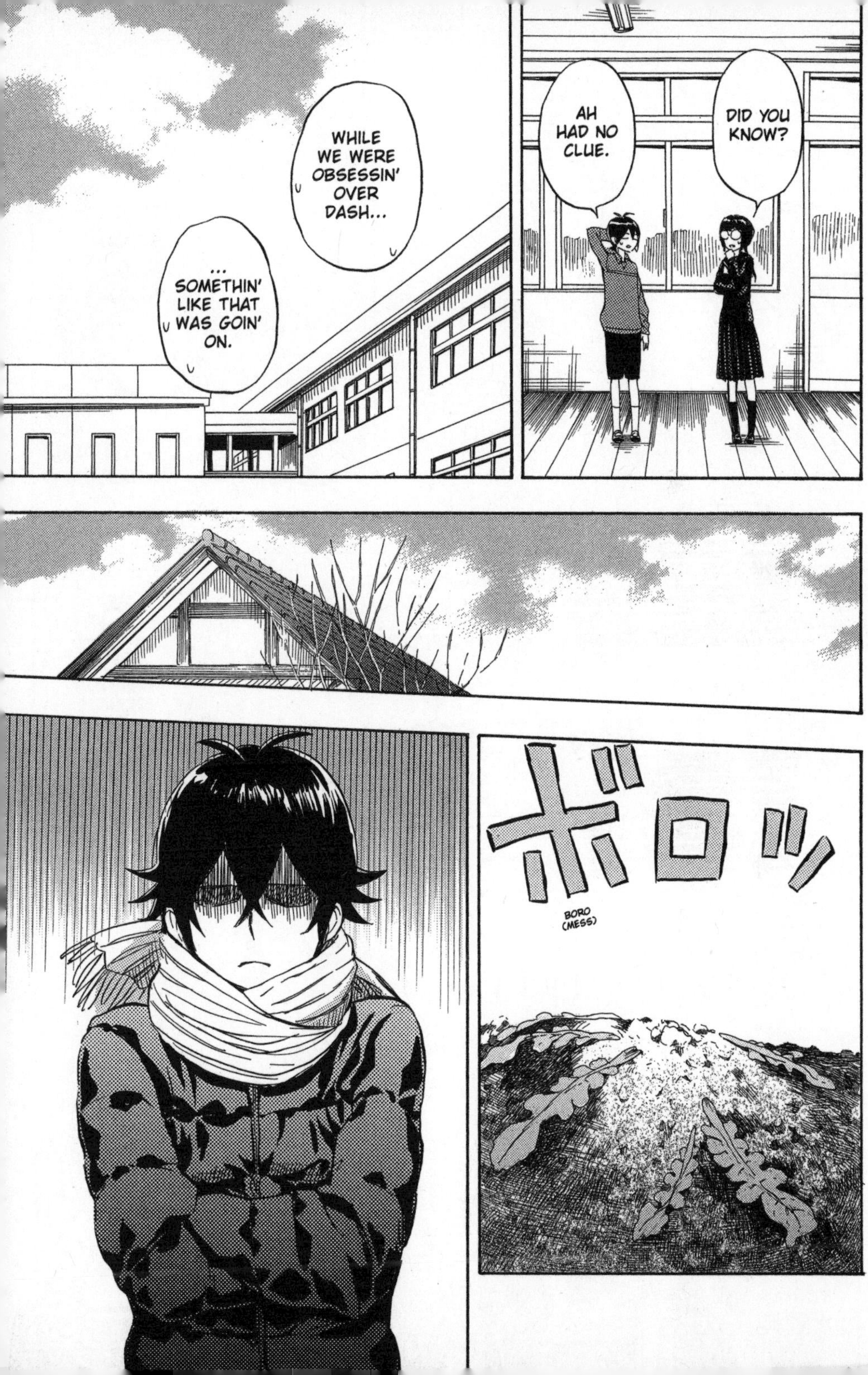
DID YOU KNOW?
AH HAD NO CLUE.
WHILE WE WERE OBSESSIN' OVER DASH...
...SOMETHIN' LIKE THAT WAS GOIN' ON.
ボロッ
BORO (MESS)

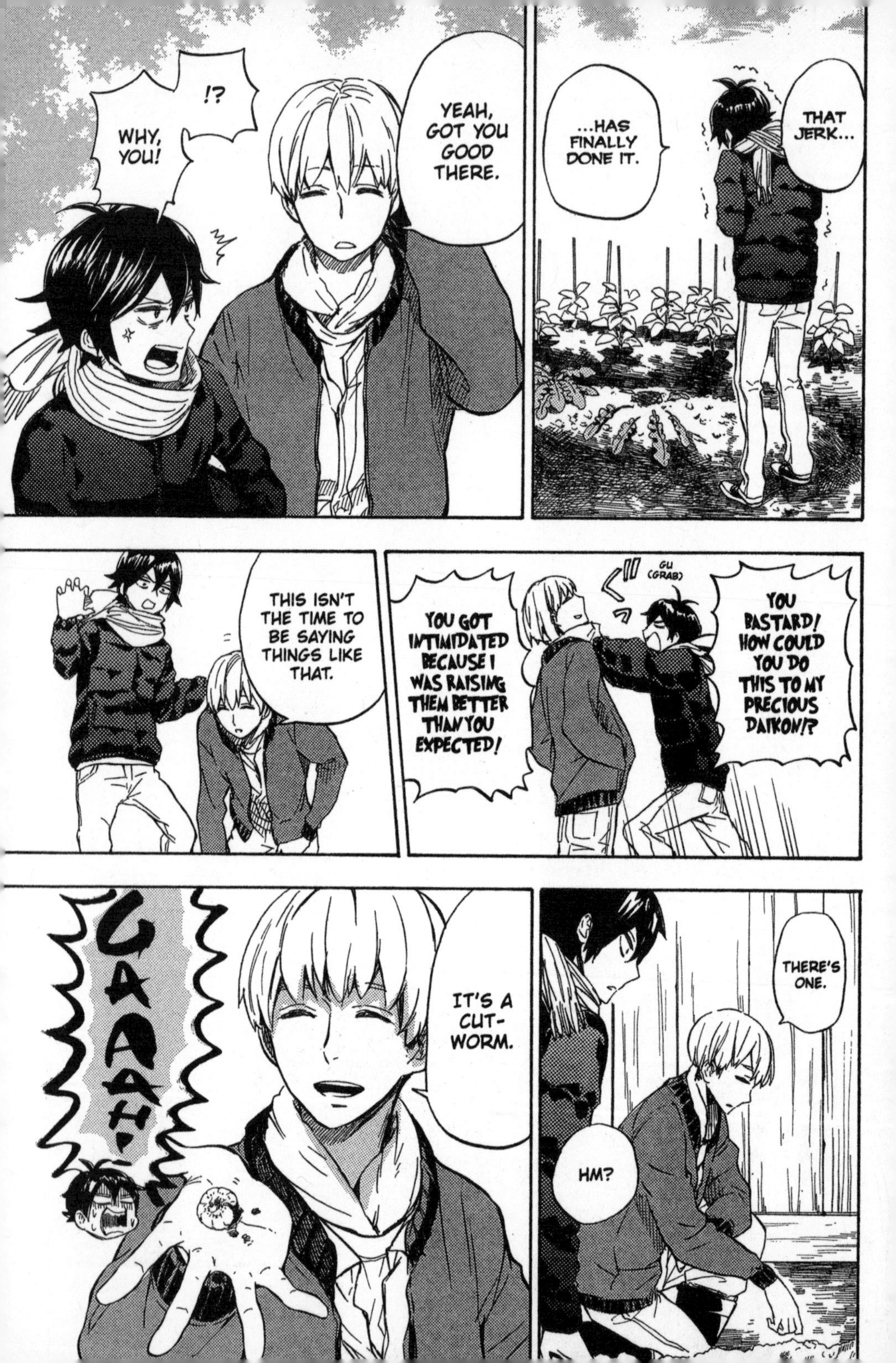
THAT JERK...
...HAS FINALLY DONE IT.
YEAH, GOT YOU GOOD THERE.
!?
WHY, YOU!
GU (GRAB)
YOU BASTARD! HOW COULD YOU DO THIS TO MY PRECIOUS DAIKON!?
YOU GOT INTIMIDATED BECAUSE I WAS RAISING THEM BETTER THAN YOU EXPECTED!
THIS ISN'T THE TIME TO BE SAYING THINGS LIKE THAT.
THERE'S ONE.
HM?
IT'S A CUT-WORM.
GAAAH!

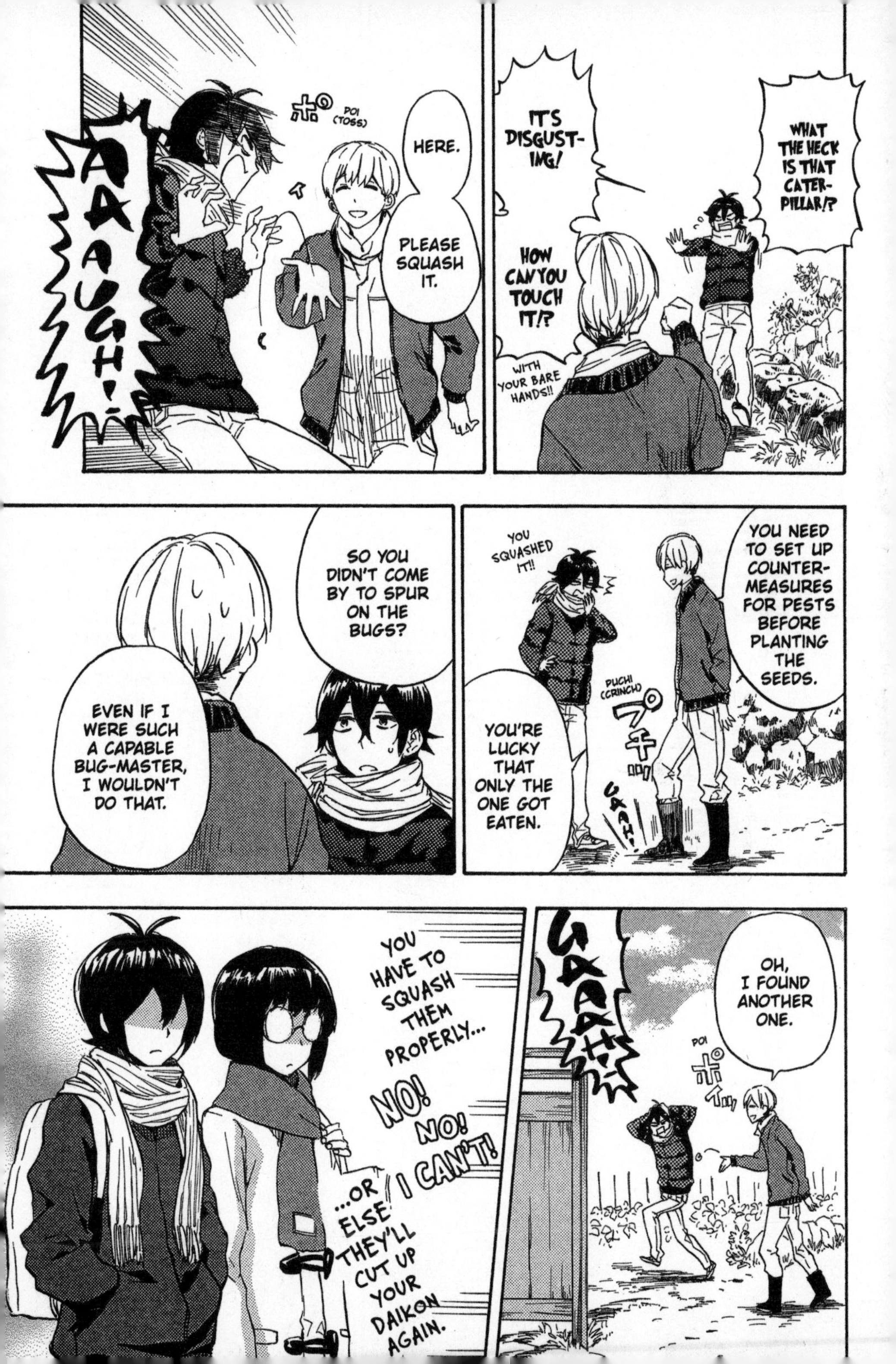
WHAT THE HECK IS THAT CATER-PILLAR!?
IT'S DISGUST-ING!
HOW CAN YOU TOUCH IT!?
WITH YOUR BARE HANDS!!
HERE.
POI (TOSS)
PLEASE SQUASH IT.
AAAUGH!-
YOU NEED TO SET UP COUNTER-MEASURES FOR PESTS BEFORE PLANTING THE SEEDS.
YOU SQUASHED IT!!
PUCHI (CRINCH)
YOU'RE LUCKY THAT ONLY THE ONE GOT EATEN.
UAAH!
SO YOU DIDN'T COME BY TO SPUR ON THE BUGS?
EVEN IF I WERE SUCH A CAPABLE BUG-MASTER, I WOULDN'T DO THAT.
OH, I FOUND ANOTHER ONE.
UAAAH!
POI
YOU HAVE TO SQUASH THEM PROPERLY...
NO! NO! I CAN'T!
...OR ELSE THEY'LL CUT UP YOUR DAIKON AGAIN.

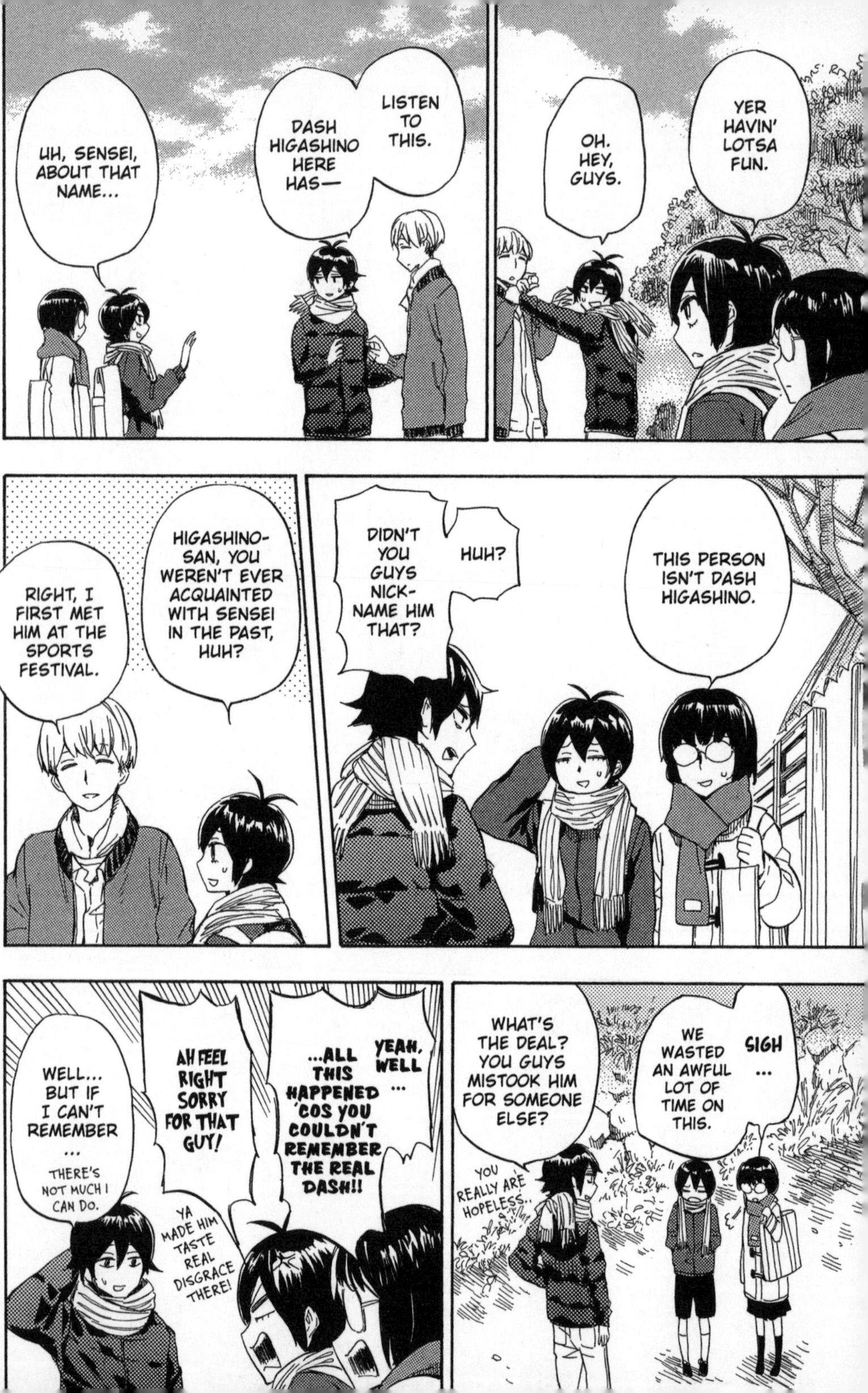

YER HAVIN' LOTSA FUN.
OH. HEY, GUYS.
LISTEN TO THIS.
DASH HIGASHINO HERE HAS—
UH, SENSEI, ABOUT THAT NAME...
THIS PERSON ISN'T DASH HIGASHINO.
HUH?
DIDN'T YOU GUYS NICK-NAME HIM THAT?
HIGASHINO-SAN, YOU WEREN'T EVER ACQUAINTED WITH SENSEI IN THE PAST, HUH?
RIGHT, I FIRST MET HIM AT THE SPORTS FESTIVAL.
SIGH...
WE WASTED AN AWFUL LOT OF TIME ON THIS.
WHAT'S THE DEAL? YOU GUYS MISTOOK HIM FOR SOMEONE ELSE?
YOU REALLY ARE HOPELESS..
YEAH, WELL...
...ALL THIS HAPPENED 'COS YOU COULDN'T REMEMBER THE REAL DASH!!
AH FEEL RIGHT SORRY FOR THAT GUY!
YA MADE HIM TASTE REAL DISGRACE THERE!
WELL... BUT IF I CAN'T REMEMBER...
THERE'S NOT MUCH I CAN DO.

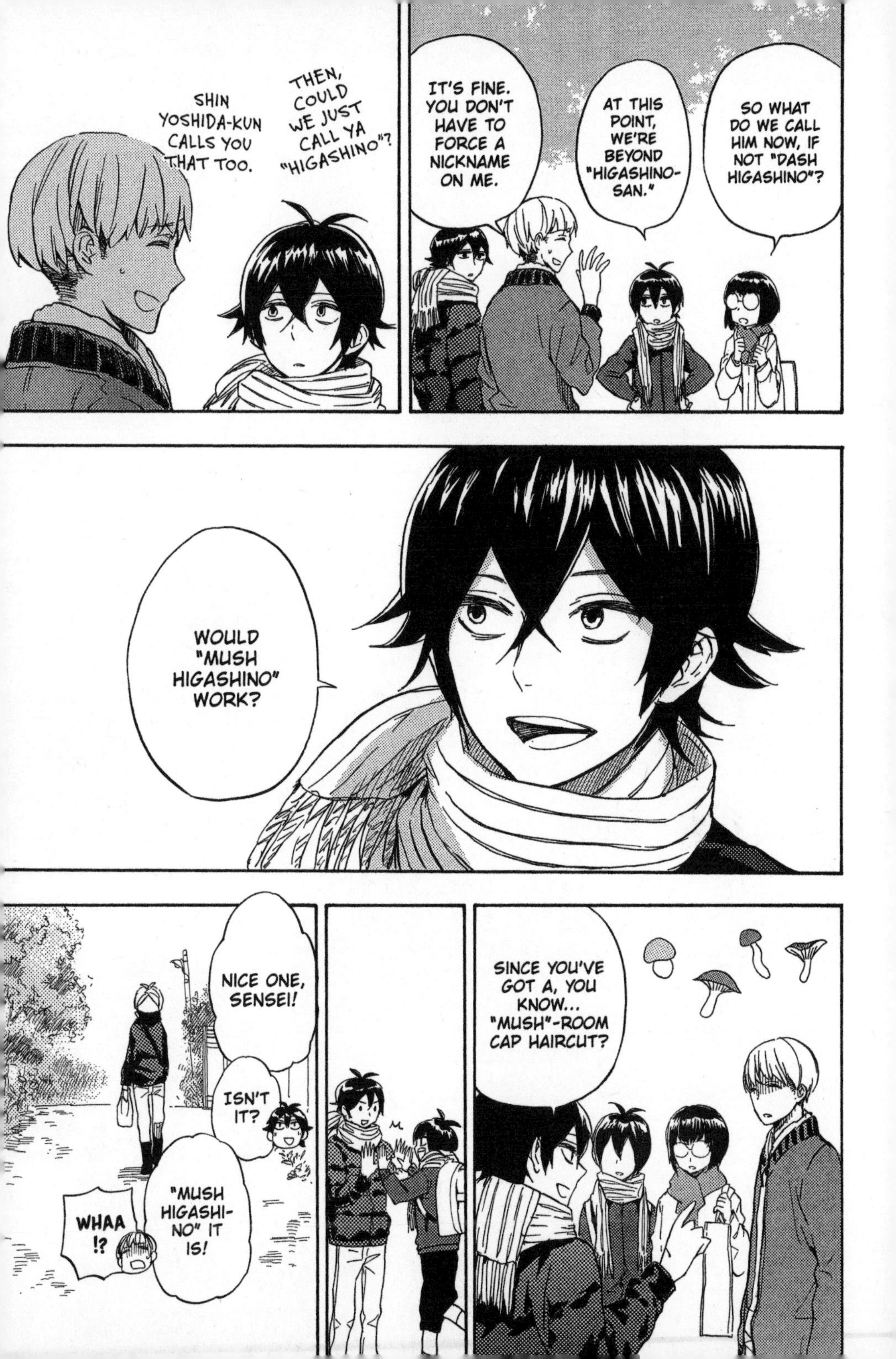
SO WHAT DO WE CALL HIM NOW, IF NOT "DASH HIGASHINO"?
AT THIS POINT, WE'RE BEYOND "HIGASHINO-SAN."
IT'S FINE. YOU DON'T HAVE TO FORCE A NICKNAME ON ME.
THEN, COULD WE JUST CALL YA "HIGASHINO"?
SHIN YOSHIDA-KUN CALLS YOU THAT TOO.
WOULD "MUSH HIGASHINO" WORK?
SINCE YOU'VE GOT A, YOU KNOW... "MUSH"-ROOM CAP HAIRCUT?
NICE ONE, SENSEI!
ISN'T IT?
"MUSH HIGASHINO" IT IS!
WHAA!?

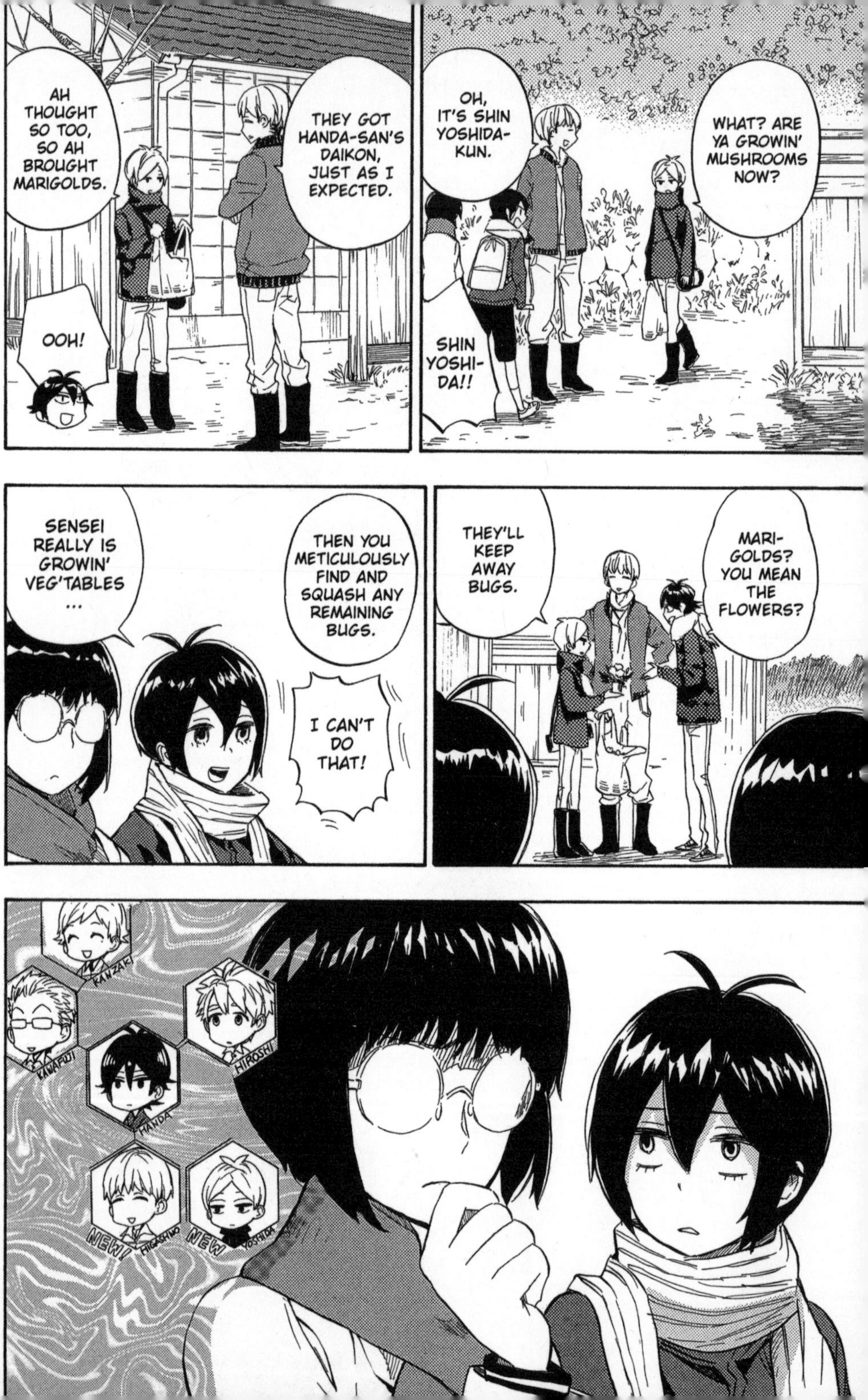
WHAT? ARE YA GROWIN' MUSHROOMS NOW?
OH, IT'S SHIN YOSHIDA-KUN.
SHIN YOSHIDA!!
THEY GOT HANDA-SAN'S DAIKON, JUST AS I EXPECTED.
AH THOUGHT SO TOO, SO AH BROUGHT MARIGOLDS.
OOH!
MARI-GOLDS? YOU MEAN THE FLOWERS?
THEY'LL KEEP AWAY BUGS.
THEN YOU METICULOUSLY FIND AND SQUASH ANY REMAINING BUGS.
SENSEI REALLY IS GROWIN' VEG'TABLES ...
I CAN'T DO THAT!
KANZAKI
KAWAFUJI
HIROSHI
HANDA
NEW!
HIGASHINO
NEW
YOSHIDA

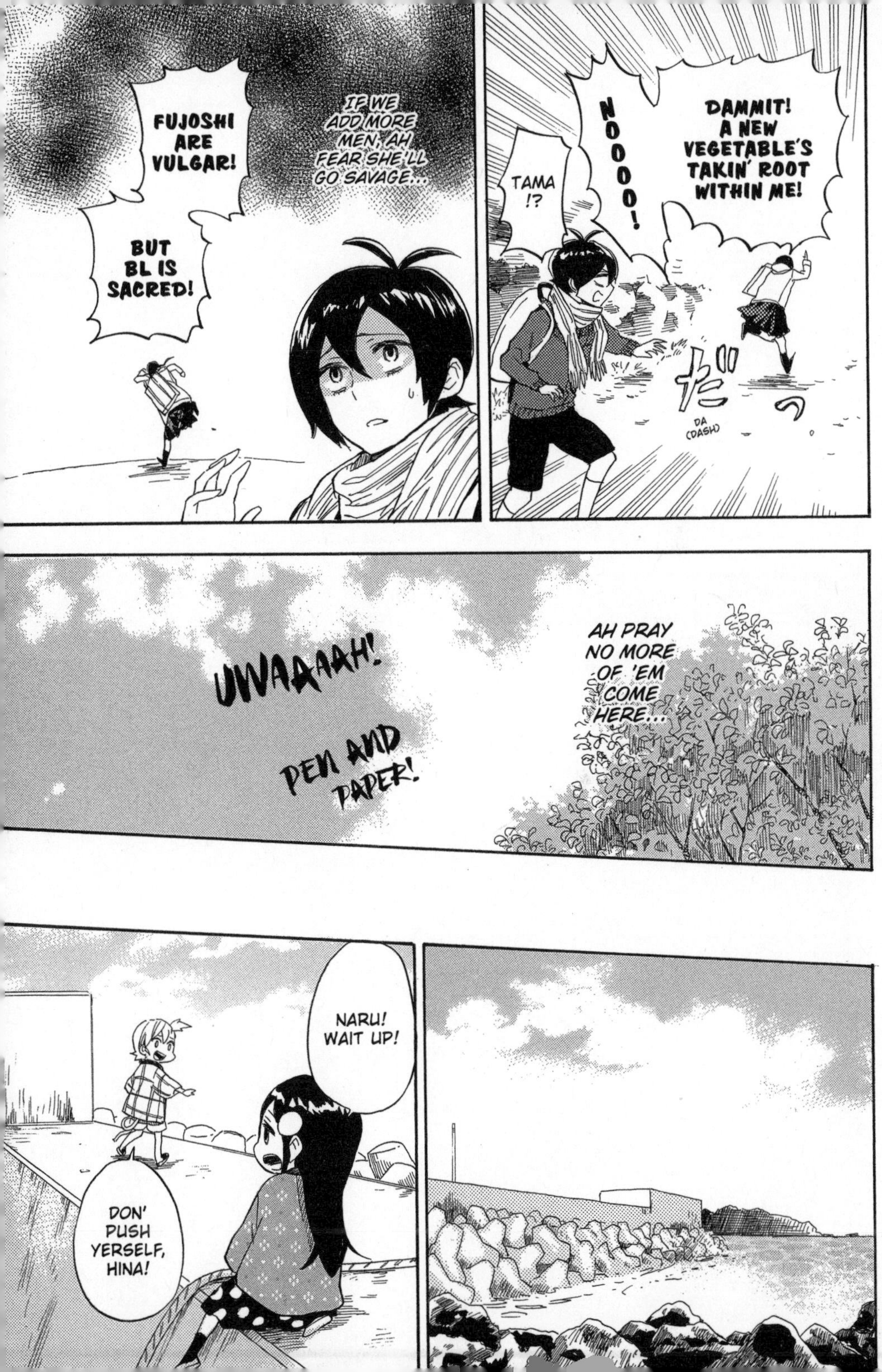

DAMMIT! A NEW VEGETABLE'S TAKIN' ROOT WITHIN ME!
NOOOOO!
TAMA !?
DA (DASH)
IF WE ADD MORE MEN, AH FEAR SHE'LL GO SAVAGE...
FUJOSHI ARE VULGAR!
BUT BL IS SACRED!
AH PRAY NO MORE OF 'EM COME HERE...
UWAAAH!
PEN AND PAPER!
NARU! WAIT UP!
DON' PUSH YERSELF, HINA!

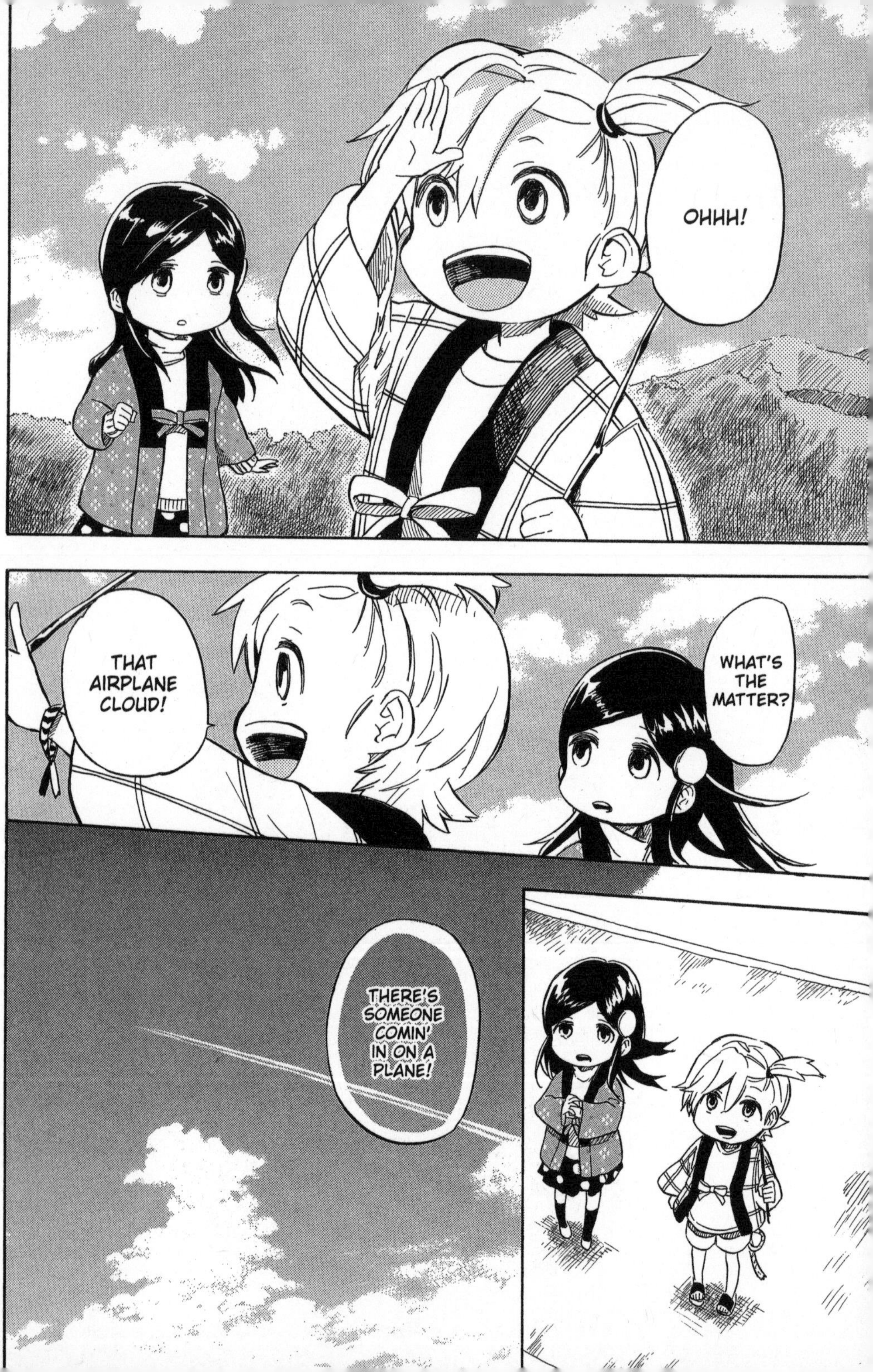
OHHH!
WHAT'S THE MATTER?
THAT AIRPLANE CLOUD!
THERE'S SOMEONE COMIN' IN ON A PLANE!

WALK
ON YER
OWN!!

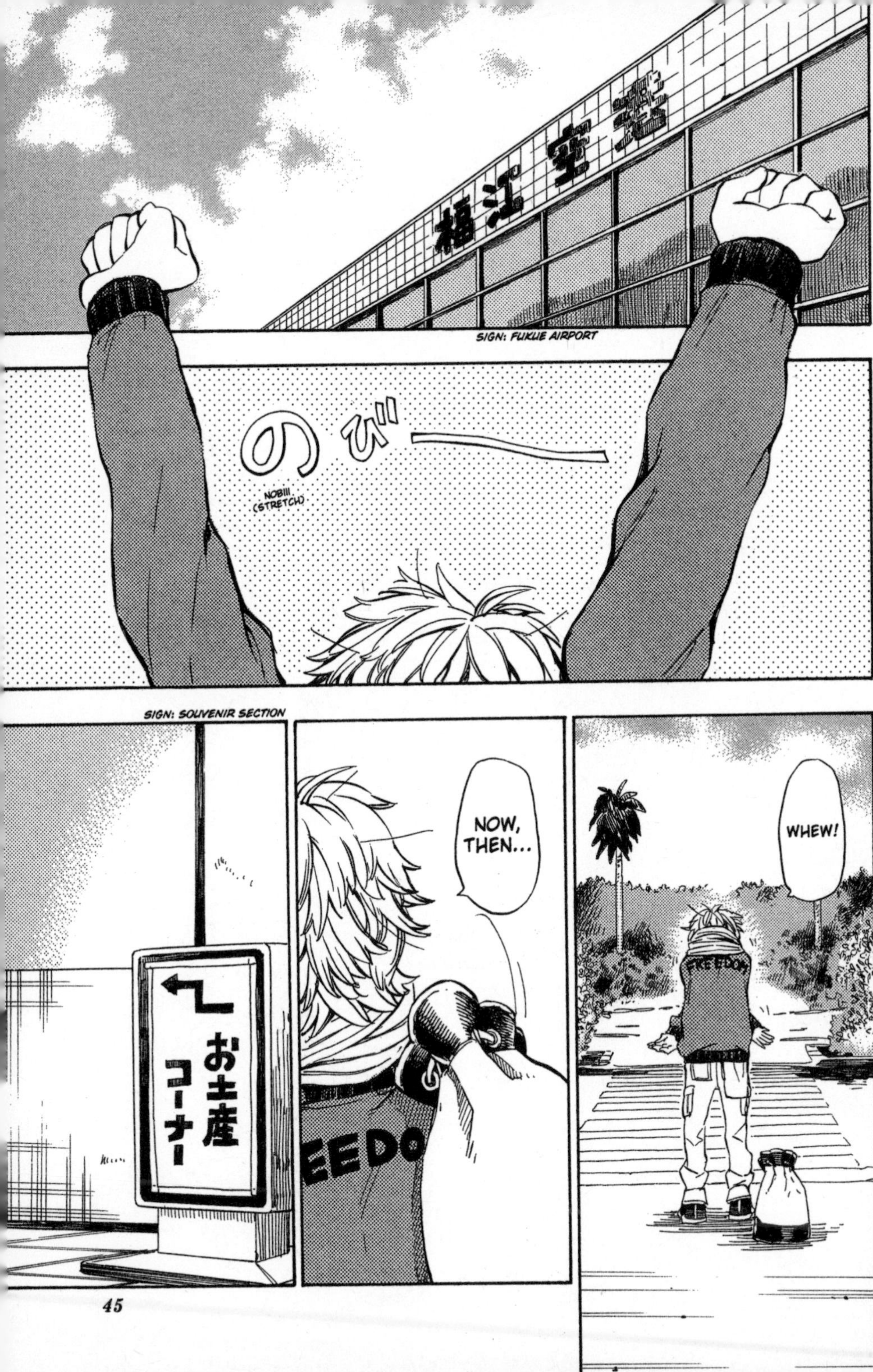
福江空港
SIGN: FUKUE AIRPORT
のび──
NOBIII (STRETCH)
WHEW!
NOW, THEN...
SIGN: SOUVENIR SECTION
お土産コーナー
EEDO

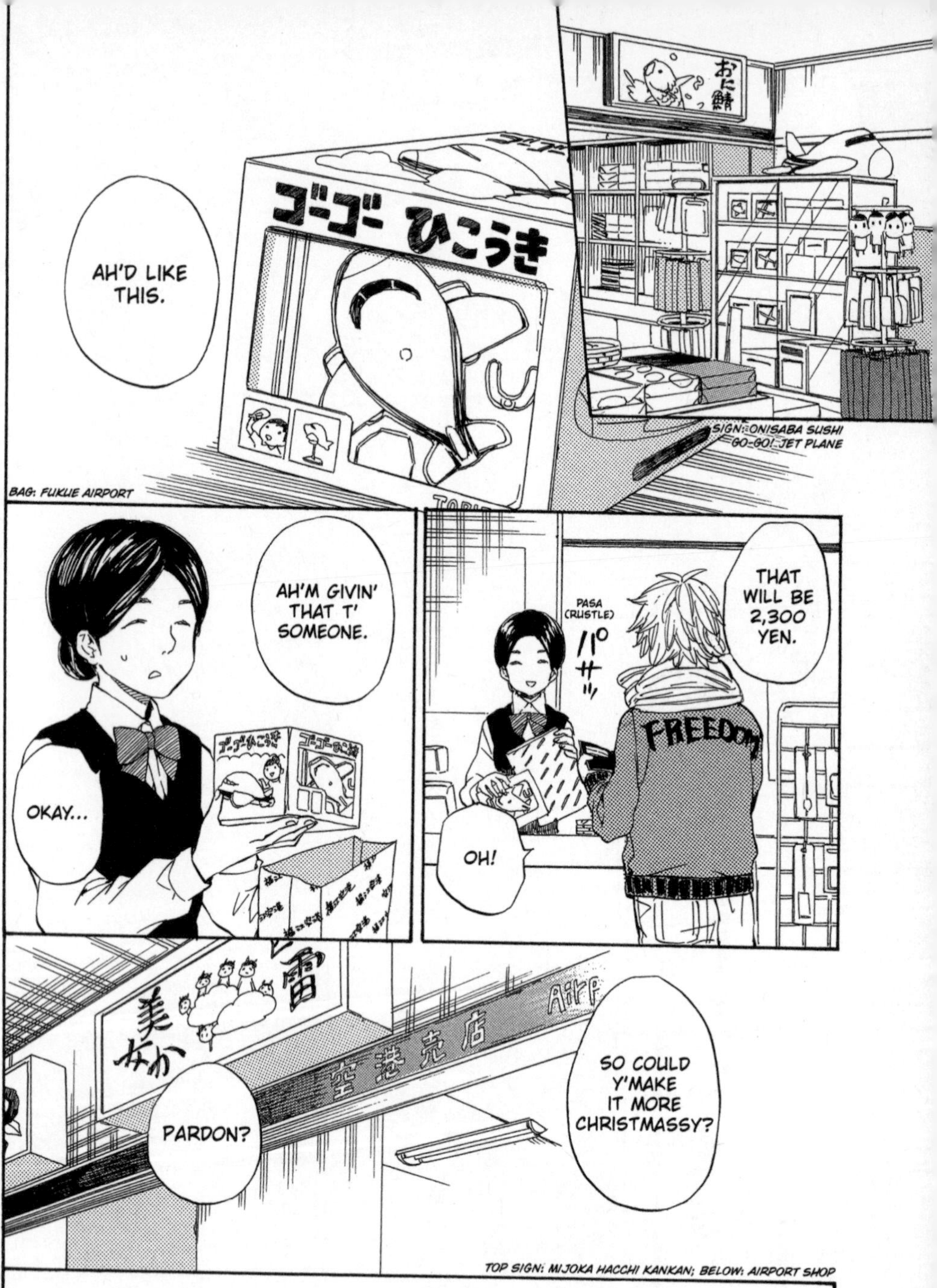
SIGN: ONISABA SUSHI
GO-GO! JET PLANE
AH'D LIKE THIS.
BAG: FUKUE AIRPORT
THAT WILL BE 2,300 YEN.
PASA (RUSTLE)
パサッ
OH!
FREEDOM
AH'M GIVIN' THAT T' SOMEONE.
OKAY...
SO COULD Y'MAKE IT MORE CHRISTMASSY?
PARDON?
TOP SIGN: MIJOKA HACCHI KANKAN; BELOW: AIRPORT SHOP

Act.90
12/24
(Translation: Christmas Eve)

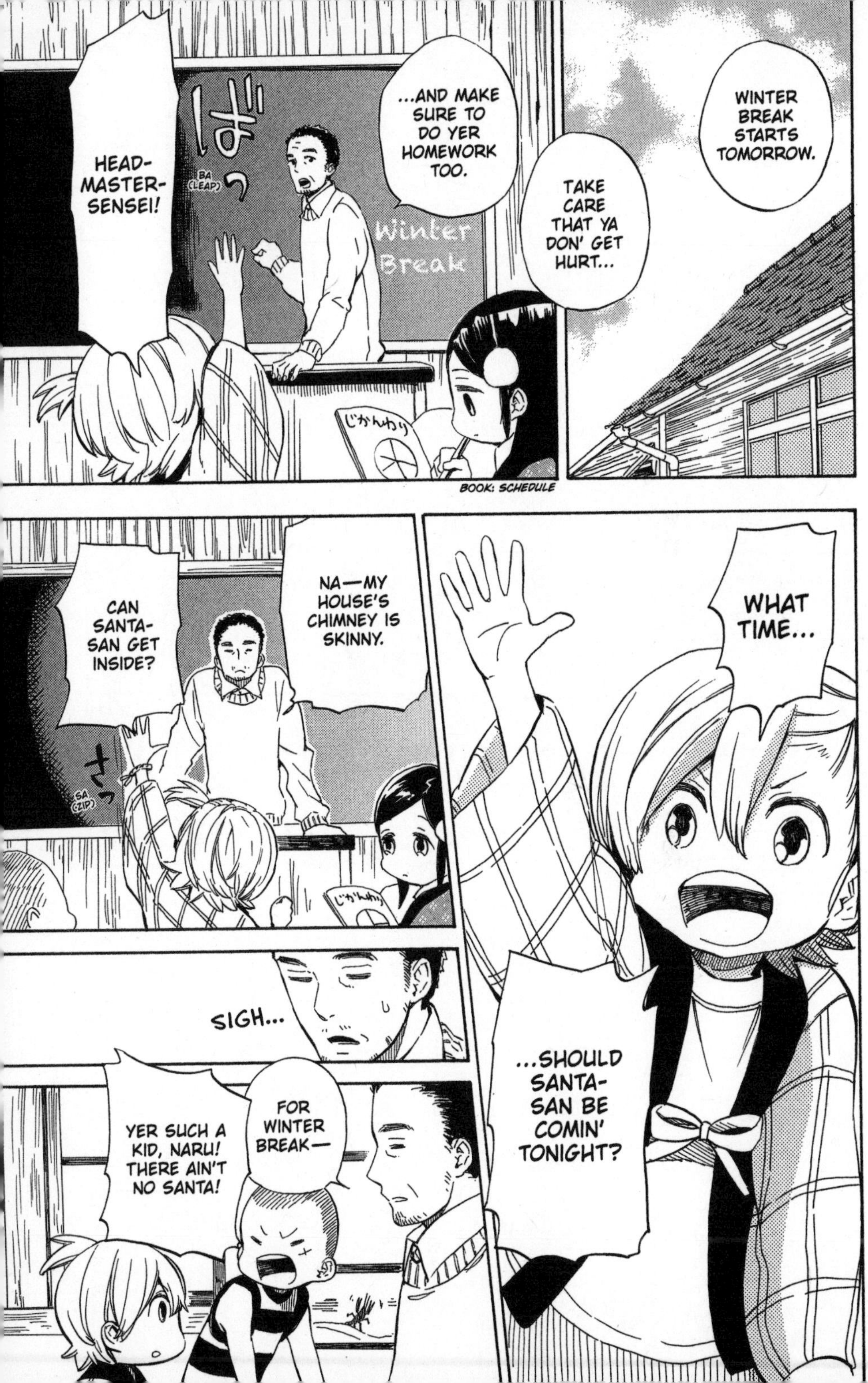
WINTER BREAK STARTS TOMORROW.
TAKE CARE THAT YA DON' GET HURT...
...AND MAKE SURE TO DO YER HOMEWORK TOO.
Winter Break
HEAD-MASTER-SENSEI!
ばっ
BA (LEAP)
じかんわり
BOOK: SCHEDULE
WHAT TIME...
...SHOULD SANTA-SAN BE COMIN' TONIGHT?
NA—MY HOUSE'S CHIMNEY IS SKINNY.
CAN SANTA-SAN GET INSIDE?
さっ
SA (ZIP)
じかんわり
SIGH...
FOR WINTER BREAK—
YER SUCH A KID, NARU! THERE AIN'T NO SANTA!

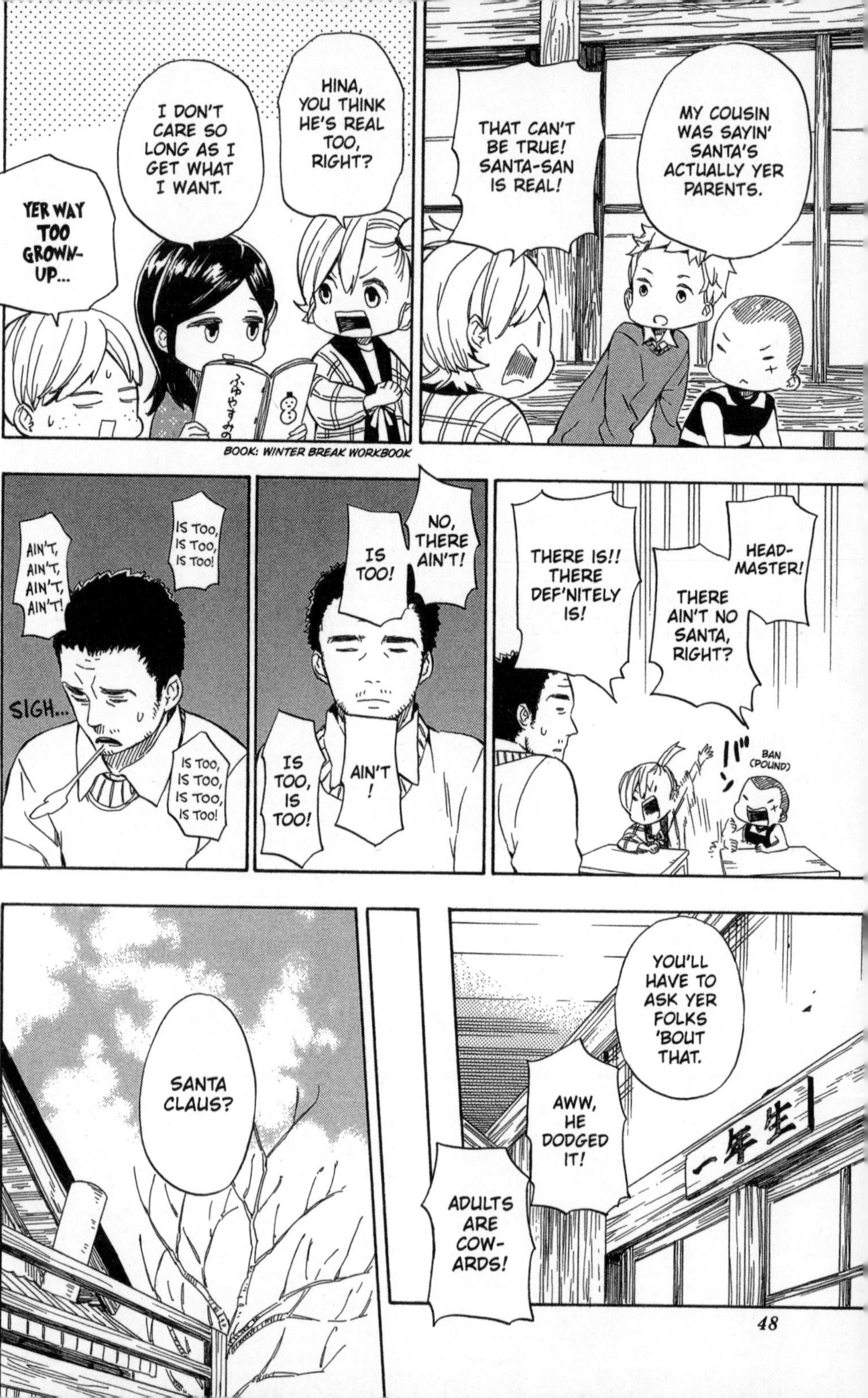
MY COUSIN WAS SAYIN' SANTA'S ACTUALLY YER PARENTS.
THAT CAN'T BE TRUE! SANTA-SAN IS REAL!
HINA, YOU THINK HE'S REAL TOO, RIGHT?
I DON'T CARE SO LONG AS I GET WHAT I WANT.
YER WAY TOO GROWN-UP...
ふゆやすみの
BOOK: WINTER BREAK WORKBOOK
HEAD-MASTER!
THERE AIN'T NO SANTA, RIGHT?
THERE IS!! THERE DEF'NITELY IS!
バ
BAN (POUND)
NO, THERE AIN'T!
IS TOO!
AIN'T!
IS TOO, IS TOO!
IS TOO, IS TOO, IS TOO!
AIN'T, AIN'T, AIN'T, AIN'T!
SIGH...
IS TOO, IS TOO, IS TOO, IS TOO!
YOU'LL HAVE TO ASK YER FOLKS 'BOUT THAT.
AWW, HE DODGED IT!
ADULTS ARE COW-ARDS!
一年生
SANTA CLAUS?

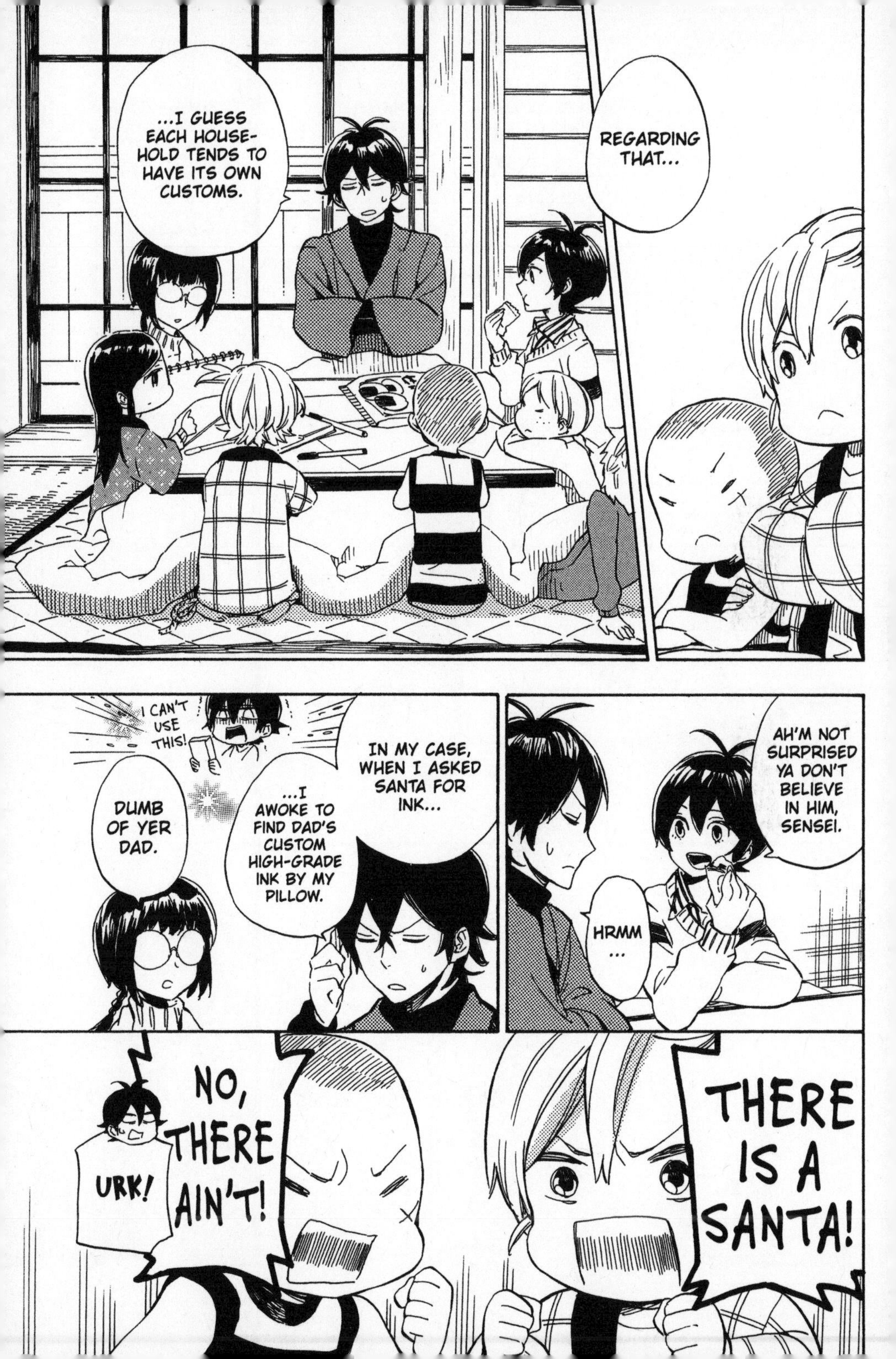
REGARDING THAT...
...I GUESS EACH HOUSEHOLD TENDS TO HAVE ITS OWN CUSTOMS.
AH'M NOT SURPRISED YA DON'T BELIEVE IN HIM, SENSEI.
HRMM ...
IN MY CASE, WHEN I ASKED SANTA FOR INK...
...I AWOKE TO FIND DAD'S CUSTOM HIGH-GRADE INK BY MY PILLOW.
I CAN'T USE THIS!
DUMB OF YER DAD.
THERE IS A SANTA!
NO, THERE AIN'T!
URK!

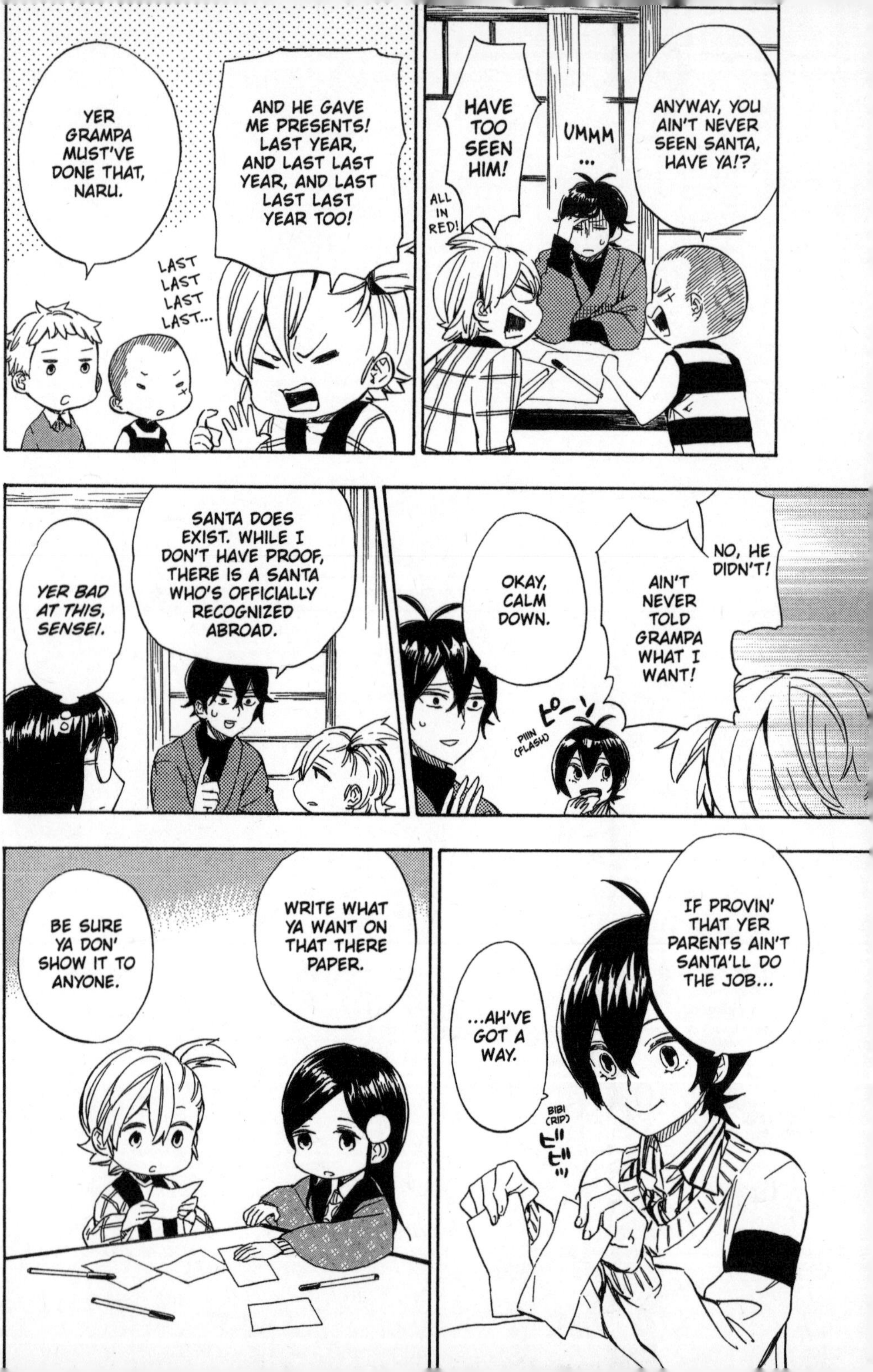
ANYWAY, YOU AIN'T NEVER SEEN SANTA, HAVE YA!?
UMMM ...
HAVE TOO SEEN HIM!
ALL IN RED!
AND HE GAVE ME PRESENTS! LAST YEAR, AND LAST LAST YEAR, AND LAST LAST LAST YEAR TOO!
YER GRAMPA MUST'VE DONE THAT, NARU.
LAST LAST LAST LAST...
NO, HE DIDN'T!
AIN'T NEVER TOLD GRAMPA WHAT I WANT!
OKAY, CALM DOWN.
ピーン
PIIIN (FLASH)
SANTA DOES EXIST. WHILE I DON'T HAVE PROOF, THERE IS A SANTA WHO'S OFFICIALLY RECOGNIZED ABROAD.
YER BAD AT THIS, SENSEI.
IF PROVIN' THAT YER PARENTS AIN'T SANTA'LL DO THE JOB...
...AH'VE GOT A WAY.
BIBI (RIP)
ビビッ
WRITE WHAT YA WANT ON THAT THERE PAPER.
BE SURE YA DON' SHOW IT TO ANYONE.

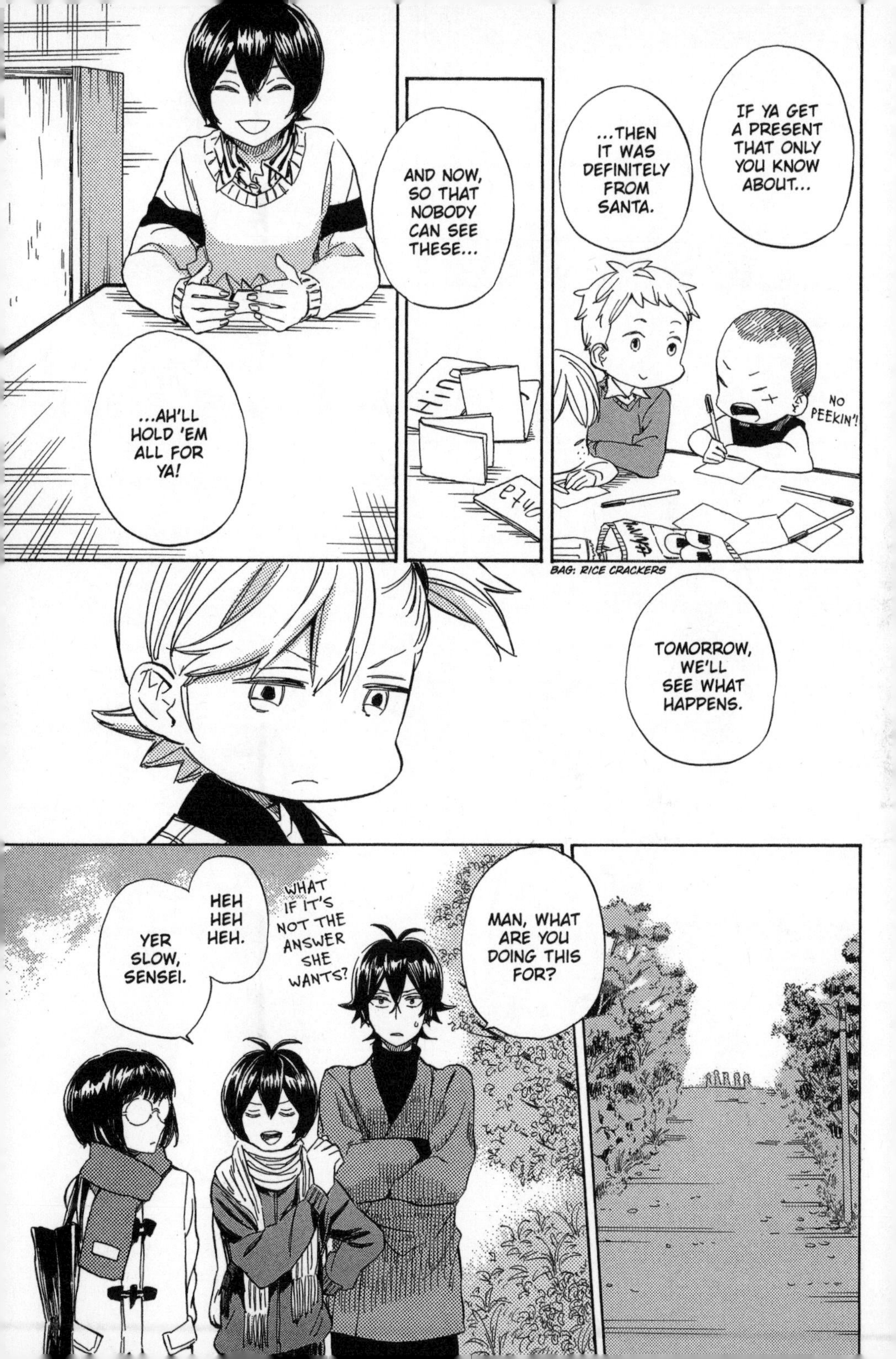
IF YA GET A PRESENT THAT ONLY YOU KNOW ABOUT...
...THEN IT WAS DEFINITELY FROM SANTA.
NO PEEKIN'!
BAG: RICE CRACKERS
AND NOW, SO THAT NOBODY CAN SEE THESE...
...AH'LL HOLD 'EM ALL FOR YA!
TOMORROW, WE'LL SEE WHAT HAPPENS.
MAN, WHAT ARE YOU DOING THIS FOR?
WHAT IF IT'S NOT THE ANSWER SHE WANTS?
HEH HEH HEH.
YER SLOW, SENSEI.

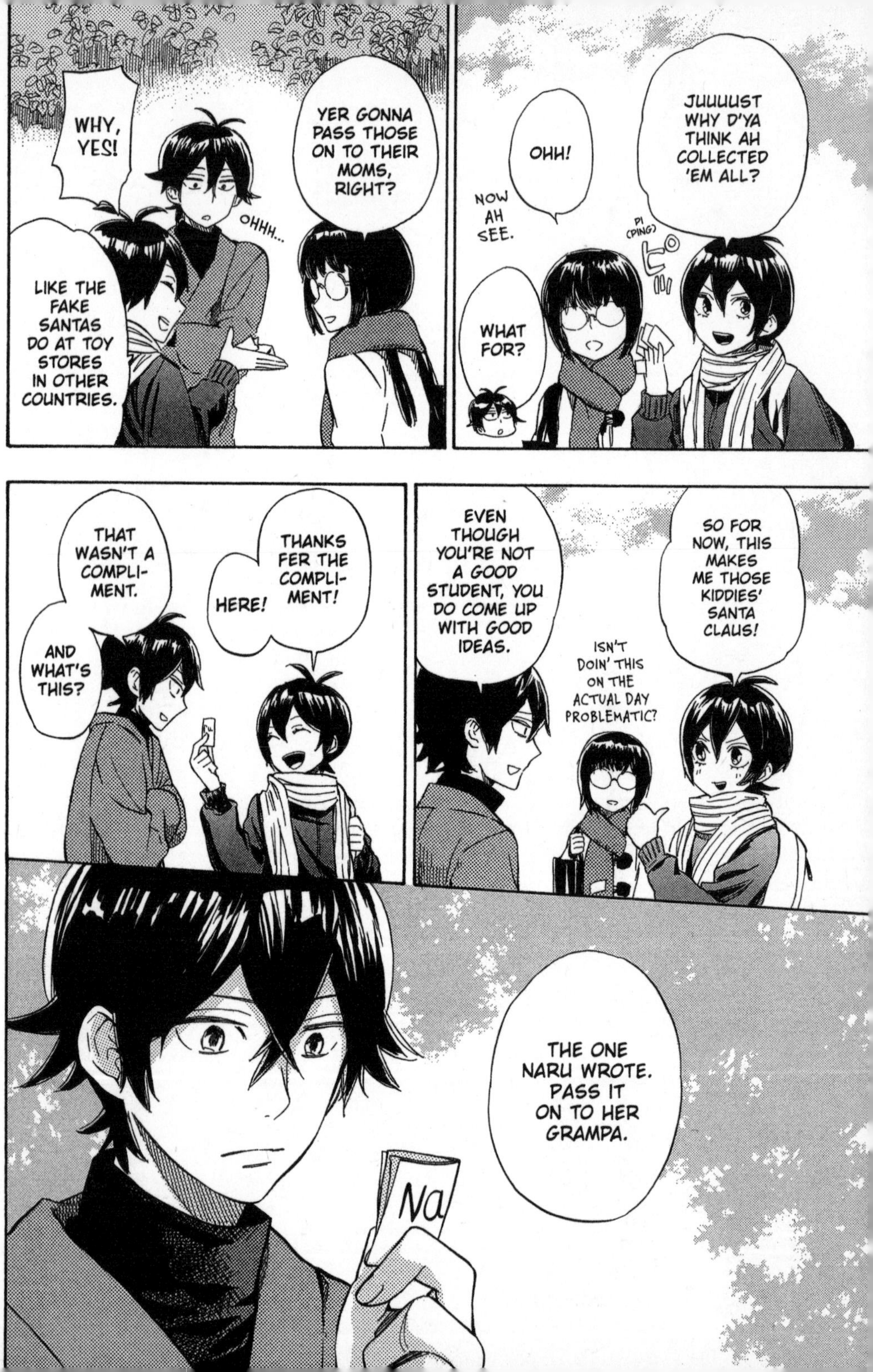
JUUUUST WHY D'YA THINK AH COLLECTED 'EM ALL?
PI (PING)
OHH!
NOW AH SEE.
WHAT FOR?
YER GONNA PASS THOSE ON TO THEIR MOMS, RIGHT?
OHHH...
WHY, YES!
LIKE THE FAKE SANTAS DO AT TOY STORES IN OTHER COUNTRIES.
SO FOR NOW, THIS MAKES ME THOSE KIDDIES' SANTA CLAUS!
ISN'T DOIN' THIS ON THE ACTUAL DAY PROBLEMATIC?
EVEN THOUGH YOU'RE NOT A GOOD STUDENT, YOU DO COME UP WITH GOOD IDEAS.
THANKS FER THE COMPLIMENT!
HERE!
THAT WASN'T A COMPLI-MENT.
AND WHAT'S THIS?
THE ONE NARU WROTE. PASS IT ON TO HER GRAMPA.
Na

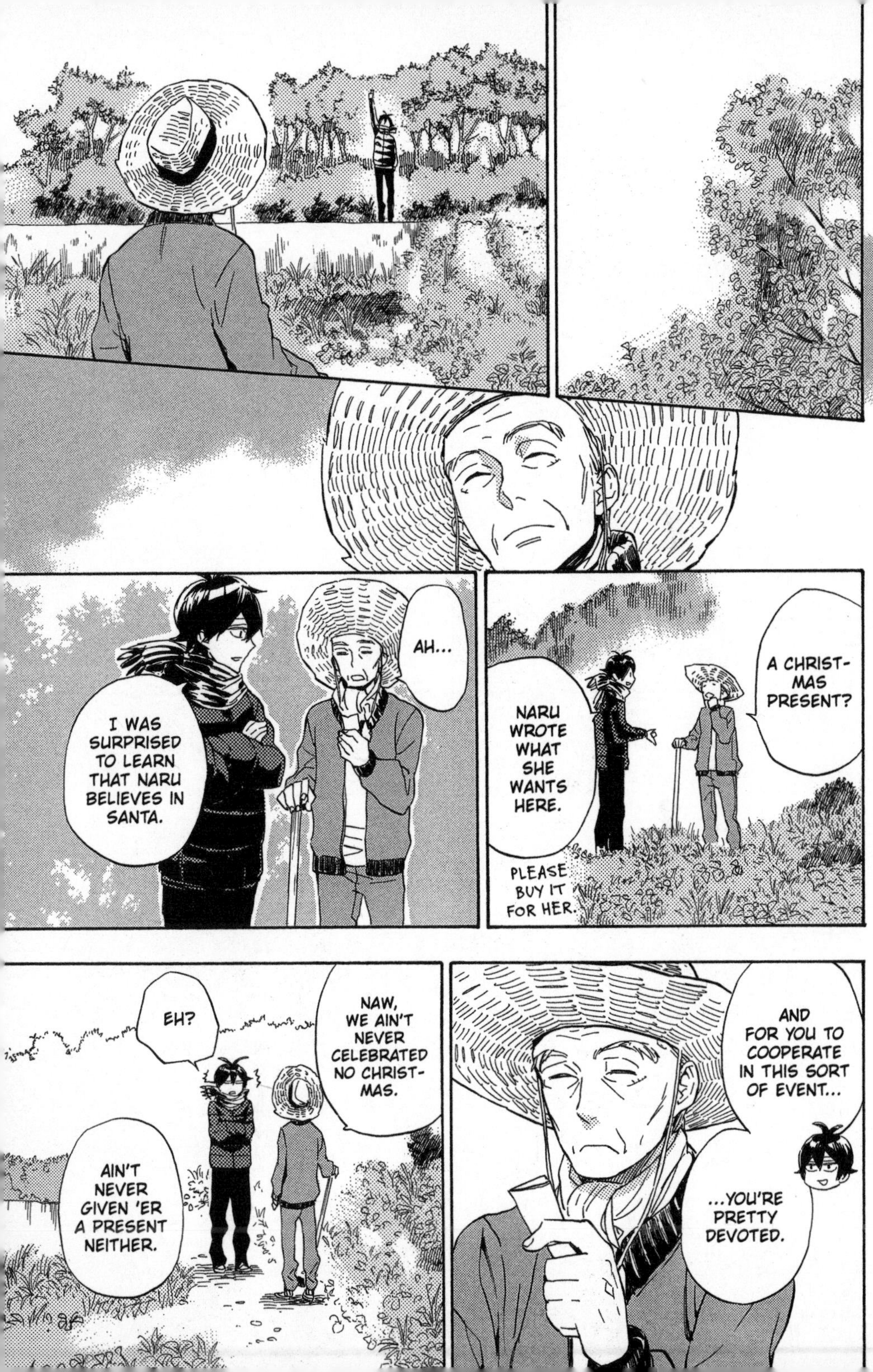
A CHRIST-MAS PRESENT?
NARU WROTE WHAT SHE WANTS HERE.
PLEASE BUY IT FOR HER.
AH...
I WAS SURPRISED TO LEARN THAT NARU BELIEVES IN SANTA.
AND FOR YOU TO COOPERATE IN THIS SORT OF EVENT...
...YOU'RE PRETTY DEVOTED.
NAW, WE AIN'T NEVER CELEBRATED NO CHRIST-MAS.
EH?
AIN'T NEVER GIVEN 'ER A PRESENT NEITHER.

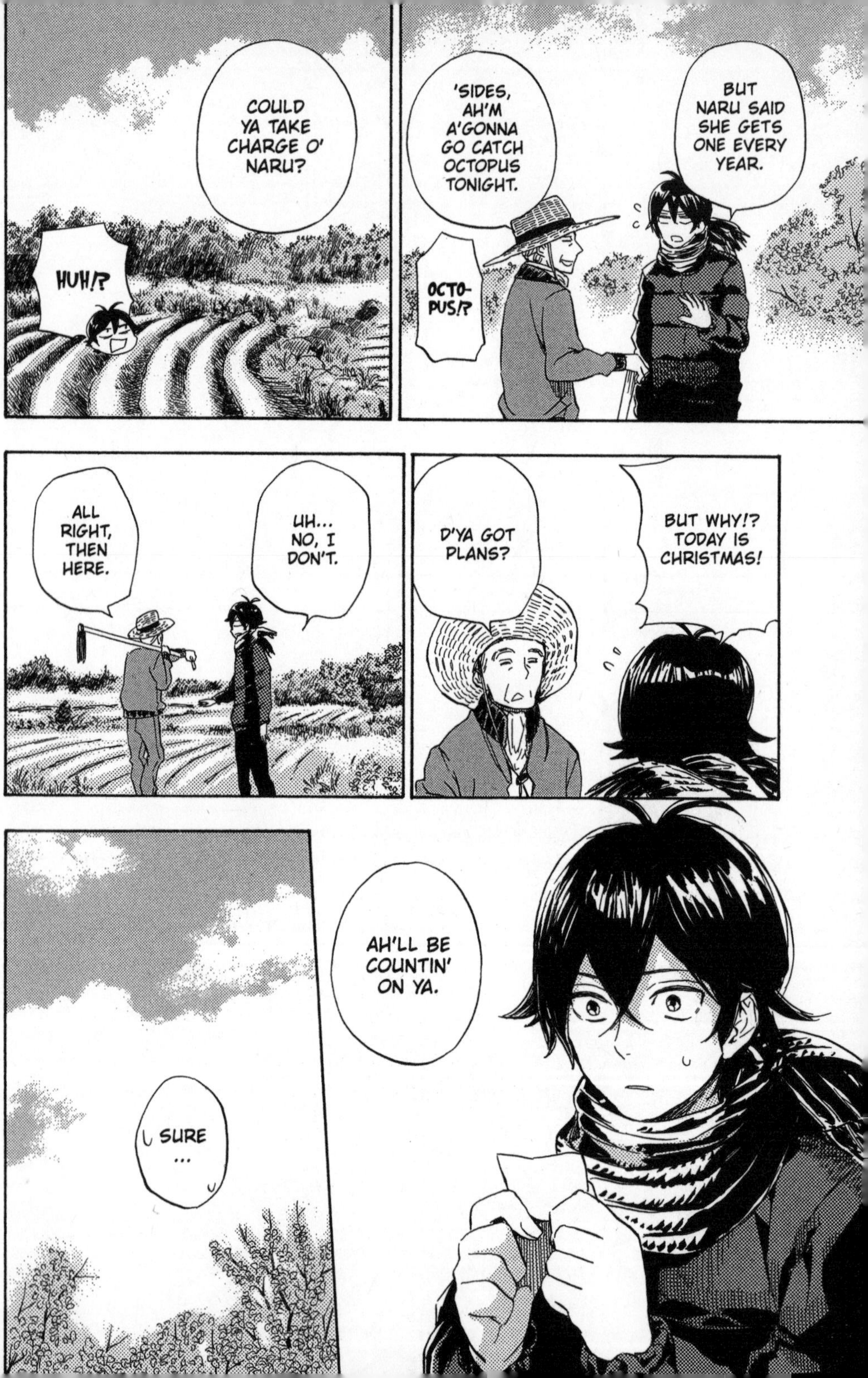
BUT NARU SAID SHE GETS ONE EVERY YEAR.
'SIDES, AH'M A'GONNA GO CATCH OCTOPUS TONIGHT.
OCTO-PUS!?
COULD YA TAKE CHARGE O' NARU?
HUH!?
BUT WHY!? TODAY IS CHRISTMAS!
D'YA GOT PLANS?
UH... NO, I DON'T.
ALL RIGHT, THEN HERE.
AH'LL BE COUNTIN' ON YA.
SURE ...

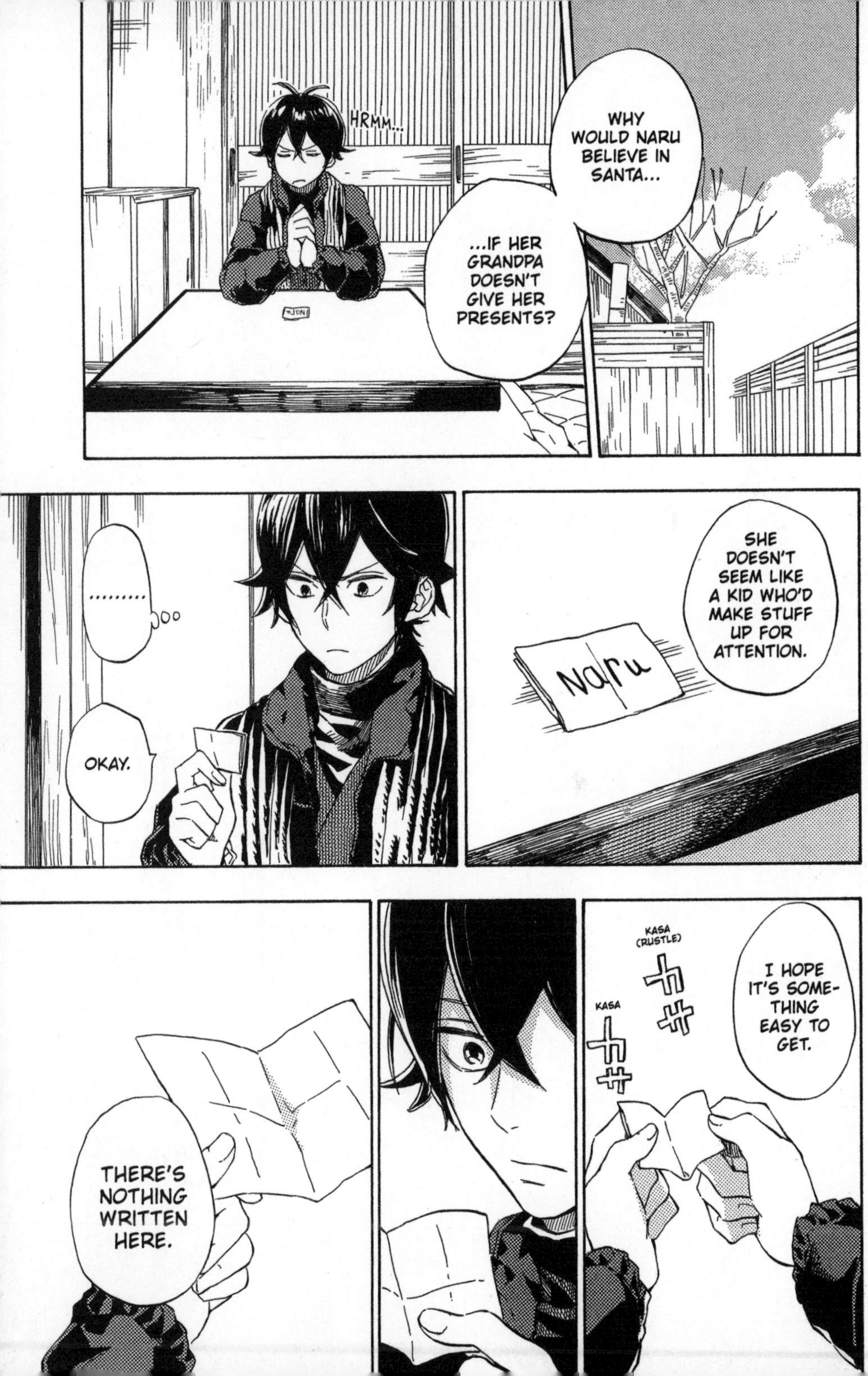
WHY WOULD NARU BELIEVE IN SANTA...
...IF HER GRANDPA DOESN'T GIVE HER PRESENTS?
HRMM...
SHE DOESN'T SEEM LIKE A KID WHO'D MAKE STUFF UP FOR ATTENTION.
Naru
....
OKAY.
KASA (RUSTLE)
KASA
I HOPE IT'S SOME-THING EASY TO GET.
THERE'S NOTHING WRITTEN HERE.

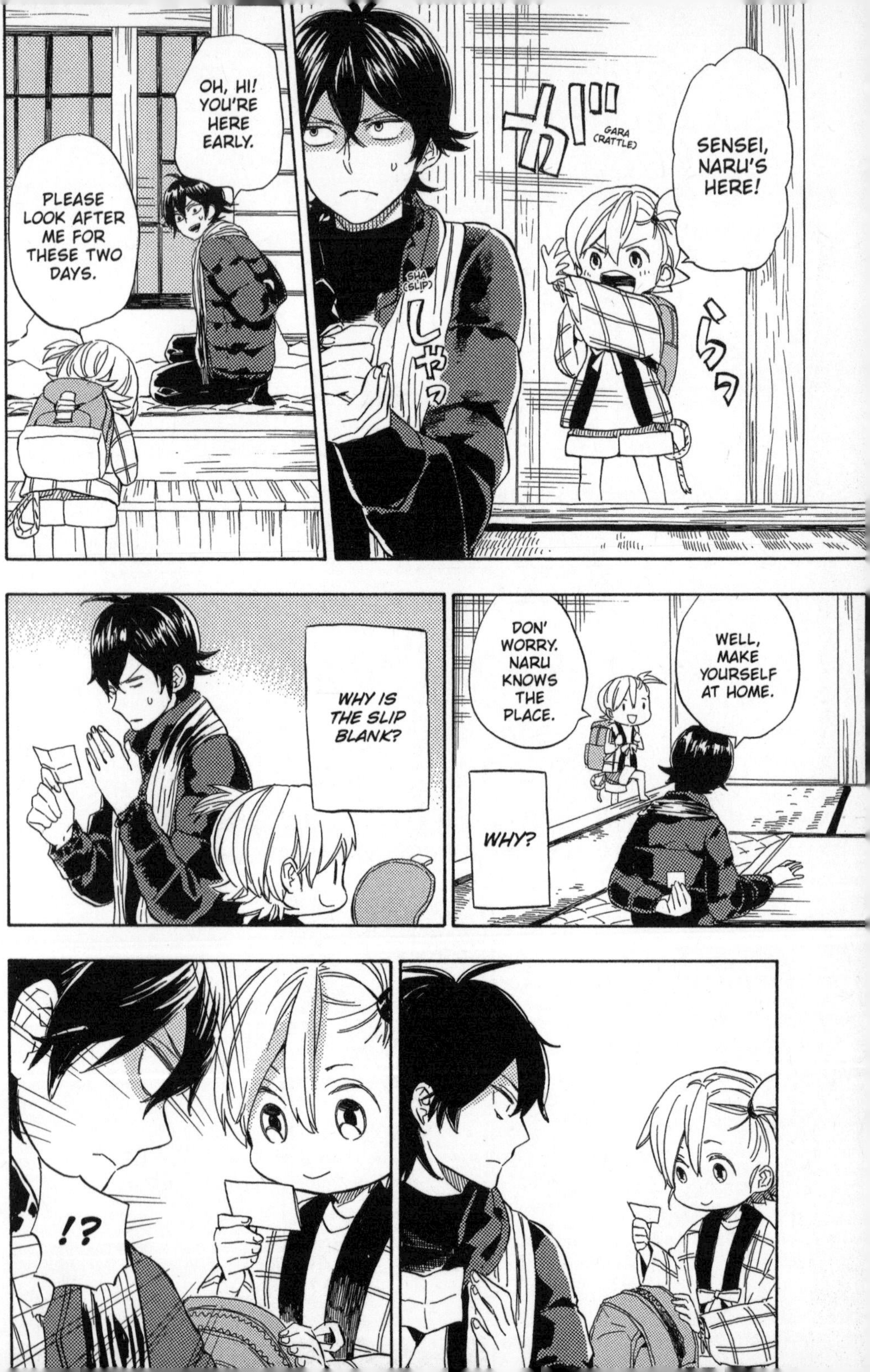
SENSEI, NARU'S HERE!
GARA (RATTLE)
SHA (SLIP)
OH, HI! YOU'RE HERE EARLY.
PLEASE LOOK AFTER ME FOR THESE TWO DAYS.
WELL, MAKE YOURSELF AT HOME.
DON' WORRY. NARU KNOWS THE PLACE.
WHY?
WHY IS THE SLIP BLANK?
!?

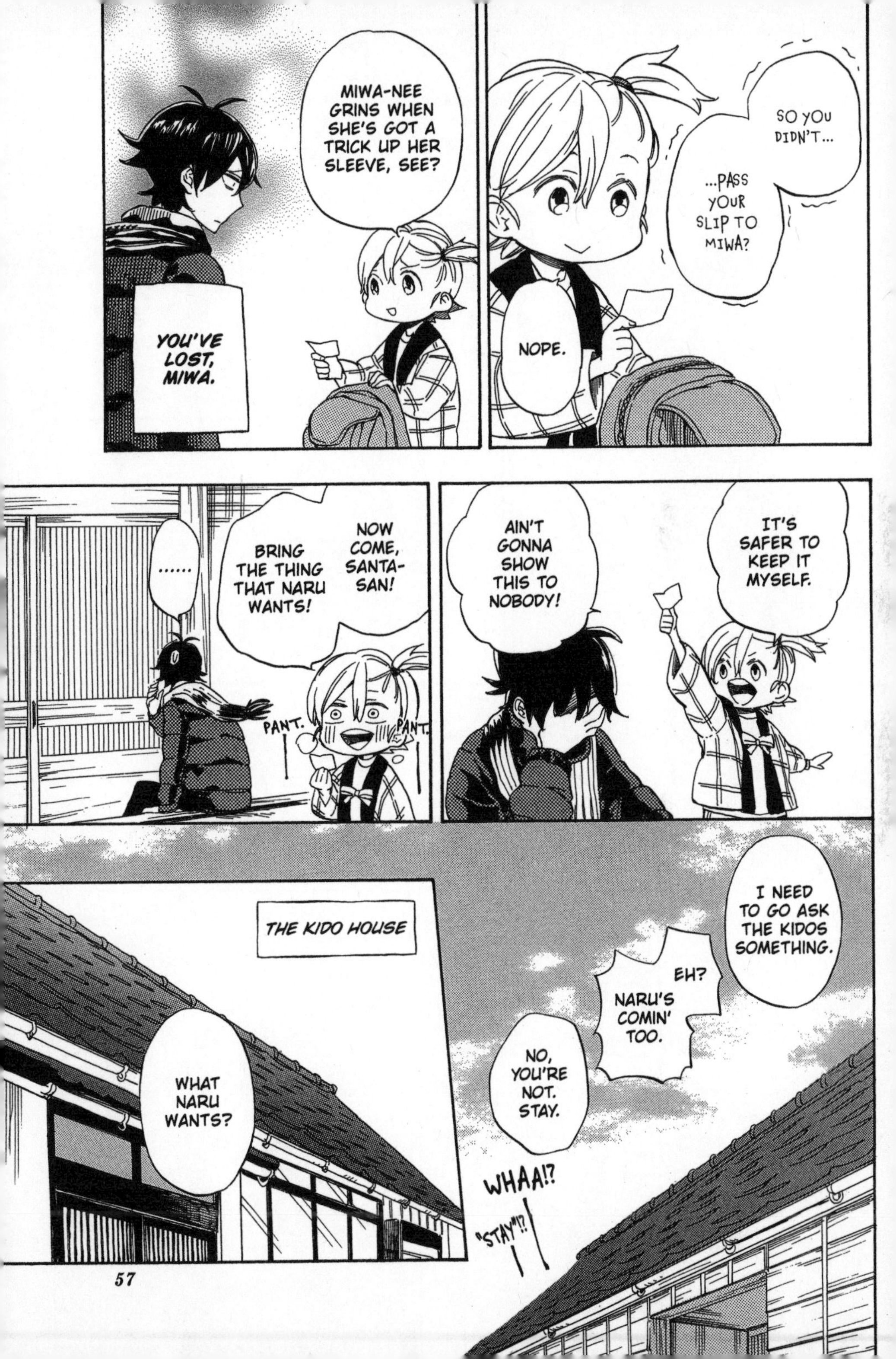
SO YOU DIDN'T...
...PASS YOUR SLIP TO MIWA?
NOPE.
MIWA-NEE GRINS WHEN SHE'S GOT A TRICK UP HER SLEEVE, SEE?
YOU'VE LOST, MIWA.
IT'S SAFER TO KEEP IT MYSELF.
AIN'T GONNA SHOW THIS TO NOBODY!
NOW COME, SANTA-SAN!
BRING THE THING THAT NARU WANTS!
PANT.
PANT.
......
I NEED TO GO ASK THE KIDOS SOMETHING.
EH? NARU'S COMIN' TOO.
NO, YOU'RE NOT. STAY.
WHAA!?
"STAY"!?
THE KIDO HOUSE
WHAT NARU WANTS?

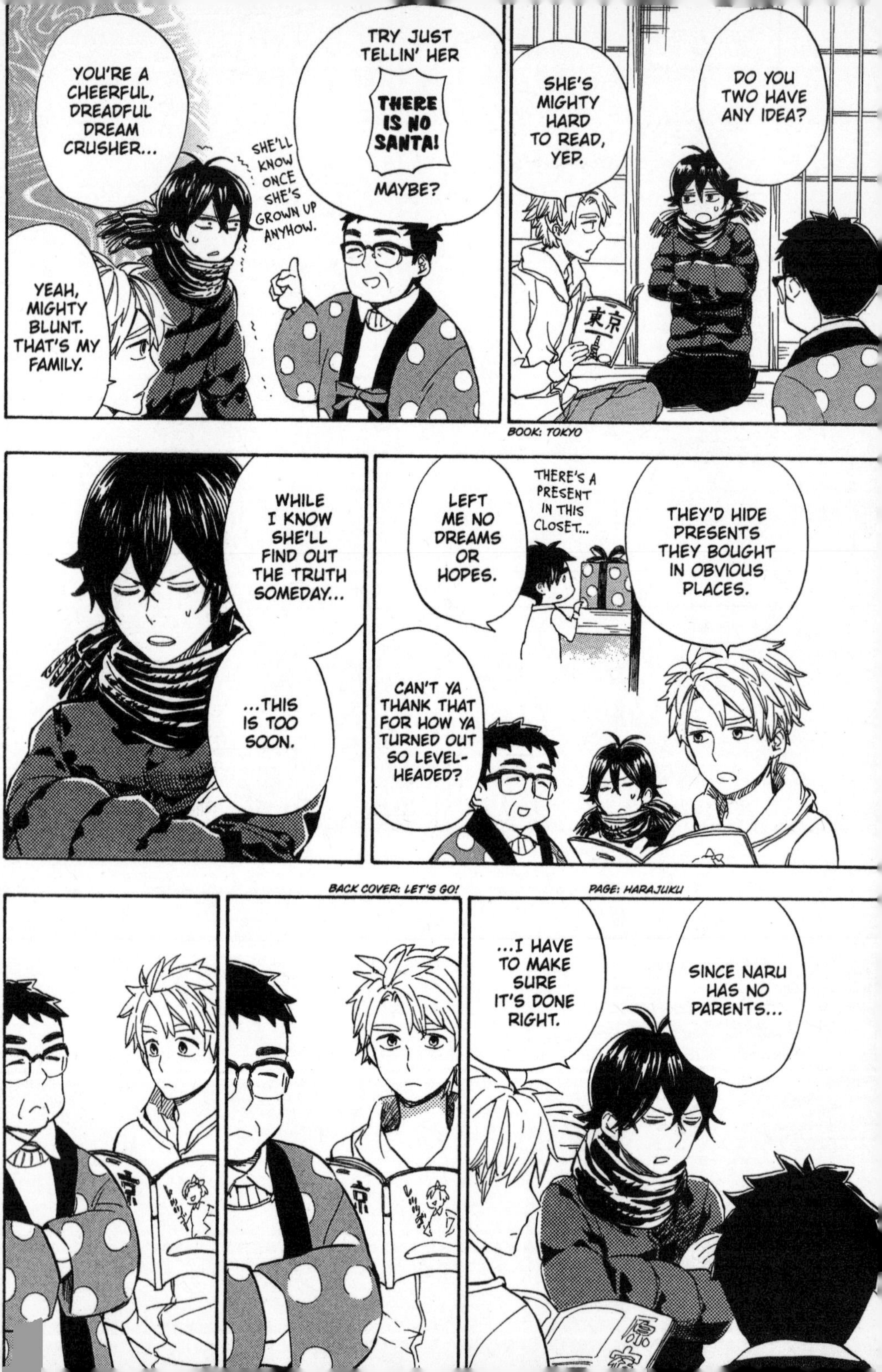
DO YOU TWO HAVE ANY IDEA?
SHE'S MIGHTY HARD TO READ, YEP.
BOOK: TOKYO
TRY JUST TELLIN' HER
THERE IS NO SANTA!
MAYBE?
SHE'LL KNOW ONCE SHE'S GROWN UP ANYHOW.
YOU'RE A CHEERFUL, DREADFUL DREAM CRUSHER...
YEAH, MIGHTY BLUNT. THAT'S MY FAMILY.
THEY'D HIDE PRESENTS THEY BOUGHT IN OBVIOUS PLACES.
THERE'S A PRESENT IN THIS CLOSET...
LEFT ME NO DREAMS OR HOPES.
CAN'T YA THANK THAT FOR HOW YA TURNED OUT SO LEVEL-HEADED?
PAGE: HARAJUKU
WHILE I KNOW SHE'LL FIND OUT THE TRUTH SOMEDAY...
...THIS IS TOO SOON.
BACK COVER: LET'S GO!
SINCE NARU HAS NO PARENTS...
...I HAVE TO MAKE SURE IT'S DONE RIGHT.

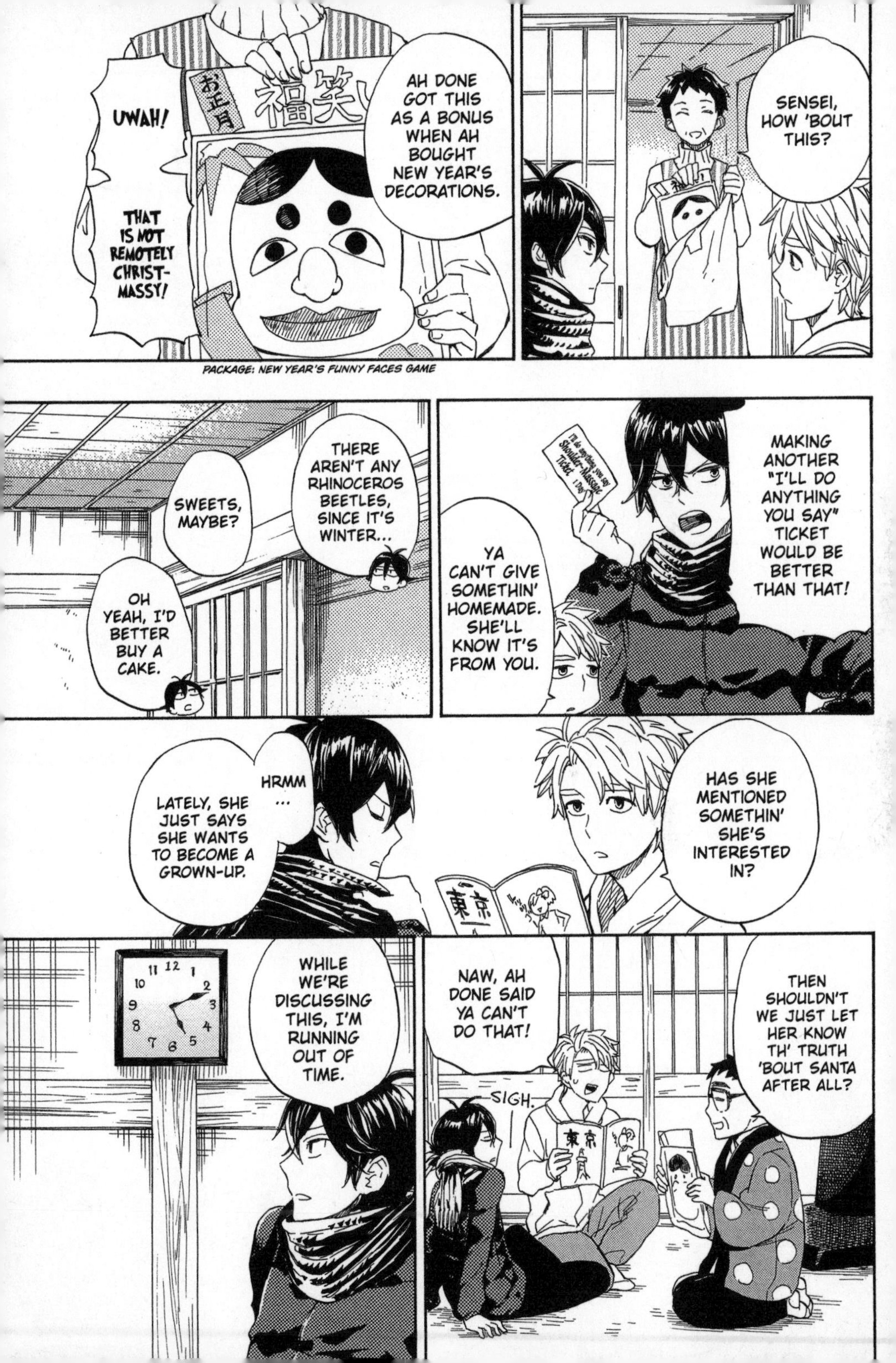
SENSEI, HOW 'BOUT THIS?
AH DONE GOT THIS AS A BONUS WHEN AH BOUGHT NEW YEAR'S DECORATIONS.
お正月
福笑い
UWAH!
THAT IS NOT REMOTELY CHRIST-MASSY!
PACKAGE: NEW YEAR'S FUNNY FACES GAME
MAKING ANOTHER "I'LL DO ANYTHING YOU SAY" TICKET WOULD BE BETTER THAN THAT!
YA CAN'T GIVE SOMETHIN' HOMEMADE. SHE'LL KNOW IT'S FROM YOU.
THERE AREN'T ANY RHINOCEROS BEETLES, SINCE IT'S WINTER...
SWEETS, MAYBE?
OH YEAH, I'D BETTER BUY A CAKE.
HAS SHE MENTIONED SOMETHIN' SHE'S INTERESTED IN?
HRMM ...
LATELY, SHE JUST SAYS SHE WANTS TO BECOME A GROWN-UP.
東京
THEN SHOULDN'T WE JUST LET HER KNOW TH' TRUTH 'BOUT SANTA AFTER ALL?
NAW, AH DONE SAID YA CAN'T DO THAT!
SIGH.
東京
WHILE WE'RE DISCUSSING THIS, I'M RUNNING OUT OF TIME.

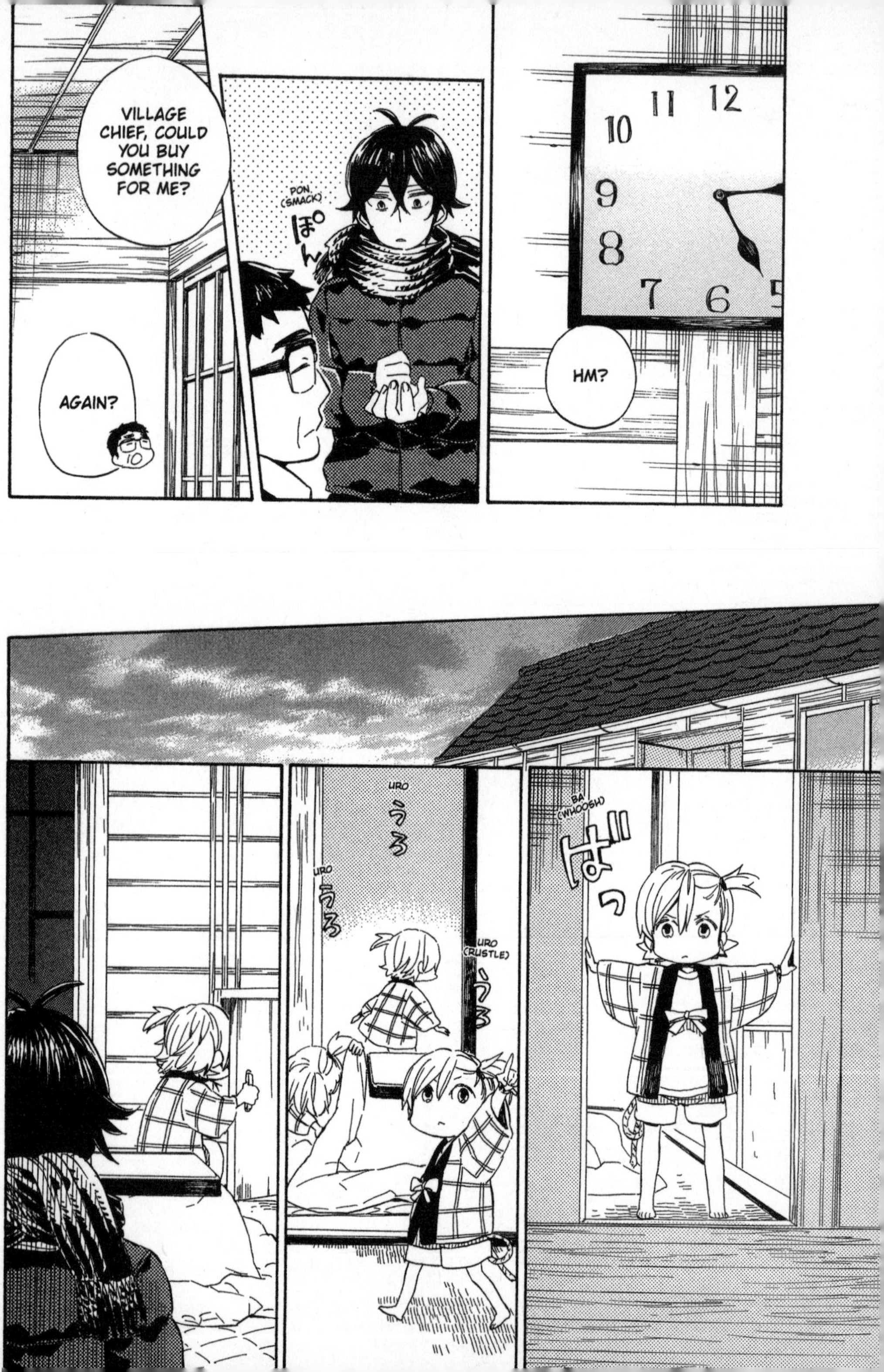

HM?
PON (SMACK)
ぽん
VILLAGE CHIEF, COULD YOU BUY SOMETHING FOR ME?
AGAIN?
BA (WHOOSH)
ばっ
URO
うろ
URO
うろ
URO (RUSTLE)
うろ

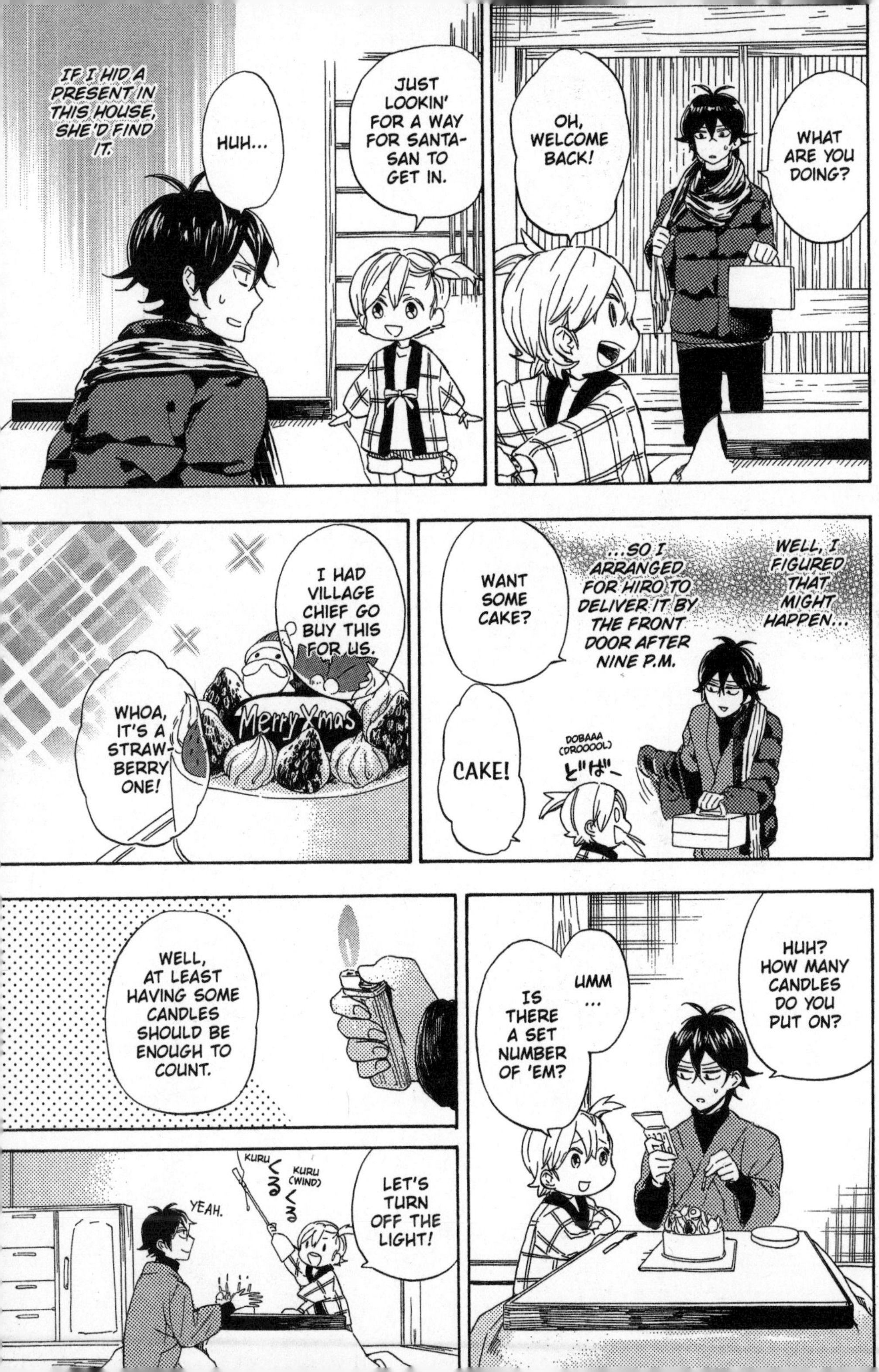
WHAT ARE YOU DOING?
OH, WELCOME BACK!
JUST LOOKIN' FOR A WAY FOR SANTA-SAN TO GET IN.
HUH...
IF I HID A PRESENT IN THIS HOUSE, SHE'D FIND IT.
WELL, I FIGURED THAT MIGHT HAPPEN...
...SO I ARRANGED FOR HIRO TO DELIVER IT BY THE FRONT DOOR AFTER NINE P.M.
WANT SOME CAKE?
DOBAAA (DROOOOL)
どばー
CAKE!
I HAD VILLAGE CHIEF GO BUY THIS FOR US.
Merry Xmas
WHOA, IT'S A STRAWBERRY ONE!
HUH? HOW MANY CANDLES DO YOU PUT ON?
UMM...
IS THERE A SET NUMBER OF 'EM?
WELL, AT LEAST HAVING SOME CANDLES SHOULD BE ENOUGH TO COUNT.
LET'S TURN OFF THE LIGHT!
KURU KURU (WIND)
くるくる
YEAH.

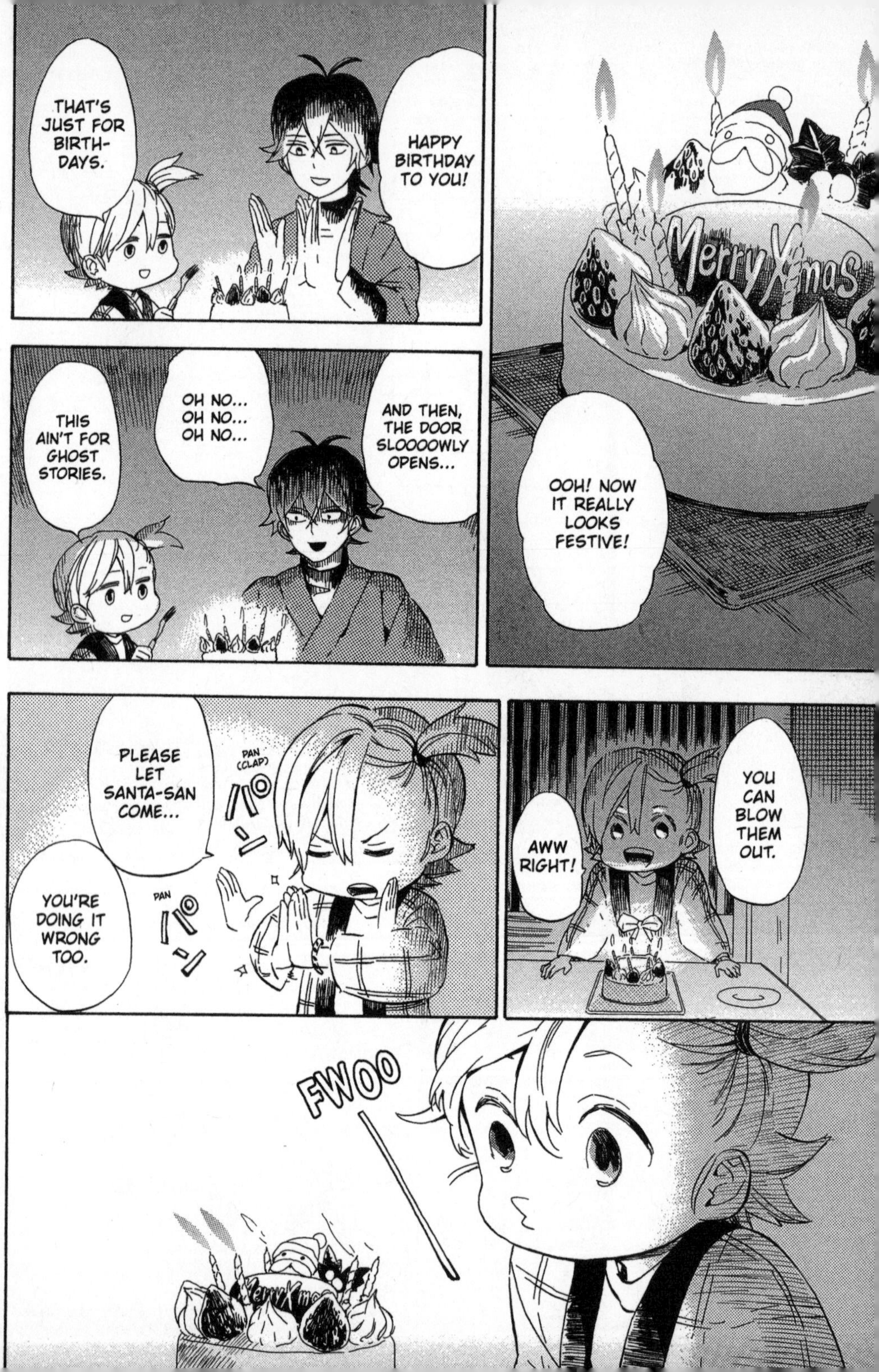
OOH! NOW IT REALLY LOOKS FESTIVE!
Merry X'mas
HAPPY BIRTHDAY TO YOU!
THAT'S JUST FOR BIRTHDAYS.
AND THEN, THE DOOR SLOOOOWLY OPENS...
OH NO... OH NO... OH NO...
THIS AIN'T FOR GHOST STORIES.
YOU CAN BLOW THEM OUT.
AWW RIGHT!
PAN (CLAP)
PLEASE LET SANTA-SAN COME...
PAN
YOU'RE DOING IT WRONG TOO.
FWOO

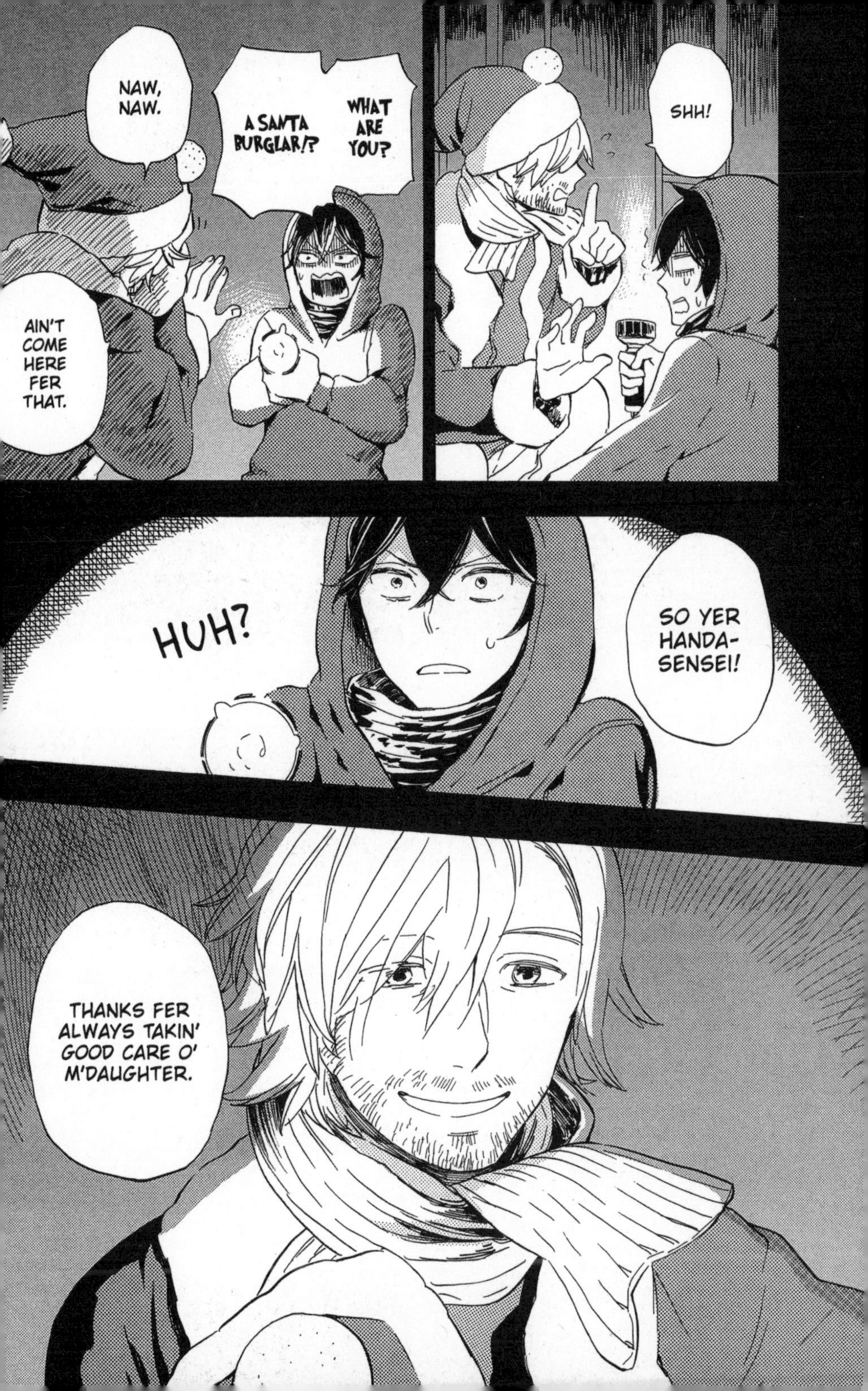
SHH!
WHAT ARE YOU?
A SANTA BURGLAR!?
NAW, NAW.
AIN'T COME HERE FER THAT.
SO YER HANDA-SENSEI!
HUH?
THANKS FER ALWAYS TAKIN' GOOD CARE O' M'DAUGHTER.

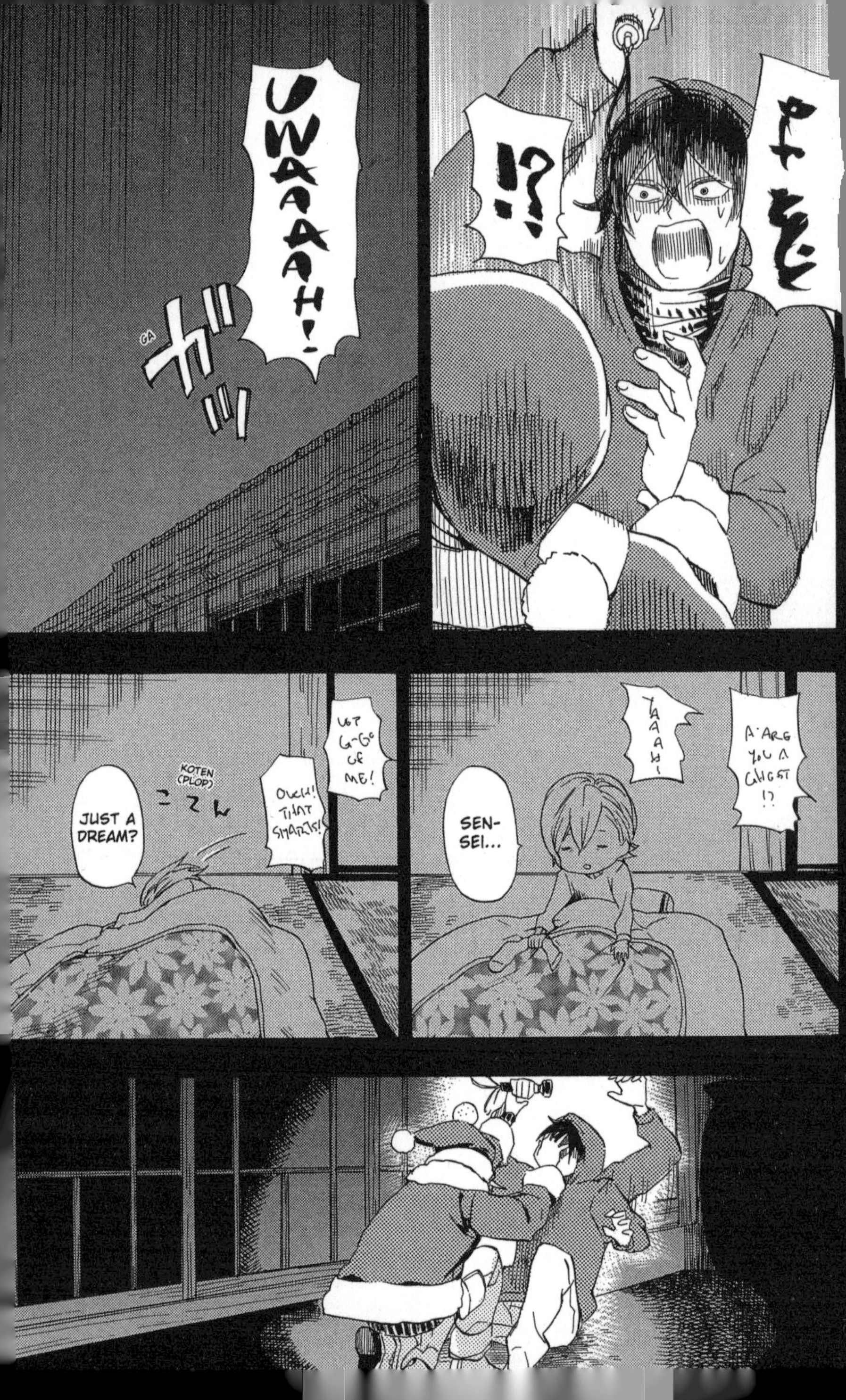
!?
UWAAAAH!
GA
ガッ
A-ARE YOU A GHOST!?
YAAAH!
SEN-SEI...
UGH G-GET OFF ME!
OUCH! THAT SMARTS!
KOTEN (PLOP)
こてん
JUST A DREAM?

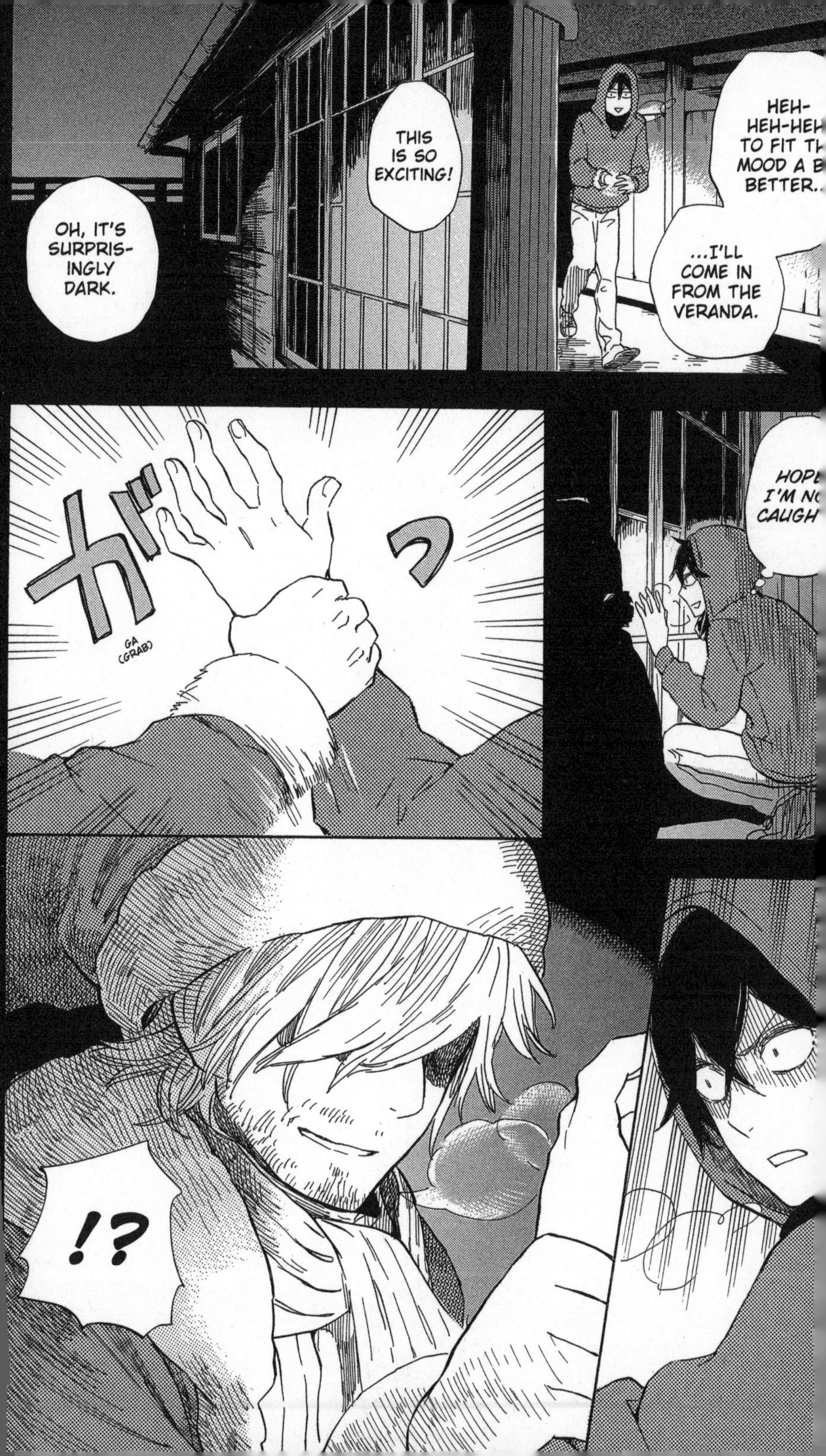
HEH-HEH-HEH TO FIT TH MOOD A B BETTER..
...I'LL COME IN FROM THE VERANDA.
THIS IS SO EXCITING!
OH, IT'S SURPRIS-INGLY DARK.
HOPE I'M NO CAUGH
ガッ
GA (GRAB)
!?

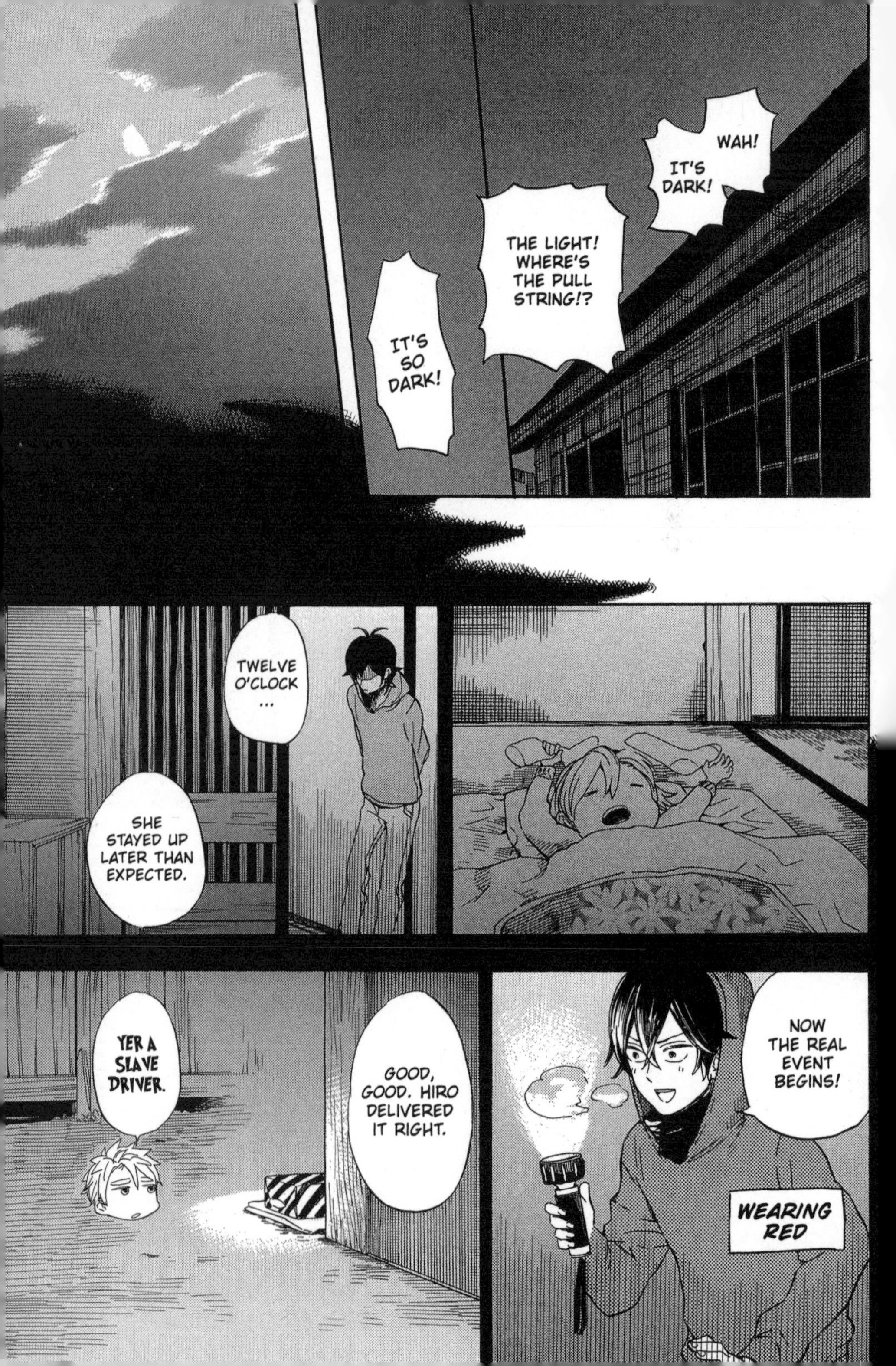
WAH! IT'S DARK!
THE LIGHT! WHERE'S THE PULL STRING!?
IT'S SO DARK!
TWELVE O'CLOCK ...
SHE STAYED UP LATER THAN EXPECTED.
NOW THE REAL EVENT BEGINS!
WEARING RED
GOOD, GOOD. HIRO DELIVERED IT RIGHT.
YER A SLAVE DRIVER.

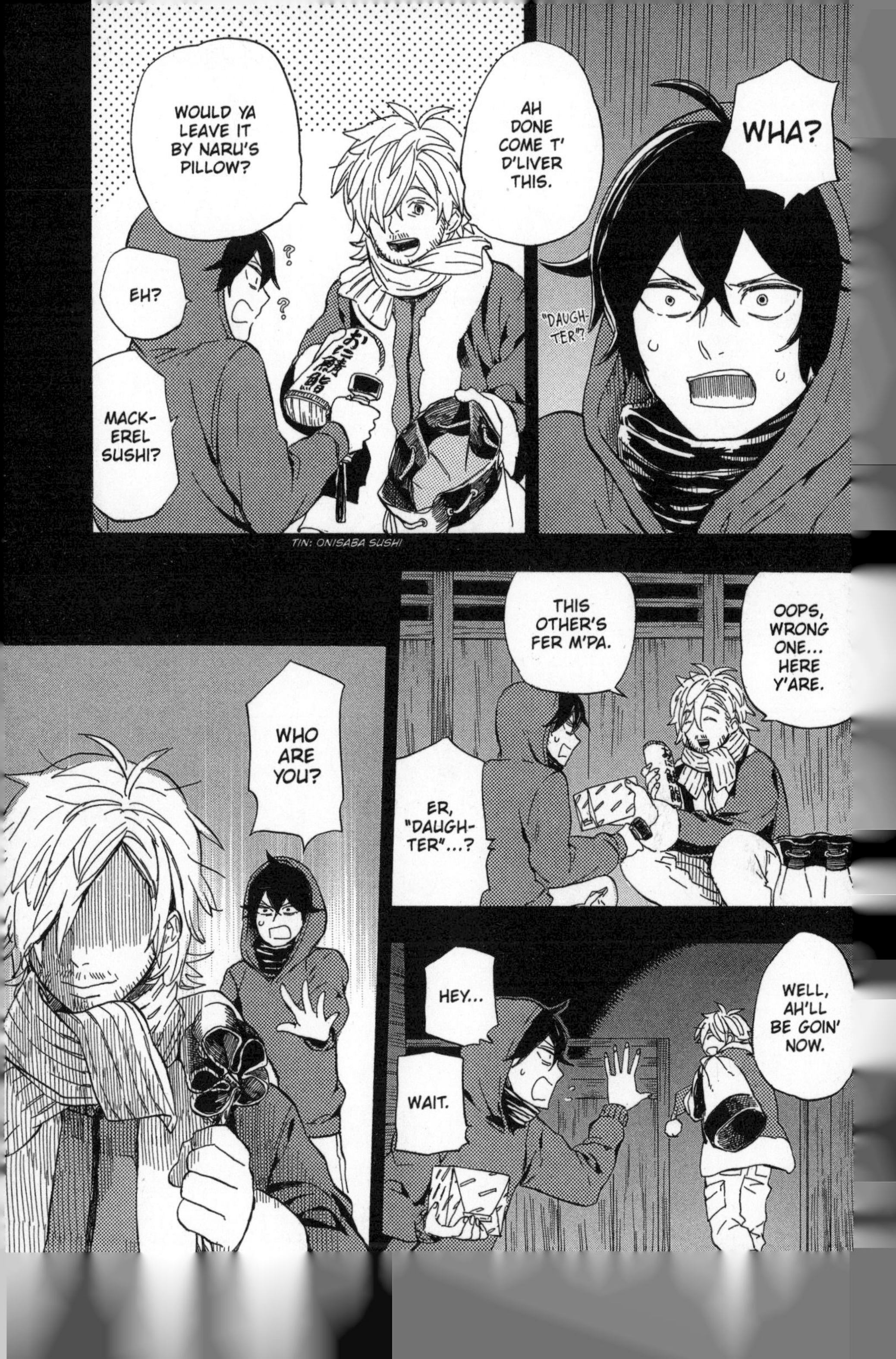
WHA?
"DAUGHTER"?
AH DONE COME T' D'LIVER THIS.
WOULD YA LEAVE IT BY NARU'S PILLOW?
EH?
MACKEREL SUSHI?
TIN: ONISABA SUSHI
OOPS, WRONG ONE... HERE Y'ARE.
THIS OTHER'S FER M'PA.
ER, "DAUGHTER"...?
WELL, AH'LL BE GOIN' NOW.
HEY...
WAIT.
WHO ARE YOU?

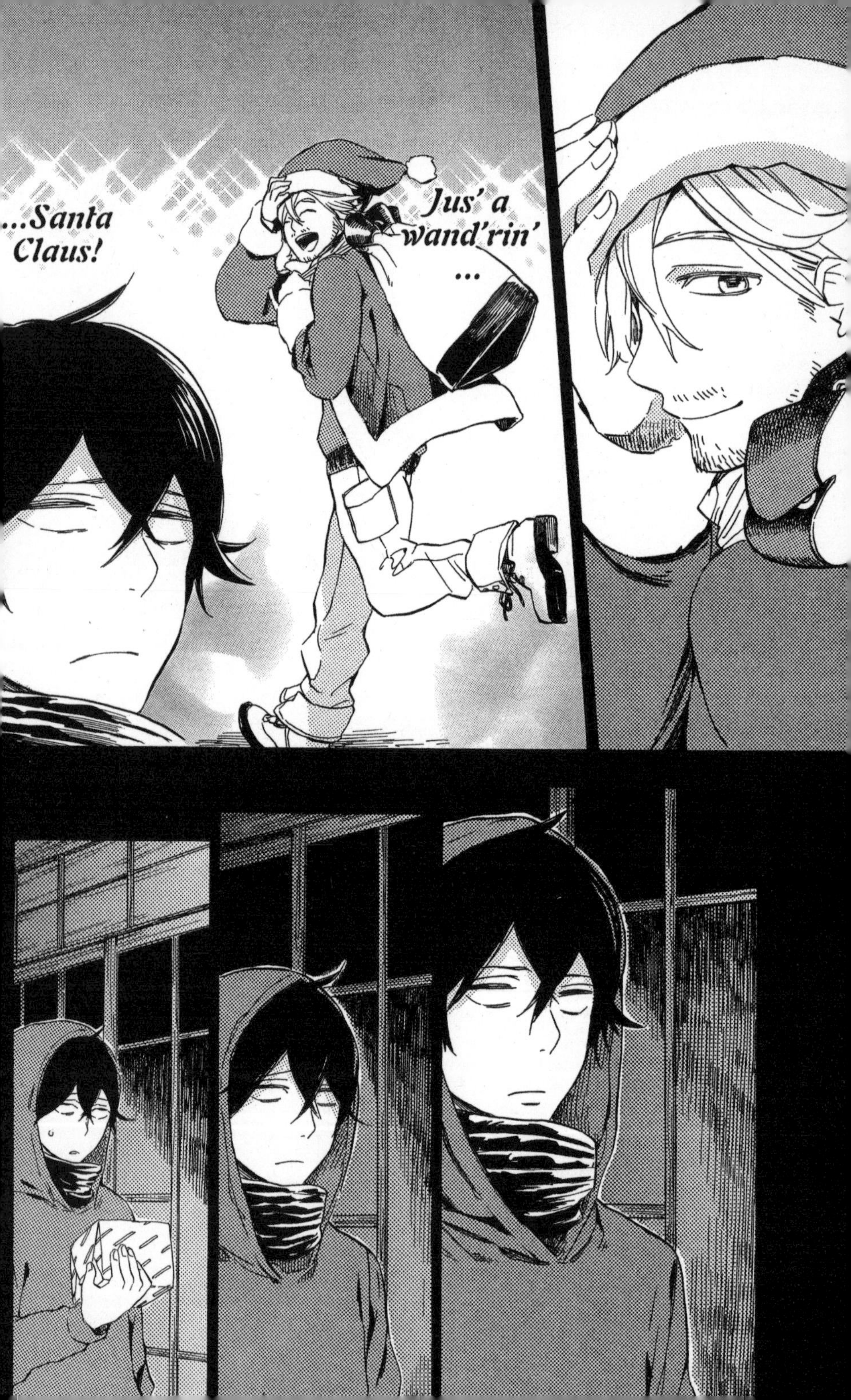
Jus' a wand'rin' ...
...Santa Claus!

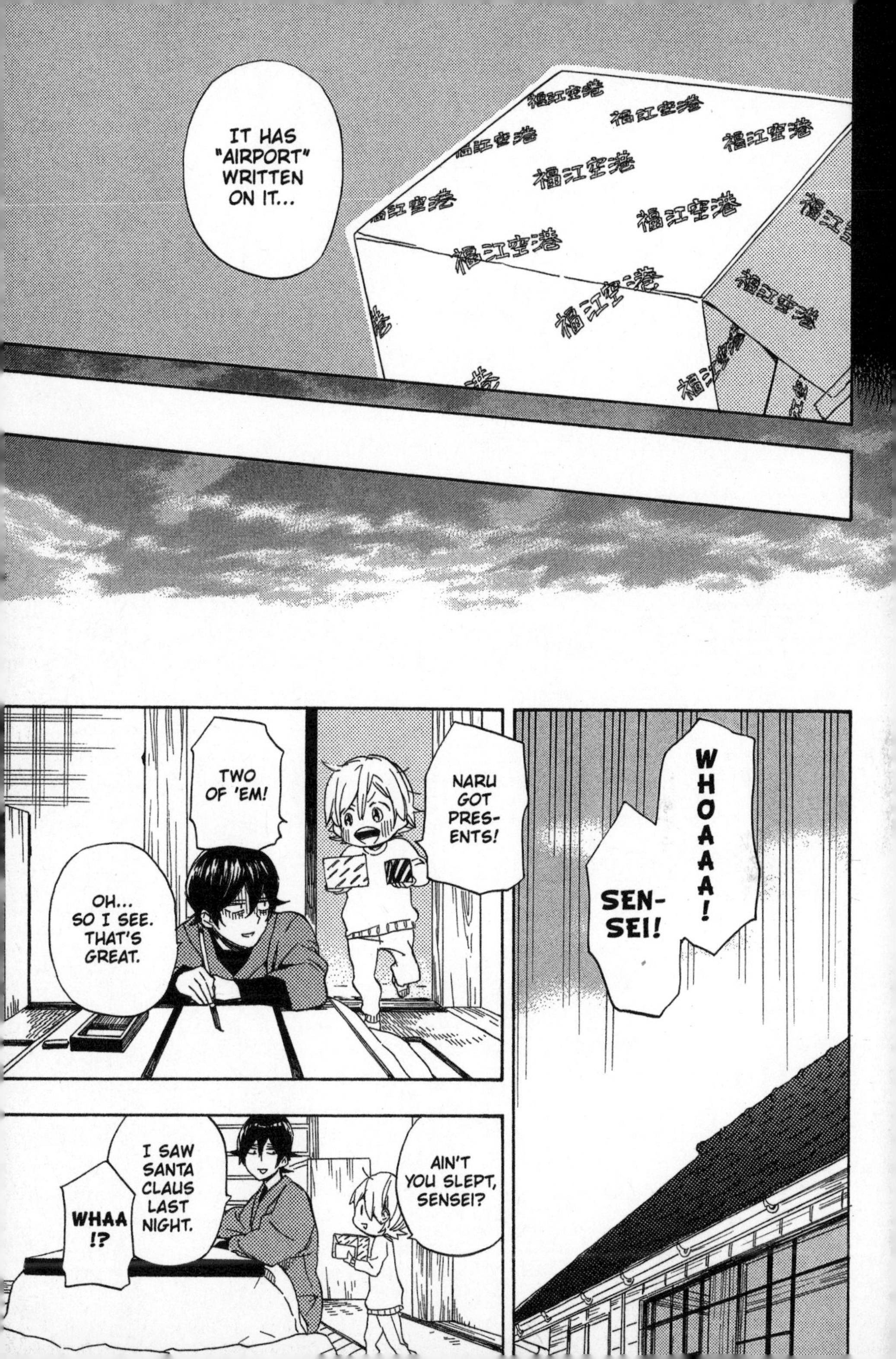
福江空港
IT HAS "AIRPORT" WRITTEN ON IT...
WHOAAAA! SEN-SEI!
NARU GOT PRES-ENTS!
TWO OF 'EM!
OH... SO I SEE. THAT'S GREAT.
AIN'T YOU SLEPT, SENSEI?
I SAW SANTA CLAUS LAST NIGHT.
WHAA!?

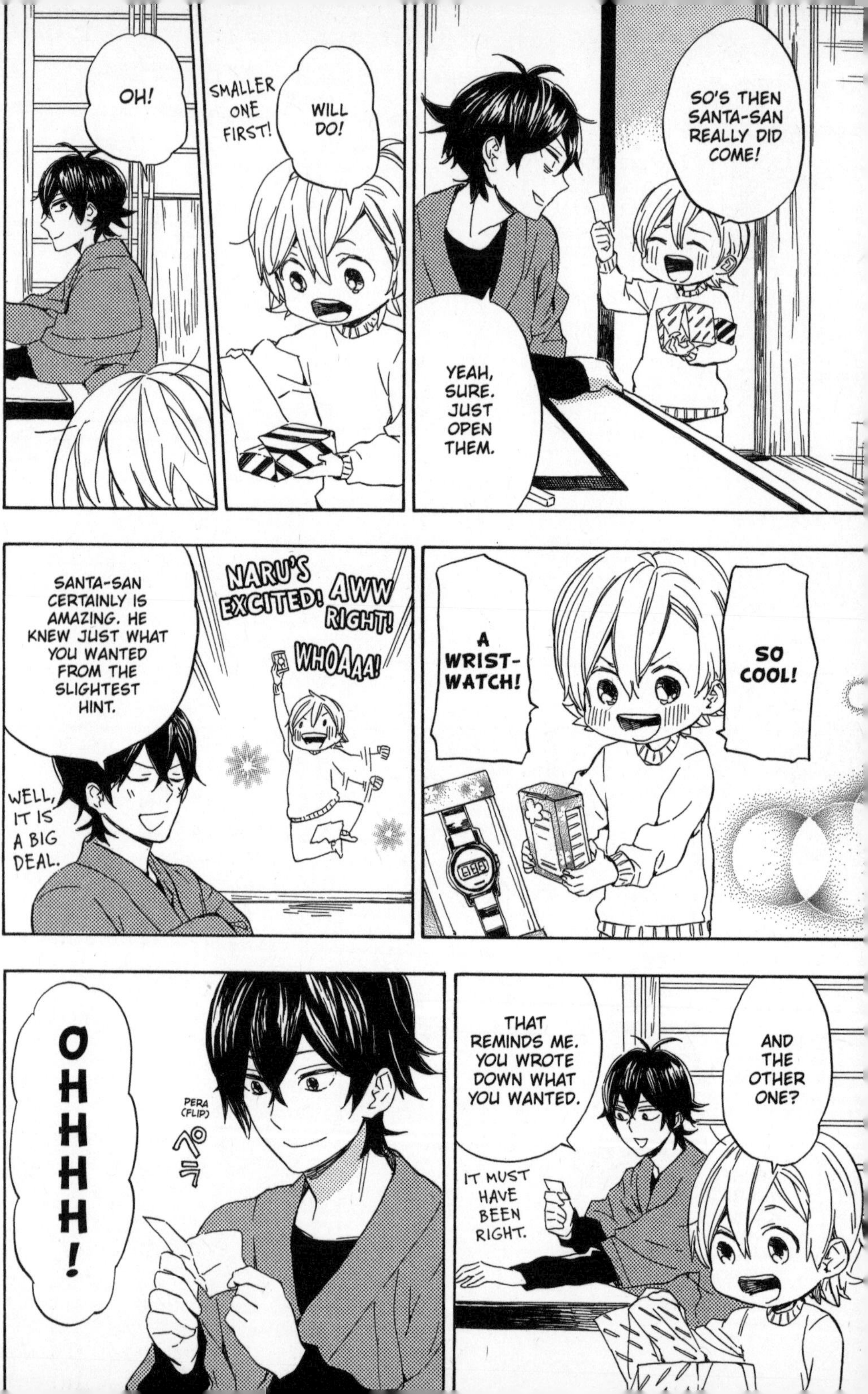
SO'S THEN SANTA-SAN REALLY DID COME!
YEAH, SURE. JUST OPEN THEM.
WILL DO!
SMALLER ONE FIRST!
OH!
SO COOL!
A WRIST-WATCH!
AWW RIGHT!
NARU'S EXCITED!
WHOAAA!
SANTA-SAN CERTAINLY IS AMAZING. HE KNEW JUST WHAT YOU WANTED FROM THE SLIGHTEST HINT.
WELL, IT IS A BIG DEAL.
AND THE OTHER ONE?
THAT REMINDS ME. YOU WROTE DOWN WHAT YOU WANTED.
IT MUST HAVE BEEN RIGHT.
PERA (FLIP)
OHHHH!

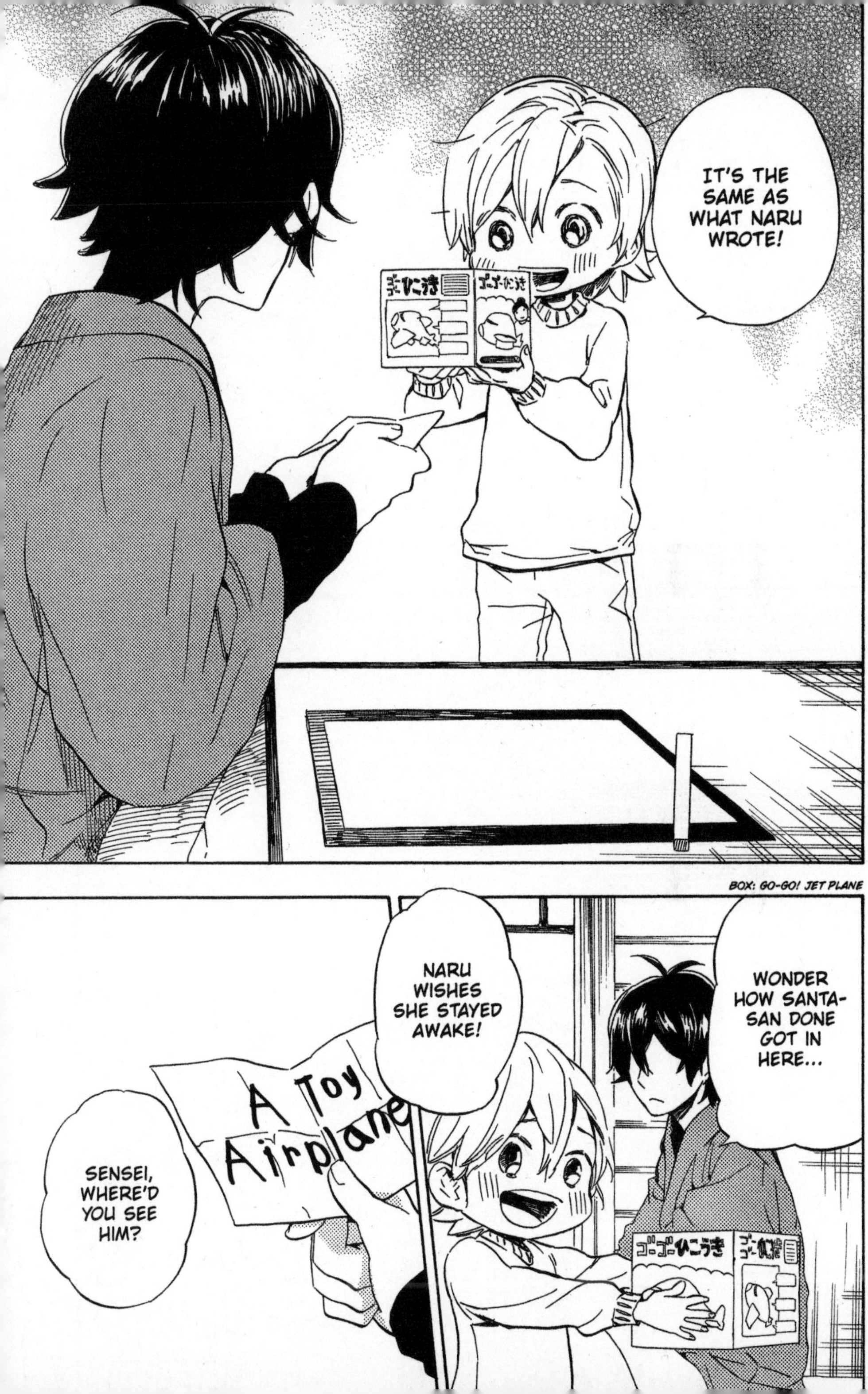
ゴーゴーひこうき
IT'S THE SAME AS WHAT NARU WROTE!
BOX: GO-GO! JET PLANE
WONDER HOW SANTA-SAN DONE GOT IN HERE...
NARU WISHES SHE STAYED AWAKE!
A Toy Airplane
SENSEI, WHERE'D YOU SEE HIM?
ゴーゴーひこうき

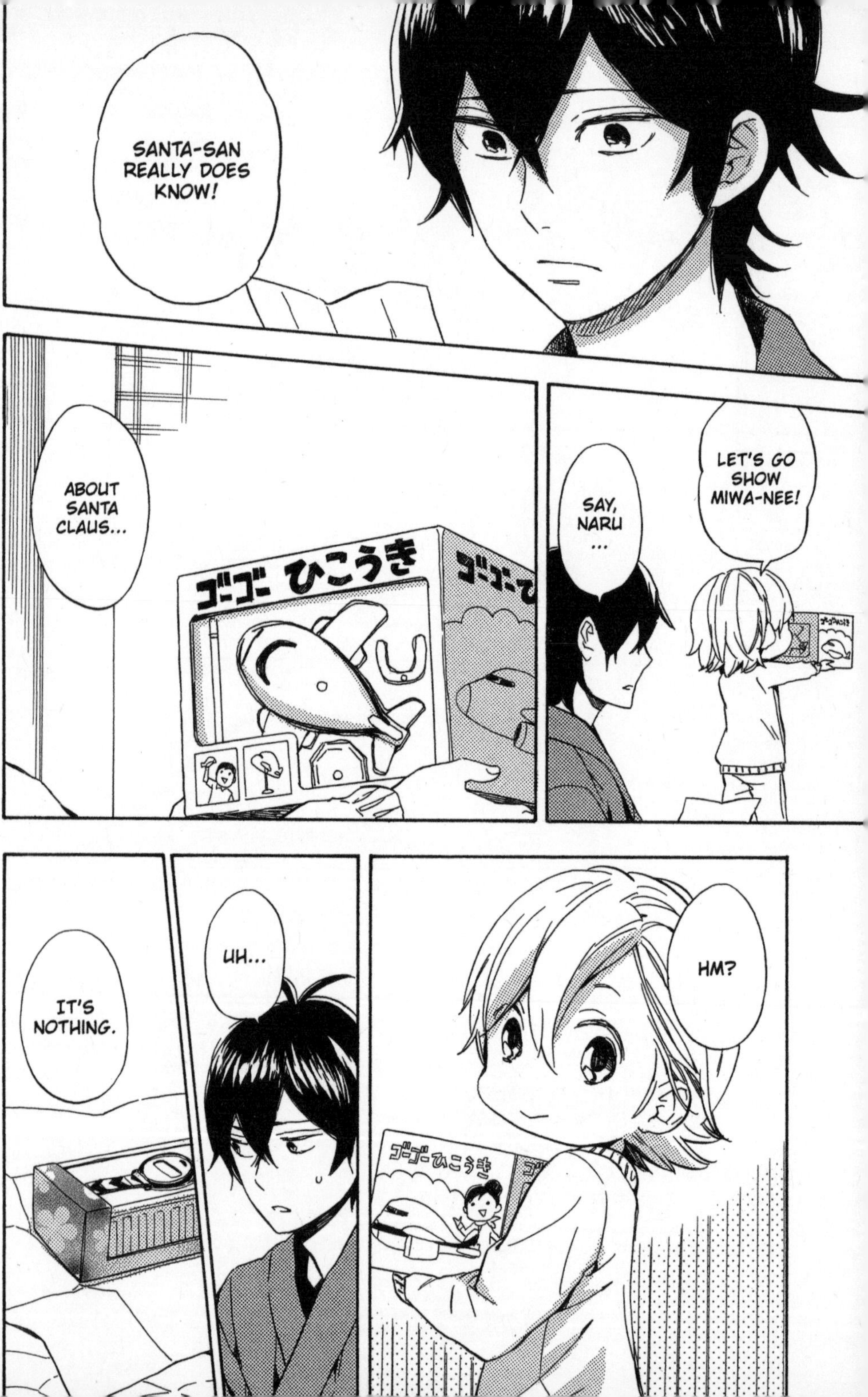
SANTA-SAN REALLY DOES KNOW!
LET'S GO SHOW MIWA-NEE!
SAY, NARU ...
ABOUT SANTA CLAUS...
ゴーゴー ひこうき
HM?
ゴーゴーひこうき
UH...
IT'S NOTHING.

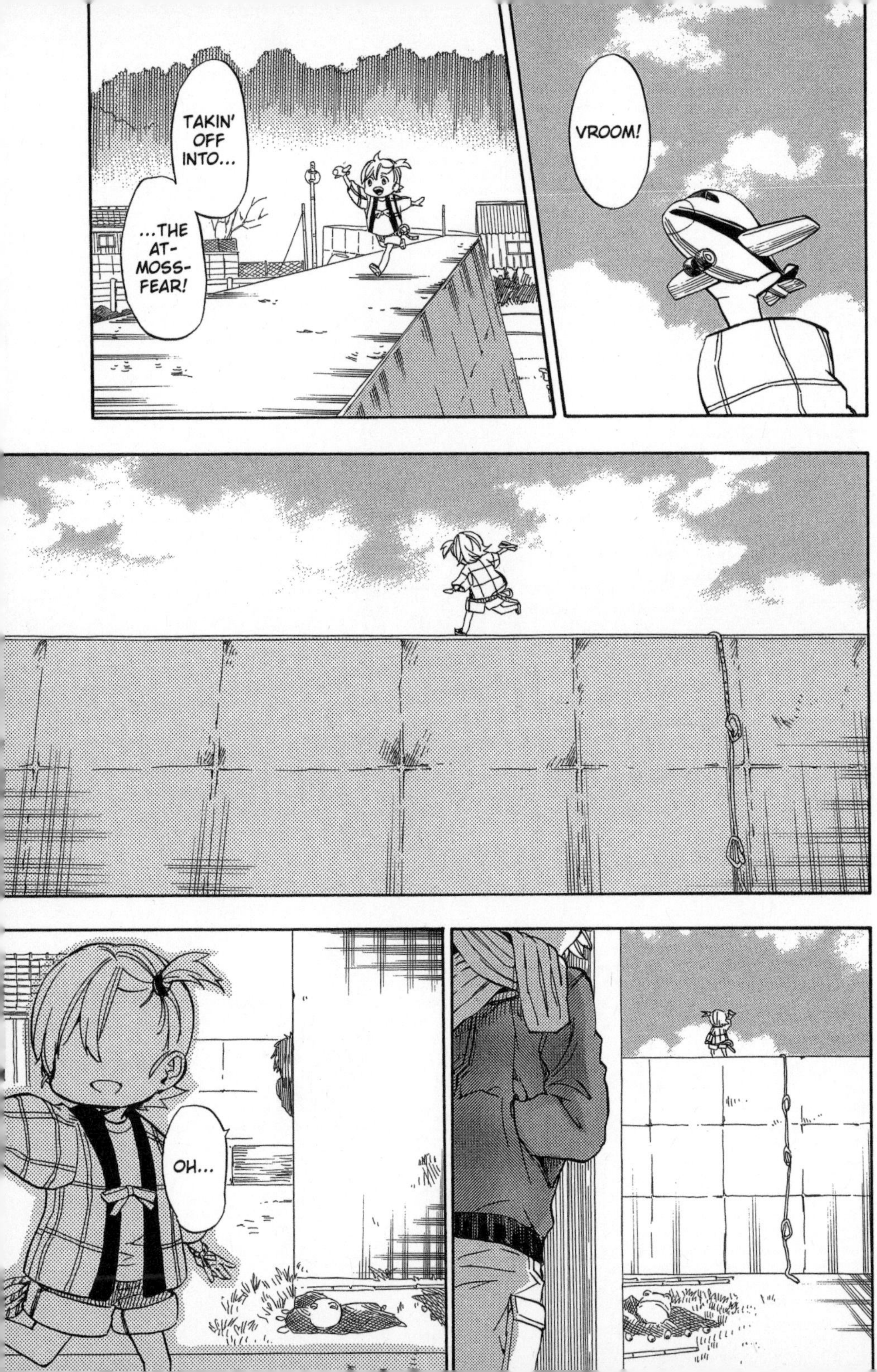
VROOM!
TAKIN' OFF INTO...
...THE AT-MOSS-FEAR!
OH...

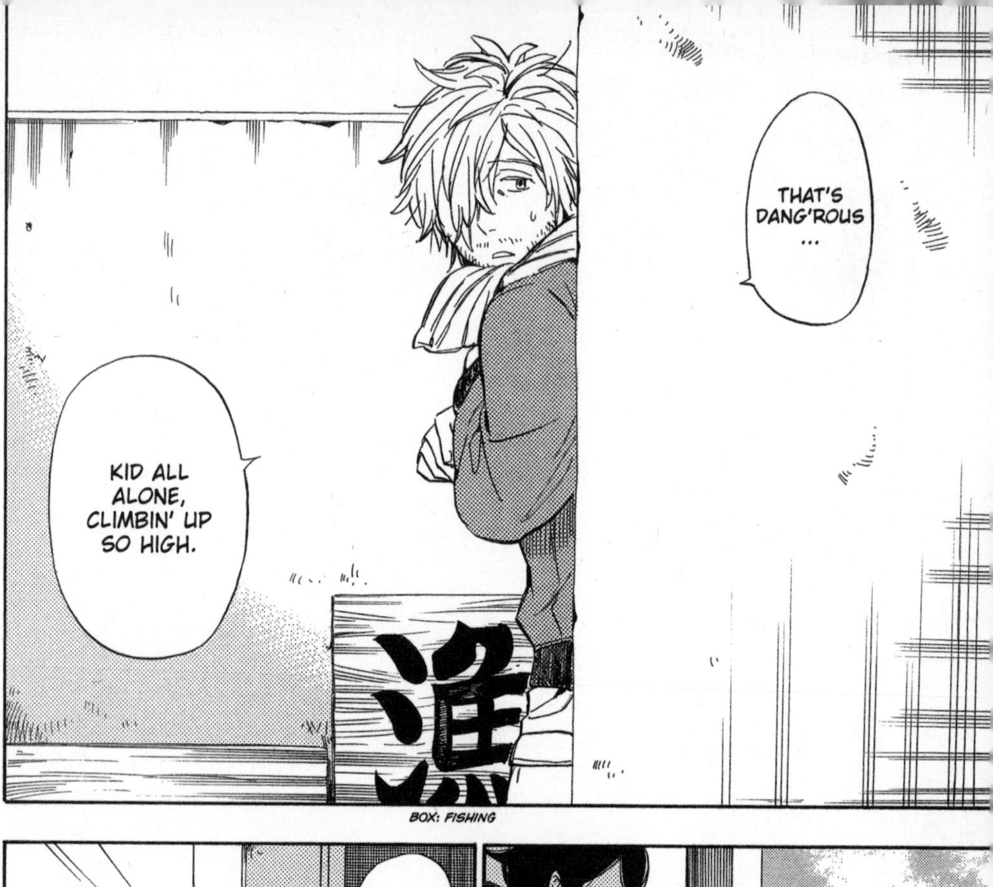
THAT'S DANG'ROUS ...
KID ALL ALONE, CLIMBIN' UP SO HIGH.

BOX: FISHING

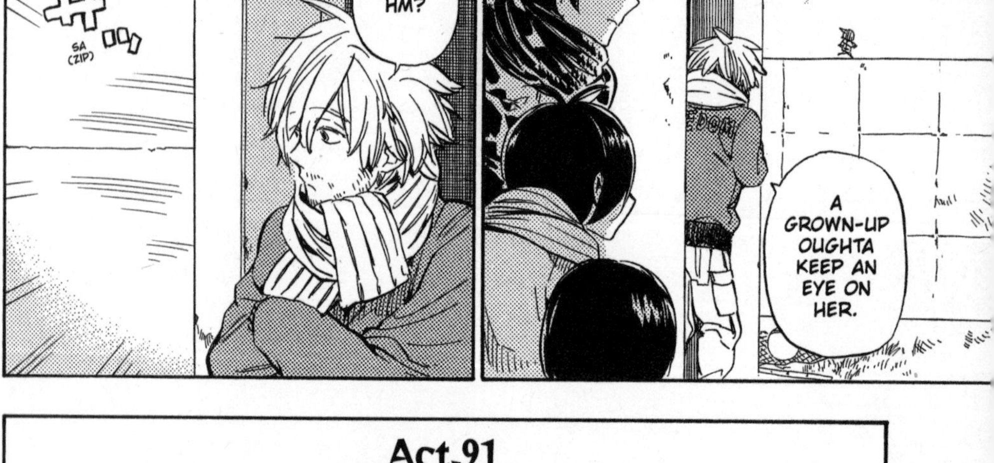
A GROWN-UP OUGHTA KEEP AN EYE ON HER.
HM?
SA (ZIP)

Act.91
THE 25TH
(Translation: It's Christmas, But More Importantly...)

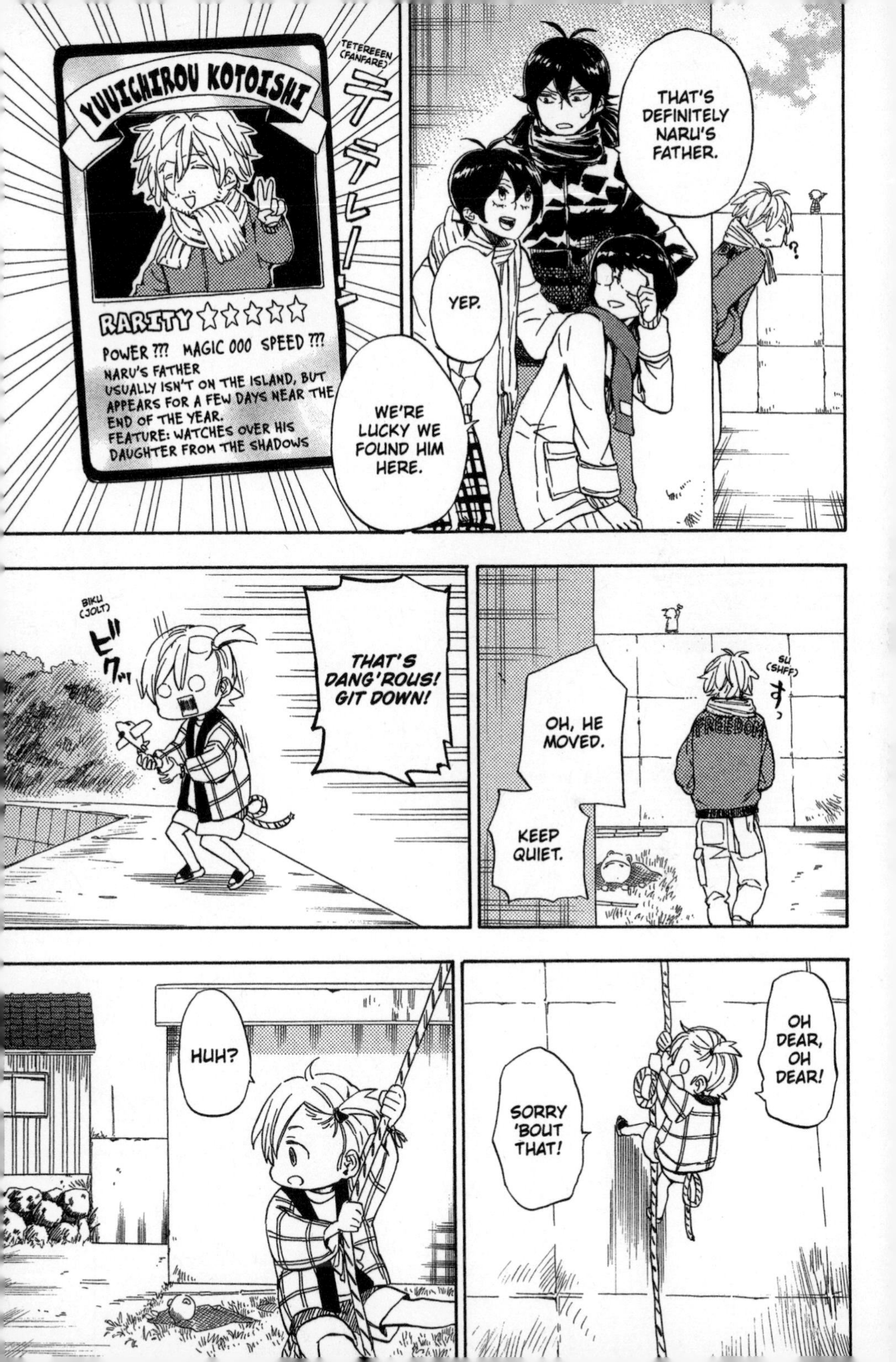
THAT'S DEFINITELY NARU'S FATHER.
YEP.
WE'RE LUCKY WE FOUND HIM HERE.
TETEREEEN (FANFARE)
YUUICHIROU KOTOISHI
RARITY ☆☆☆☆☆
POWER ??? MAGIC 000 SPEED ???
NARU'S FATHER
USUALLY ISN'T ON THE ISLAND, BUT APPEARS FOR A FEW DAYS NEAR THE END OF THE YEAR.
FEATURE: WATCHES OVER HIS DAUGHTER FROM THE SHADOWS
SU (SHFF)
OH, HE MOVED.
KEEP QUIET.
BIKU (JOLT)
THAT'S DANG'ROUS! GIT DOWN!
OH DEAR, OH DEAR!
SORRY 'BOUT THAT!
HUH?

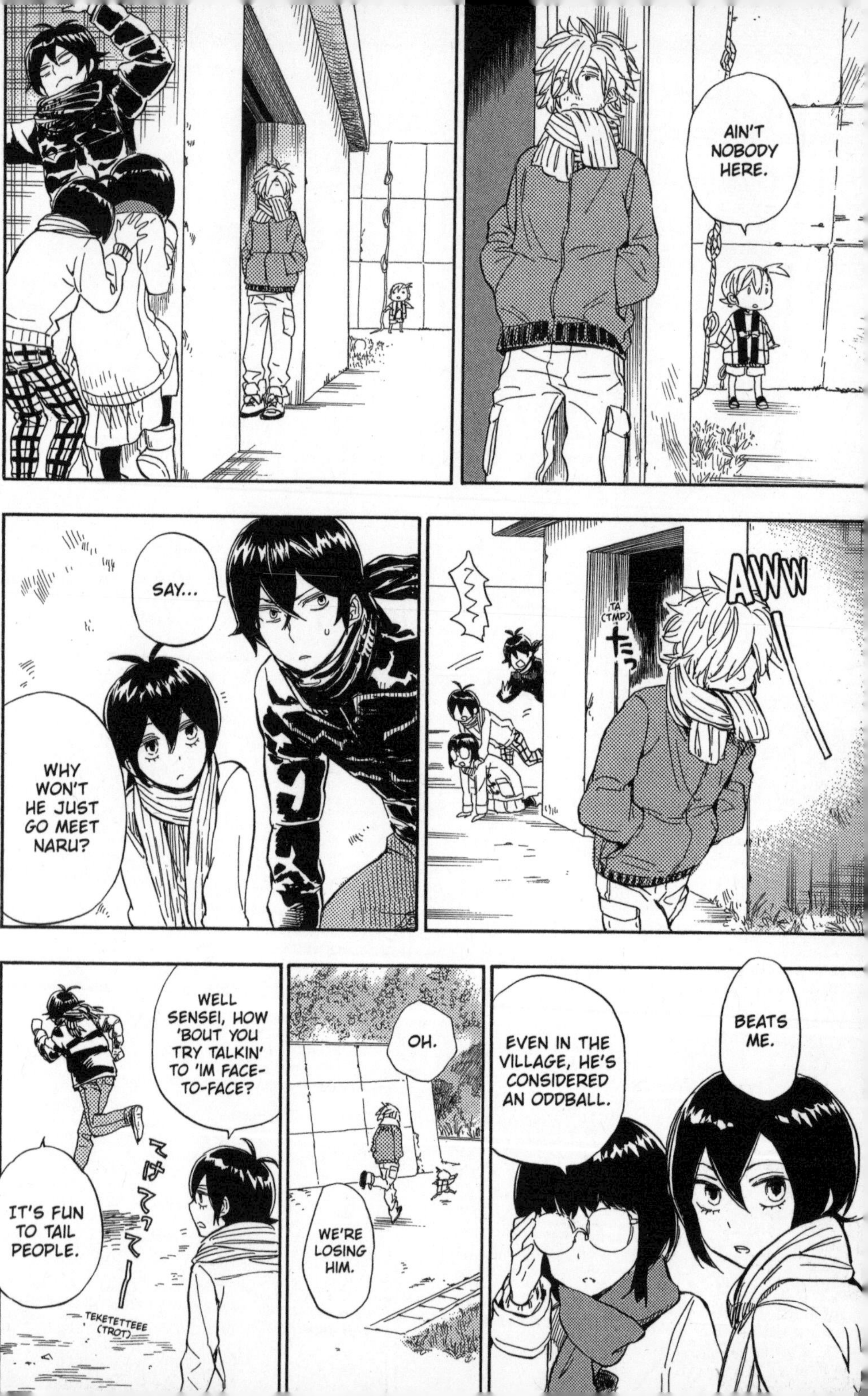
AIN'T NOBODY HERE.
AWW
TA (TMP)
たっ
SAY...
WHY WON'T HE JUST GO MEET NARU?
BEATS ME.
EVEN IN THE VILLAGE, HE'S CONSIDERED AN ODDBALL.
OH.
WE'RE LOSING HIM.
WELL SENSEI, HOW 'BOUT YOU TRY TALKIN' TO 'IM FACE-TO-FACE?
IT'S FUN TO TAIL PEOPLE.
てけてってー
TEKETETTEEE (TROT)

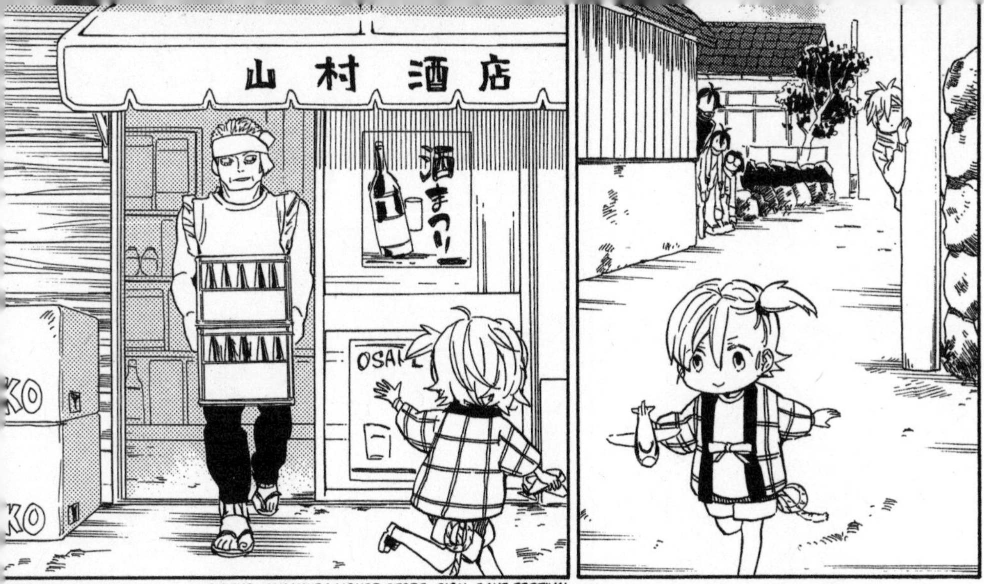
山村酒店
酒まつり!

AWNING: YAMAMURA LIQUOR STORE; SIGN: SAKE FESTIVAL

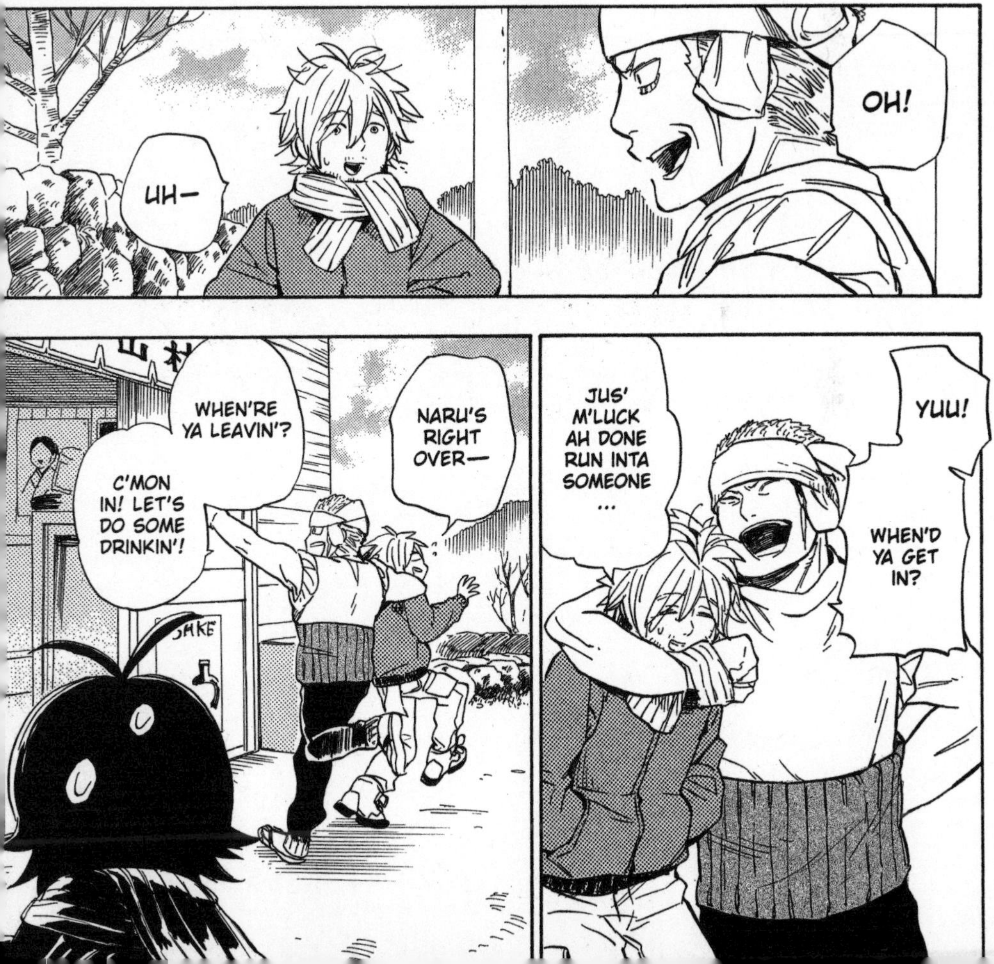
OH!
UH—
YUU!
WHEN'D YA GET IN?
JUS' M'LUCK AH DONE RUN INTA SOMEONE ...
NARU'S RIGHT OVER—
WHEN'RE YA LEAVIN'?
C'MON IN! LET'S DO SOME DRINKIN'!

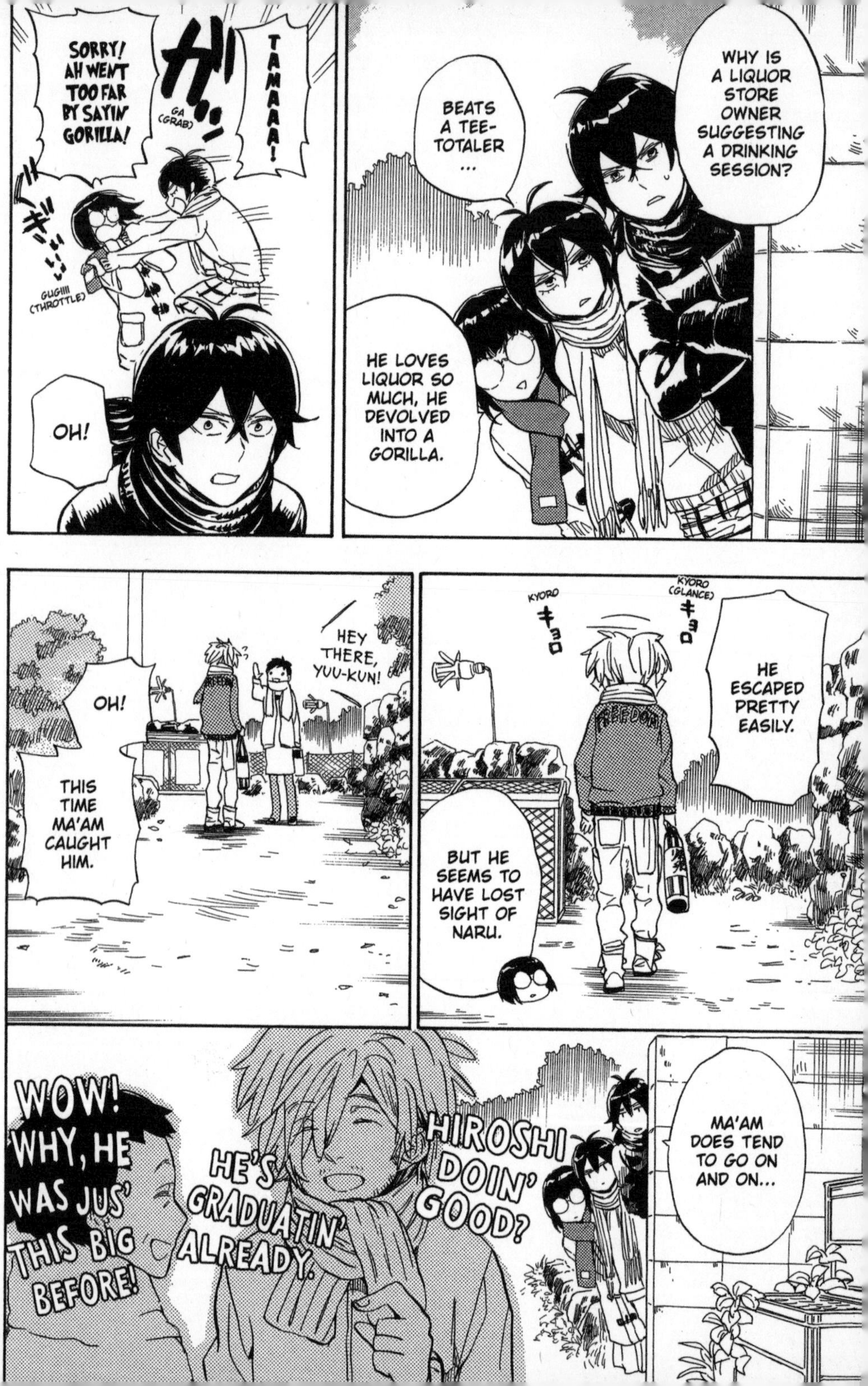

WHY IS A LIQUOR STORE OWNER SUGGESTING A DRINKING SESSION?
BEATS A TEE-TOTALER ...
HE LOVES LIQUOR SO MUCH, HE DEVOLVED INTO A GORILLA.
TAMAAAA!
GA (GRAB)
SORRY! AH WENT TOO FAR BY SAYIN' GORILLA!
GUGIII (THROTTLE)
OH!
KYORO (GLANCE)
KYORO
HE ESCAPED PRETTY EASILY.
BUT HE SEEMS TO HAVE LOST SIGHT OF NARU.
HEY THERE, YUU-KUN!
OH!
THIS TIME MA'AM CAUGHT HIM.
MA'AM DOES TEND TO GO ON AND ON...
HIROSHI DOIN' GOOD?
HE'S GRADUATIN' ALREADY.
WOW! WHY, HE WAS JUS' THIS BIG BEFORE!

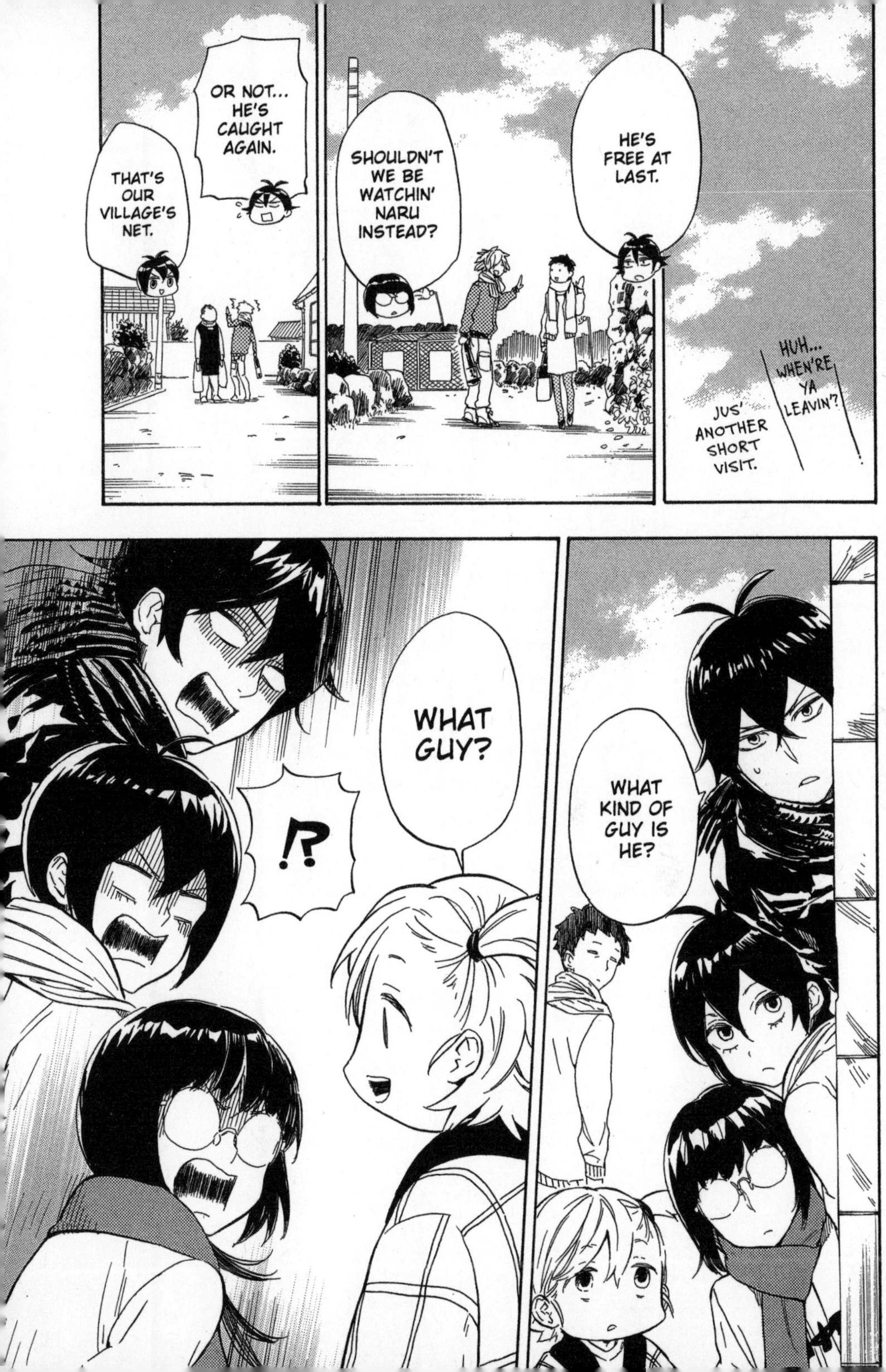
HE'S FREE AT LAST.
HUH... WHEN'RE YA LEAVIN'?
JUS' ANOTHER SHORT VISIT.
SHOULDN'T WE BE WATCHIN' NARU INSTEAD?
OR NOT... HE'S CAUGHT AGAIN.
THAT'S OUR VILLAGE'S NET.
WHAT KIND OF GUY IS HE?
WHAT GUY?
!?

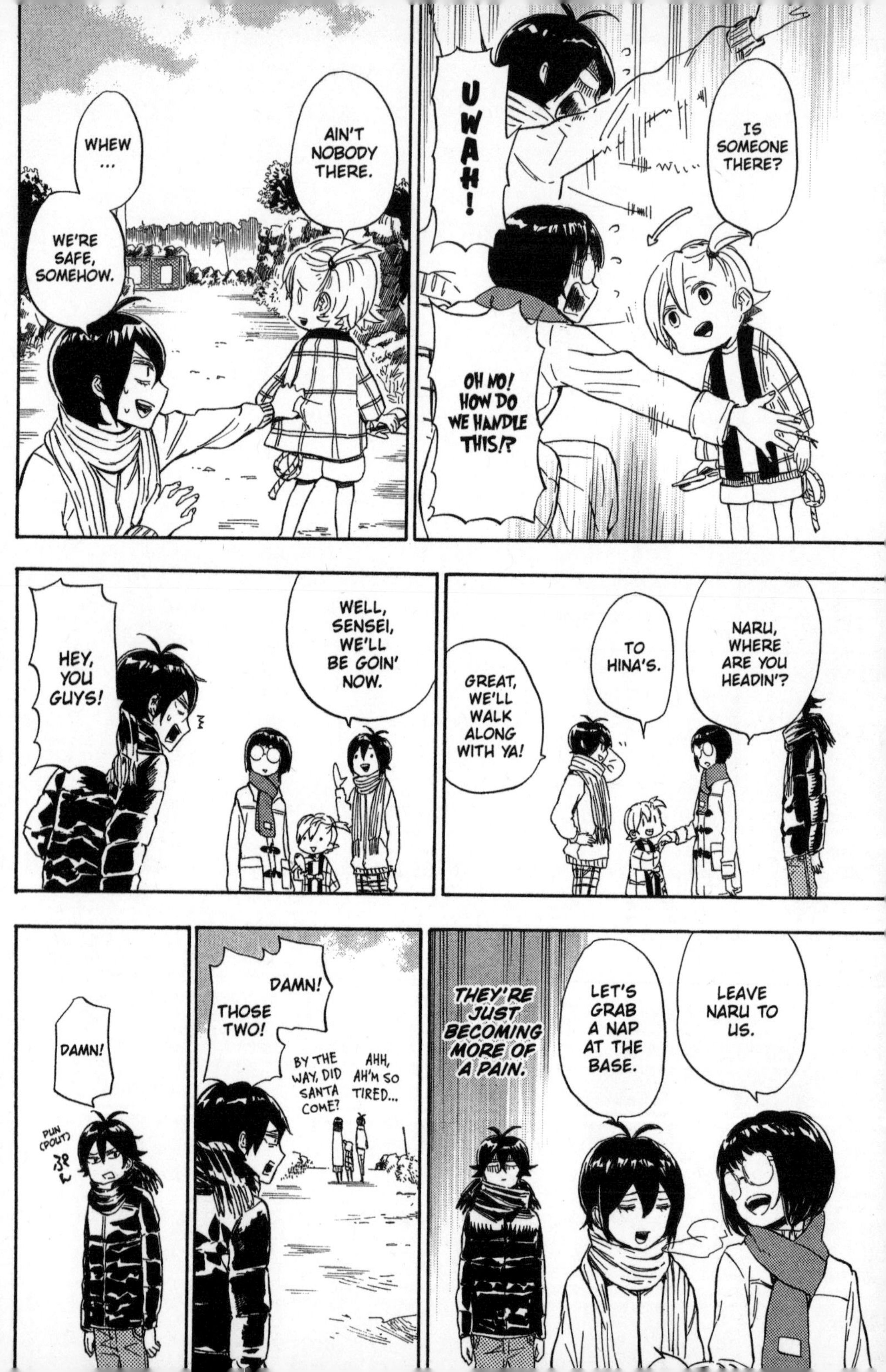
IS SOMEONE THERE?
UWAH!
OH NO! HOW DO WE HANDLE THIS!?
AIN'T NOBODY THERE.
WHEW ...
WE'RE SAFE, SOMEHOW.
NARU, WHERE ARE YOU HEADIN'?
TO HINA'S.
GREAT, WE'LL WALK ALONG WITH YA!
WELL, SENSEI, WE'LL BE GOIN' NOW.
HEY, YOU GUYS!
LEAVE NARU TO US.
LET'S GRAB A NAP AT THE BASE.
THEY'RE JUST BECOMING MORE OF A PAIN.
DAMN!
THOSE TWO!
AHH, AH'M SO TIRED...
BY THE WAY, DID SANTA COME?
DAMN!
PUN (POUT)
ぷん

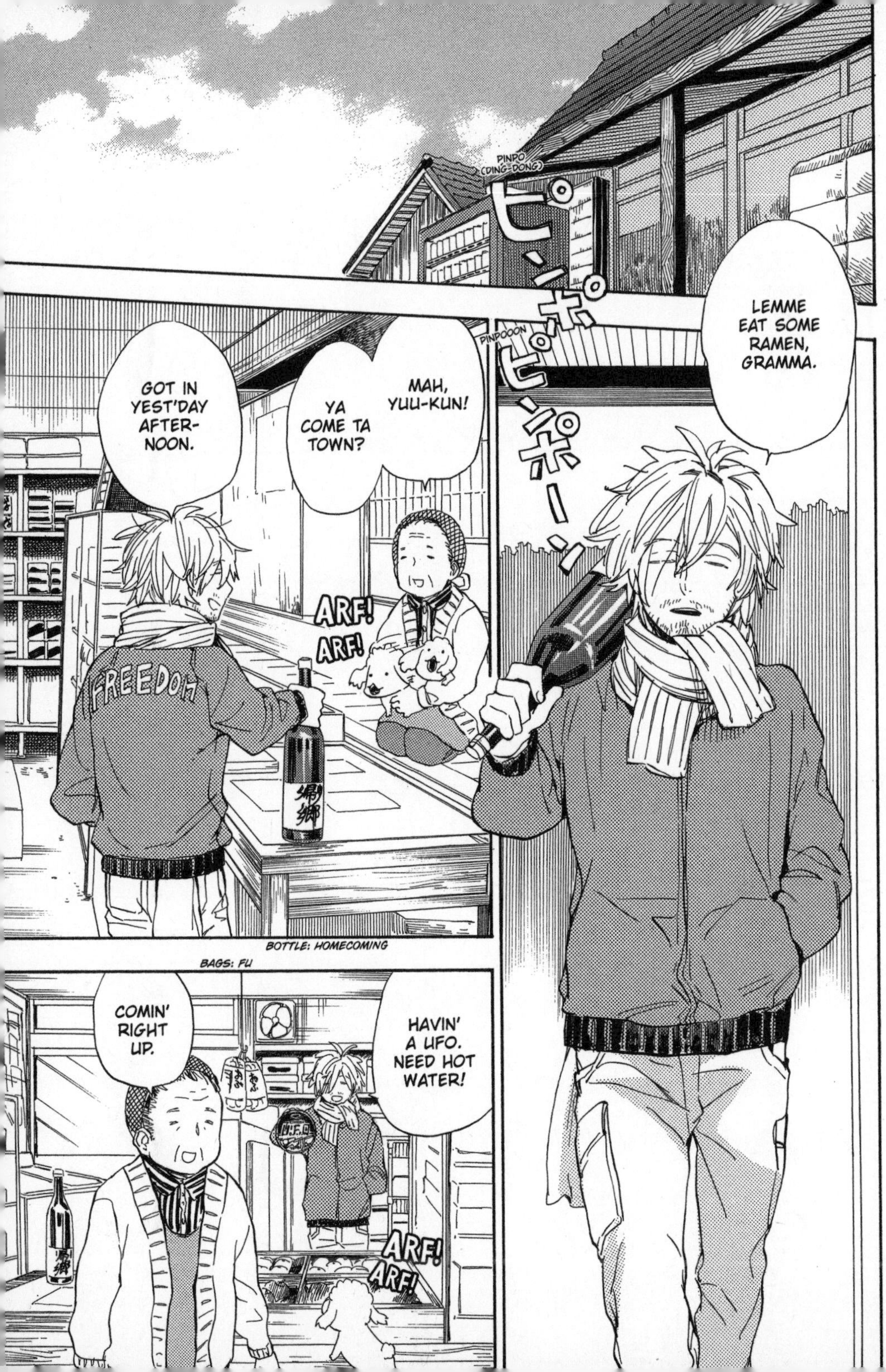
PINPO (DING-DONG)
ピンポ
PINPOOON
ピンポーン
LEMME EAT SOME RAMEN, GRAMMA.
MAH, YUU-KUN! YA COME TA TOWN?
GOT IN YEST'DAY AFTERNOON.
ARF! ARF!
BOTTLE: HOMECOMING
HAVIN' A UFO. NEED HOT WATER!
COMIN' RIGHT UP.
ARF! ARF!
BAGS: FU

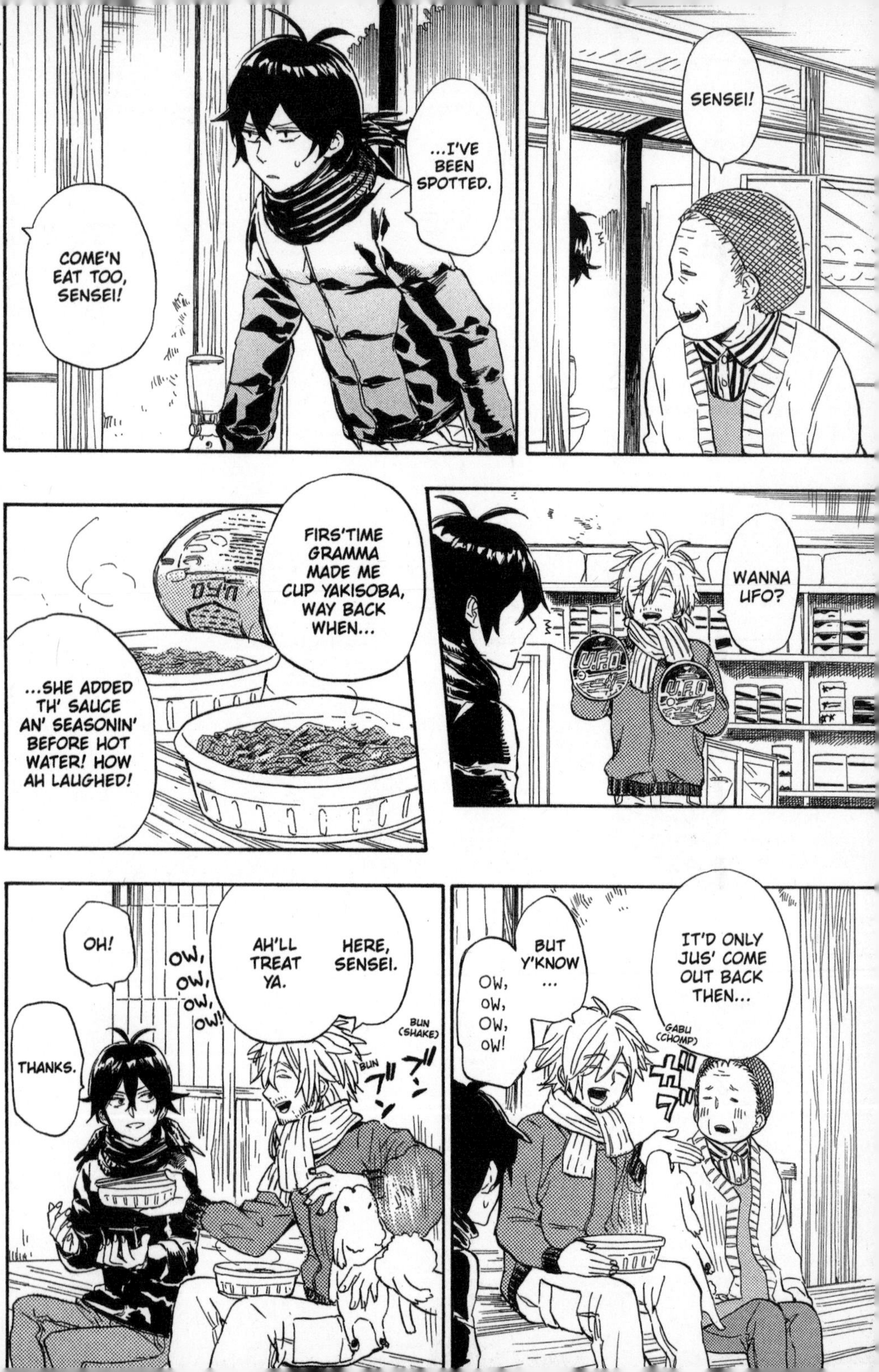
SENSEI!
...I'VE BEEN SPOTTED.
COME'N EAT TOO, SENSEI!
WANNA UFO?
U.F.O
FIRS'TIME GRAMMA MADE ME CUP YAKISOBA, WAY BACK WHEN...
...SHE ADDED TH' SAUCE AN' SEASONIN' BEFORE HOT WATER! HOW AH LAUGHED!
IT'D ONLY JUS' COME OUT BACK THEN...
GABU (CHOMP)
BUT Y'KNOW...
OW, OW, OW, OW!
HERE, SENSEI.
AH'LL TREAT YA.
BUN (SHAKE)
OW, OW, OW, OW!
OH!
THANKS.

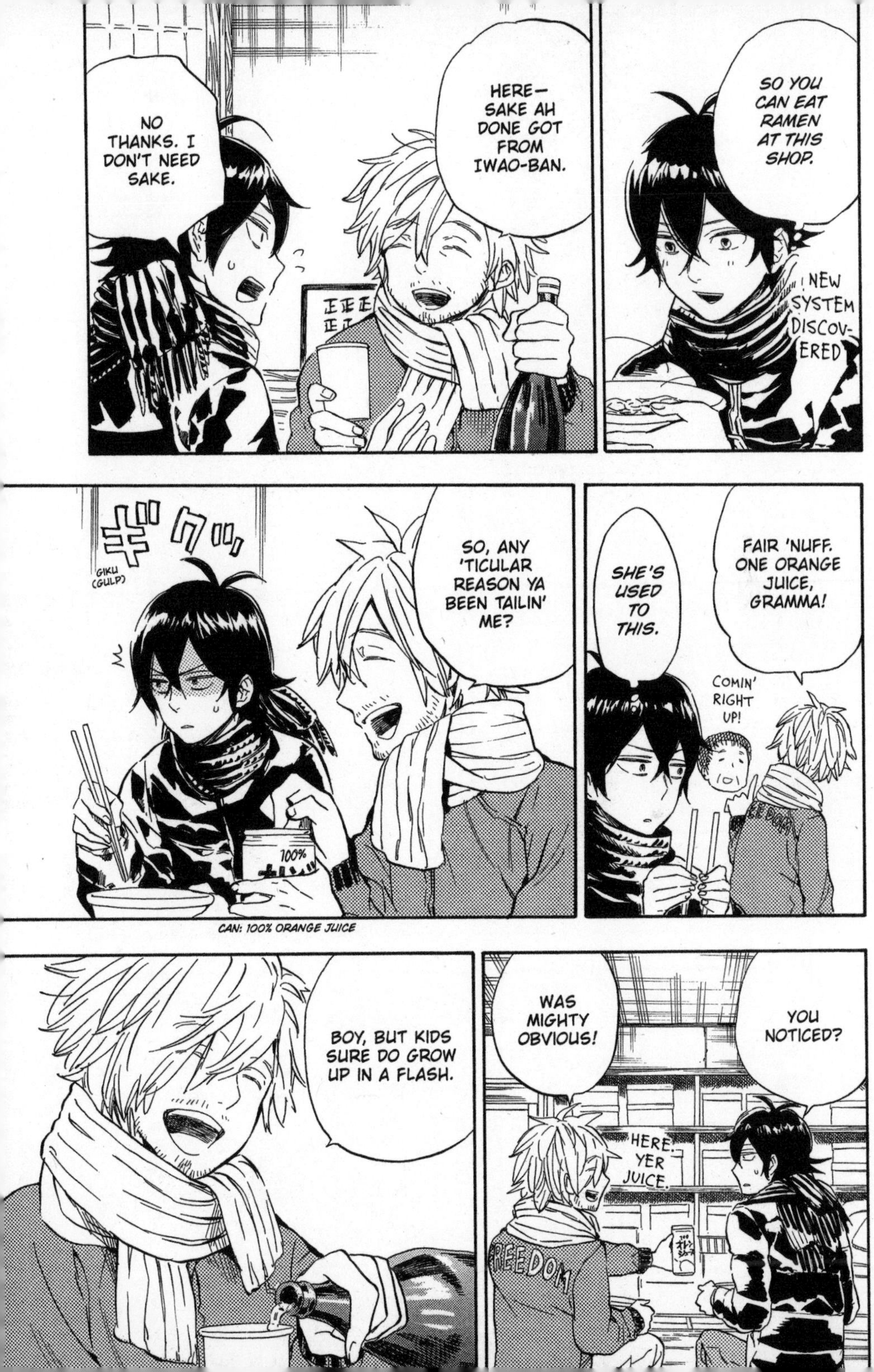
SO YOU CAN EAT RAMEN AT THIS SHOP.
NEW SYSTEM DISCOVERED
HERE— SAKE AH DONE GOT FROM IWAO-BAN.
NO THANKS. I DON'T NEED SAKE.
FAIR 'NUFF. ONE ORANGE JUICE, GRAMMA!
SHE'S USED TO THIS.
COMIN' RIGHT UP!
SO, ANY 'TICULAR REASON YA BEEN TAILIN' ME?
ギクッ
GIKU (GULP)
100%
CAN: 100% ORANGE JUICE
YOU NOTICED?
WAS MIGHTY OBVIOUS!
HERE. YER JUICE.
FREEDOM
BOY, BUT KIDS SURE DO GROW UP IN A FLASH.

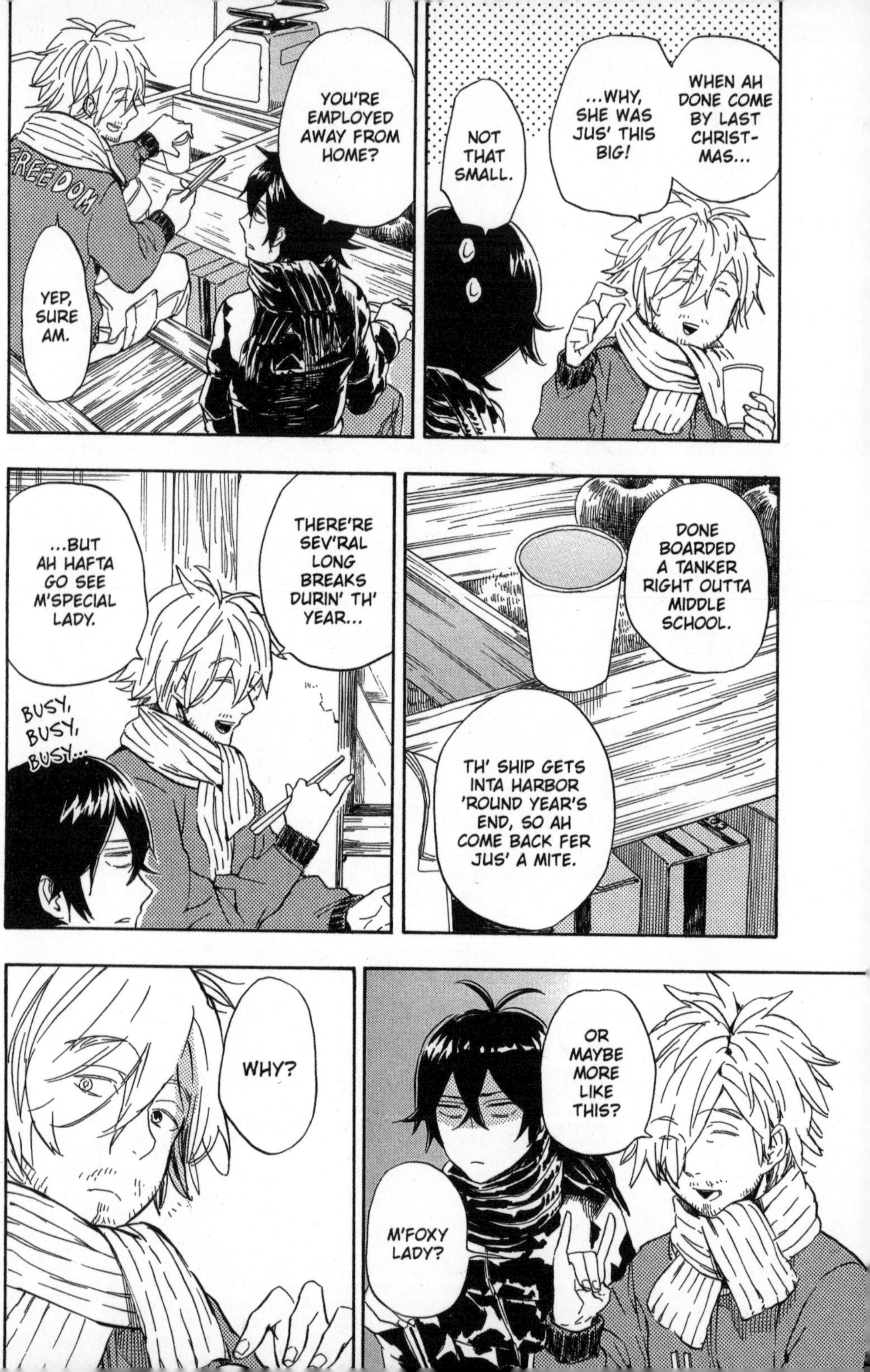
WHEN AH DONE COME BY LAST CHRISTMAS...
...WHY, SHE WAS JUS' THIS BIG!
NOT THAT SMALL.
YOU'RE EMPLOYED AWAY FROM HOME?
YEP, SURE AM.
DONE BOARDED A TANKER RIGHT OUTTA MIDDLE SCHOOL.
TH' SHIP GETS INTA HARBOR 'ROUND YEAR'S END, SO AH COME BACK FER JUS' A MITE.
THERE'RE SEV'RAL LONG BREAKS DURIN' TH' YEAR...
...BUT AH HAFTA GO SEE M'SPECIAL LADY.
BUSY, BUSY, BUSY...
OR MAYBE MORE LIKE THIS?
M'FOXY LADY?
WHY?

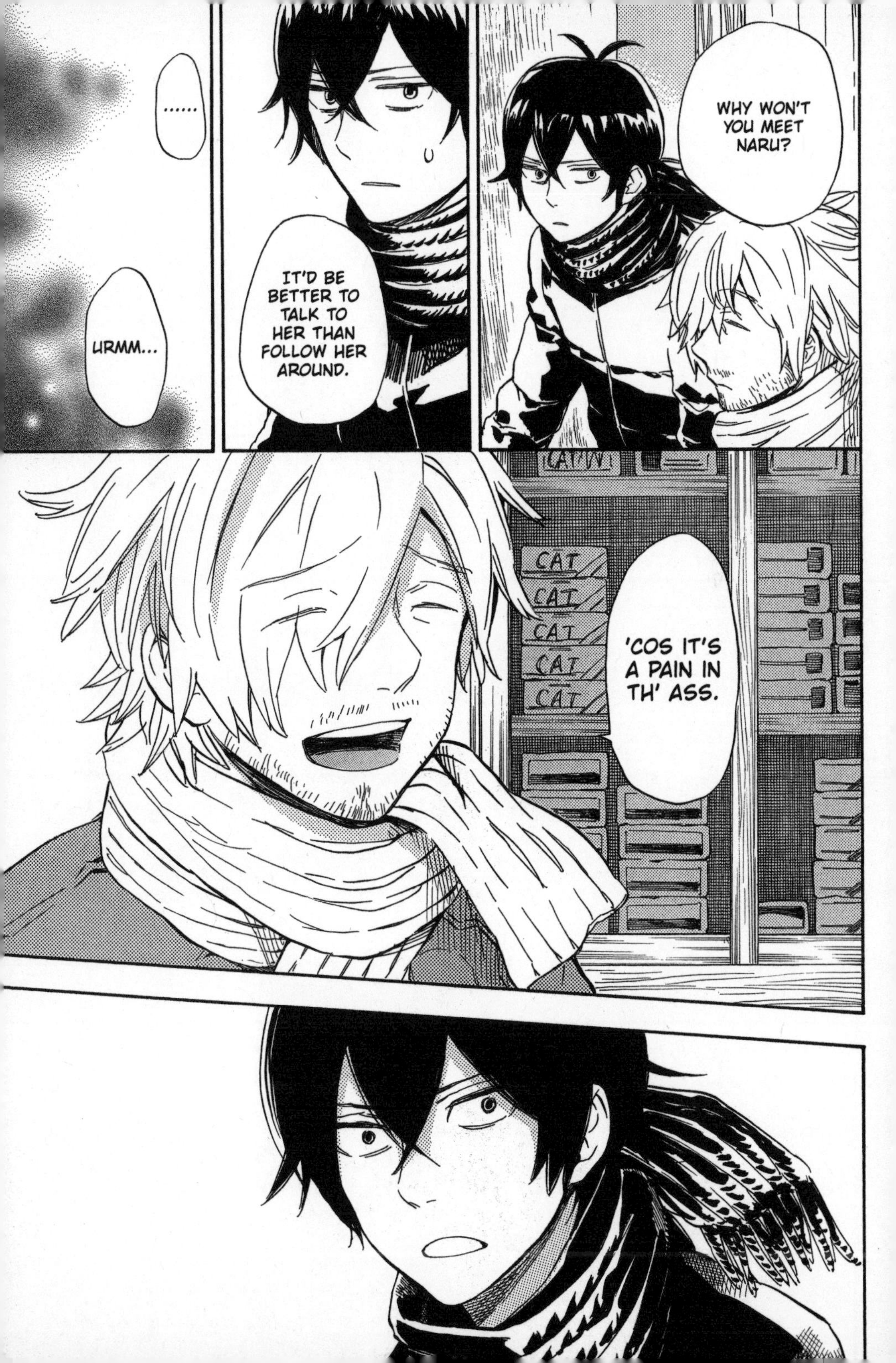
WHY WON'T YOU MEET NARU?
IT'D BE BETTER TO TALK TO HER THAN FOLLOW HER AROUND.
......
URMM...
'COS IT'S A PAIN IN TH' ASS.
CAT
CAT
CAT
CAT
CAT

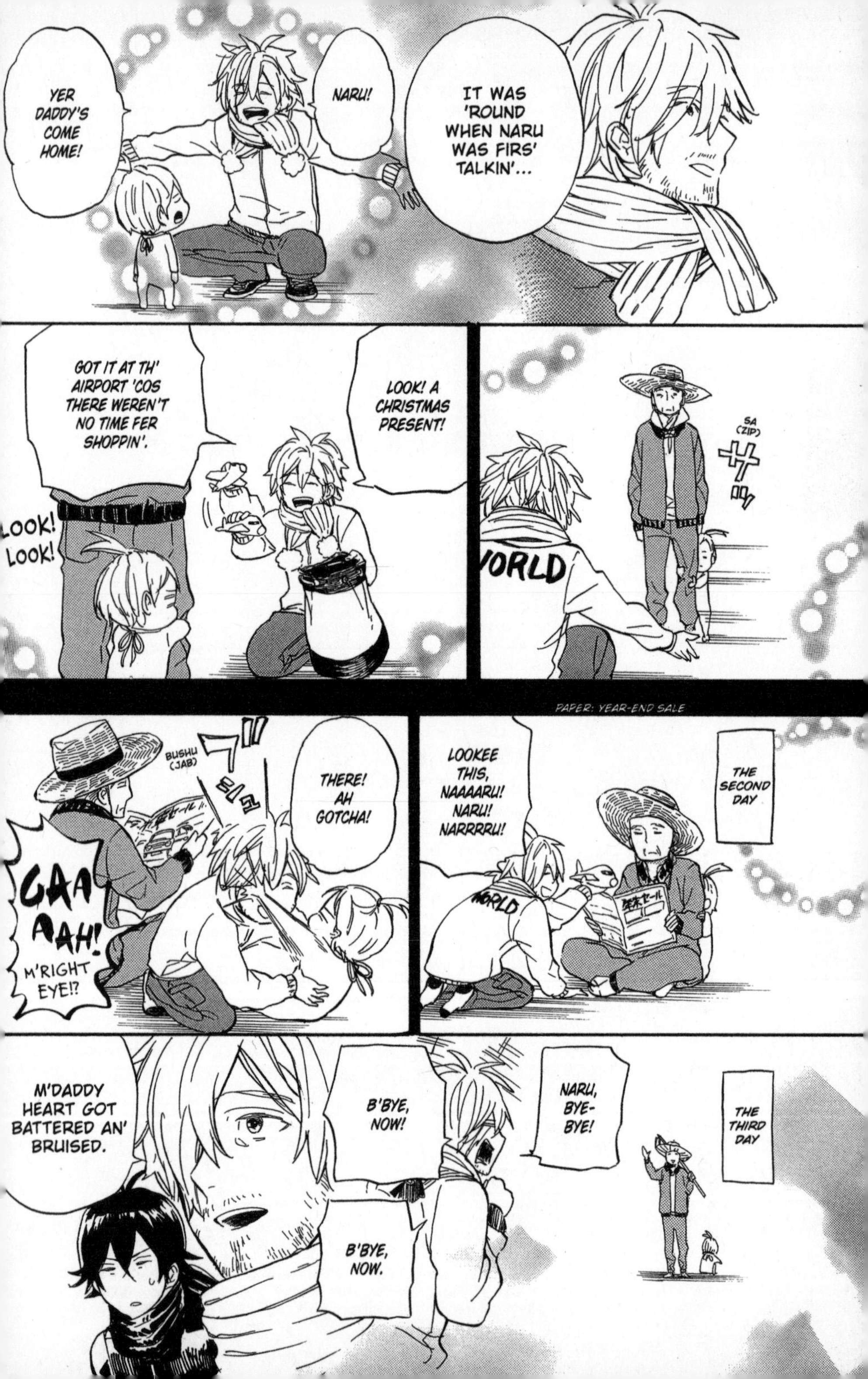
IT WAS 'ROUND WHEN NARU WAS FIRS' TALKIN'...
NARU!
YER DADDY'S COME HOME!
SA (ZIP)
LOOK! A CHRISTMAS PRESENT!
GOT IT AT TH' AIRPORT 'COS THERE WEREN'T NO TIME FER SHOPPIN'.
LOOK! LOOK!
THE SECOND DAY
LOOKEE THIS, NAAAARU! NARU! NARRRRU!
PAPER: YEAR-END SALE
THERE! AH GOTCHA!
BUSHU (JAB)
GAAAAH!
M'RIGHT EYE!?
THE THIRD DAY
NARU, BYE-BYE!
B'YE, NOW!
B'BYE, NOW.
M'DADDY HEART GOT BATTERED AN' BRUISED.

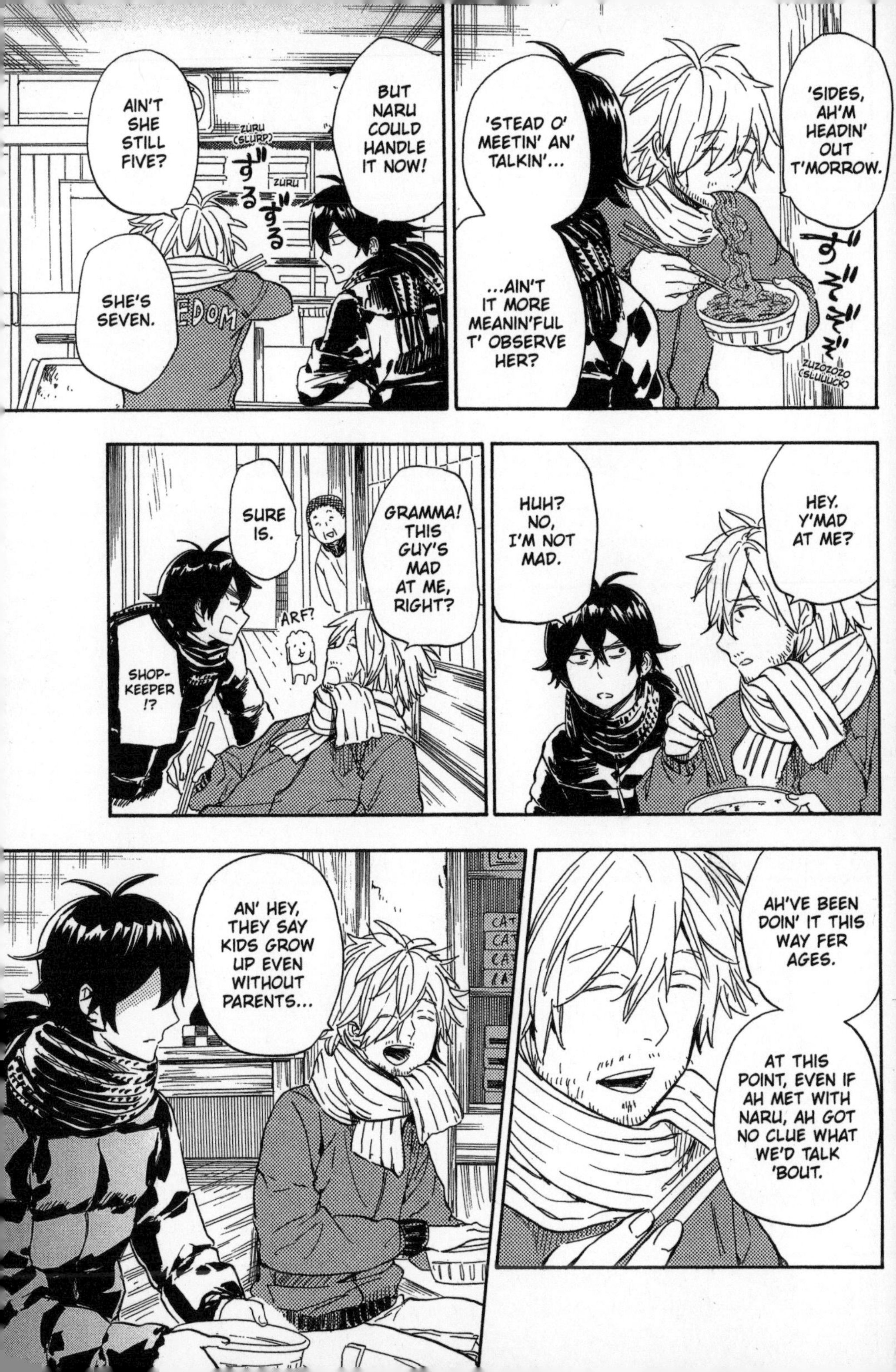
'SIDES, AH'M HEADIN' OUT T'MORROW.
ZUZOZOZO (SLUUUCK)
'STEAD O' MEETIN' AN' TALKIN'...
...AIN'T IT MORE MEANIN'FUL T' OBSERVE HER?
BUT NARU COULD HANDLE IT NOW!
AIN'T SHE STILL FIVE?
ずる
ZURU (SLURP)
ずる
ZURU
SHE'S SEVEN.
HEY. Y'MAD AT ME?
HUH? NO, I'M NOT MAD.
GRAMMA! THIS GUY'S MAD AT ME, RIGHT?
SURE IS.
ARF?
SHOP-KEEPER!?
AH'VE BEEN DOIN' IT THIS WAY FER AGES.
AT THIS POINT, EVEN IF AH MET WITH NARU, AH GOT NO CLUE WHAT WE'D TALK 'BOUT.
AN' HEY, THEY SAY KIDS GROW UP EVEN WITHOUT PARENTS...

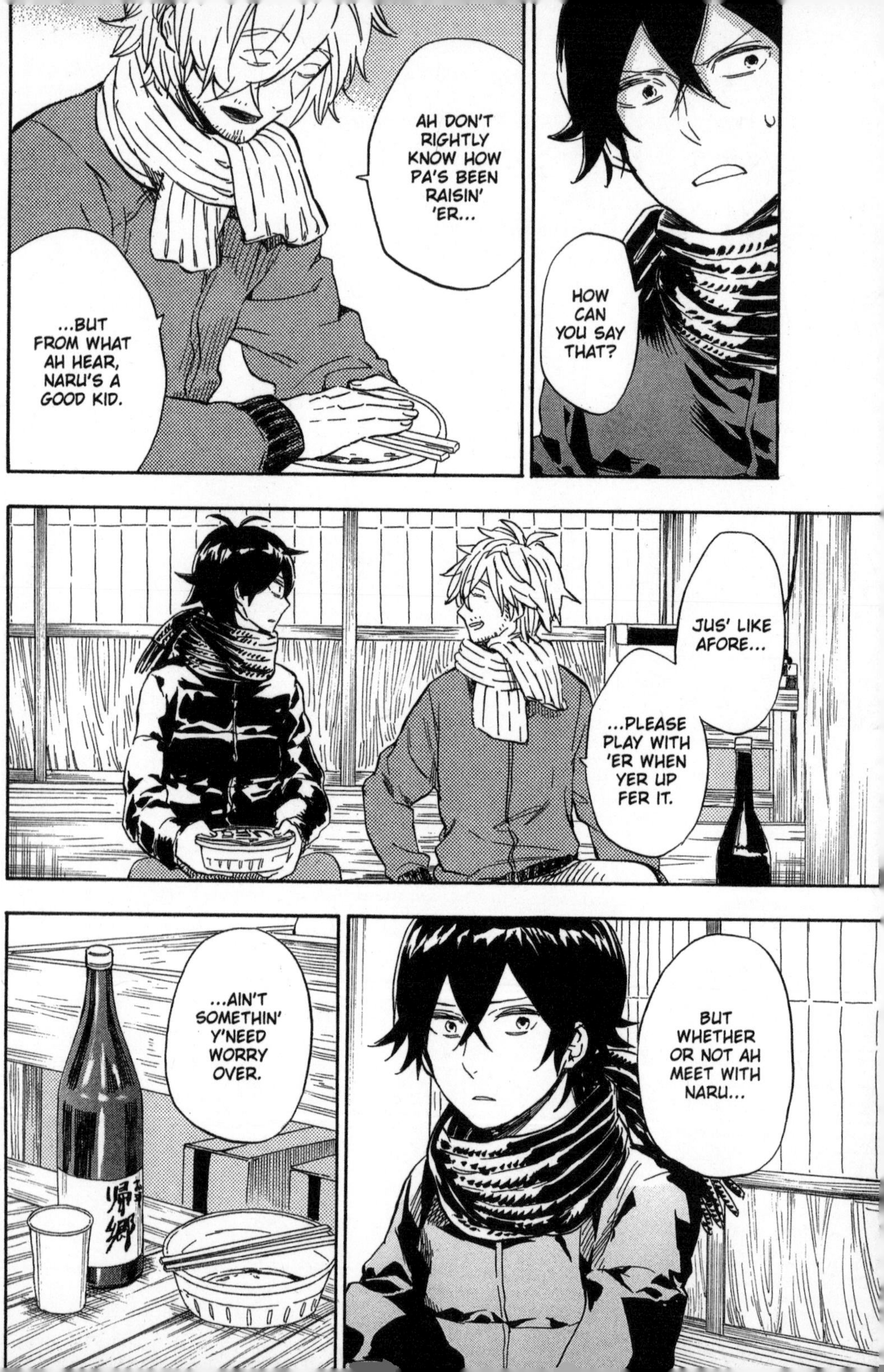
HOW CAN YOU SAY THAT?
AH DON'T RIGHTLY KNOW HOW PA'S BEEN RAISIN' 'ER...
...BUT FROM WHAT AH HEAR, NARU'S A GOOD KID.
JUS' LIKE AFORE...
...PLEASE PLAY WITH 'ER WHEN YER UP FER IT.
BUT WHETHER OR NOT AH MEET WITH NARU...
...AIN'T SOMETHIN' Y'NEED WORRY OVER.
帰郷

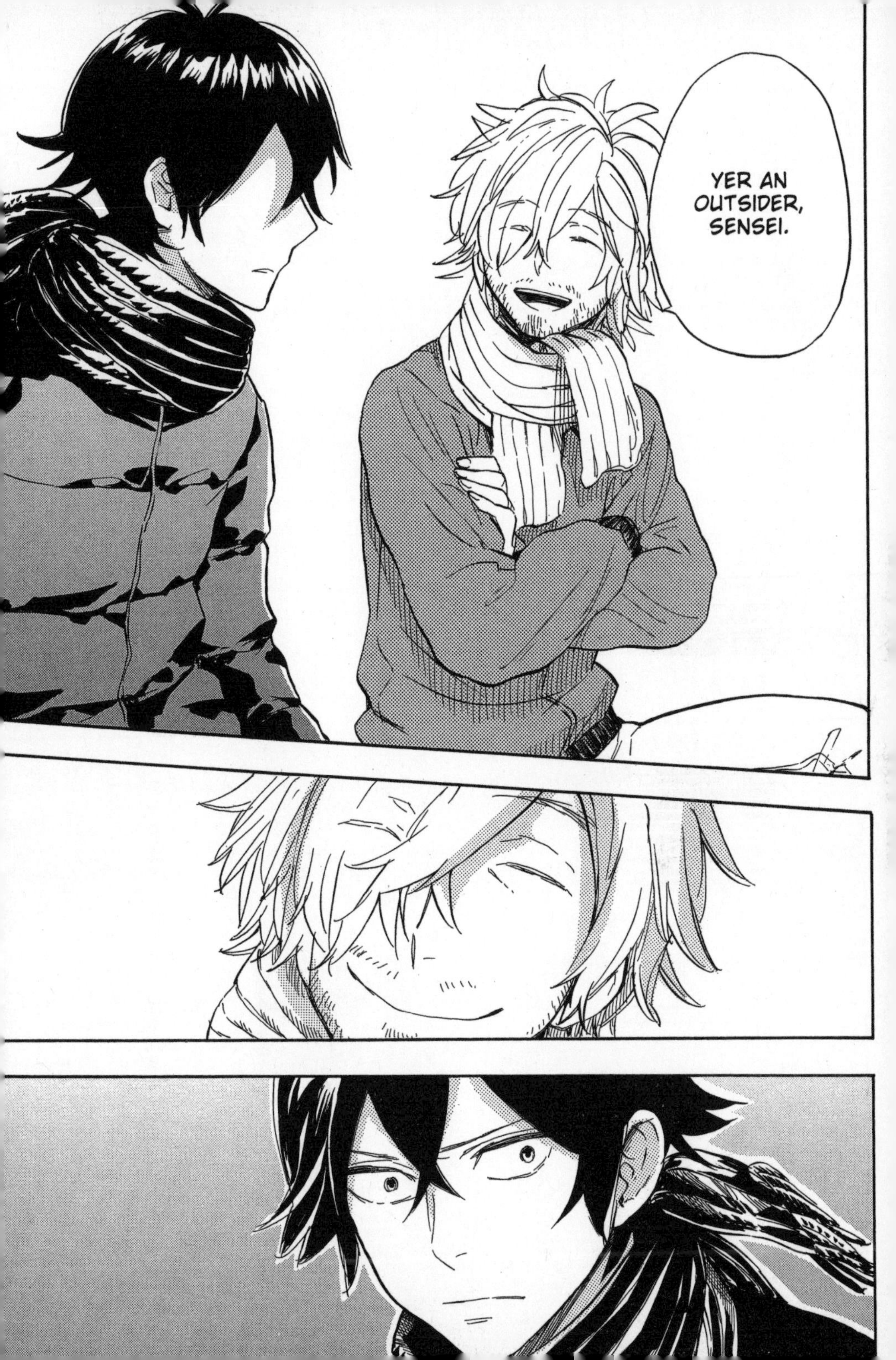
YER AN OUTSIDER, SENSEI.

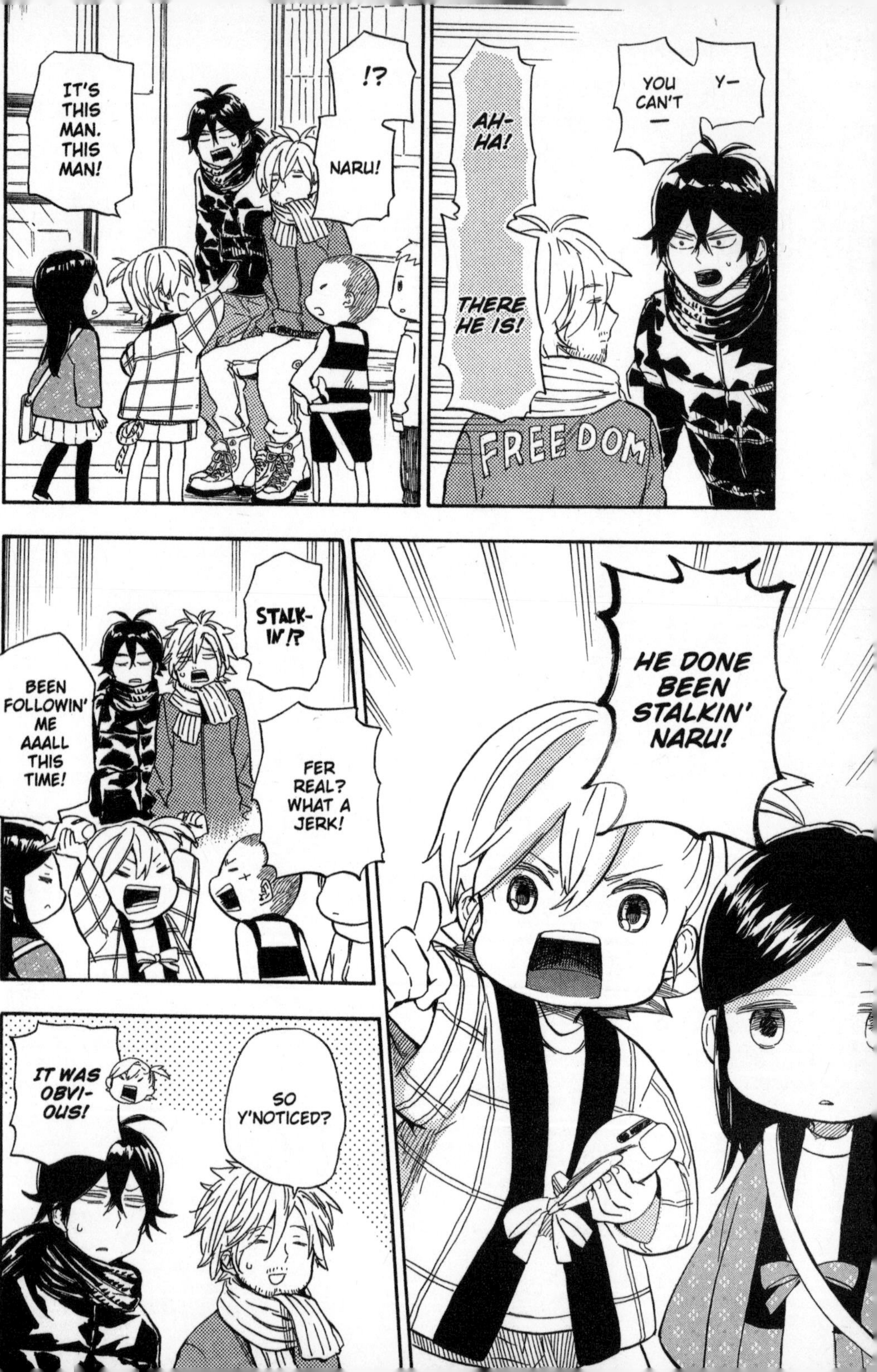
Y— YOU CAN'T —
AH-HA!
THERE HE IS!
FREEDOM
!?
NARU!
IT'S THIS MAN. THIS MAN!
HE DONE BEEN STALKIN' NARU!
STALK-IN'!?
FER REAL? WHAT A JERK!
BEEN FOLLOWIN' ME AAALL THIS TIME!
SO Y'NOTICED?
IT WAS OBVI-OUS!

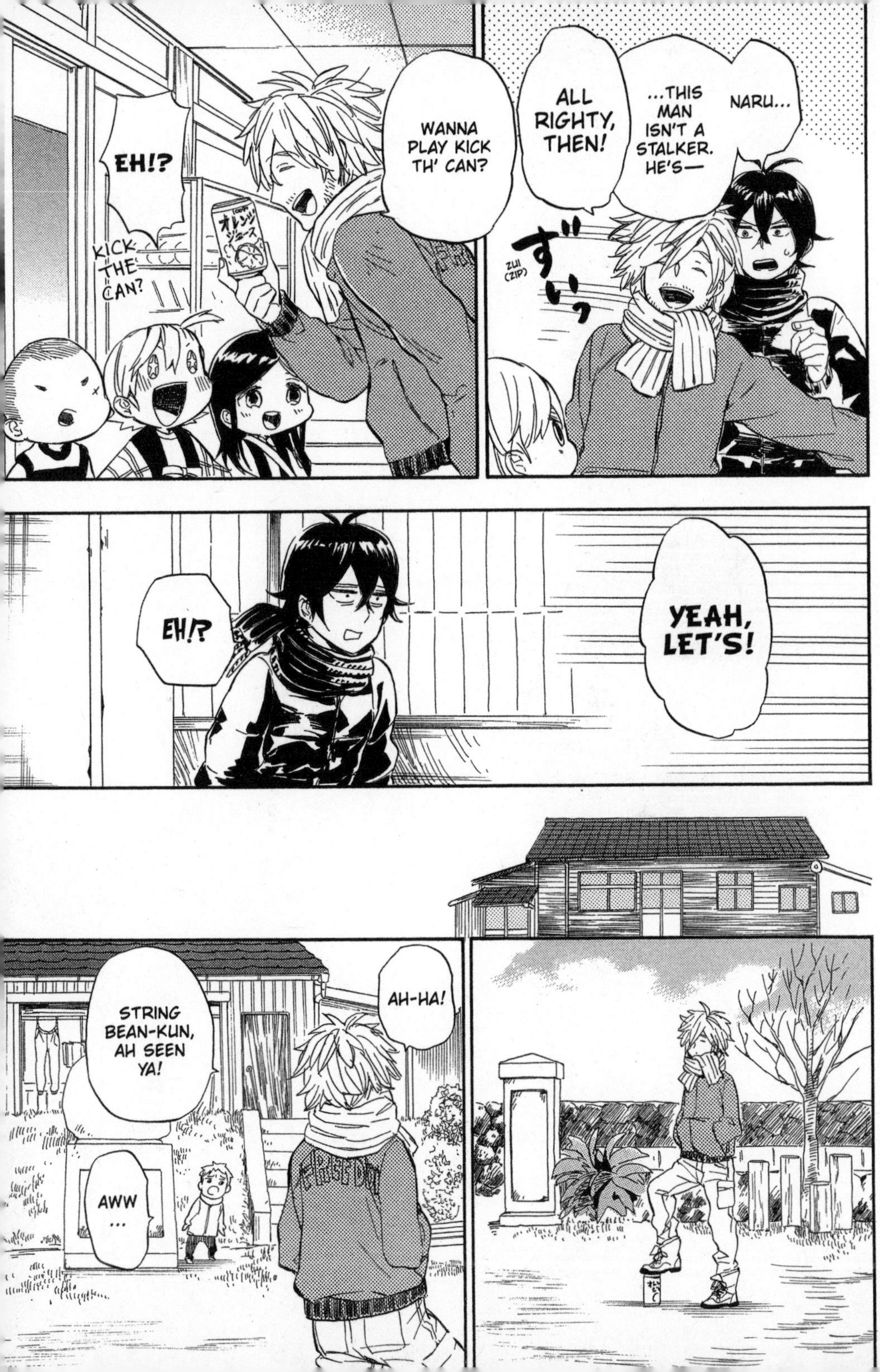
NARU...
...THIS MAN ISN'T A STALKER. HE'S—
ALL RIGHTY, THEN!
ZUI (ZIP)
WANNA PLAY KICK TH' CAN?
EH!?
KICK THE CAN?
YEAH, LET'S!
EH!?
AH-HA!
STRING BEAN-KUN, AH SEEN YA!
AWW ...

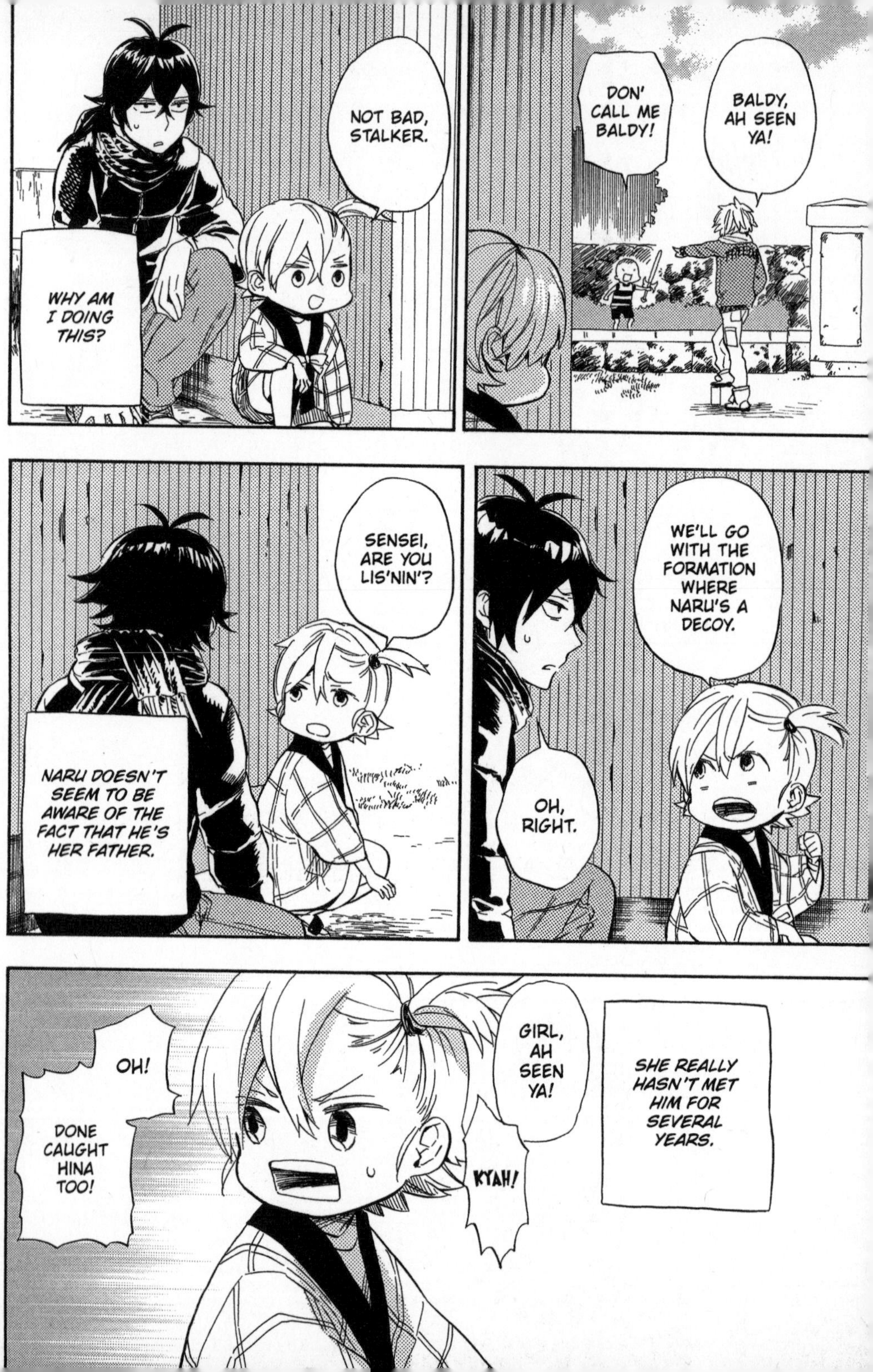
BALDY, AH SEEN YA!
DON' CALL ME BALDY!
NOT BAD, STALKER.
WHY AM I DOING THIS?
WE'LL GO WITH THE FORMATION WHERE NARU'S A DECOY.
OH, RIGHT.
SENSEI, ARE YOU LIS'NIN'?
NARU DOESN'T SEEM TO BE AWARE OF THE FACT THAT HE'S HER FATHER.
SHE REALLY HASN'T MET HIM FOR SEVERAL YEARS.
GIRL, AH SEEN YA!
KYAH!
OH!
DONE CAUGHT HINA TOO!

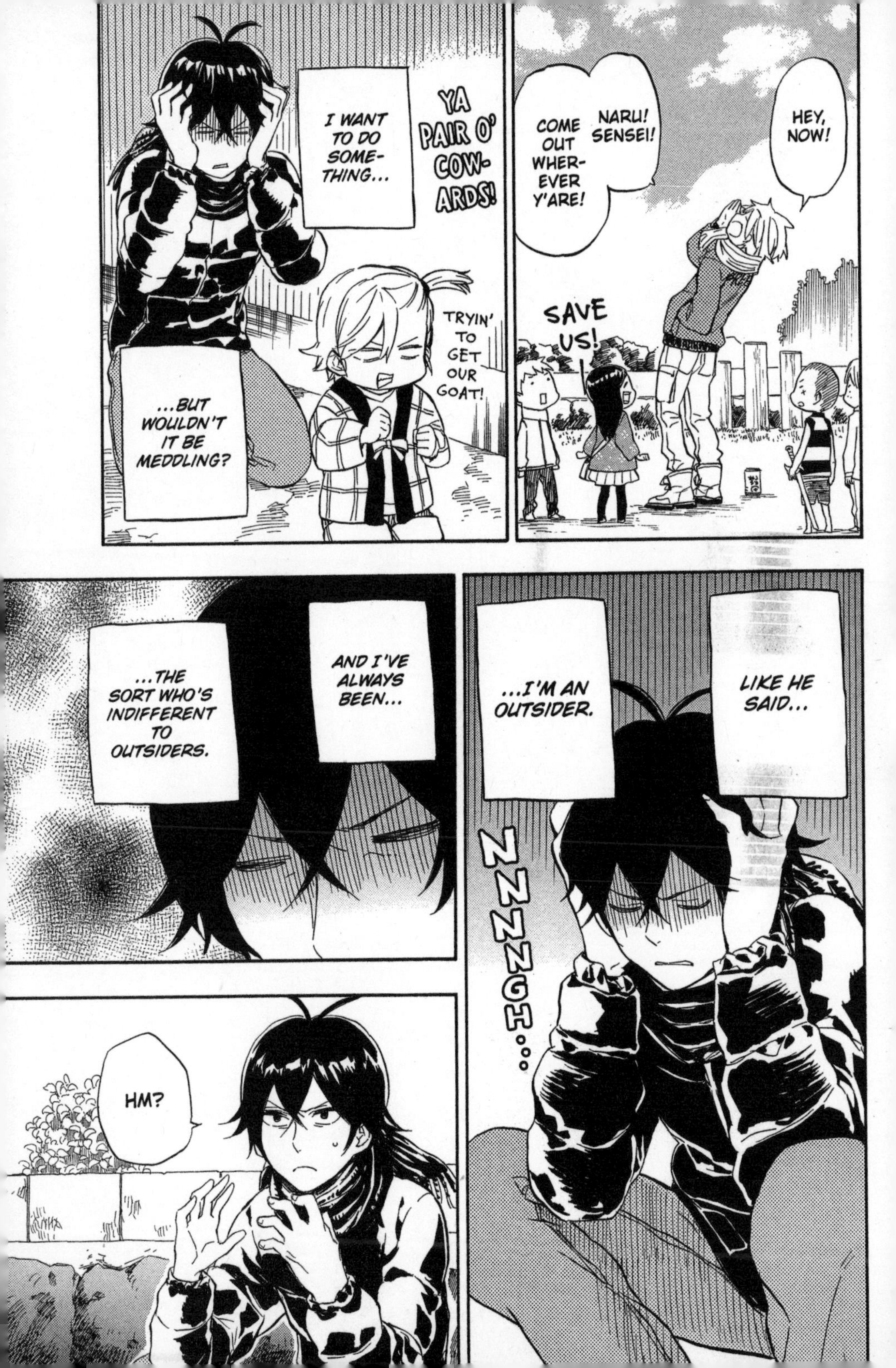
HEY, NOW!
NARU! SENSEI!
COME OUT WHER-EVER Y'ARE!
SAVE US!
YA PAIR O' COW-ARDS!
I WANT TO DO SOME-THING...
TRYIN' TO GET OUR GOAT!
...BUT WOULDN'T IT BE MEDDLING?
LIKE HE SAID...
...I'M AN OUTSIDER.
NNNNGH...
AND I'VE ALWAYS BEEN...
...THE SORT WHO'S INDIFFERENT TO OUTSIDERS.
HM?

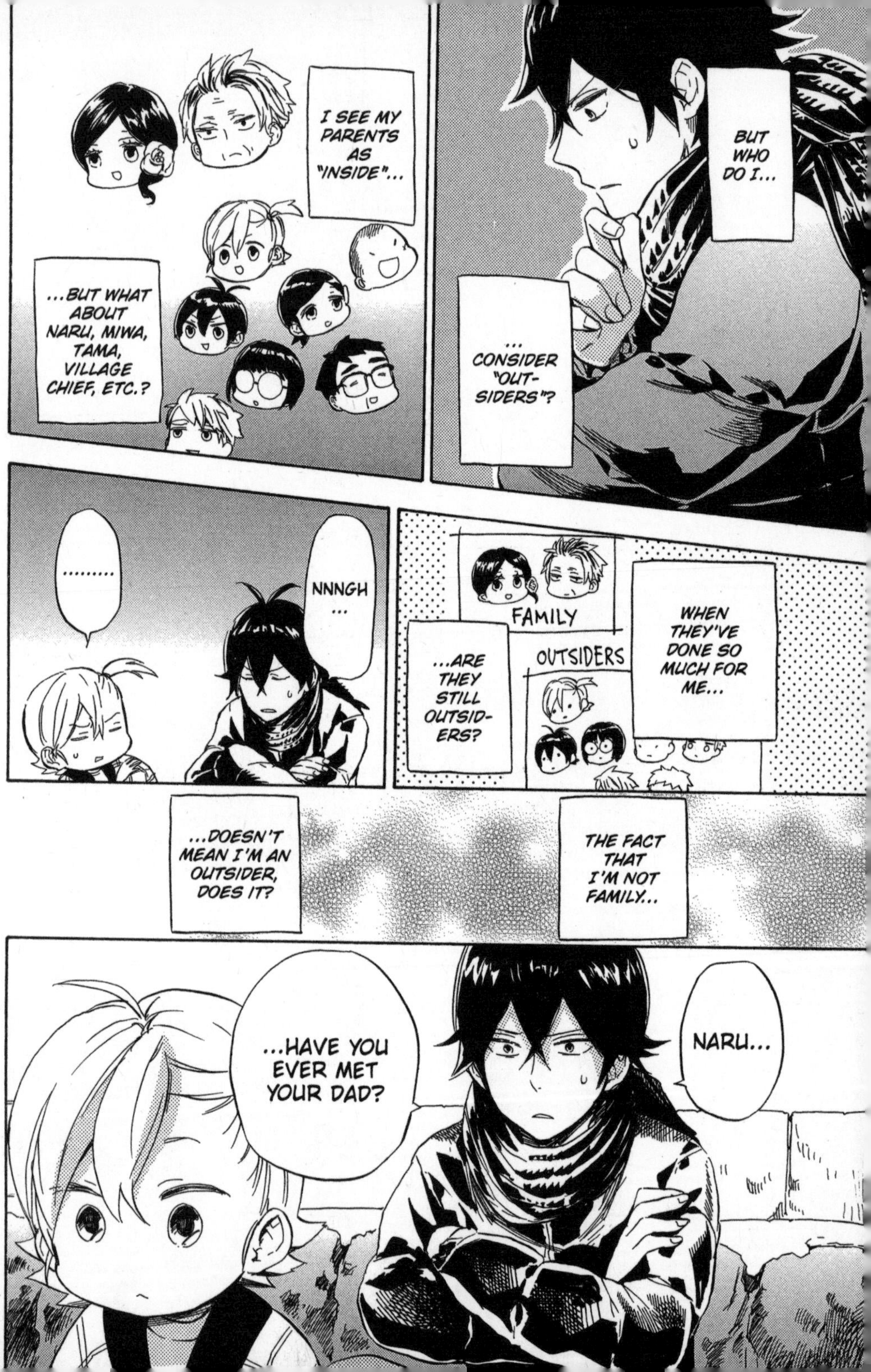
BUT WHO DO I...
...CONSIDER "OUT-SIDERS"?
I SEE MY PARENTS AS "INSIDE"...
...BUT WHAT ABOUT NARU, MIWA, TAMA, VILLAGE CHIEF, ETC.?
FAMILY
WHEN THEY'VE DONE SO MUCH FOR ME...
OUTSIDERS
...ARE THEY STILL OUTSID-ERS?
NNNGH ...
....
THE FACT THAT I'M NOT FAMILY...
...DOESN'T MEAN I'M AN OUTSIDER, DOES IT?
NARU...
...HAVE YOU EVER MET YOUR DAD?

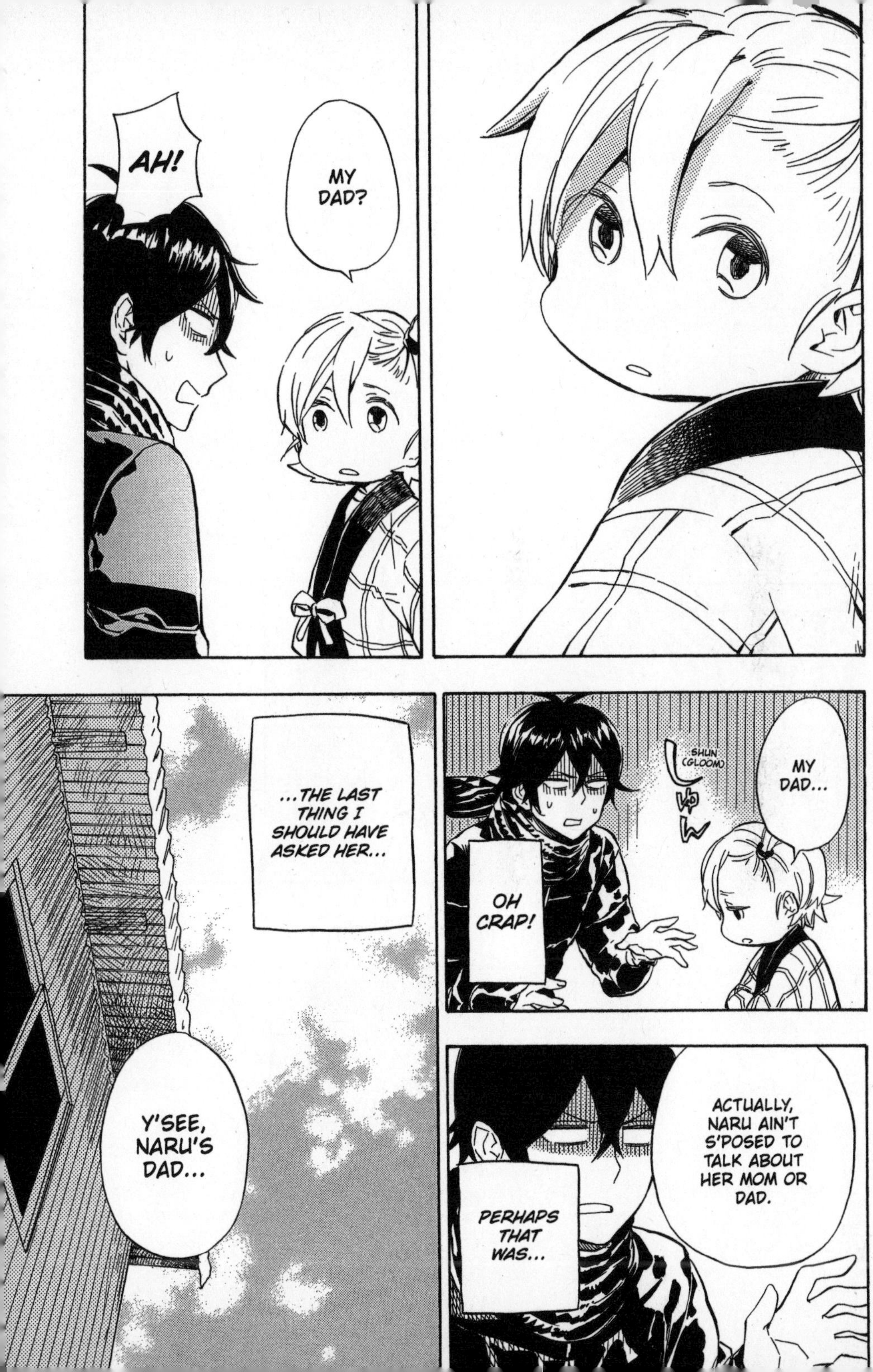
MY DAD?
AH!
MY DAD...
しゅん
SHUN (GLOOM)
OH CRAP!
ACTUALLY, NARU AIN'T S'POSED TO TALK ABOUT HER MOM OR DAD.
PERHAPS THAT WAS...
...THE LAST THING I SHOULD HAVE ASKED HER...
Y'SEE, NARU'S DAD...

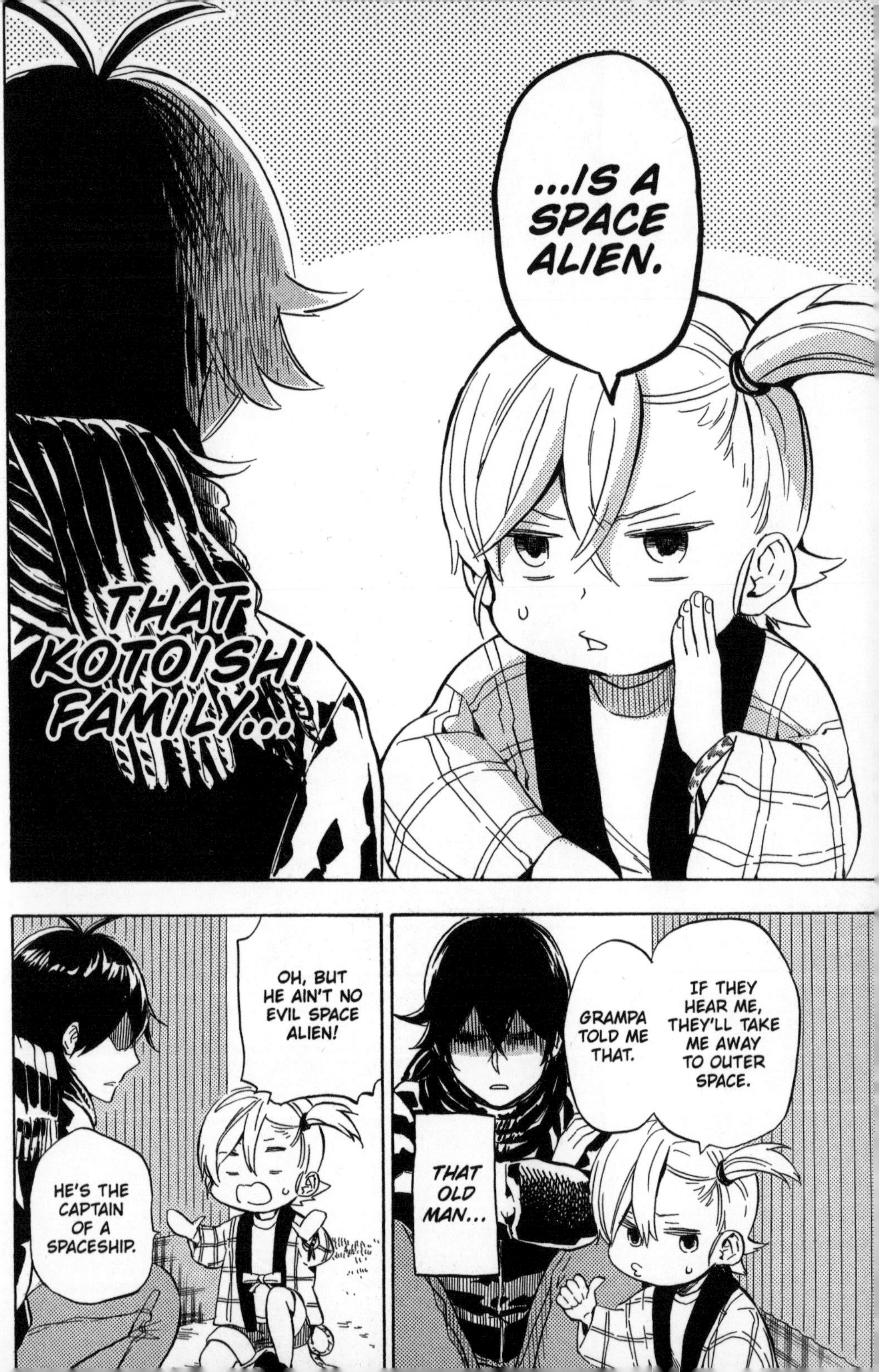
THAT KOTOISHI FAMILY...
...IS A SPACE ALIEN.
IF THEY HEAR ME, THEY'LL TAKE ME AWAY TO OUTER SPACE.
GRAMPA TOLD ME THAT.
THAT OLD MAN...
OH, BUT HE AIN'T NO EVIL SPACE ALIEN!
HE'S THE CAPTAIN OF A SPACESHIP.

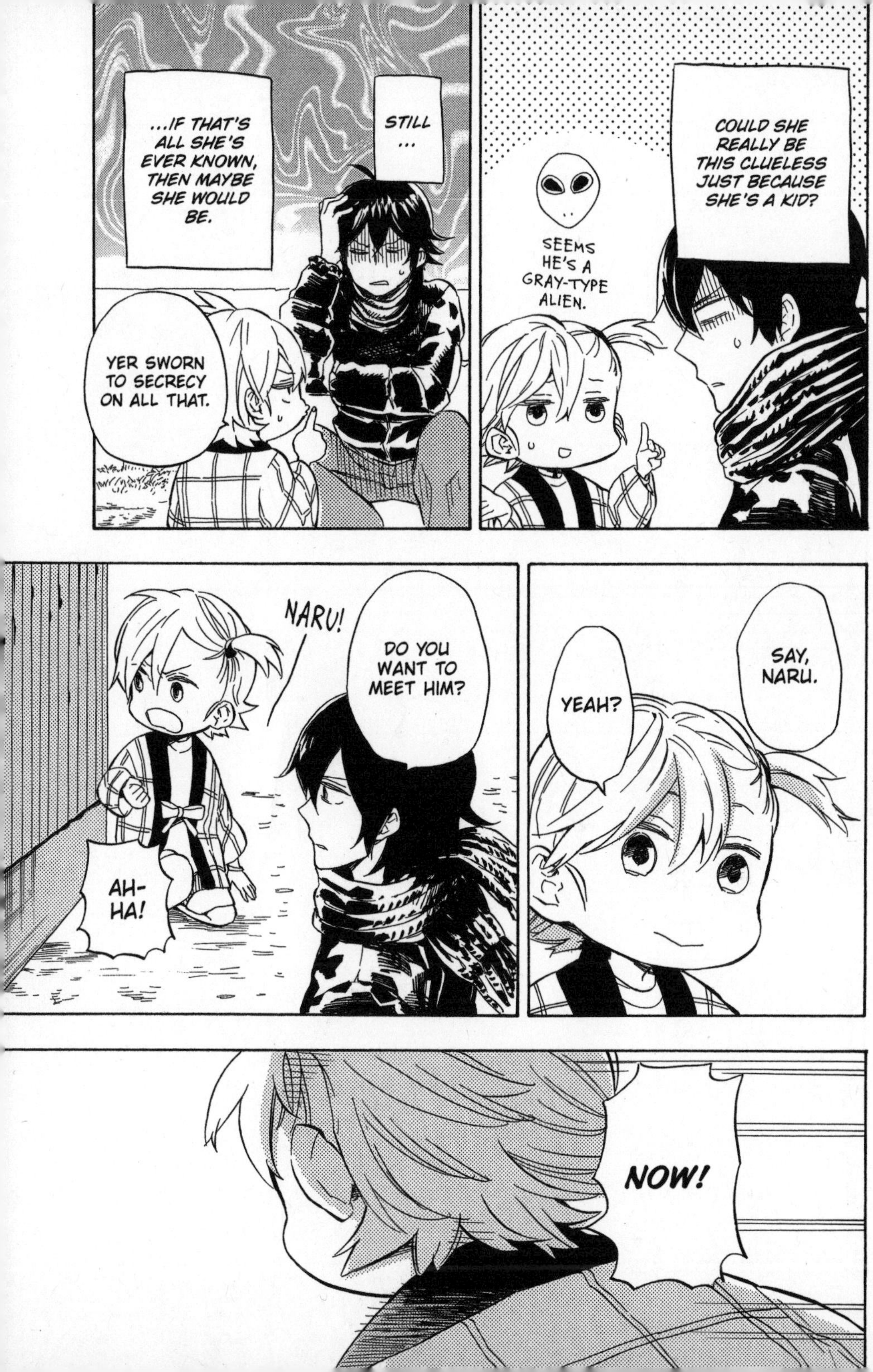
COULD SHE REALLY BE THIS CLUELESS JUST BECAUSE SHE'S A KID?
SEEMS HE'S A GRAY-TYPE ALIEN.
STILL ...
...IF THAT'S ALL SHE'S EVER KNOWN, THEN MAYBE SHE WOULD BE.
YER SWORN TO SECRECY ON ALL THAT.
SAY, NARU.
YEAH?
DO YOU WANT TO MEET HIM?
NARU!
AH-HA!
NOW!

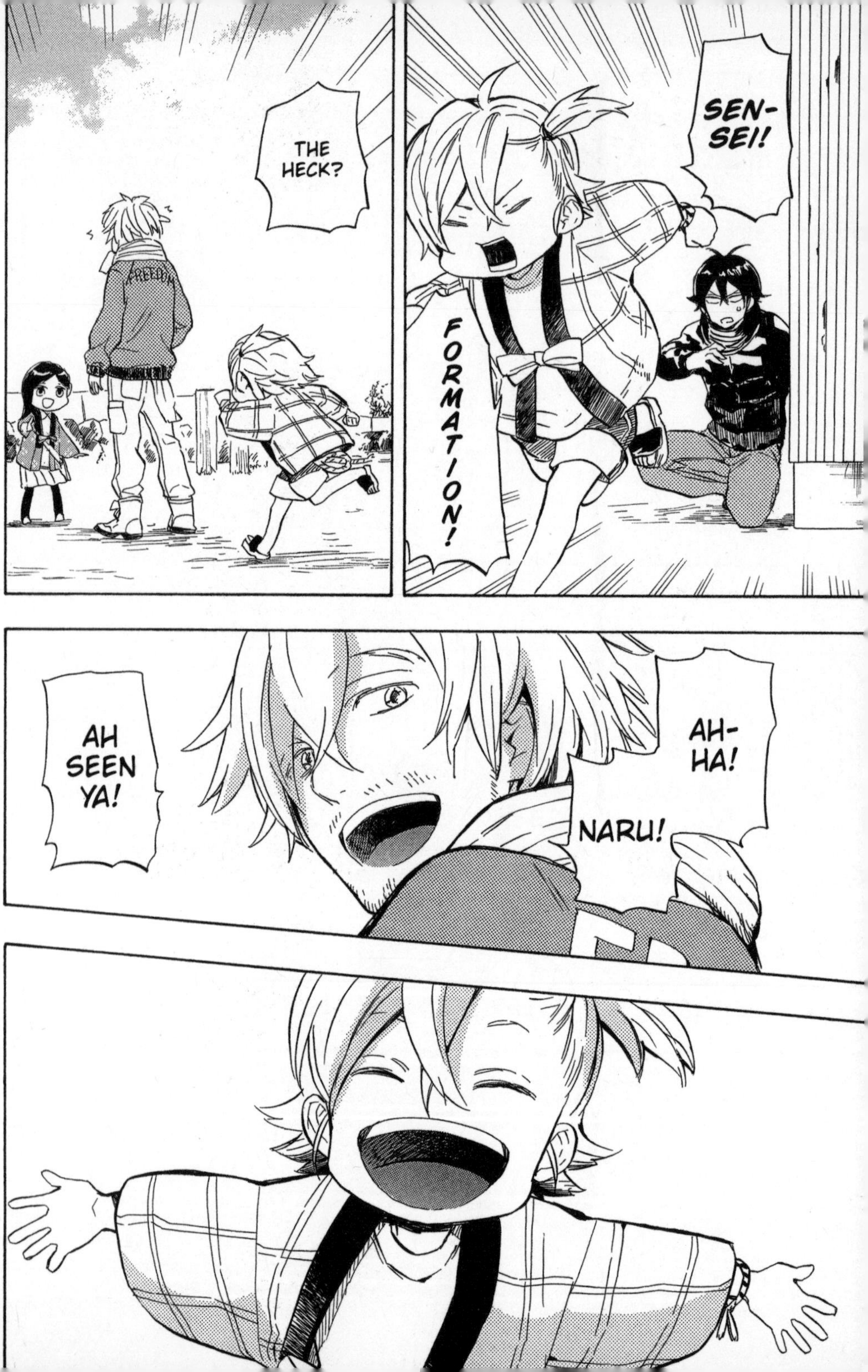
SEN-SEI!
FORMATION!
THE HECK?
AH-HA!
NARU!
AH SEEN YA!

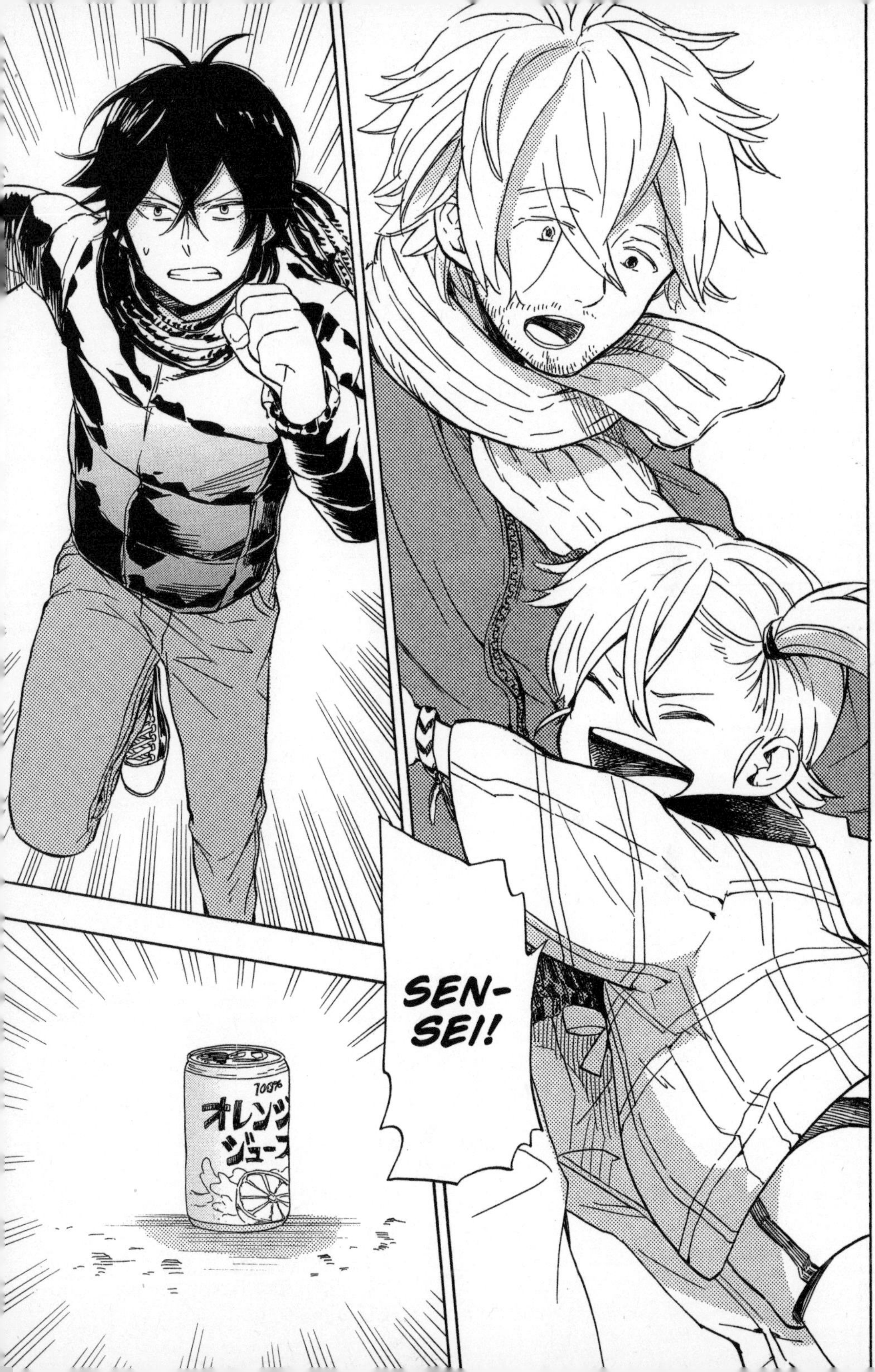
SEN-SEI!

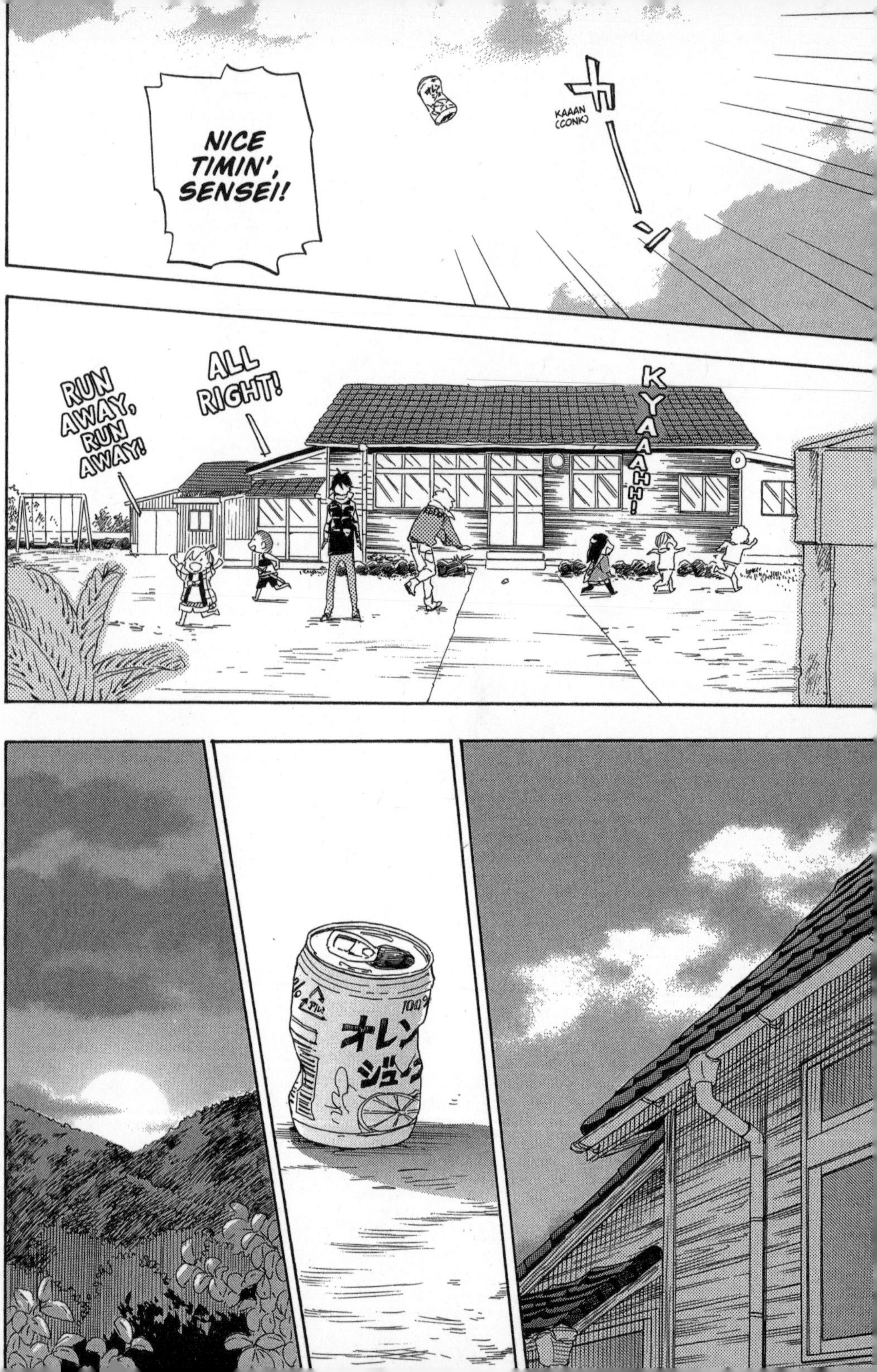

KAAAN (CONK)
NICE TIMIN', SENSEI!
KYAAAAHH!
ALL RIGHT!
RUN AWAY, RUN AWAY!

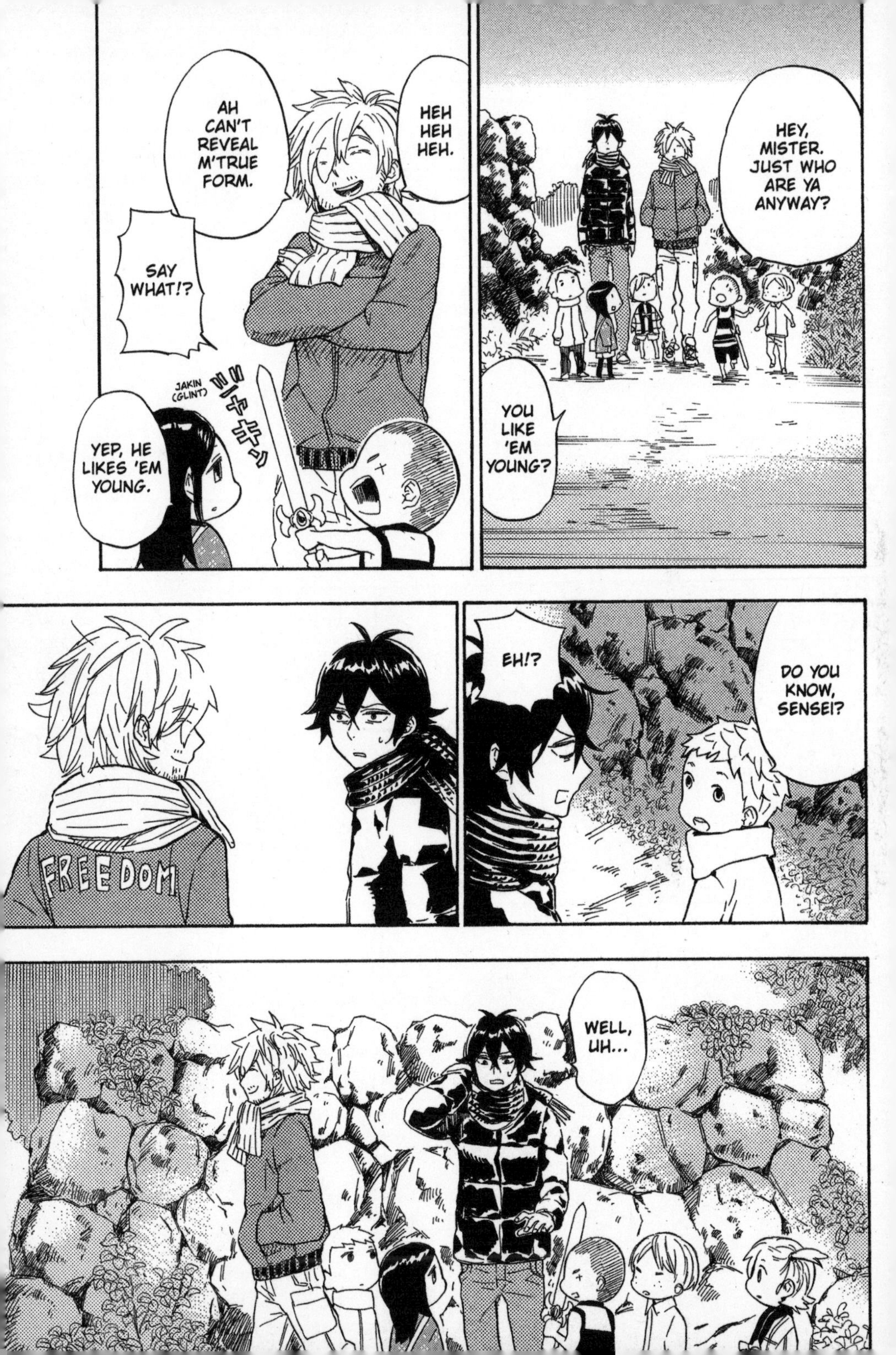
HEY, MISTER. JUST WHO ARE YA ANYWAY?
YOU LIKE 'EM YOUNG?
HEH HEH HEH.
AH CAN'T REVEAL M'TRUE FORM.
SAY WHAT!?
JAKIN (GLINT)
YEP, HE LIKES 'EM YOUNG.
DO YOU KNOW, SENSEI?
EH!?
FREEDOM
WELL, UH...

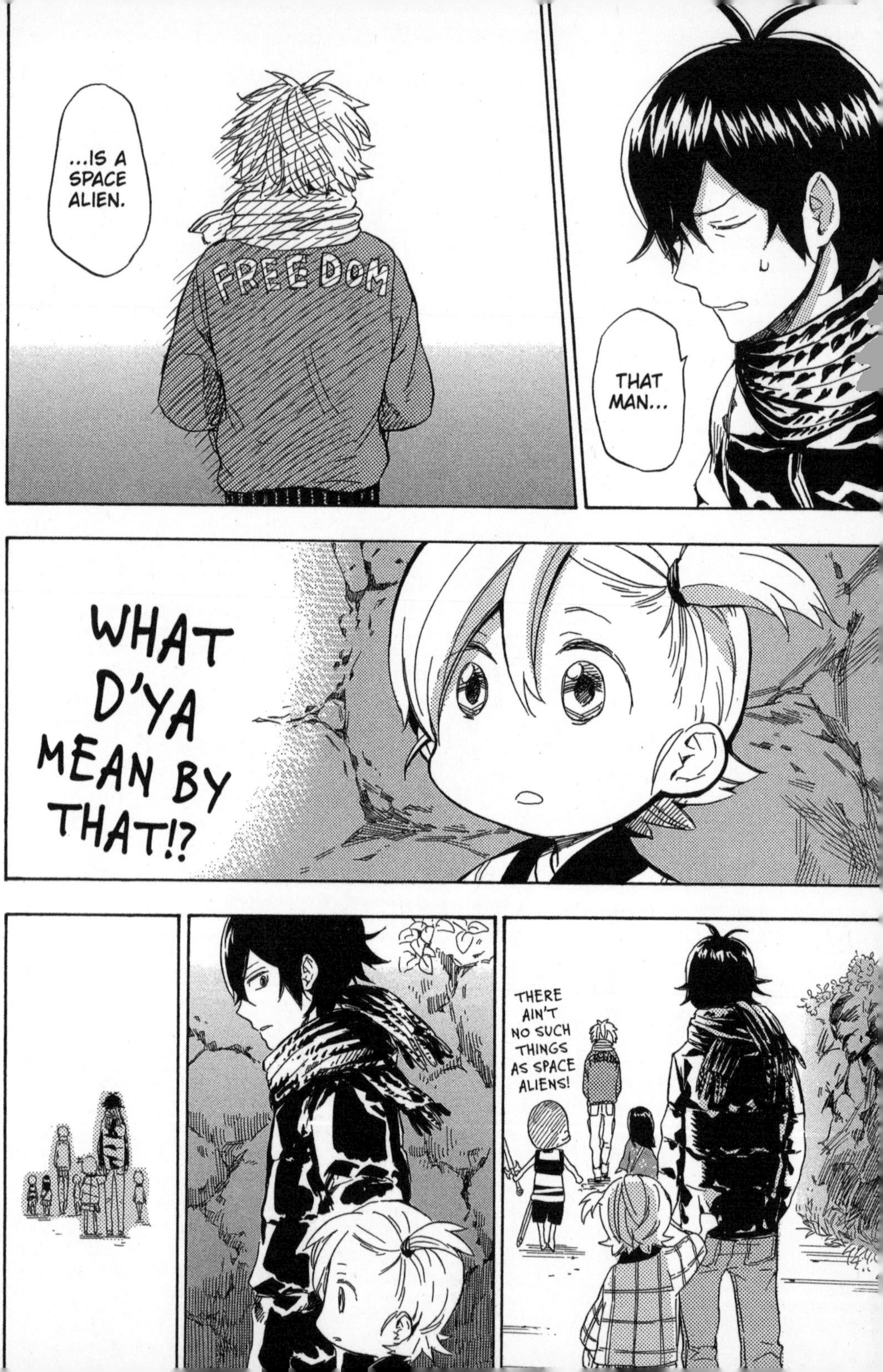
THAT MAN...
...IS A SPACE ALIEN.
FREEDOM
WHAT D'YA MEAN BY THAT!?
THERE AIN'T NO SUCH THINGS AS SPACE ALIENS!

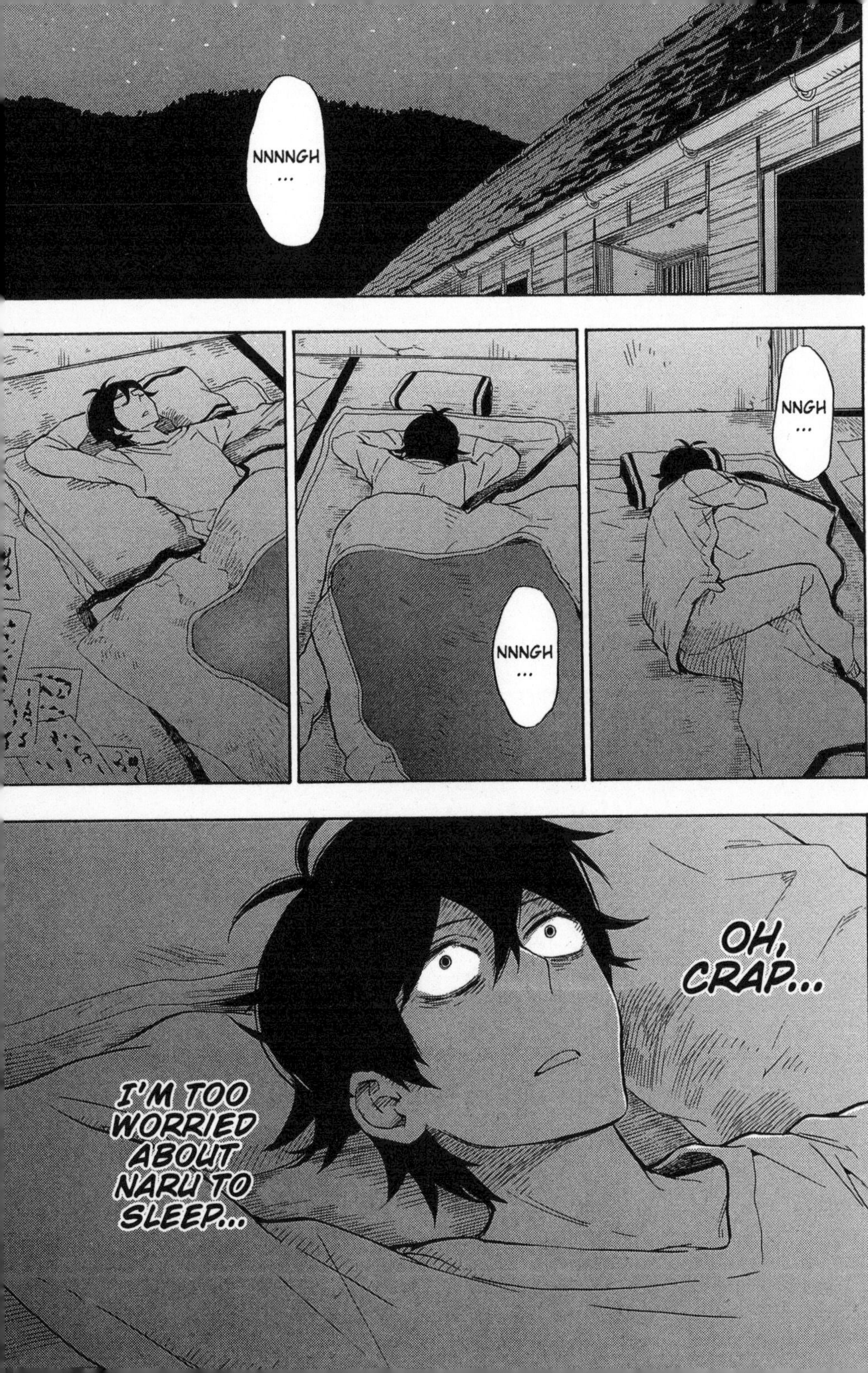
NNNNGH...
NNGH...
NNNNGH...
OH, CRAP...
I'M TOO WORRIED ABOUT NARU TO SLEEP...

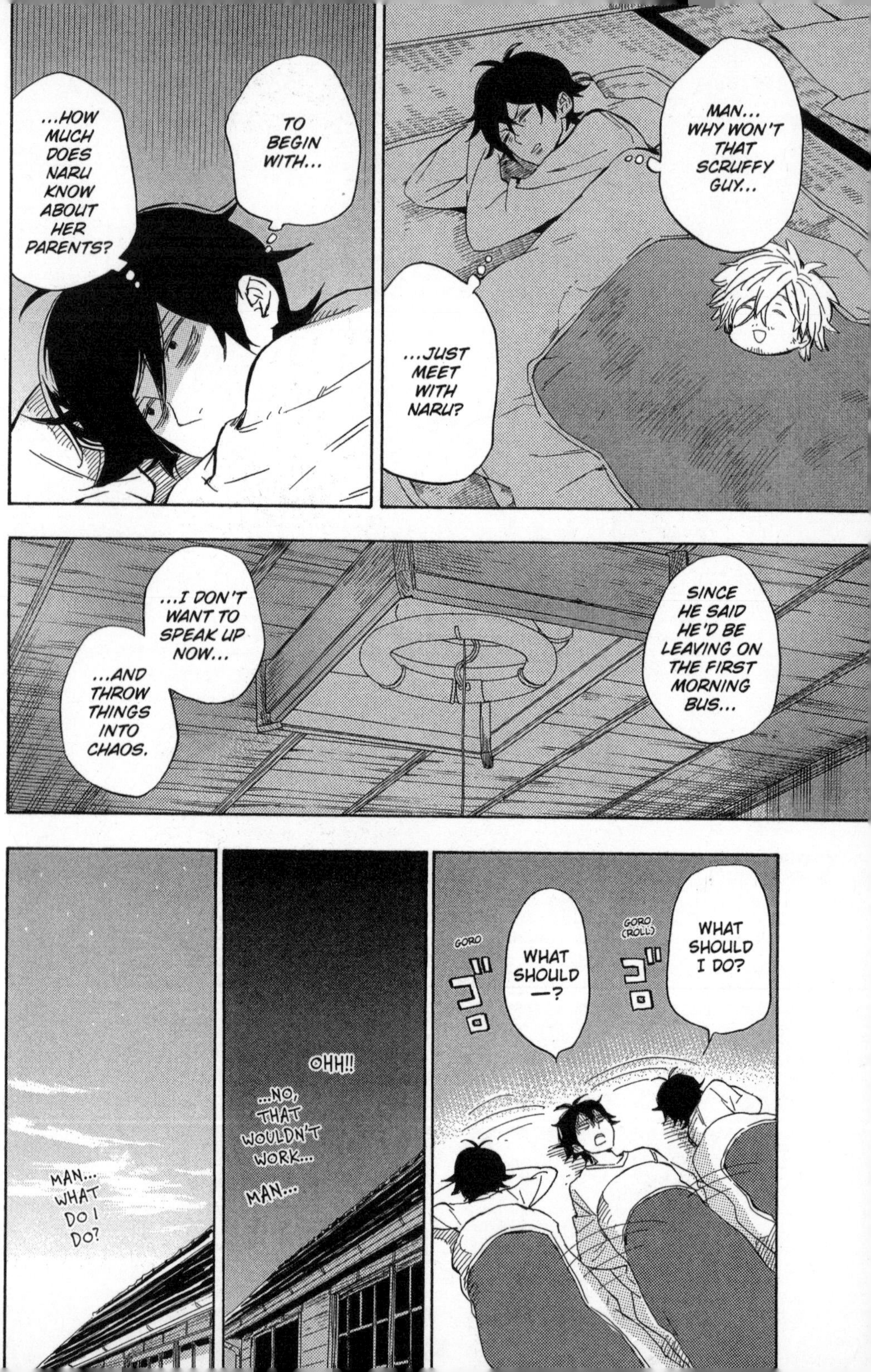
MAN... WHY WON'T THAT SCRUFFY GUY...
...JUST MEET WITH NARU?
TO BEGIN WITH...
...HOW MUCH DOES NARU KNOW ABOUT HER PARENTS?
SINCE HE SAID HE'D BE LEAVING ON THE FIRST MORNING BUS...
...I DON'T WANT TO SPEAK UP NOW...
...AND THROW THINGS INTO CHAOS.
WHAT SHOULD I DO?
ゴロ
GORO (ROLL)
WHAT SHOULD—?
ゴロ
GORO
OHH!!
...NO, THAT WOULDN'T WORK...
MAN...
MAN... WHAT DO I DO?

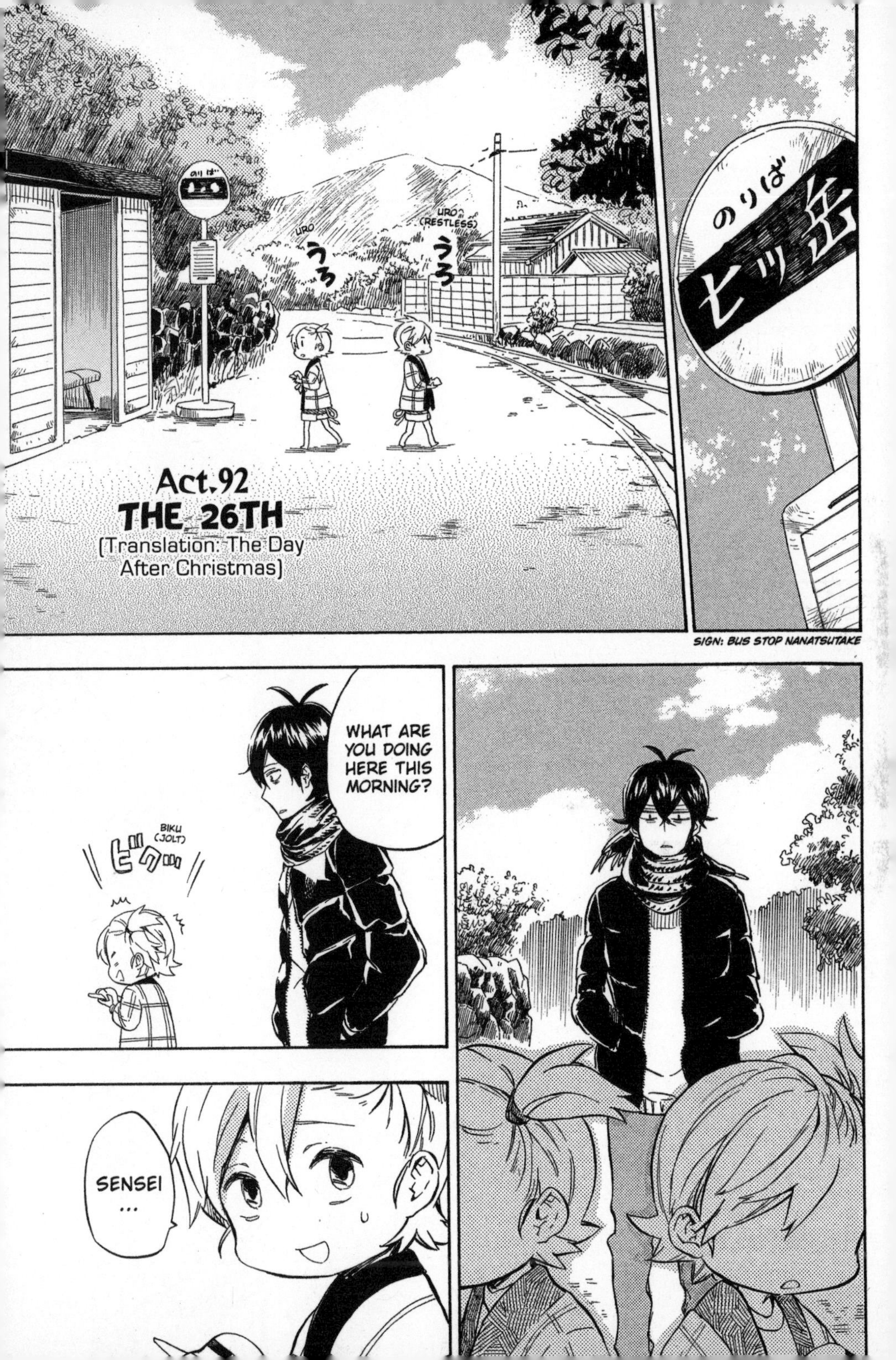
のりば
七ッ岳
URO (RESTLESS)
うろ
URO
うろ
Act.92
THE 26TH
(Translation: The Day After Christmas)
SIGN: BUS STOP NANATSUTAKE
WHAT ARE YOU DOING HERE THIS MORNING?
BIKU (JOLT)
ビクッ
SENSEI ...

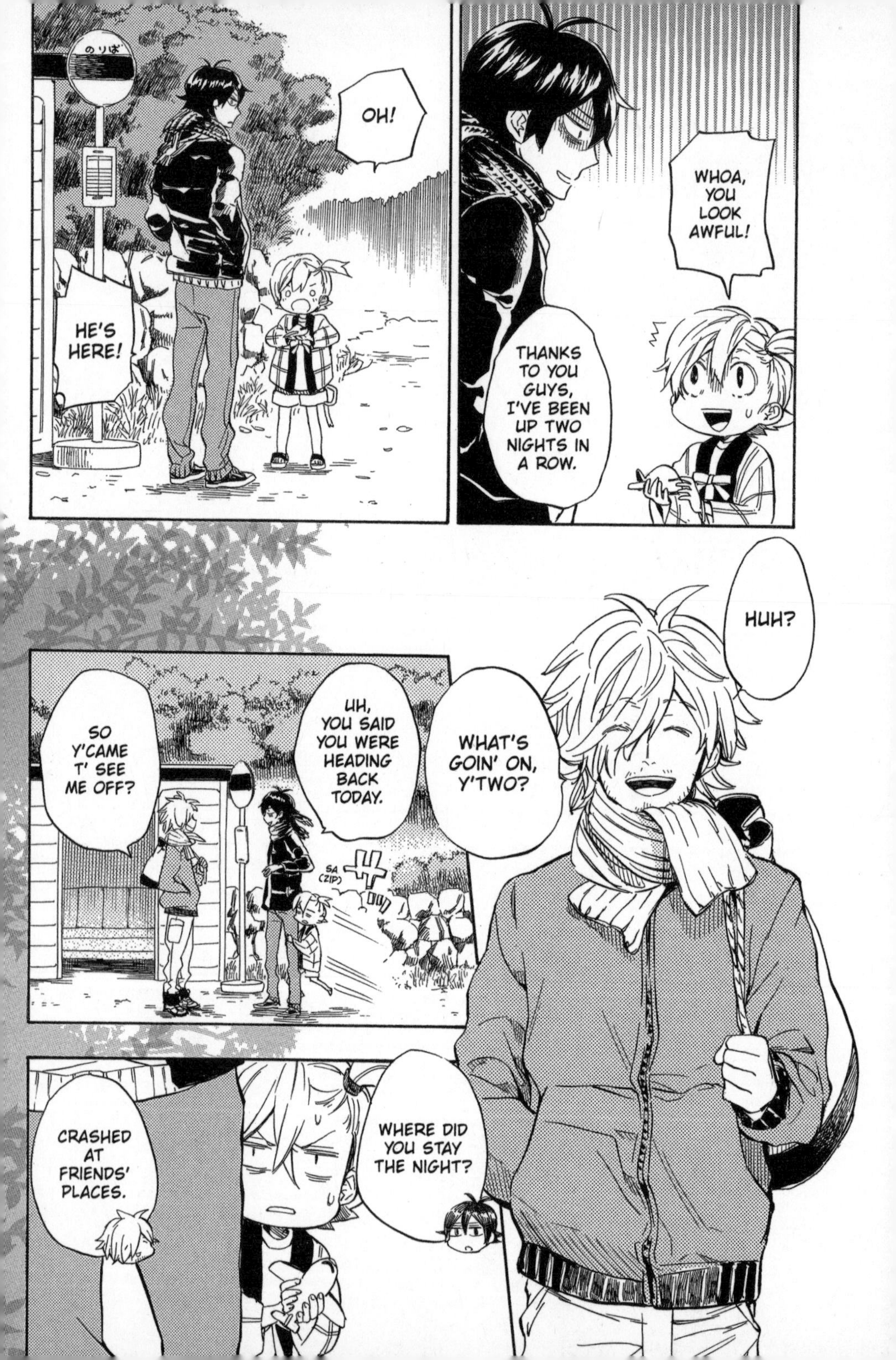
WHOA, YOU LOOK AWFUL!
THANKS TO YOU GUYS, I'VE BEEN UP TWO NIGHTS IN A ROW.
OH!
HE'S HERE!
HUH?
WHAT'S GOIN' ON, Y'TWO?
UH, YOU SAID YOU WERE HEADING BACK TODAY.
SO Y'CAME T' SEE ME OFF?
SA (ZIP)
WHERE DID YOU STAY THE NIGHT?
CRASHED AT FRIENDS' PLACES.

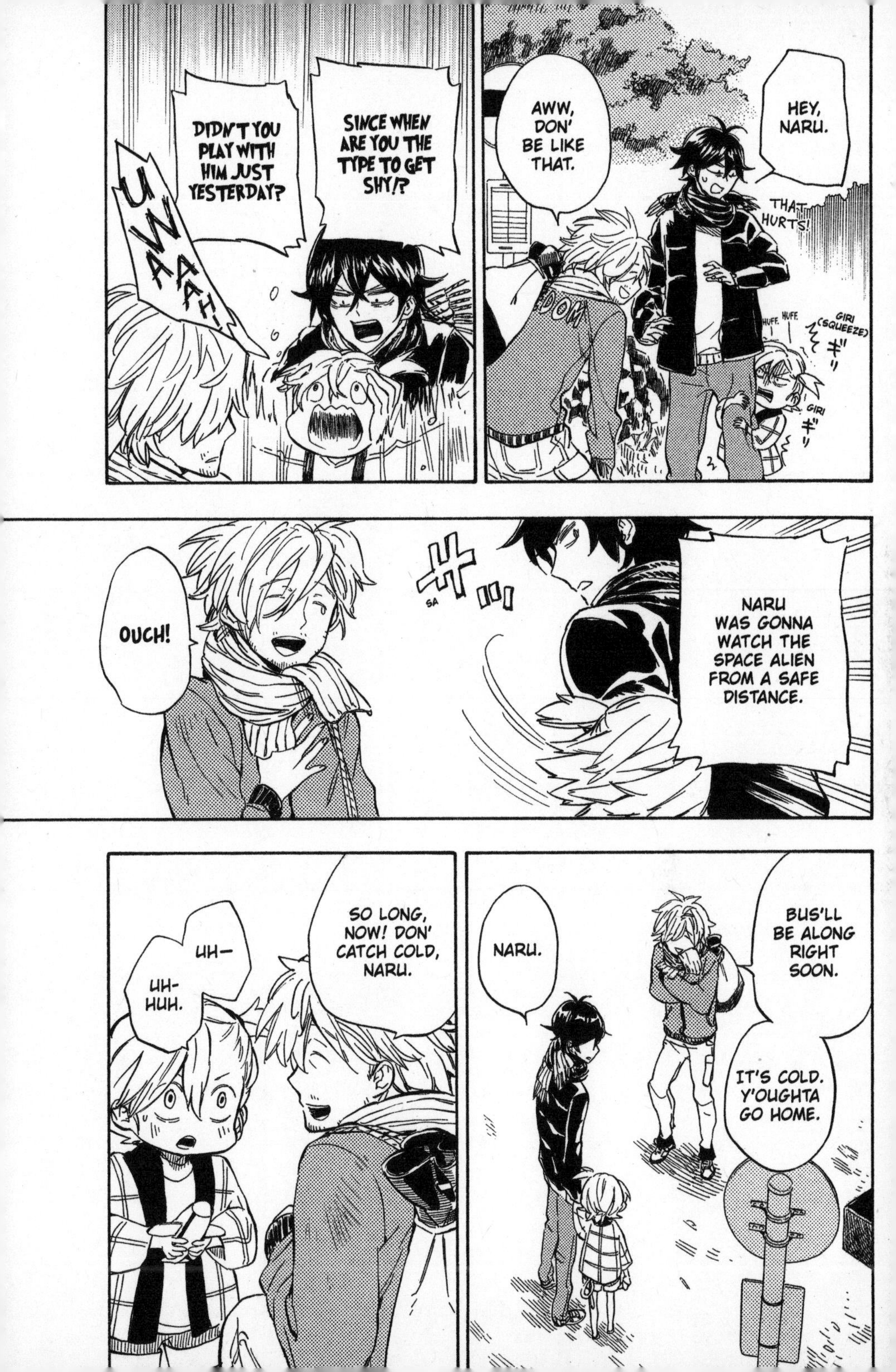
HEY, NARU.
THAT HURTS!
AWW, DON' BE LIKE THAT.
HUFF. HUFF.
GIRI (SQUEEZE)
ギリ
GIRI
ギリ
SINCE WHEN ARE YOU THE TYPE TO GET SHY!?
DIDN'T YOU PLAY WITH HIM JUST YESTERDAY?
UWAAAH!
NARU WAS GONNA WATCH THE SPACE ALIEN FROM A SAFE DISTANCE.
SA
サッ
OUCH!
BUS'LL BE ALONG RIGHT SOON.
IT'S COLD. Y'OUGHTA GO HOME.
NARU.
SO LONG, NOW! DON' CATCH COLD, NARU.
UH—
UH-HUH.

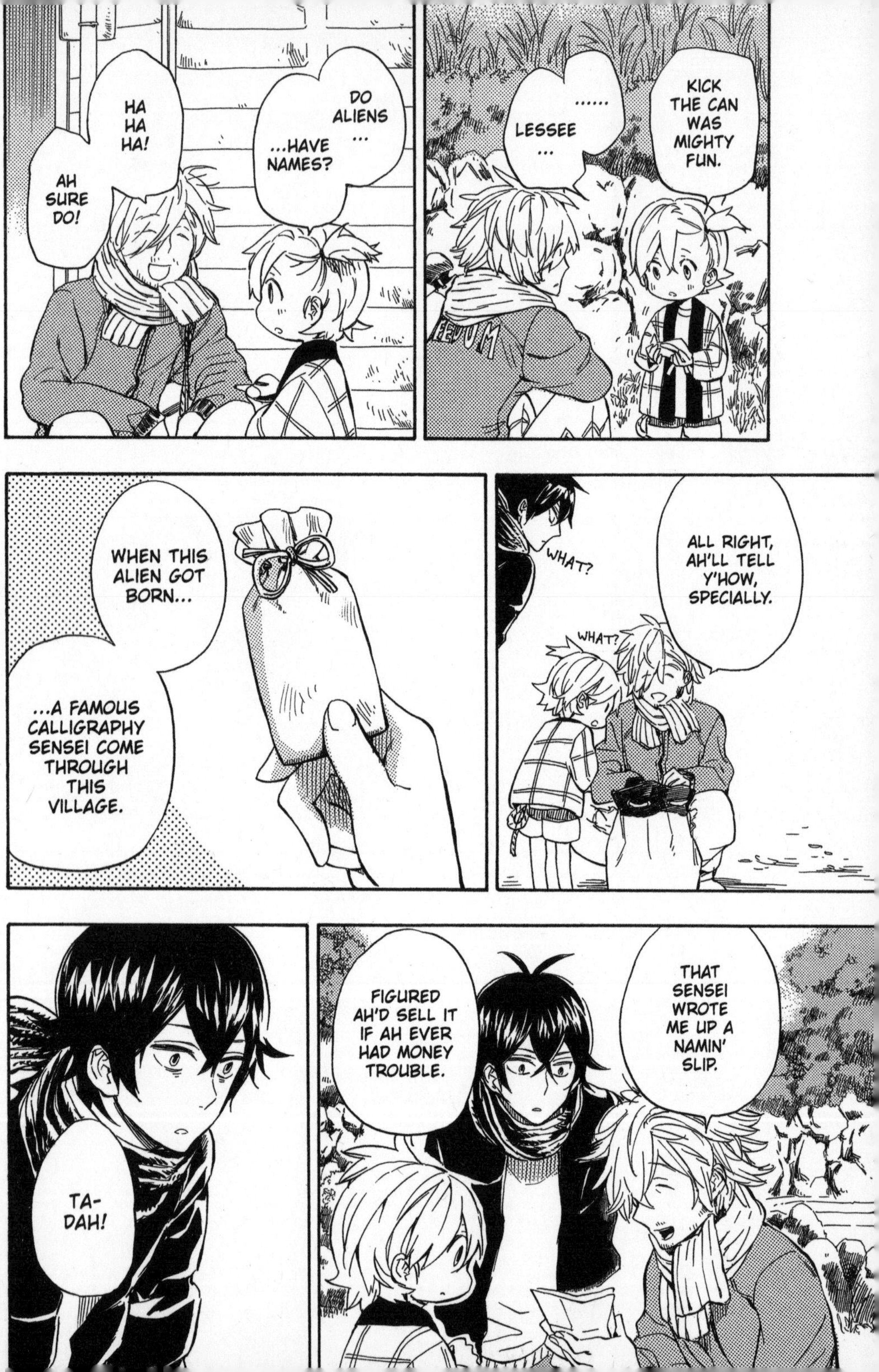
KICK THE CAN WAS MIGHTY FUN.
......
LESSEE ...
DO ALIENS ...
...HAVE NAMES?
HA HA HA!
AH SURE DO!
ALL RIGHT, AH'LL TELL Y'HOW, SPECIALLY.
WHAT?
WHAT?
WHEN THIS ALIEN GOT BORN...
...A FAMOUS CALLIGRAPHY SENSEI COME THROUGH THIS VILLAGE.
THAT SENSEI WROTE ME UP A NAMIN' SLIP.
FIGURED AH'D SELL IT IF AH EVER HAD MONEY TROUBLE.
TA-DAH!

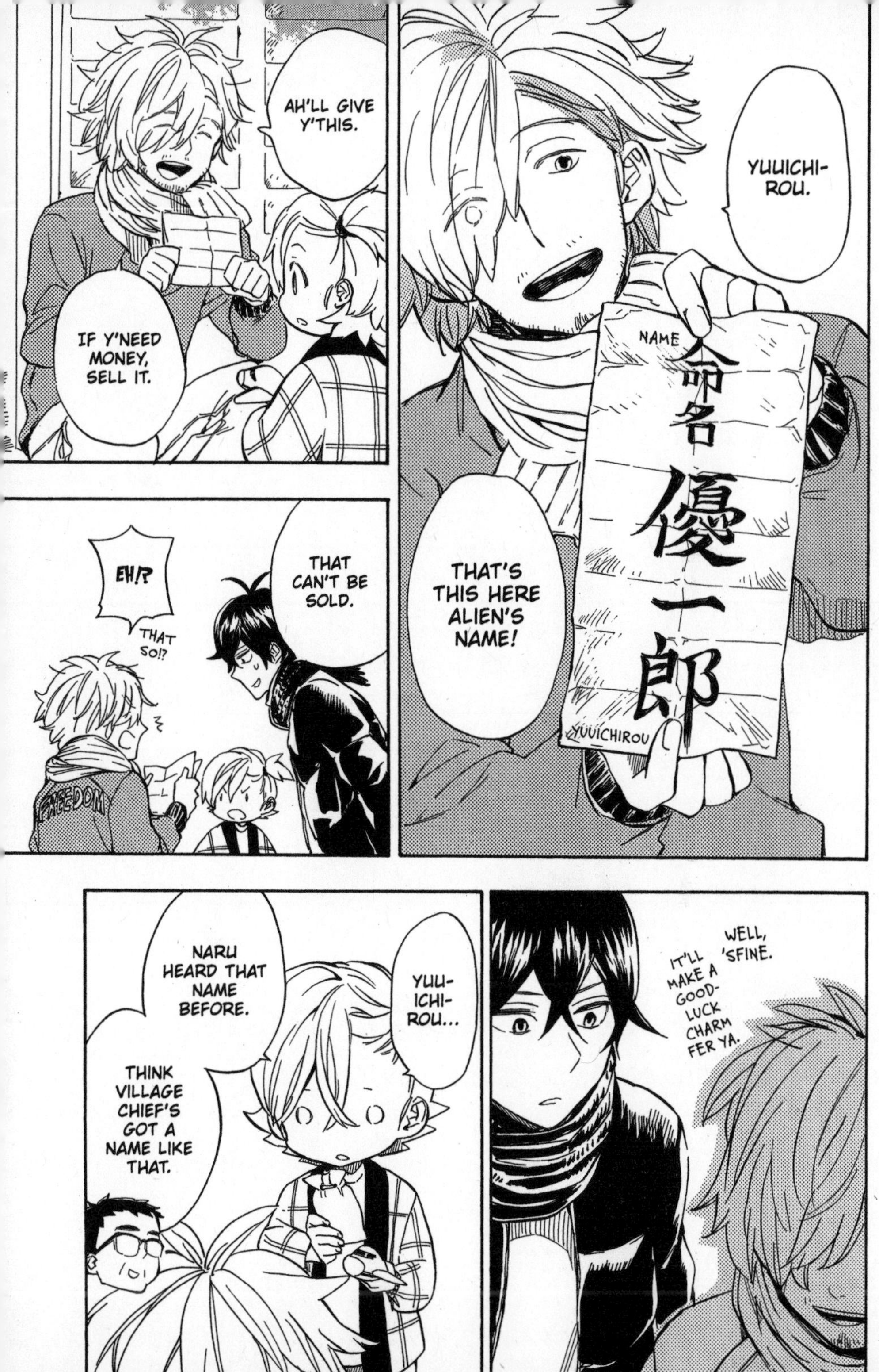
YUUICHI-ROU.
NAME
命名
優一郎
YUUICHIROU
THAT'S THIS HERE ALIEN'S NAME!
AH'LL GIVE Y'THIS.
IF Y'NEED MONEY, SELL IT.
THAT CAN'T BE SOLD.
EH!?
THAT SO!?
FREEDOM
WELL, 'SFINE.
IT'LL MAKE A GOOD-LUCK CHARM FER YA.
YUU-ICHI-ROU...
NARU HEARD THAT NAME BEFORE.
THINK VILLAGE CHIEF'S GOT A NAME LIKE THAT.

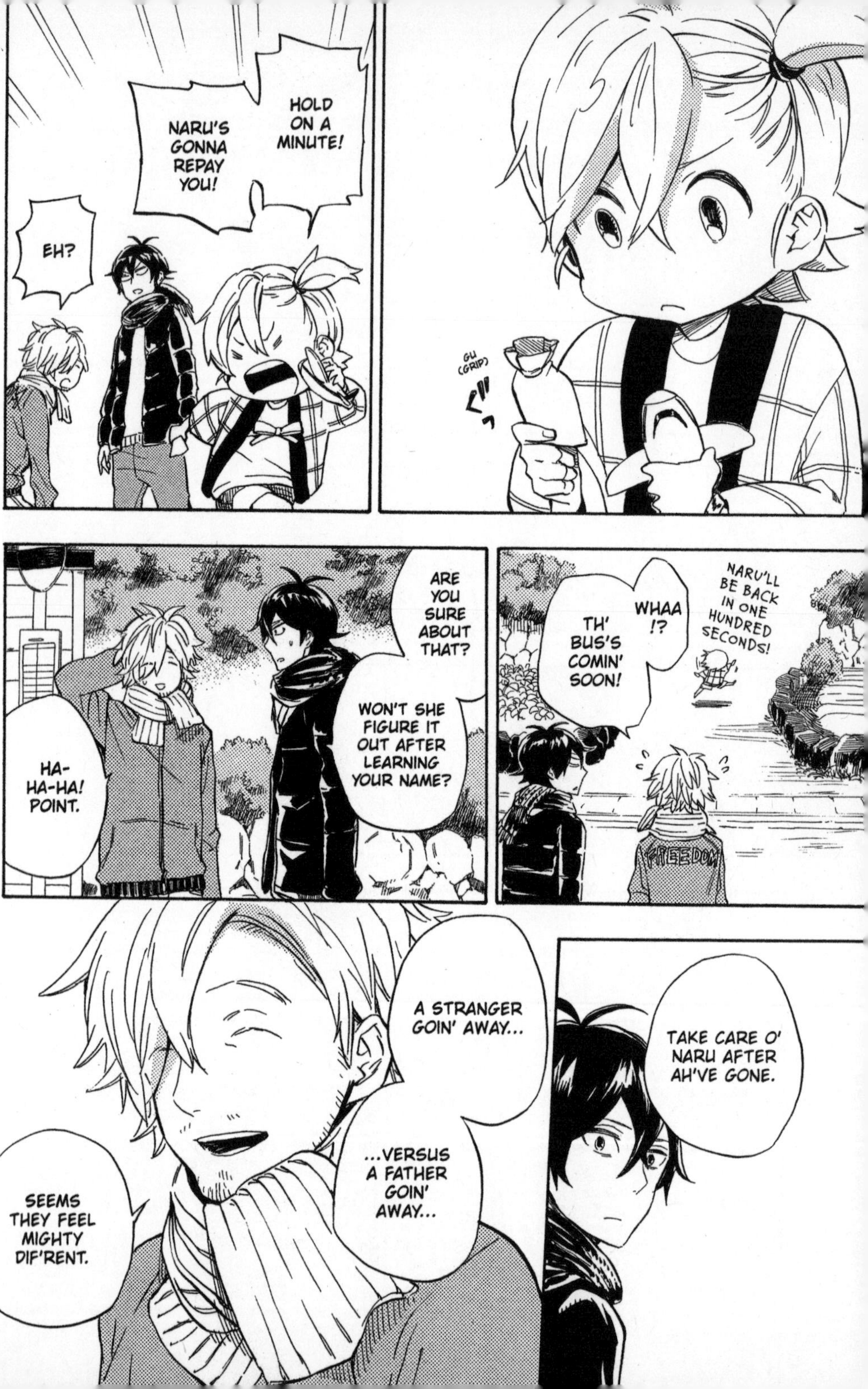
GU (GRIP)
HOLD ON A MINUTE!
NARU'S GONNA REPAY YOU!
EH?
NARU'LL BE BACK IN ONE HUNDRED SECONDS!
WHAA !?
TH' BUS'S COMIN' SOON!
FREEDOM
ARE YOU SURE ABOUT THAT?
WON'T SHE FIGURE IT OUT AFTER LEARNING YOUR NAME?
HA-HA-HA! POINT.
TAKE CARE O' NARU AFTER AH'VE GONE.
A STRANGER GOIN' AWAY...
...VERSUS A FATHER GOIN' AWAY...
SEEMS THEY FEEL MIGHTY DIF'RENT.

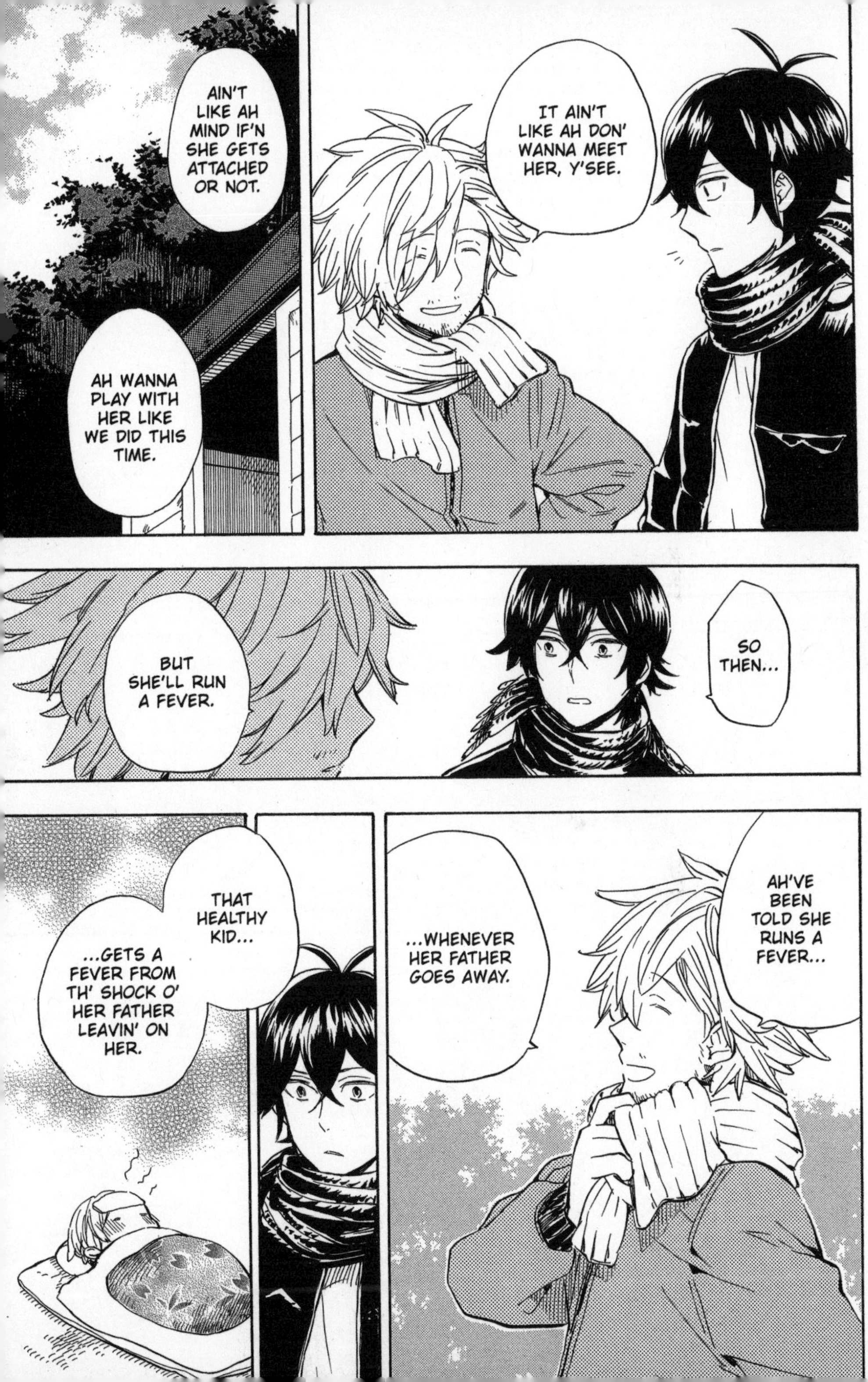
IT AIN'T LIKE AH DON' WANNA MEET HER, Y'SEE.
AIN'T LIKE AH MIND IF'N SHE GETS ATTACHED OR NOT.
AH WANNA PLAY WITH HER LIKE WE DID THIS TIME.
SO THEN...
BUT SHE'LL RUN A FEVER.
AH'VE BEEN TOLD SHE RUNS A FEVER...
...WHENEVER HER FATHER GOES AWAY.
THAT HEALTHY KID...
...GETS A FEVER FROM TH' SHOCK O' HER FATHER LEAVIN' ON HER.

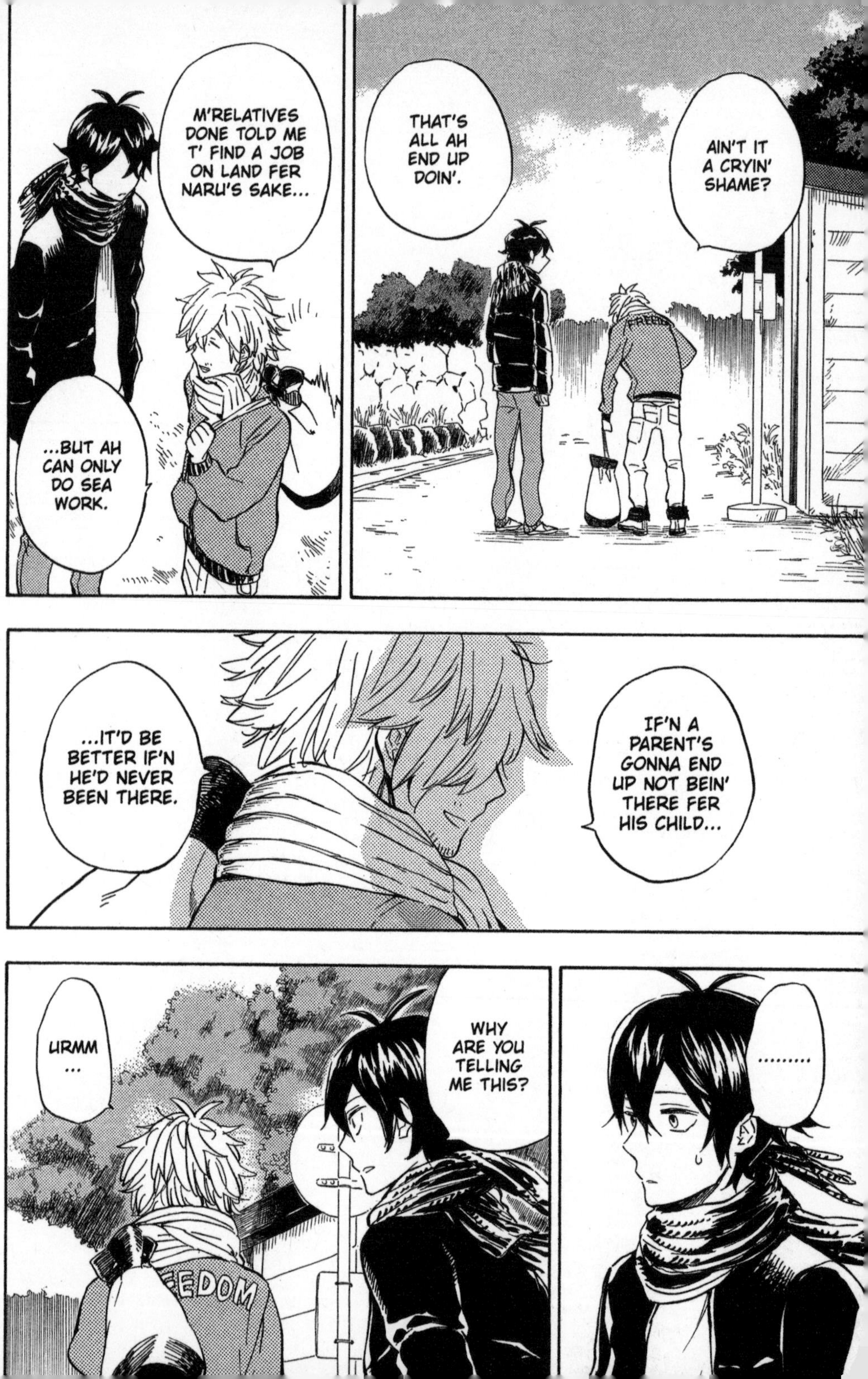
AIN'T IT A CRYIN' SHAME?
THAT'S ALL AH END UP DOIN'.
M'RELATIVES DONE TOLD ME T' FIND A JOB ON LAND FER NARU'S SAKE...
...BUT AH CAN ONLY DO SEA WORK.
IF'N A PARENT'S GONNA END UP NOT BEIN' THERE FER HIS CHILD...
...IT'D BE BETTER IF'N HE'D NEVER BEEN THERE.
....
WHY ARE YOU TELLING ME THIS?
URMM...
EEDOM

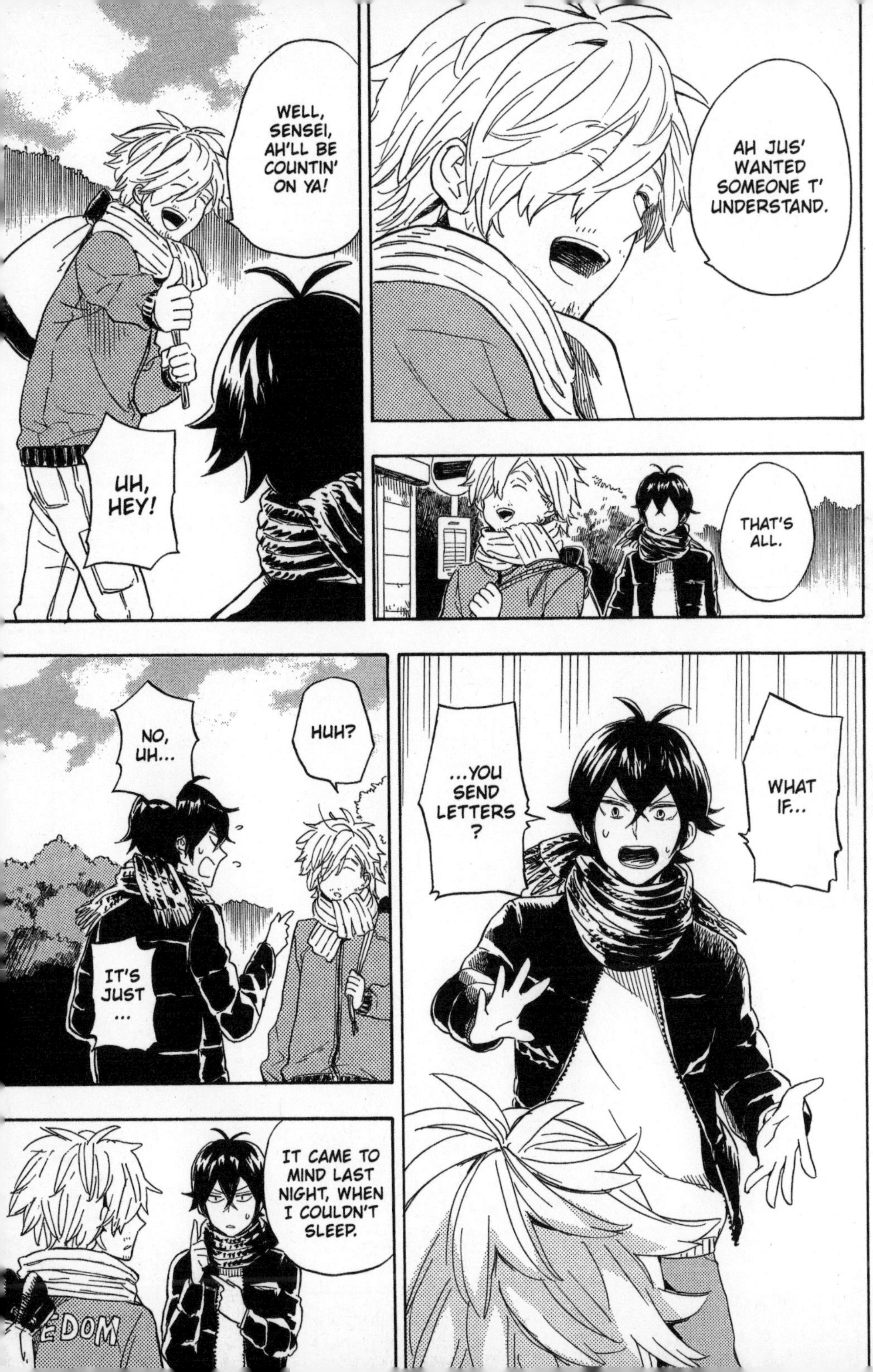
AH JUS' WANTED SOMEONE T' UNDERSTAND.
THAT'S ALL.
WELL, SENSEI, AH'LL BE COUNTIN' ON YA!
UH, HEY!
WHAT IF...
...YOU SEND LETTERS ?
HUH?
NO, UH...
IT'S JUST ...
IT CAME TO MIND LAST NIGHT, WHEN I COULDN'T SLEEP.

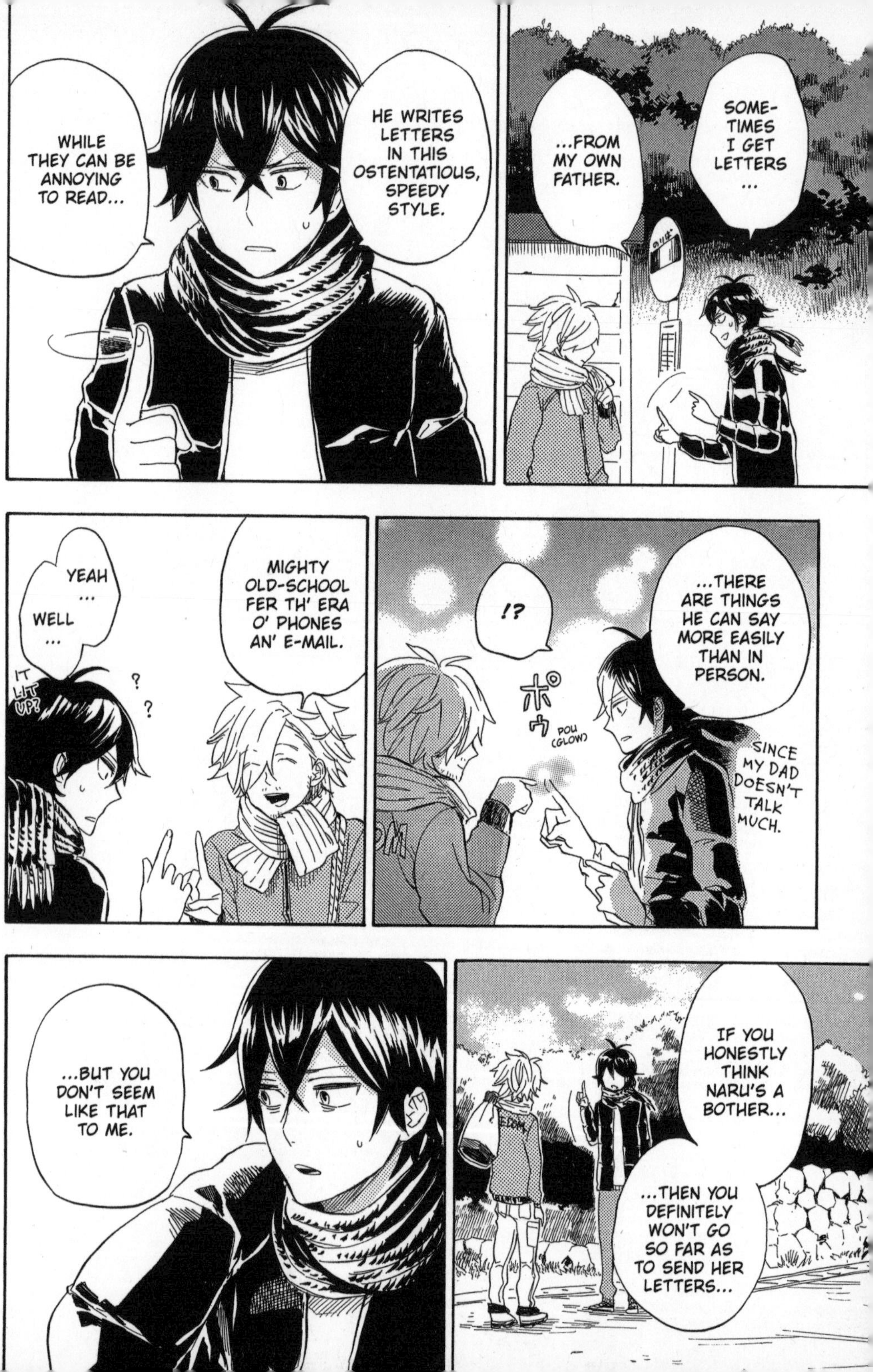

SOME-TIMES I GET LETTERS ...
...FROM MY OWN FATHER.
HE WRITES LETTERS IN THIS OSTENTATIOUS, SPEEDY STYLE.
WHILE THEY CAN BE ANNOYING TO READ...
...THERE ARE THINGS HE CAN SAY MORE EASILY THAN IN PERSON.
SINCE MY DAD DOESN'T TALK MUCH.
!?
ポゥ
POU (GLOW)
MIGHTY OLD-SCHOOL FER TH' ERA O' PHONES AN' E-MAIL.
YEAH ... WELL ...
IT LIT UP?
? ?
IF YOU HONESTLY THINK NARU'S A BOTHER...
...THEN YOU DEFINITELY WON'T GO SO FAR AS TO SEND HER LETTERS...
...BUT YOU DON'T SEEM LIKE THAT TO ME.

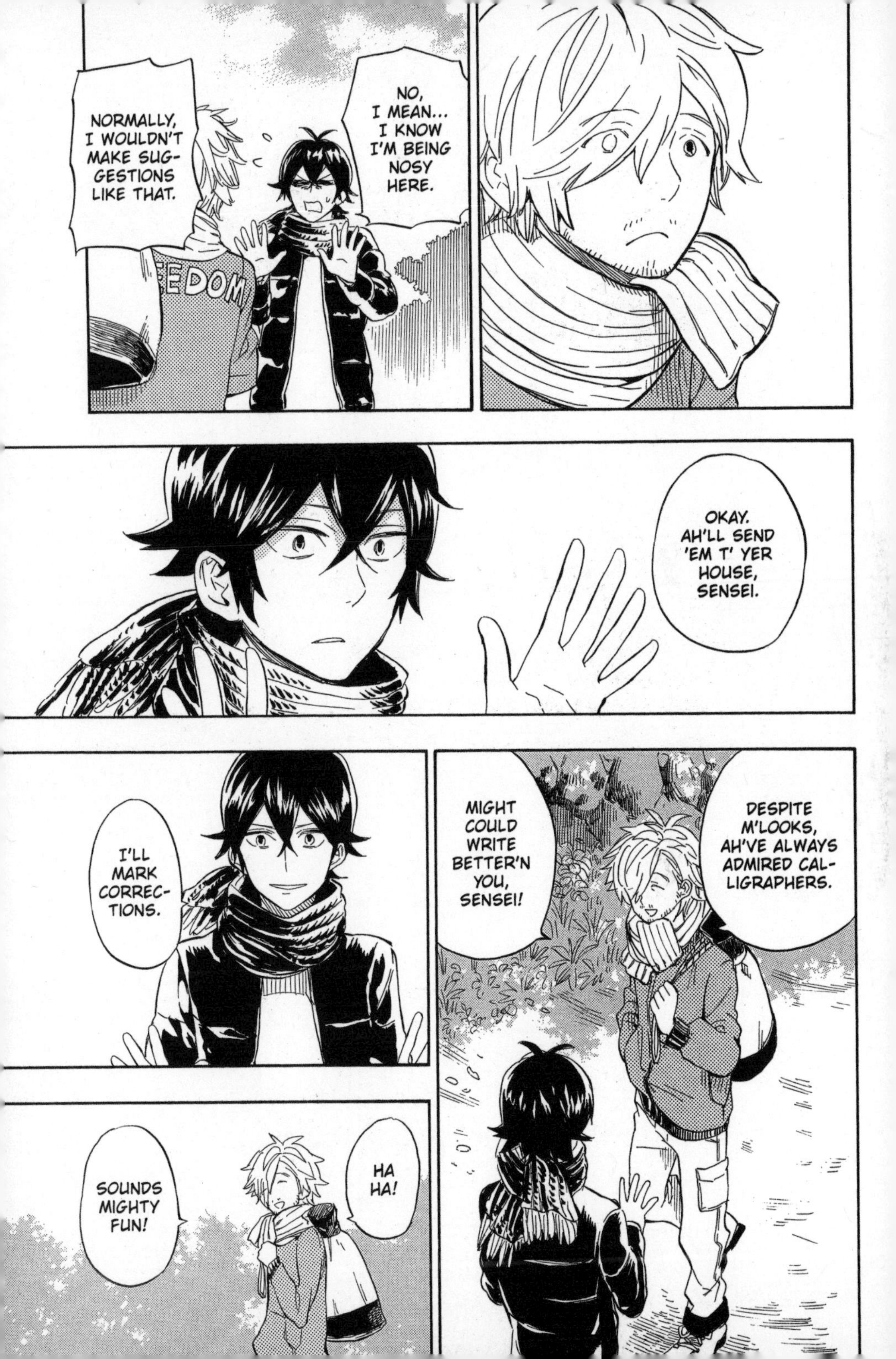
NO, I MEAN... I KNOW I'M BEING NOSY HERE.
NORMALLY, I WOULDN'T MAKE SUGGESTIONS LIKE THAT.
EDOM
OKAY. AH'LL SEND 'EM T' YER HOUSE, SENSEI.
DESPITE M'LOOKS, AH'VE ALWAYS ADMIRED CALLIGRAPHERS.
MIGHT COULD WRITE BETTER'N YOU, SENSEI!
I'LL MARK CORRECTIONS.
HA HA!
SOUNDS MIGHTY FUN!

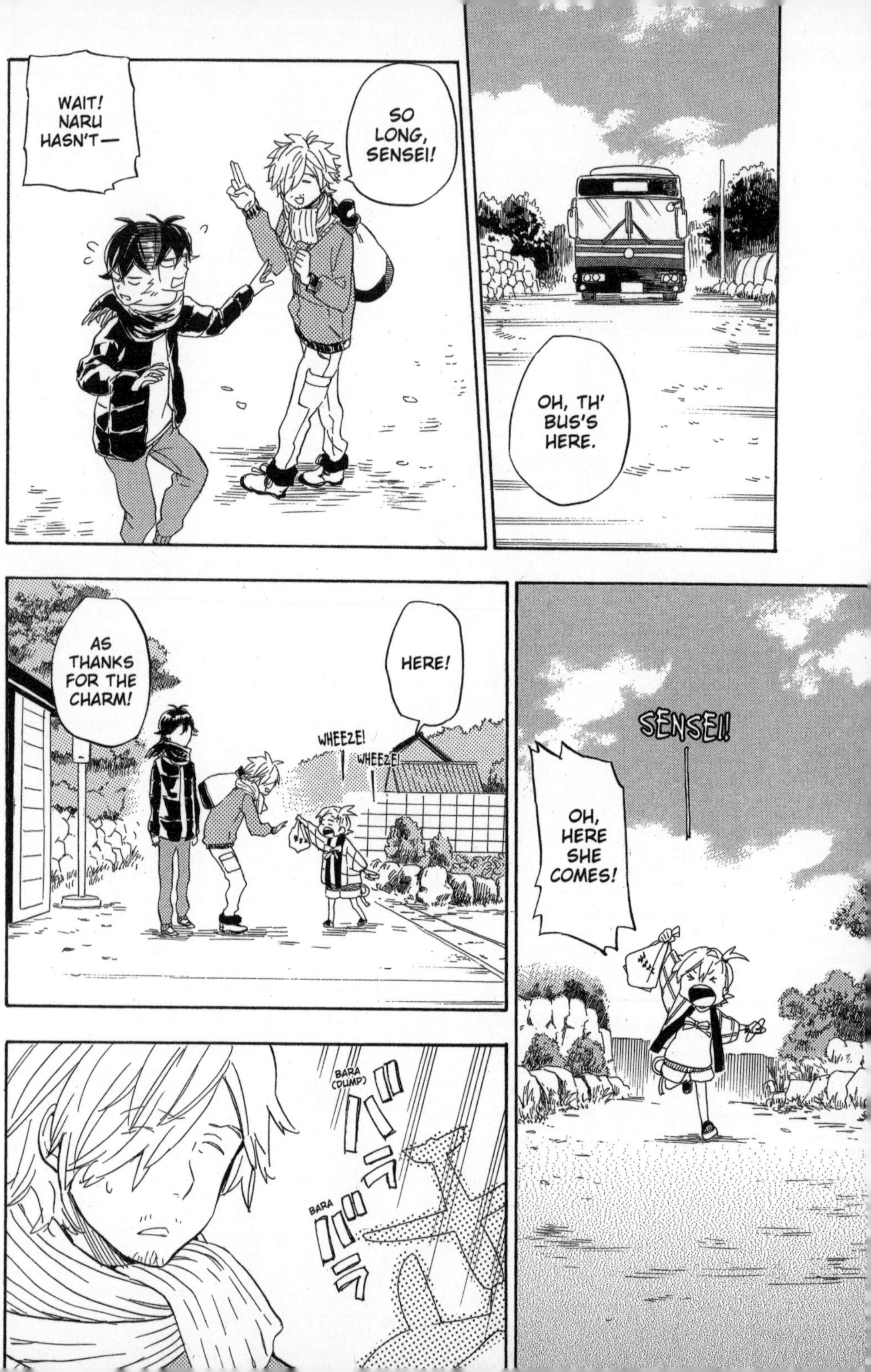
OH, TH' BUS'S HERE.
SO LONG, SENSEI!
WAIT! NARU HASN'T—
SENSEI!
OH, HERE SHE COMES!
HERE!
WHEEZE!
WHEEZE!
AS THANKS FOR THE CHARM!
BARA (DUMP)
BARA

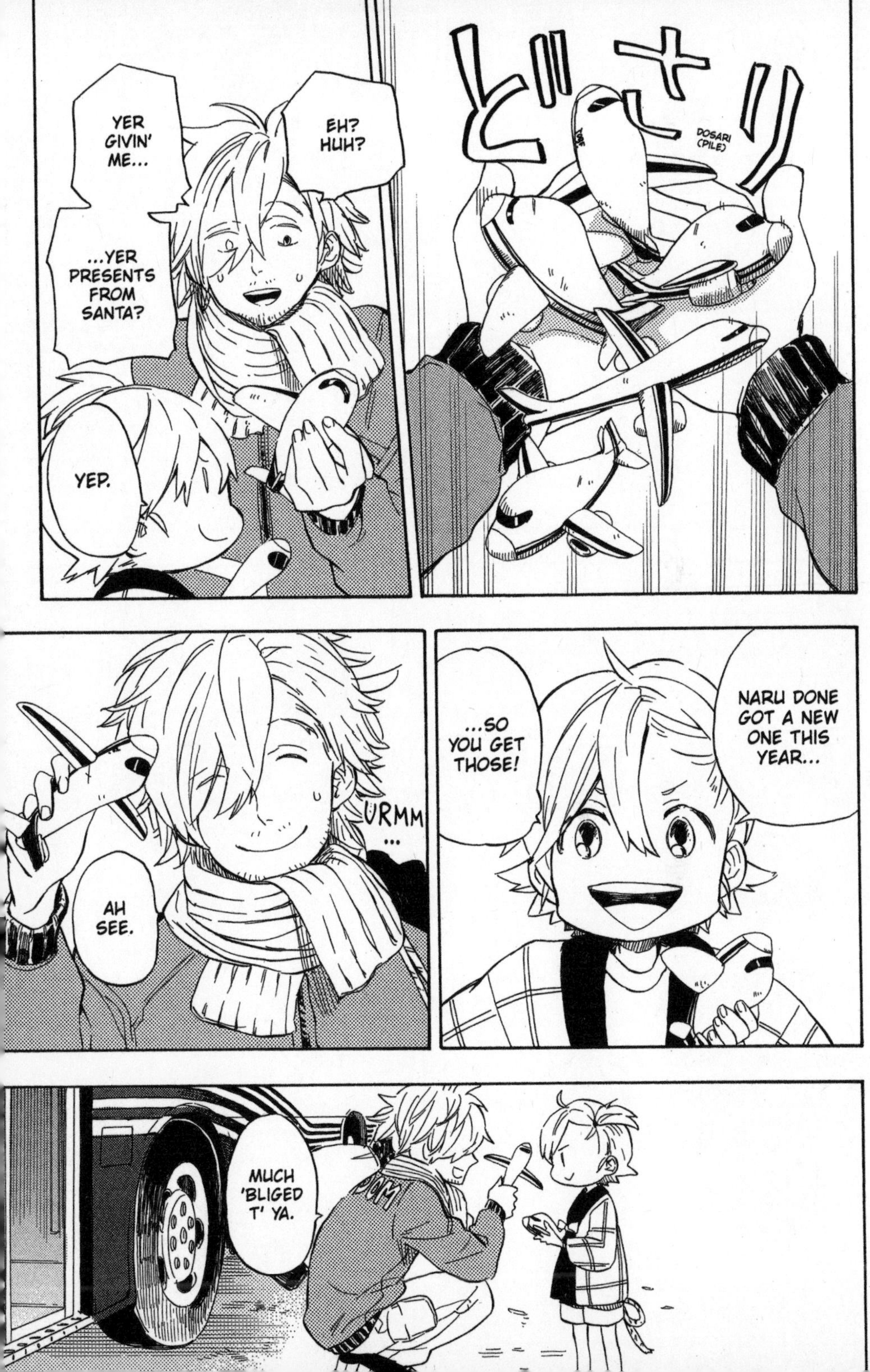
どさり
DOSARI (PILE)
EH? HUH?
YER GIVIN' ME...
...YER PRESENTS FROM SANTA?
YEP.
NARU DONE GOT A NEW ONE THIS YEAR...
...SO YOU GET THOSE!
URMM ...
AH SEE.
MUCH 'BLIGED T' YA.

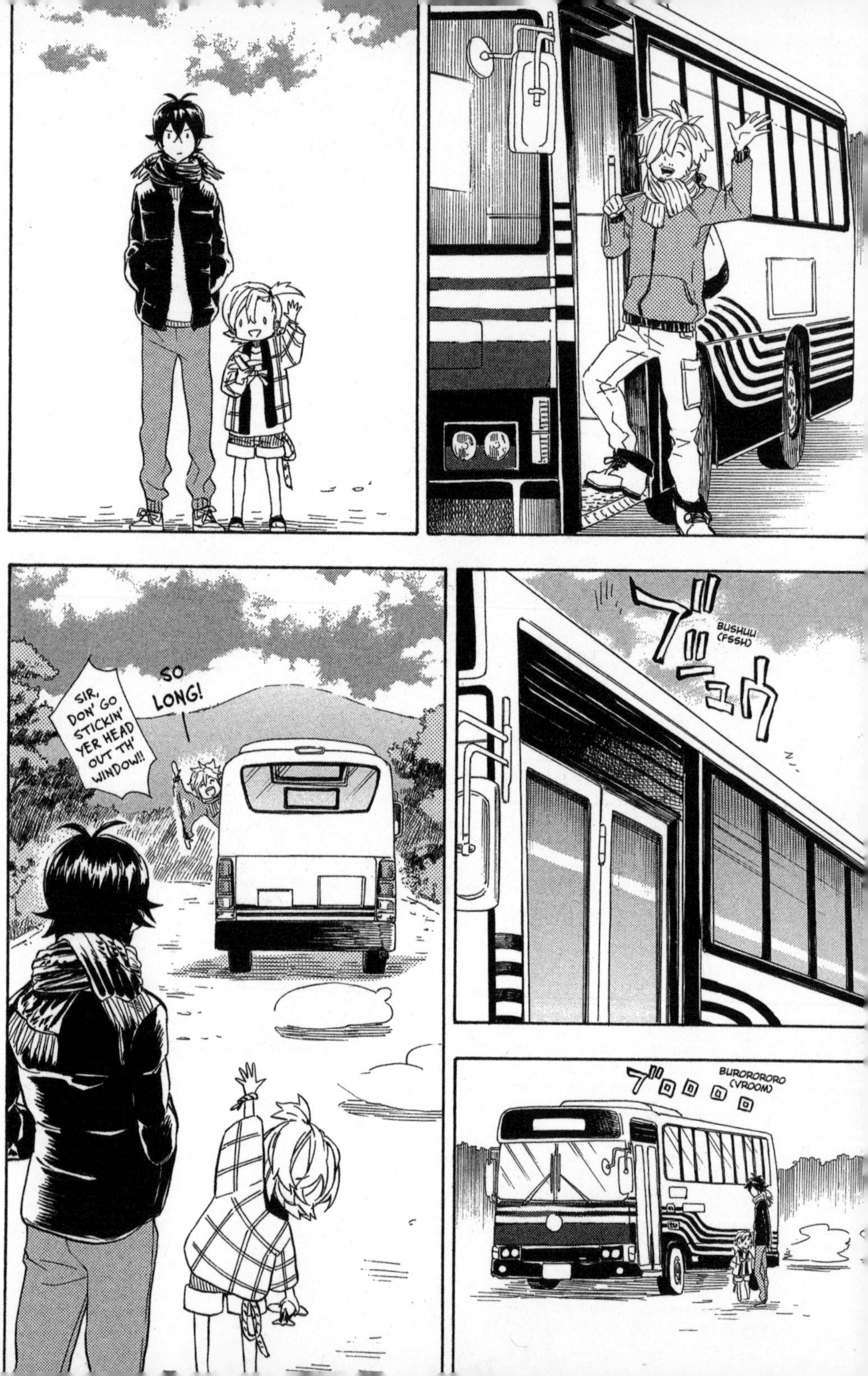
ブシュウ
BUSHUU (FSSH)
ブロロロロ
BURORORO (VROOM)
SO LONG!
SIR, DON' GO STICKIN' YER HEAD OUT TH' WINDOW!!

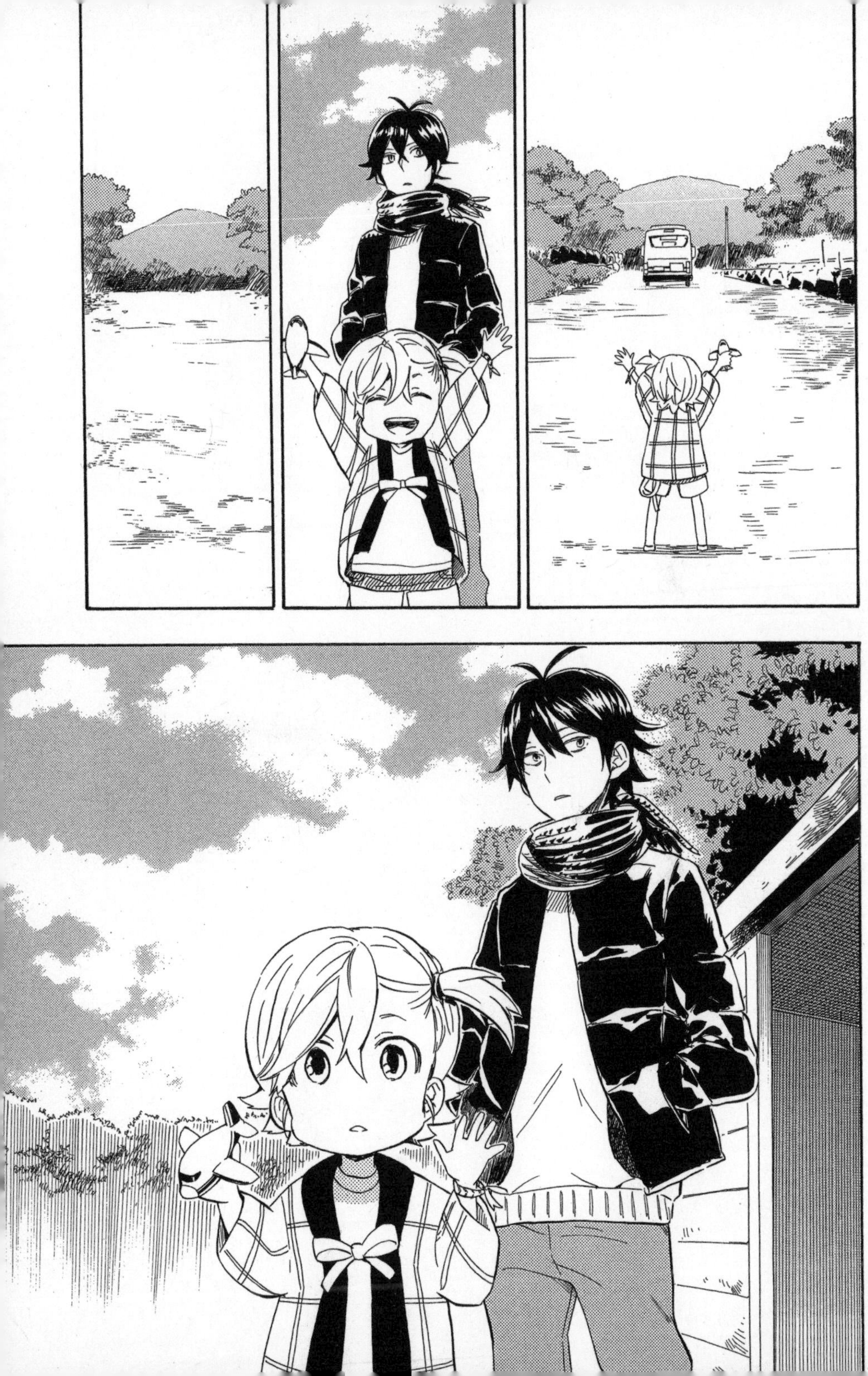

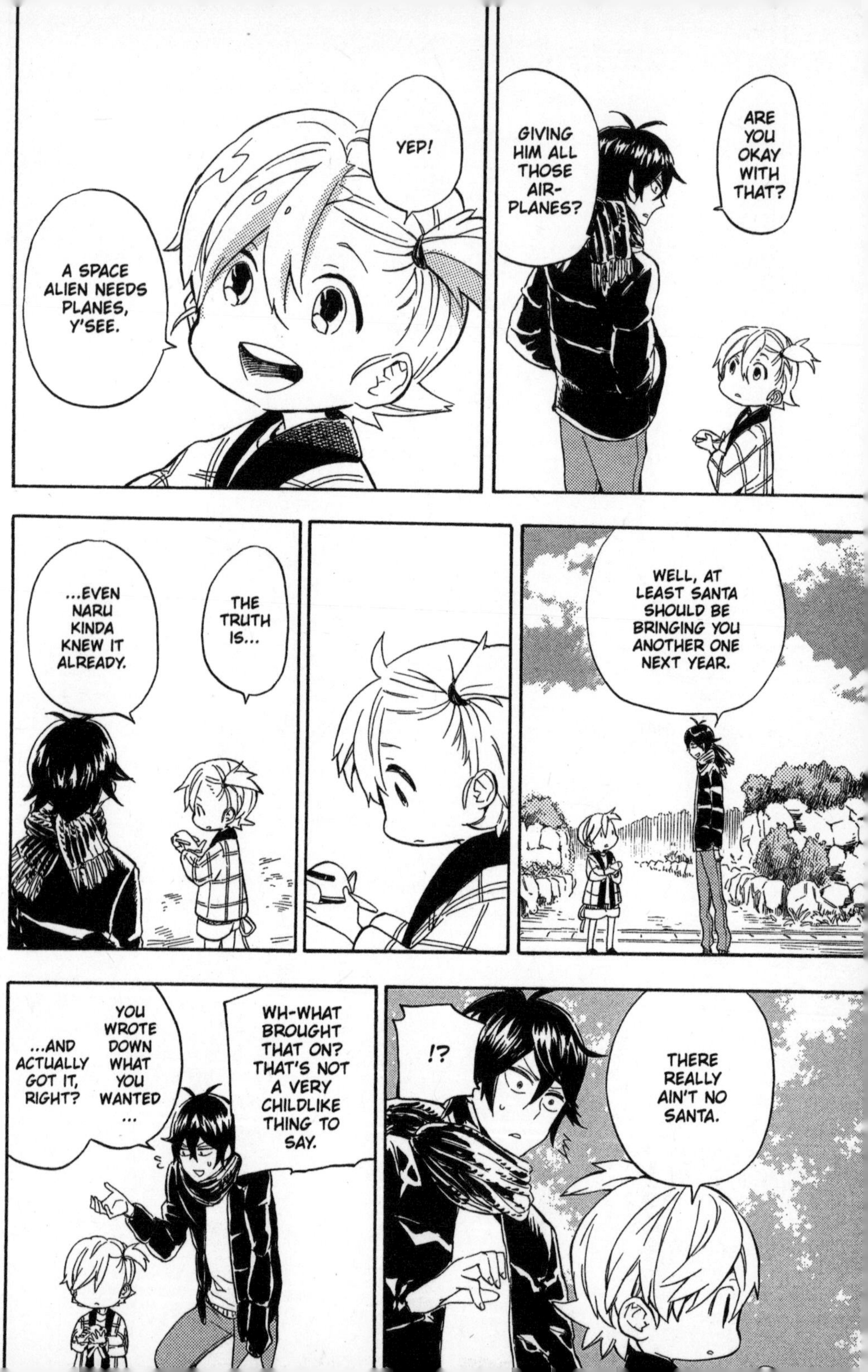
ARE YOU OKAY WITH THAT?
GIVING HIM ALL THOSE AIR-PLANES?
YEP!
A SPACE ALIEN NEEDS PLANES, Y'SEE.
WELL, AT LEAST SANTA SHOULD BE BRINGING YOU ANOTHER ONE NEXT YEAR.
THE TRUTH IS...
...EVEN NARU KINDA KNEW IT ALREADY.
THERE REALLY AIN'T NO SANTA.
!?
WH-WHAT BROUGHT THAT ON? THAT'S NOT A VERY CHILDLIKE THING TO SAY.
YOU WROTE DOWN WHAT YOU WANTED ...
...AND ACTUALLY GOT IT, RIGHT?

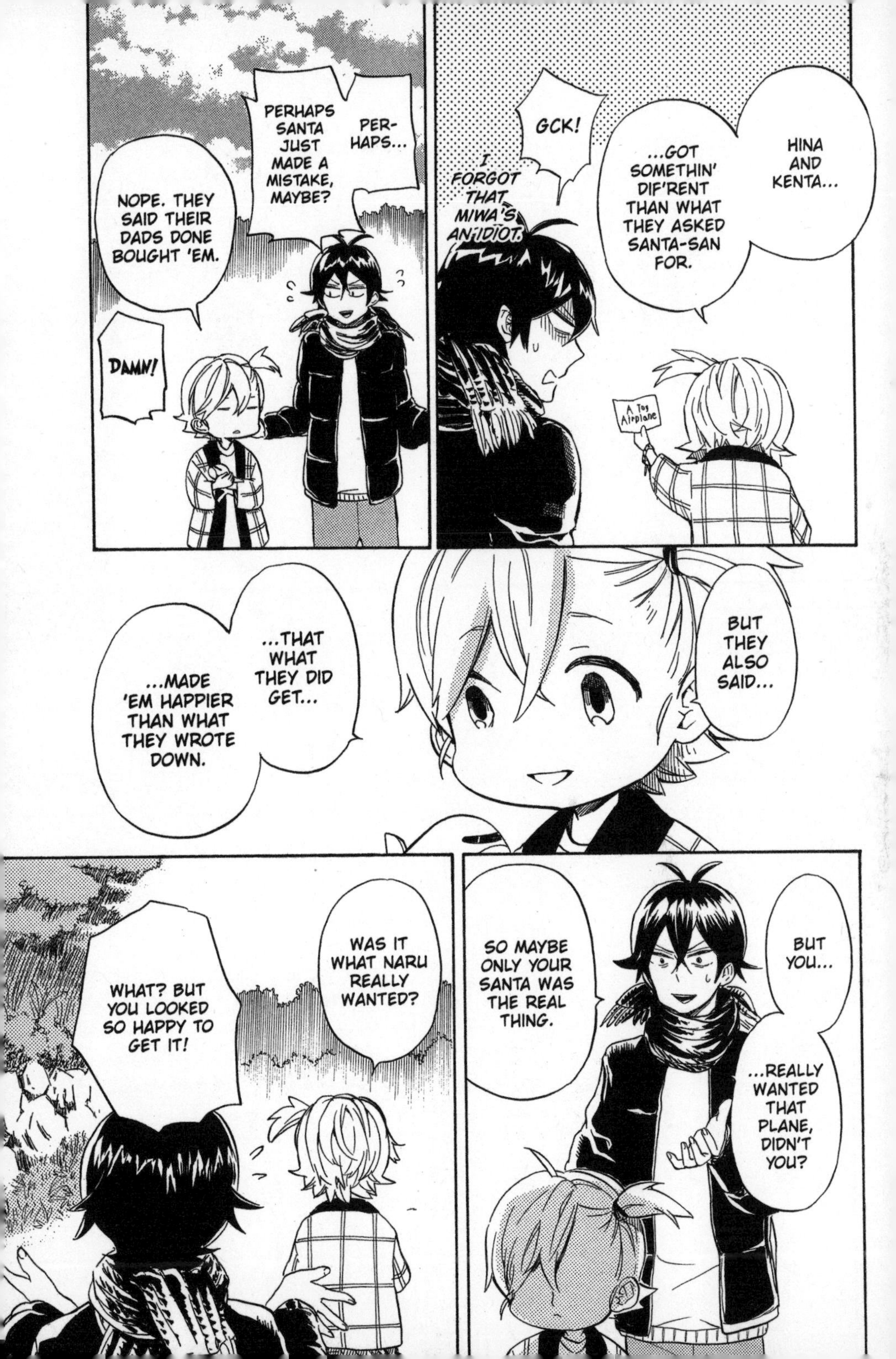
HINA AND KENTA...
...GOT SOMETHIN' DIF'RENT THAN WHAT THEY ASKED SANTA-SAN FOR.
GCK!
I FORGOT THAT MIWA'S AN IDIOT.
A Toy Airplane
PER-HAPS...
PERHAPS SANTA JUST MADE A MISTAKE, MAYBE?
NOPE. THEY SAID THEIR DADS DONE BOUGHT 'EM.
DAMN!
BUT THEY ALSO SAID...
...THAT WHAT THEY DID GET...
...MADE 'EM HAPPIER THAN WHAT THEY WROTE DOWN.
BUT YOU...
...REALLY WANTED THAT PLANE, DIDN'T YOU?
SO MAYBE ONLY YOUR SANTA WAS THE REAL THING.
WAS IT WHAT NARU REALLY WANTED?
WHAT? BUT YOU LOOKED SO HAPPY TO GET IT!

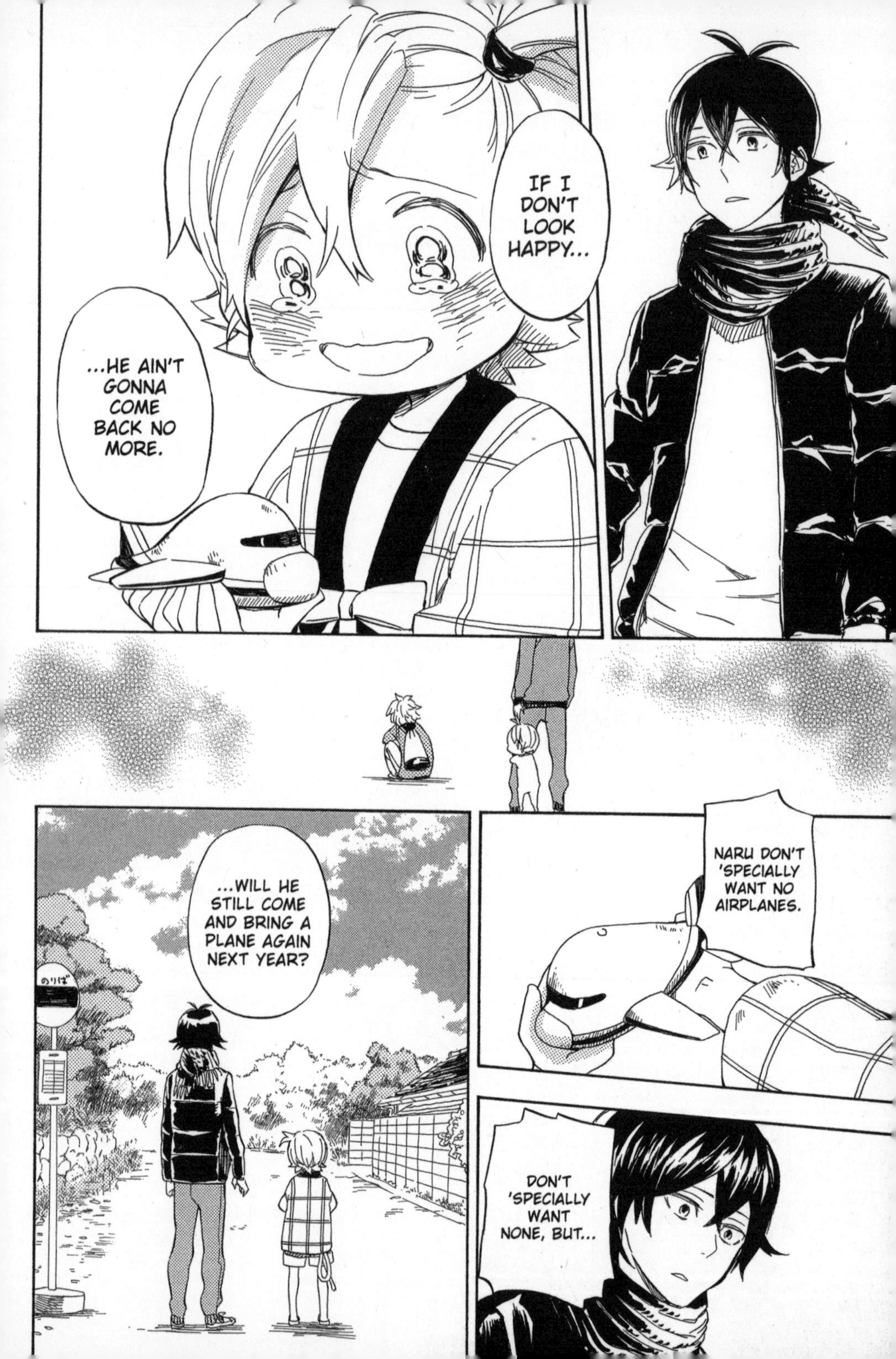
IF I DON'T LOOK HAPPY...
...HE AIN'T GONNA COME BACK NO MORE.
NARU DON'T 'SPECIALLY WANT NO AIRPLANES.
DON'T 'SPECIALLY WANT NONE, BUT...
...WILL HE STILL COME AND BRING A PLANE AGAIN NEXT YEAR?
のりば

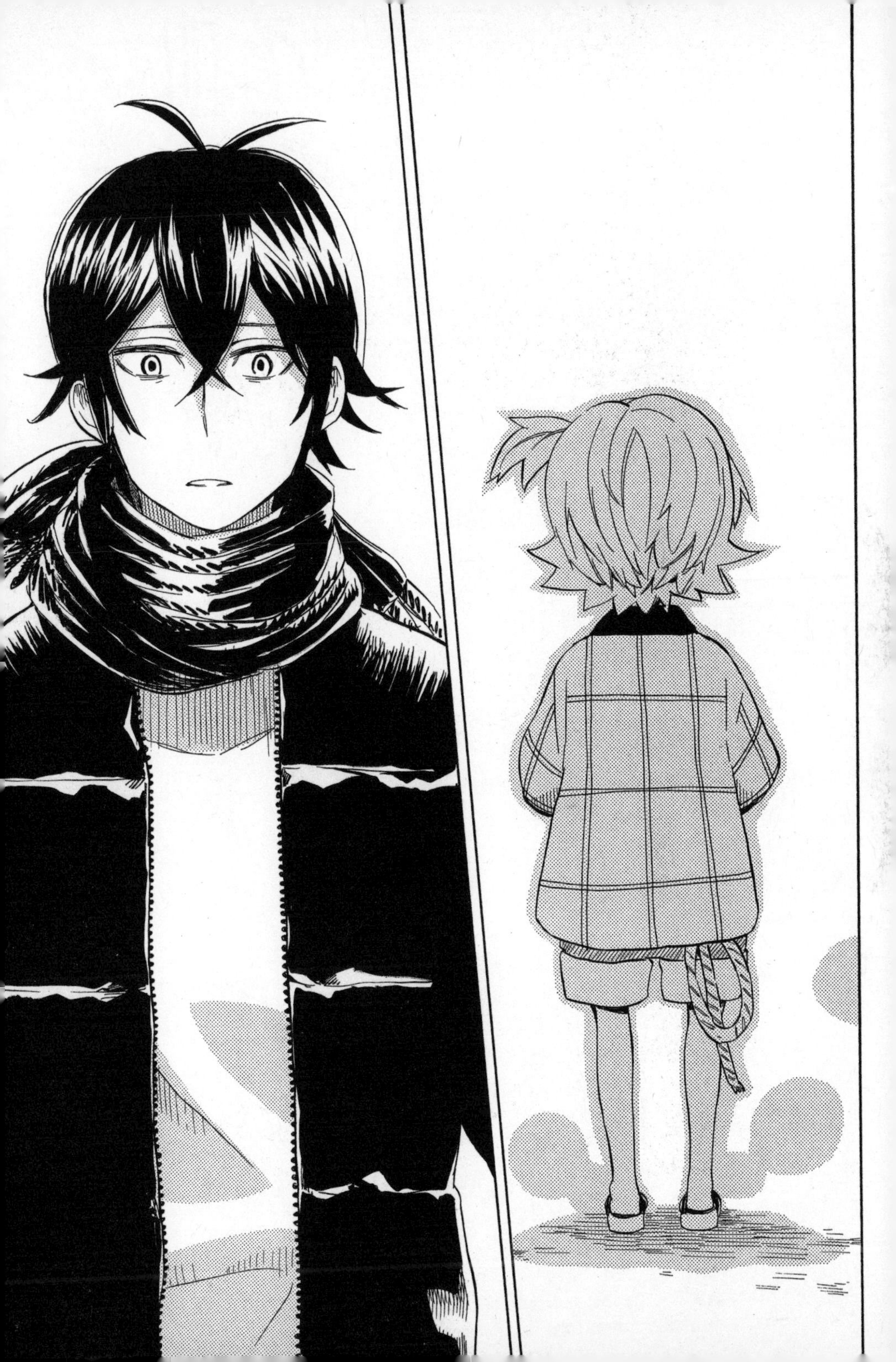

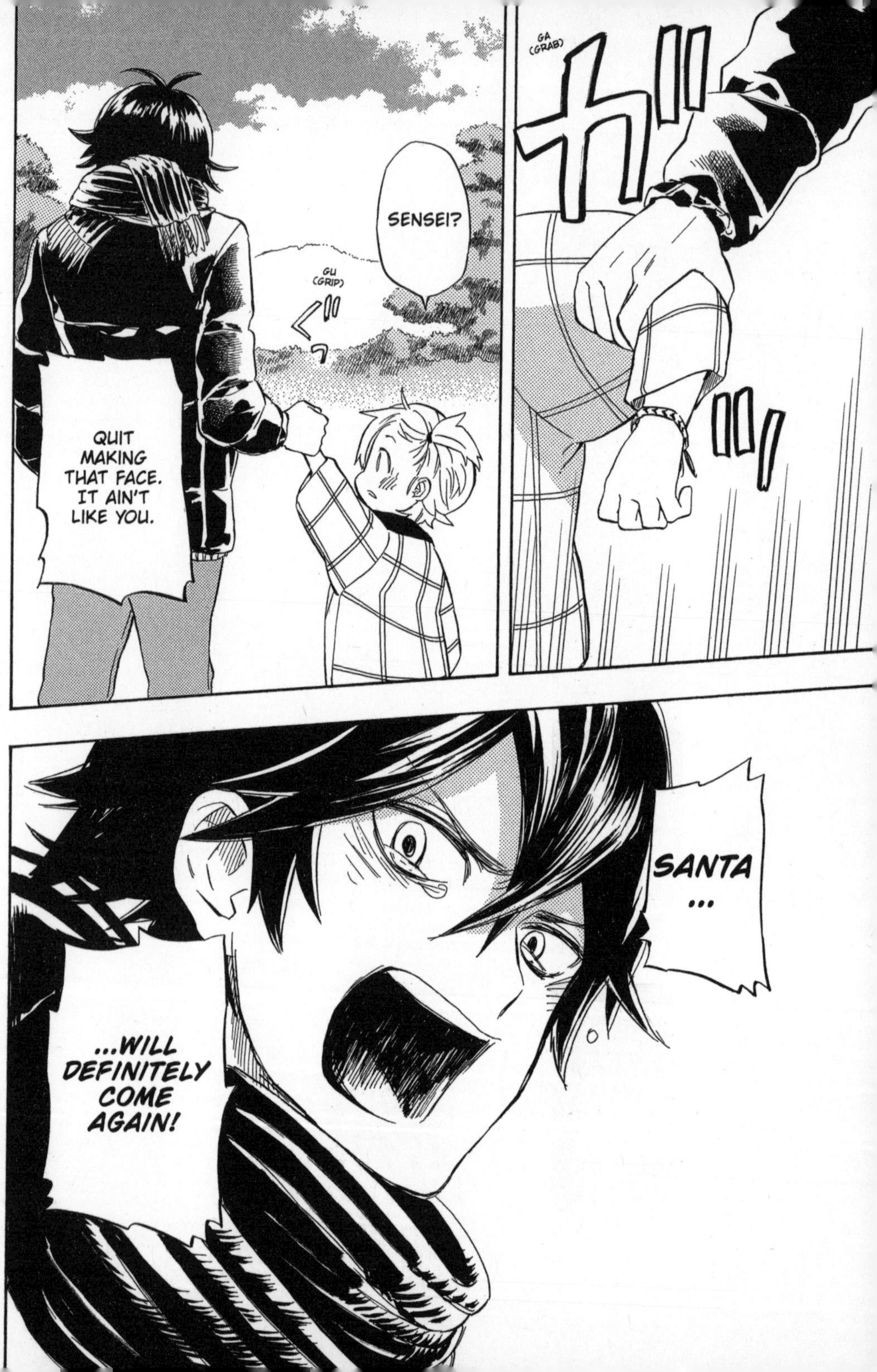
GA (GRAB)
SENSEI?
GU (GRIP)
QUIT MAKING THAT FACE. IT AIN'T LIKE YOU.
SANTA ...
...WILL DEFINITELY COME AGAIN!

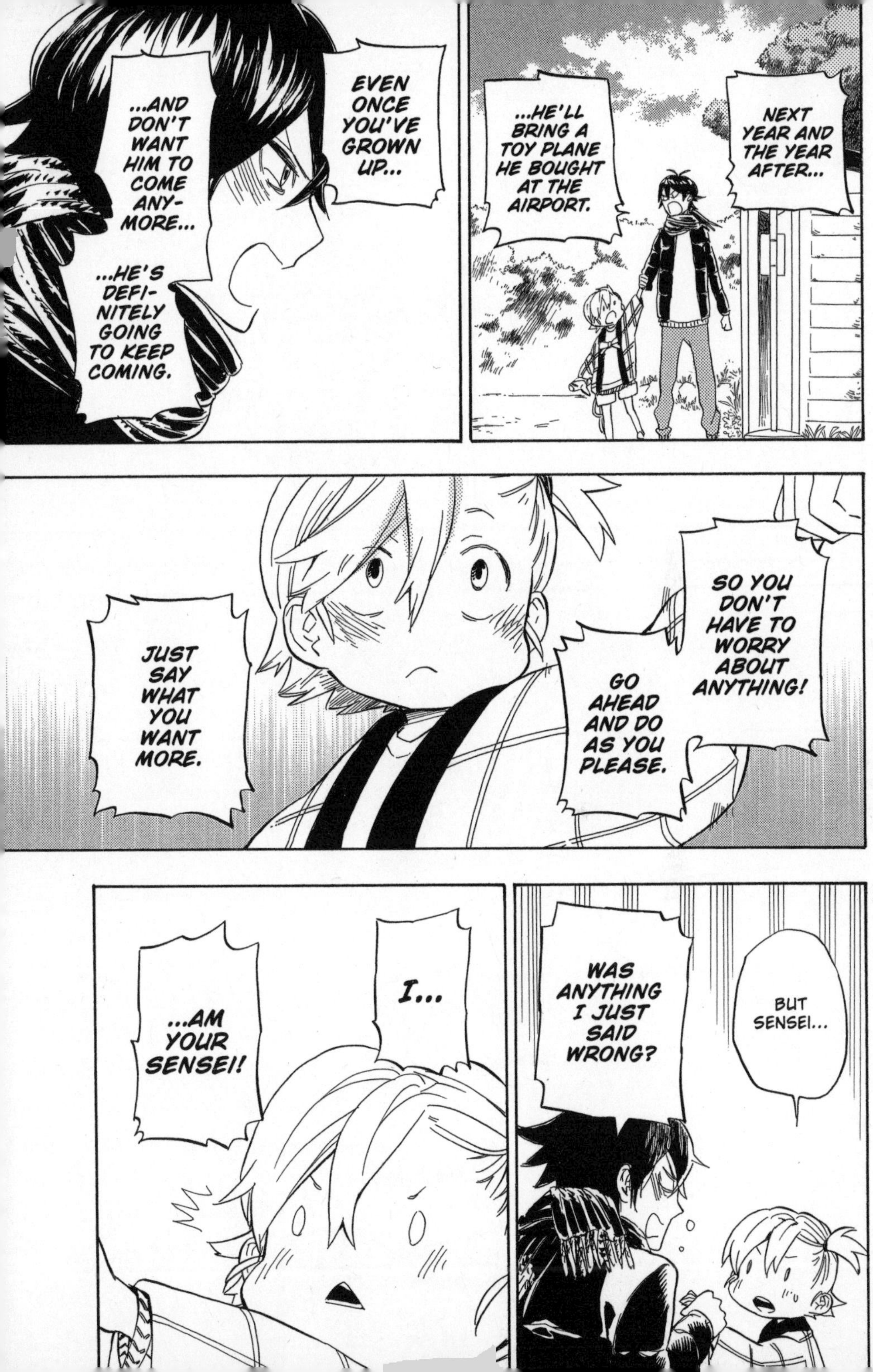
NEXT YEAR AND THE YEAR AFTER...
...HE'LL BRING A TOY PLANE HE BOUGHT AT THE AIRPORT.
EVEN ONCE YOU'VE GROWN UP...
...AND DON'T WANT HIM TO COME ANYMORE...
...HE'S DEFINITELY GOING TO KEEP COMING.
SO YOU DON'T HAVE TO WORRY ABOUT ANYTHING!
GO AHEAD AND DO AS YOU PLEASE.
JUST SAY WHAT YOU WANT MORE.
BUT SENSEI...
WAS ANYTHING I JUST SAID WRONG?
I...
...AM YOUR SENSEI!

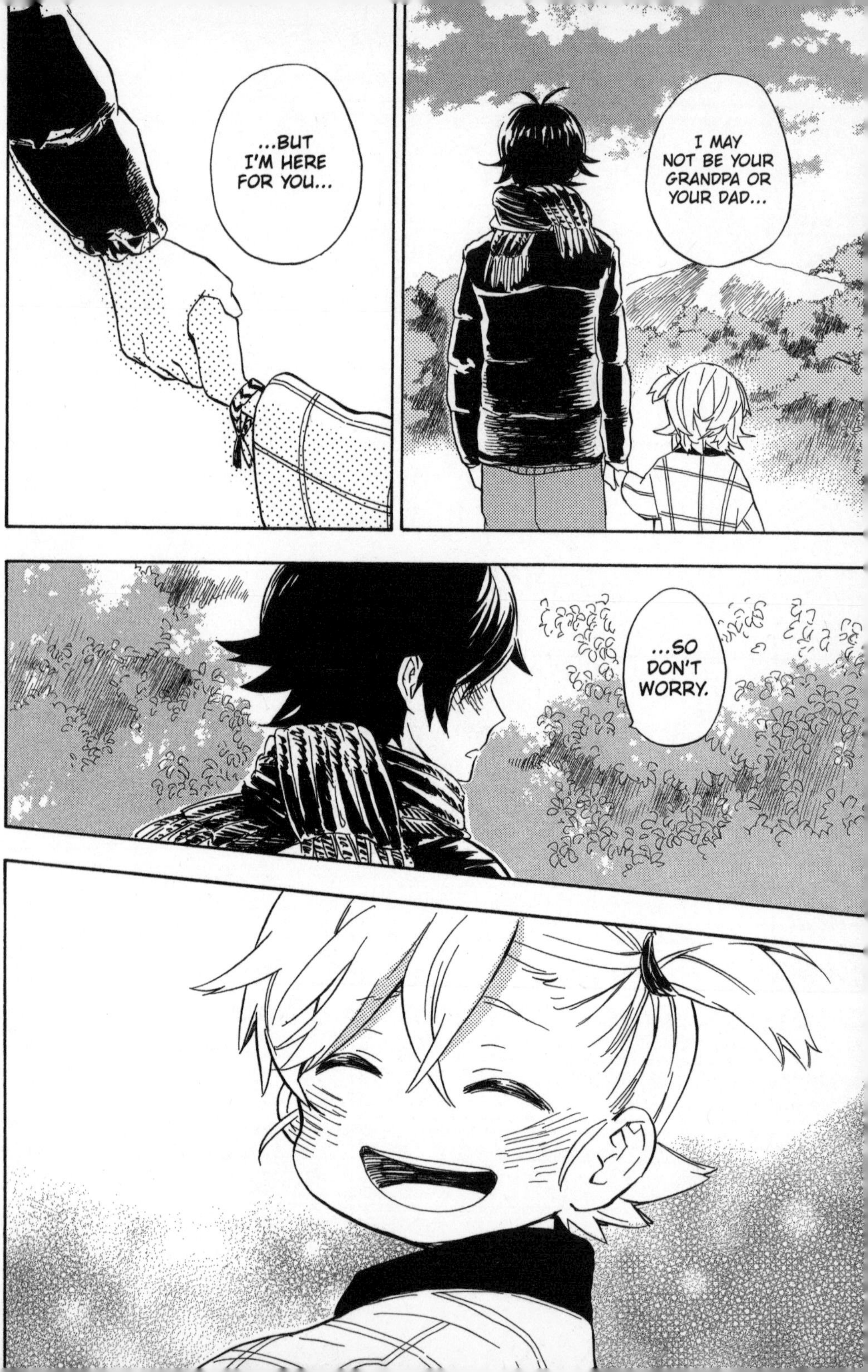
I MAY NOT BE YOUR GRANDPA OR YOUR DAD...
...BUT I'M HERE FOR YOU...
...SO DON'T WORRY.

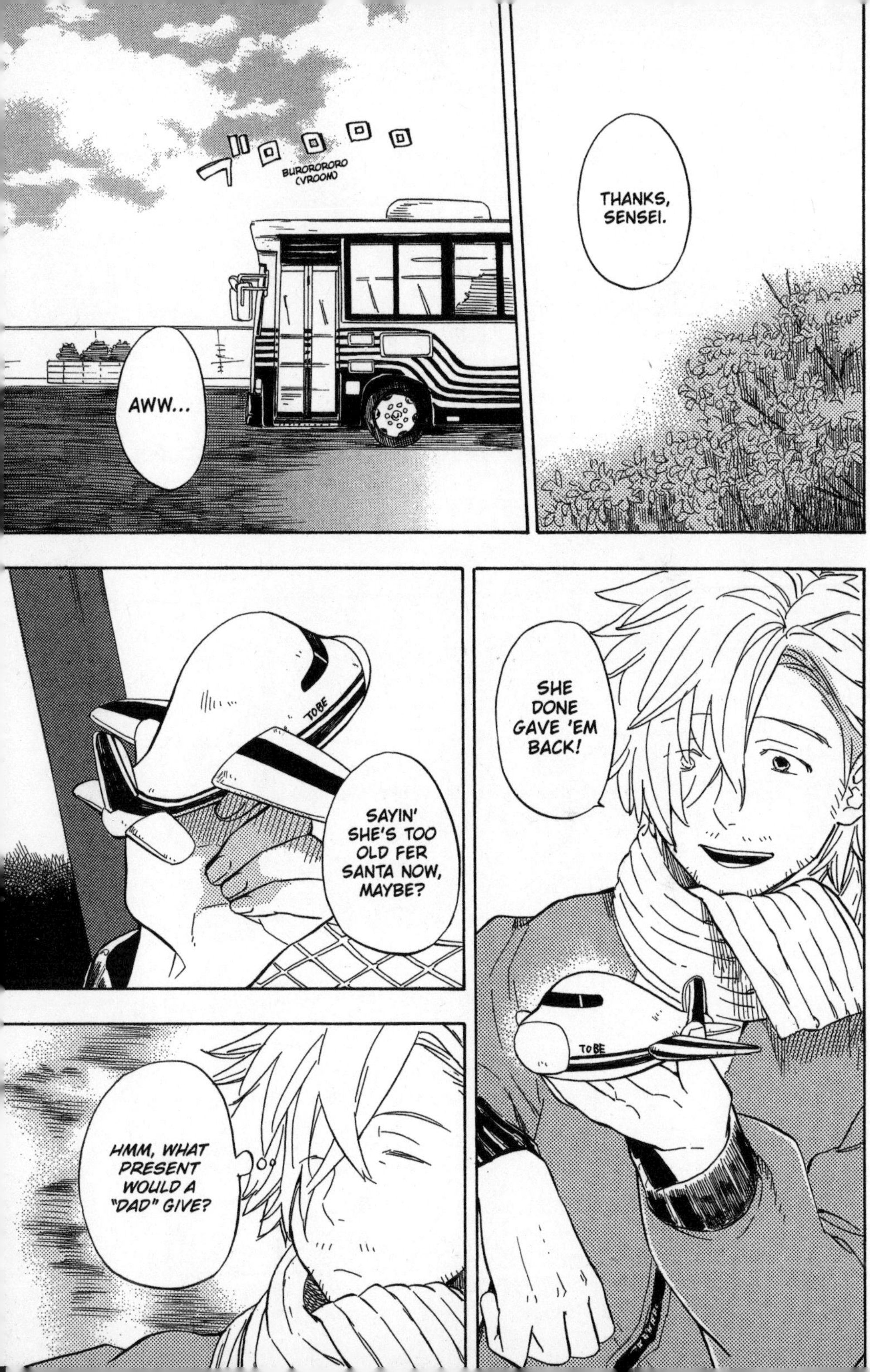
THANKS, SENSEI.
ブロロロロ
BURORORORO (VROOM)
AWW...
SHE DONE GAVE 'EM BACK!
SAYIN' SHE'S TOO OLD FER SANTA NOW, MAYBE?
HMM, WHAT PRESENT WOULD A "DAD" GIVE?

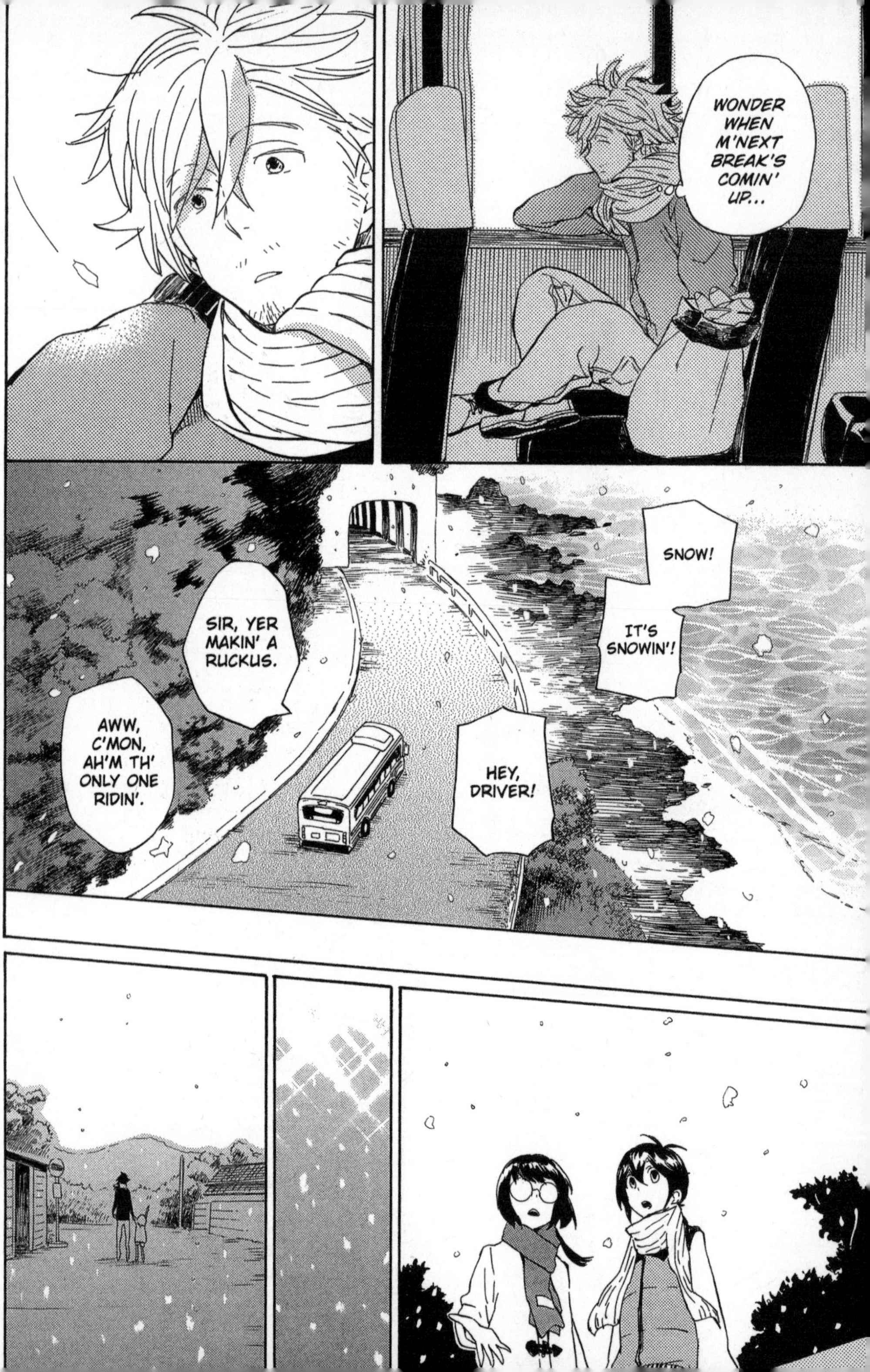
WONDER WHEN M'NEXT BREAK'S COMIN' UP...
SNOW!
IT'S SNOWIN'!
HEY, DRIVER!
SIR, YER MAKIN' A RUCKUS.
AWW, C'MON, AH'M TH' ONLY ONE RIDIN'.

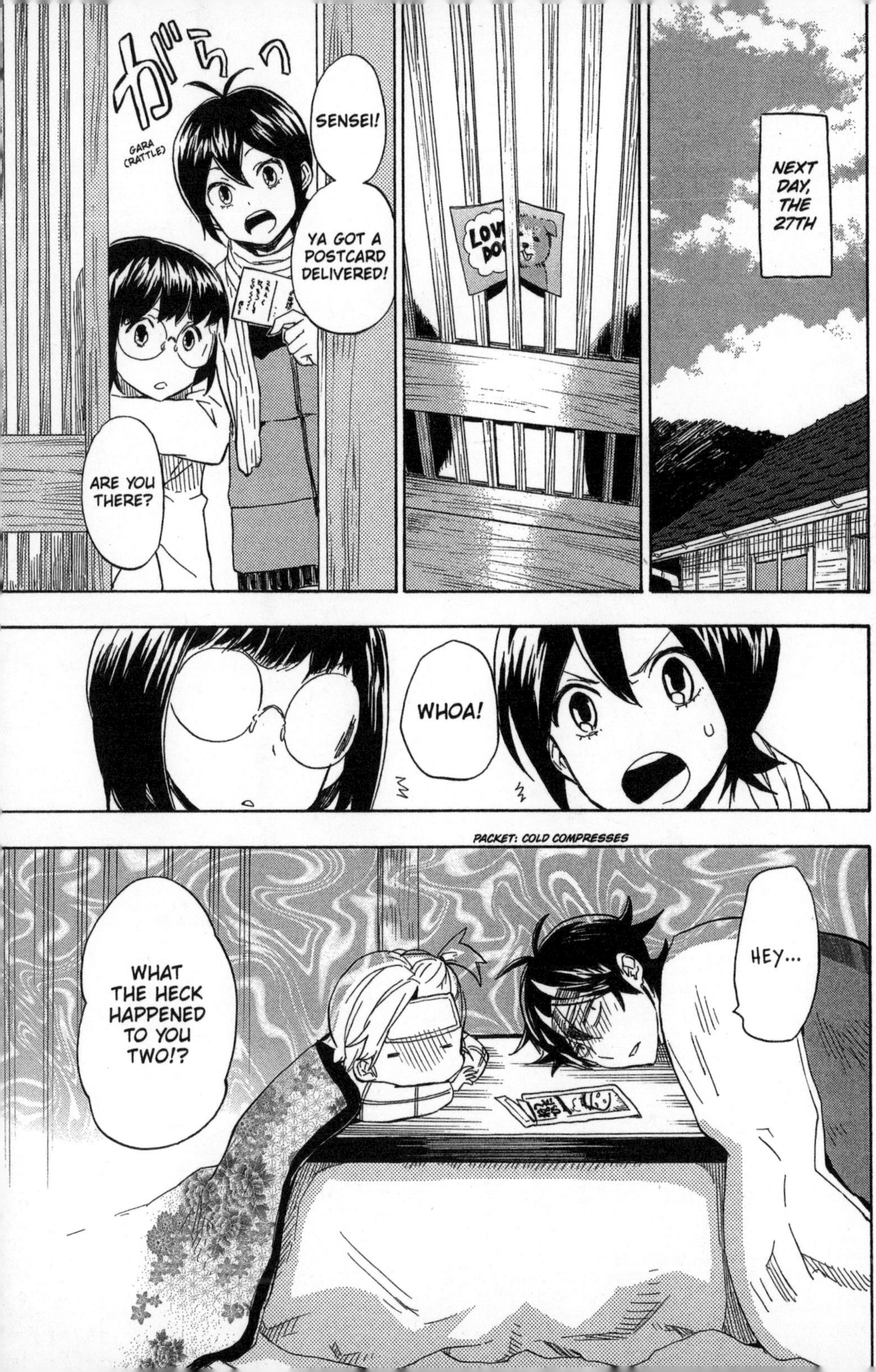
NEXT DAY, THE 27TH
がらっ
GARA (RATTLE)
SENSEI!
YA GOT A POSTCARD DELIVERED!
ARE YOU THERE?
WHOA!
PACKET: COLD COMPRESSES
HEY...
WHAT THE HECK HAPPENED TO YOU TWO!?

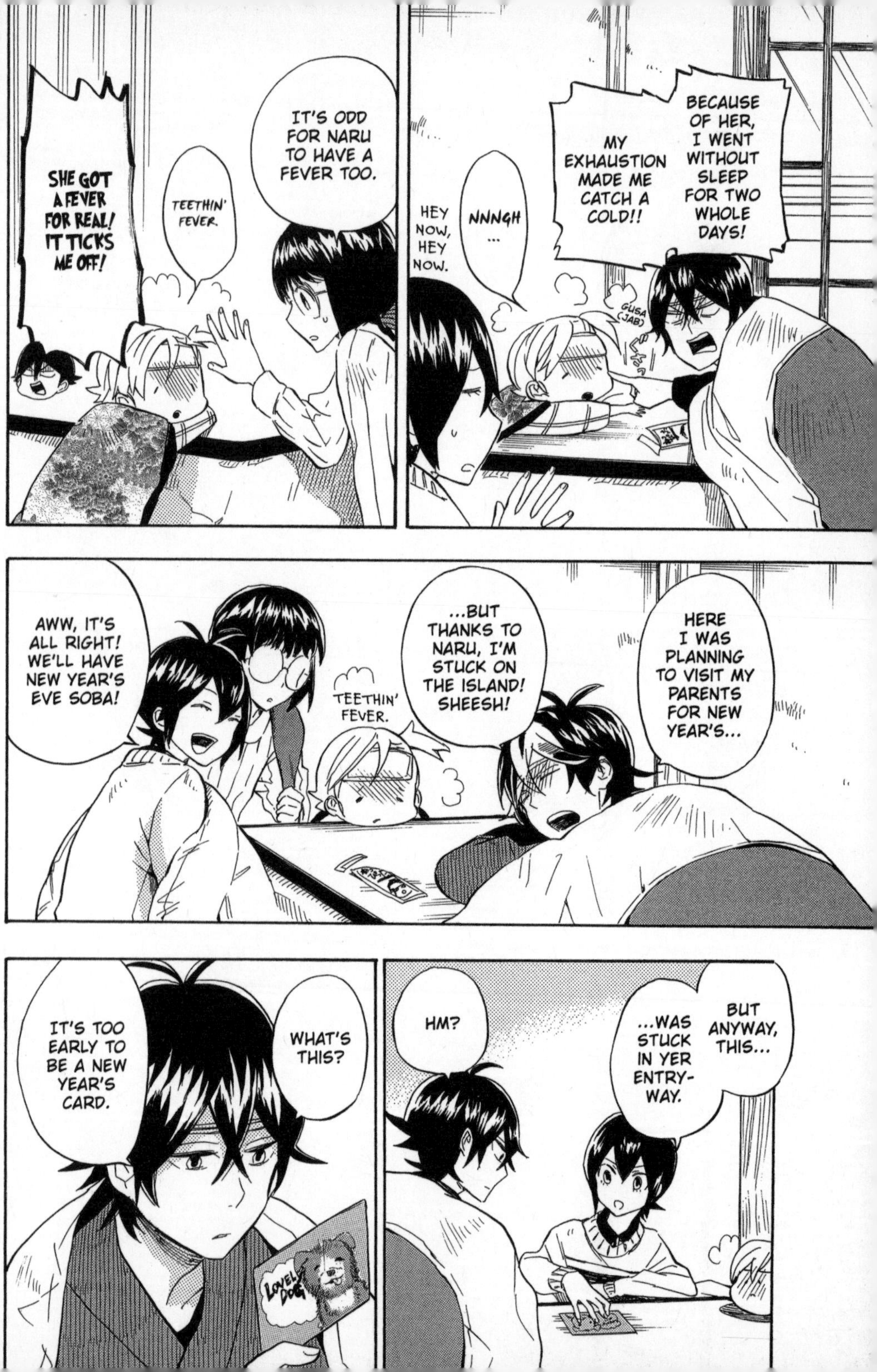
BECAUSE OF HER, I WENT WITHOUT SLEEP FOR TWO WHOLE DAYS!
MY EXHAUSTION MADE ME CATCH A COLD!!
GUSA (JAB)
NNNGH ...
HEY NOW, HEY NOW.
IT'S ODD FOR NARU TO HAVE A FEVER TOO.
TEETHIN' FEVER.
SHE GOT A FEVER FOR REAL! IT TICKS ME OFF!
HERE I WAS PLANNING TO VISIT MY PARENTS FOR NEW YEAR'S...
...BUT THANKS TO NARU, I'M STUCK ON THE ISLAND! SHEESH!
TEETHIN' FEVER.
AWW, IT'S ALL RIGHT! WE'LL HAVE NEW YEAR'S EVE SOBA!
BUT ANYWAY, THIS...
...WAS STUCK IN YER ENTRY-WAY.
HM?
WHAT'S THIS?
IT'S TOO EARLY TO BE A NEW YEAR'S CARD.
LOVELY DOG

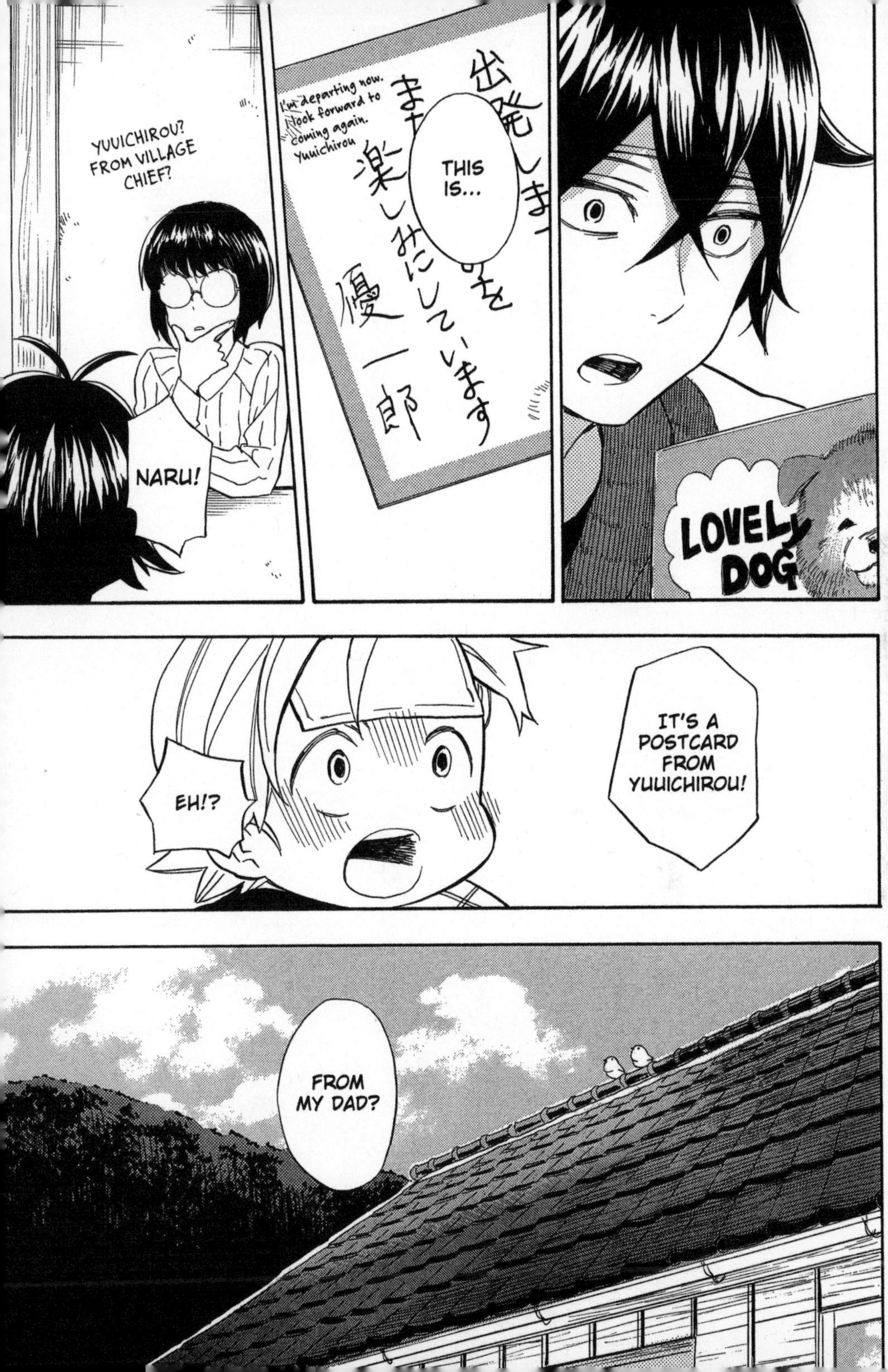
LOVELY DOG
THIS IS...
楽しみにしています
優一郎
I'm departing now. I look forward to coming again. Yuuichirou
YUUICHIROU? FROM VILLAGE CHIEF?
NARU!
IT'S A POSTCARD FROM YUUICHIROU!
EH!?
FROM MY DAD?

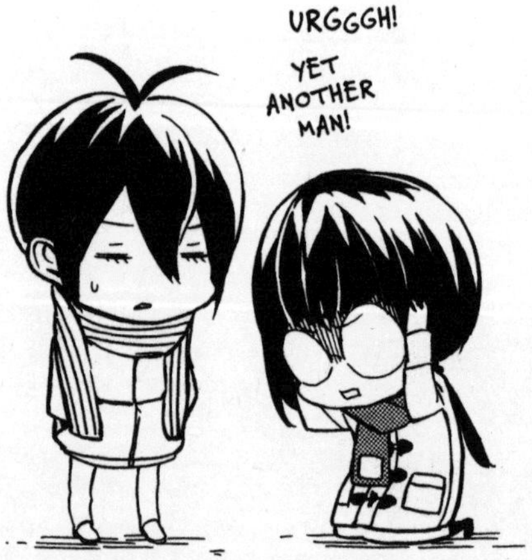
URGGGH!
YET ANOTHER MAN!

Act.92.5 ONE COLD DAY (Special Addendum)

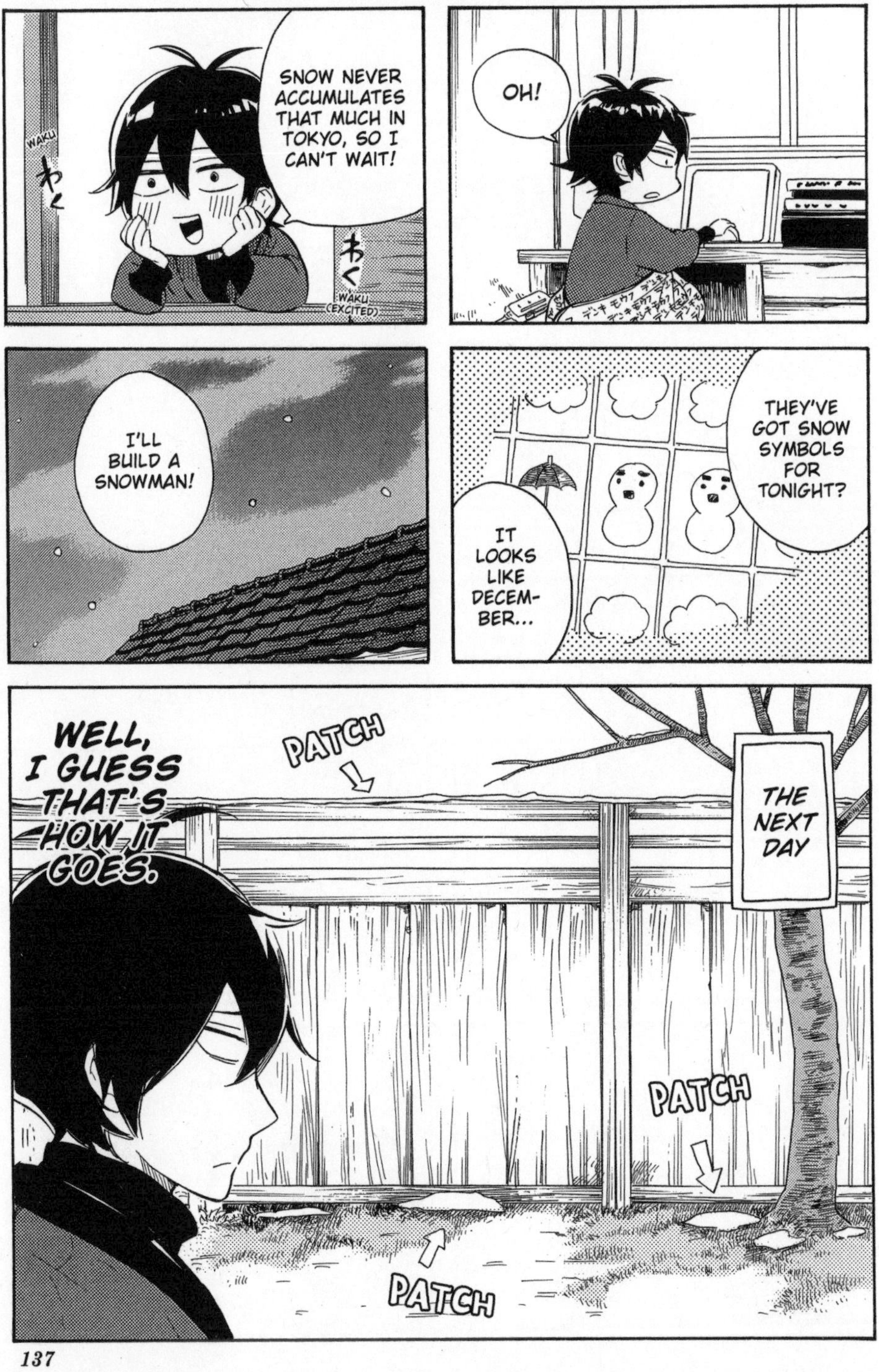
OH!
SNOW NEVER ACCUMULATES THAT MUCH IN TOKYO, SO I CAN'T WAIT!
わく
WAKU
わく
WAKU (EXCITED)
THEY'VE GOT SNOW SYMBOLS FOR TONIGHT?
IT LOOKS LIKE DECEM-BER...
I'LL BUILD A SNOWMAN!
THE NEXT DAY
PATCH
PATCH
PATCH
WELL, I GUESS THAT'S HOW IT GOES.

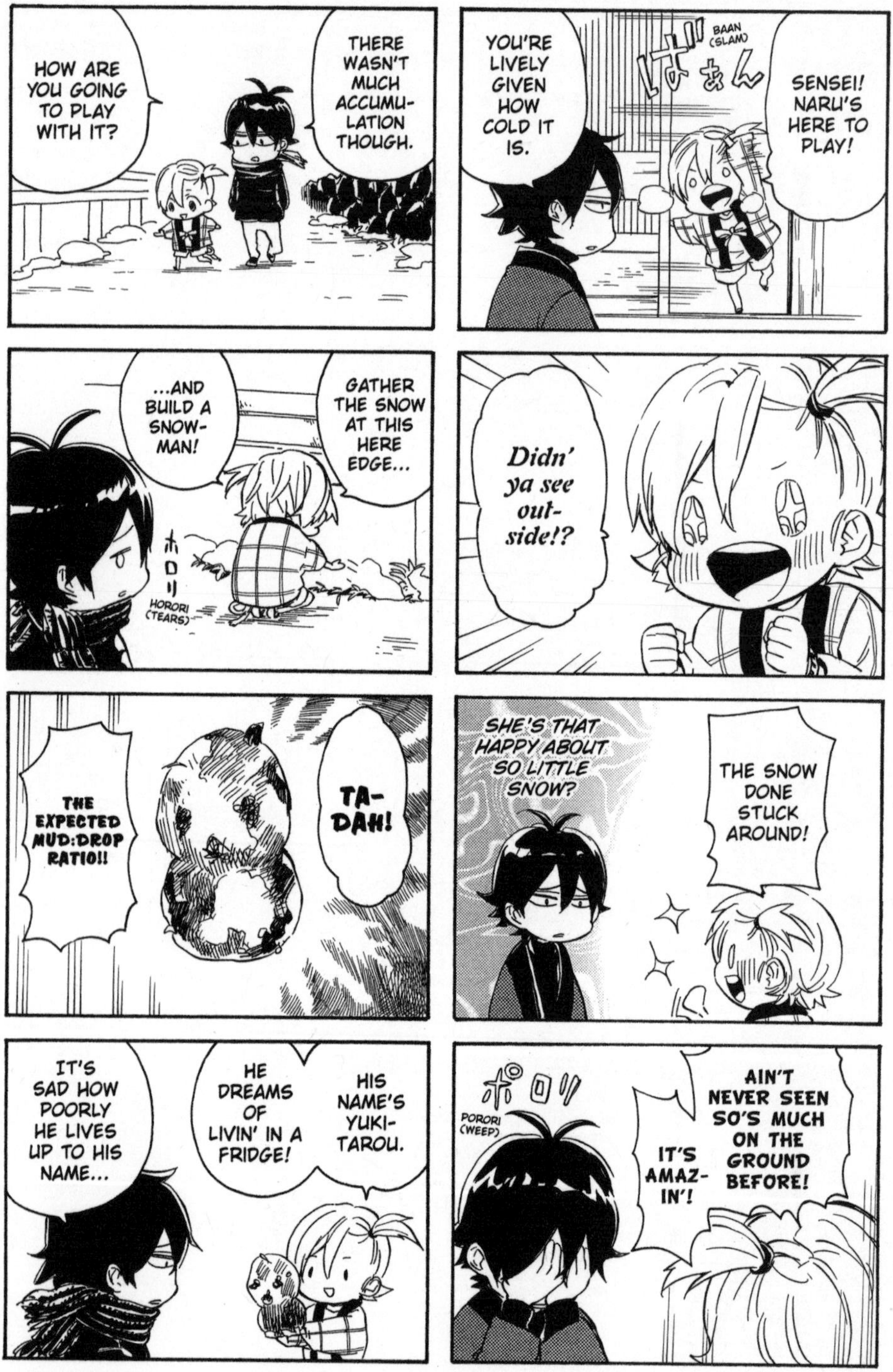
SENSEI! NARU'S HERE TO PLAY!
ばぁん
BAAN (SLAM)
YOU'RE LIVELY GIVEN HOW COLD IT IS.
THERE WASN'T MUCH ACCUMULATION THOUGH.
HOW ARE YOU GOING TO PLAY WITH IT?
Didn' ya see outside!?
GATHER THE SNOW AT THIS HERE EDGE...
...AND BUILD A SNOWMAN!
ホロリ
HORORI (TEARS)
THE SNOW DONE STUCK AROUND!
SHE'S THAT HAPPY ABOUT SO LITTLE SNOW?
TA-DAH!
THE EXPECTED MUD:DROP RATIO!!
AIN'T NEVER SEEN SO'S MUCH ON THE GROUND BEFORE!
IT'S AMAZIN'!
ポロリ
PORORI (WEEP)
HIS NAME'S YUKITAROU.
HE DREAMS OF LIVIN' IN A FRIDGE!
IT'S SAD HOW POORLY HE LIVES UP TO HIS NAME...

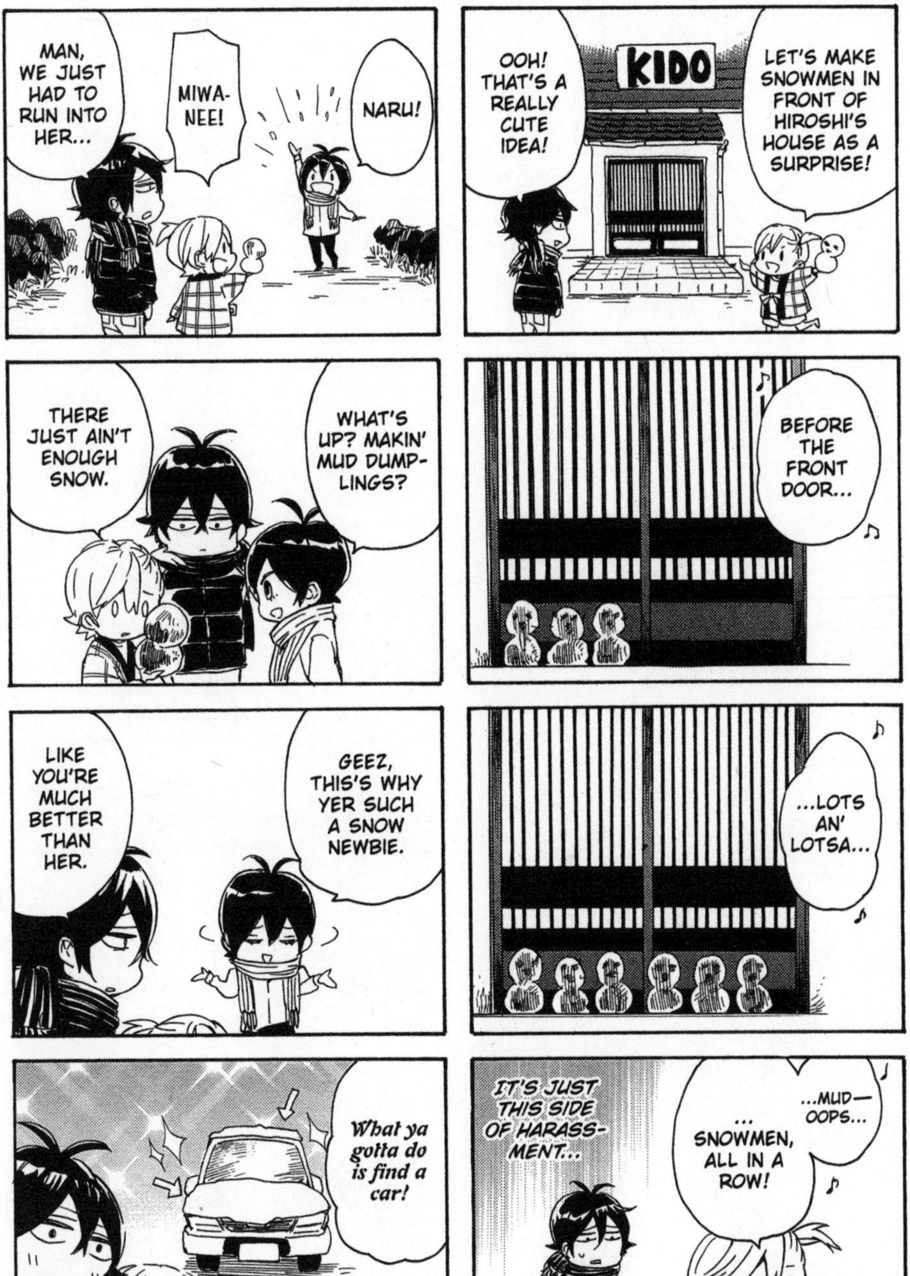

LET'S MAKE SNOWMEN IN FRONT OF HIROSHI'S HOUSE AS A SURPRISE!
KIDO
OOH! THAT'S A REALLY CUTE IDEA!
BEFORE THE FRONT DOOR...
...LOTS AN' LOTSA...
...MUD— OOPS...
... SNOWMEN, ALL IN A ROW!
IT'S JUST THIS SIDE OF HARASS-MENT...
NARU!
MIWA-NEE!
MAN, WE JUST HAD TO RUN INTO HER...
WHAT'S UP? MAKIN' MUD DUMP-LINGS?
THERE JUST AIN'T ENOUGH SNOW.
GEEZ, THIS'S WHY YER SUCH A SNOW NEWBIE.
LIKE YOU'RE MUCH BETTER THAN HER.
What ya gotta do is find a car!

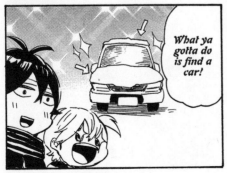

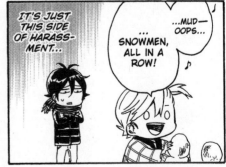

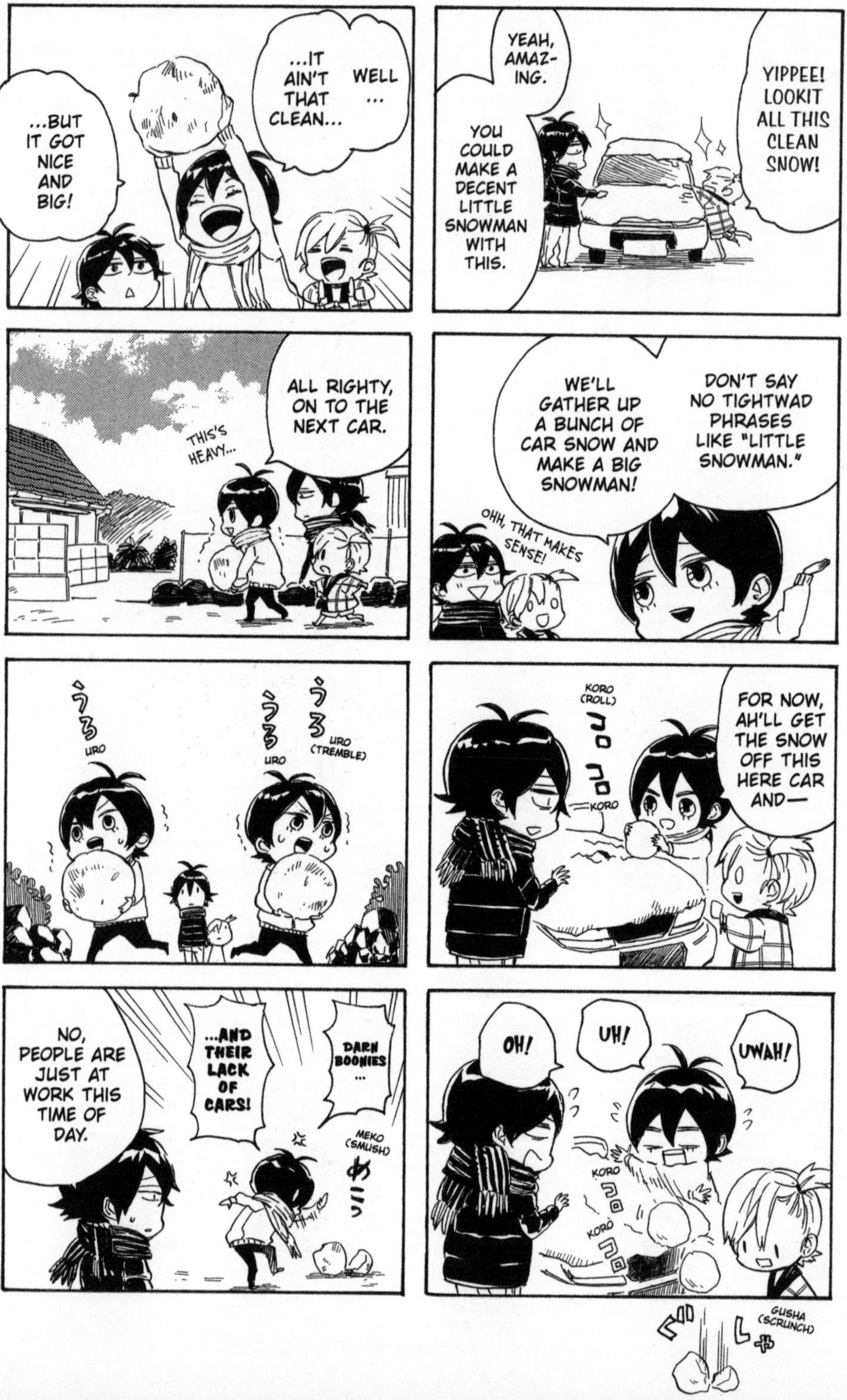
YIPPEE! LOOKIT ALL THIS CLEAN SNOW!
YEAH, AMAZ-ING.
YOU COULD MAKE A DECENT LITTLE SNOWMAN WITH THIS.
WELL ...
...IT AIN'T THAT CLEAN...
...BUT IT GOT NICE AND BIG!
DON'T SAY NO TIGHTWAD PHRASES LIKE "LITTLE SNOWMAN."
WE'LL GATHER UP A BUNCH OF CAR SNOW AND MAKE A BIG SNOWMAN!
OHH, THAT MAKES SENSE!
ALL RIGHTY, ON TO THE NEXT CAR.
THIS'S HEAVY...
FOR NOW, AH'LL GET THE SNOW OFF THIS HERE CAR AND—
KORO (ROLL)
コロ
コロ
KORO
うろ
URO (TREMBLE)
うろ
URO
うろ
URO
UWAH!
UH!
OH!
KORO
コロ
KORO
コロ
GUSHA (SCRUNCH)
ぐしゃ
DARN BOONIES ...
...AND THEIR LACK OF CARS!
MEKO (SMUSH)
めこっ
NO, PEOPLE ARE JUST AT WORK THIS TIME OF DAY.

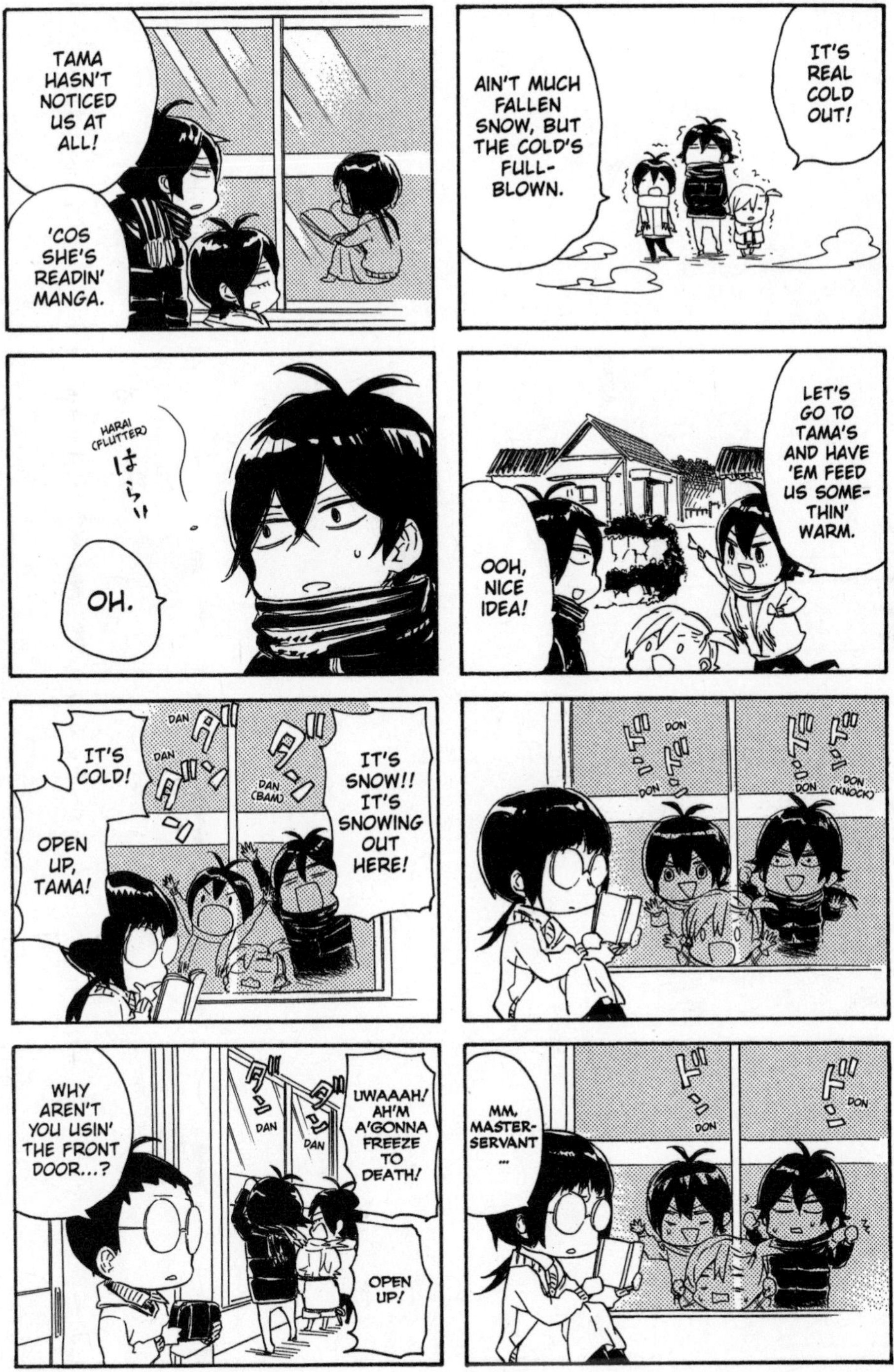
IT'S REAL COLD OUT!
AIN'T MUCH FALLEN SNOW, BUT THE COLD'S FULL-BLOWN.
TAMA HASN'T NOTICED US AT ALL!
'COS SHE'S READIN' MANGA.
LET'S GO TO TAMA'S AND HAVE 'EM FEED US SOME-THIN' WARM.
OOH, NICE IDEA!
HARAI (FLUTTER)
はらい
OH.
DON
DON
DON
DON (KNOCK)
IT'S SNOW!! IT'S SNOWING OUT HERE!
DAN (BAM)
DAN
DAN
IT'S COLD!
OPEN UP, TAMA!
DON
DON
MM, MASTER-SERVANT ...
UWAAAH! AH'M A'GONNA FREEZE TO DEATH!
DAN
DAN
WHY AREN'T YOU USIN' THE FRONT DOOR...?
OPEN UP!

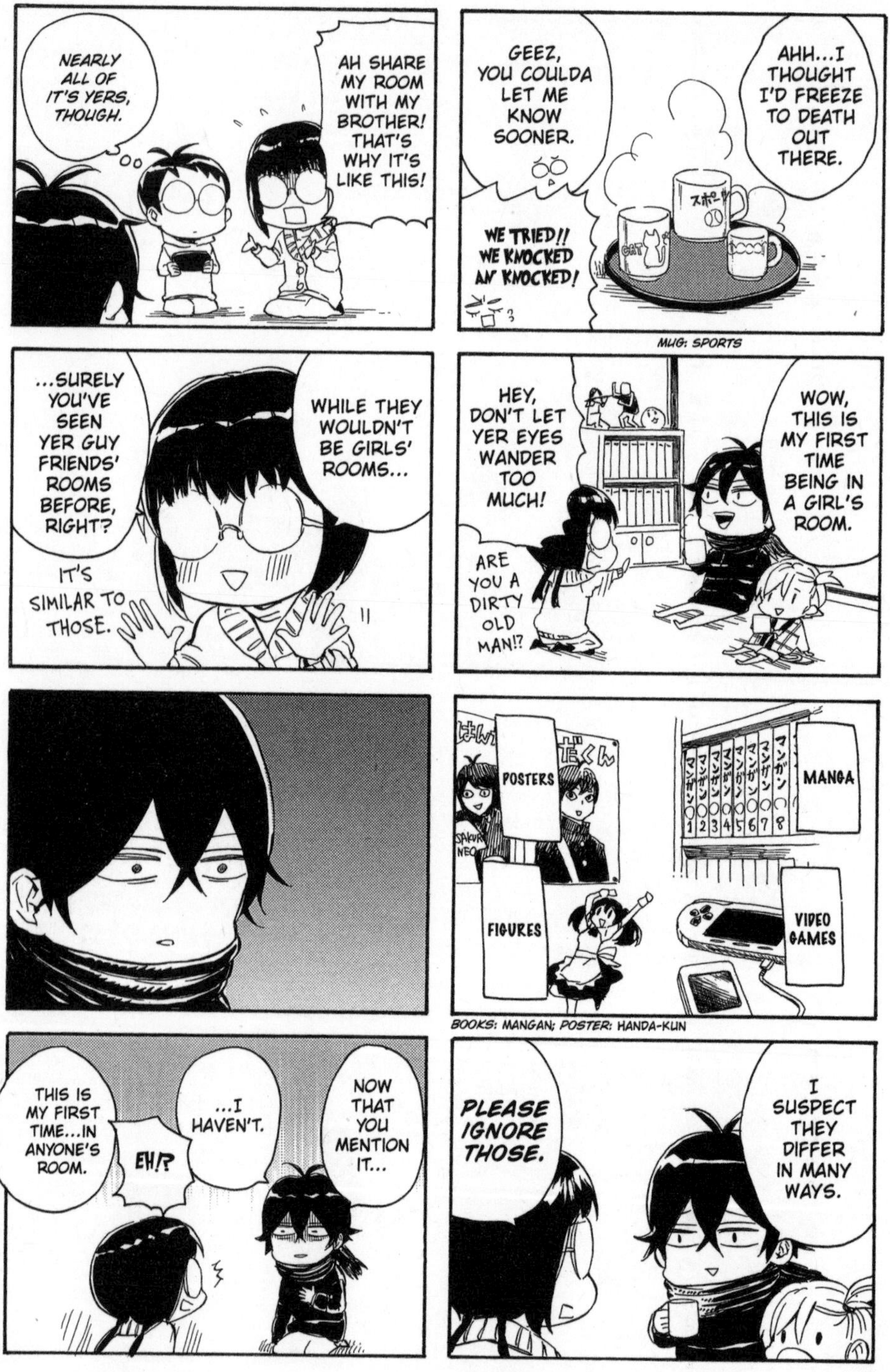
AHH...I THOUGHT I'D FREEZE TO DEATH OUT THERE.
GEEZ, YOU COULDA LET ME KNOW SOONER.
WE TRIED!! WE KNOCKED AN' KNOCKED!
MUG: SPORTS
WOW, THIS IS MY FIRST TIME BEING IN A GIRL'S ROOM.
HEY, DON'T LET YER EYES WANDER TOO MUCH!
ARE YOU A DIRTY OLD MAN!?
MANGA
POSTERS
VIDEO GAMES
FIGURES
BOOKS: MANGAN; POSTER: HANDA-KUN
I SUSPECT THEY DIFFER IN MANY WAYS.
PLEASE IGNORE THOSE.
AH SHARE MY ROOM WITH MY BROTHER! THAT'S WHY IT'S LIKE THIS!
NEARLY ALL OF IT'S YERS, THOUGH.
WHILE THEY WOULDN'T BE GIRLS' ROOMS...
...SURELY YOU'VE SEEN YER GUY FRIENDS' ROOMS BEFORE, RIGHT?
IT'S SIMILAR TO THOSE.
NOW THAT YOU MENTION IT...
...I HAVEN'T.
EH!?
THIS IS MY FIRST TIME...IN ANYONE'S ROOM.

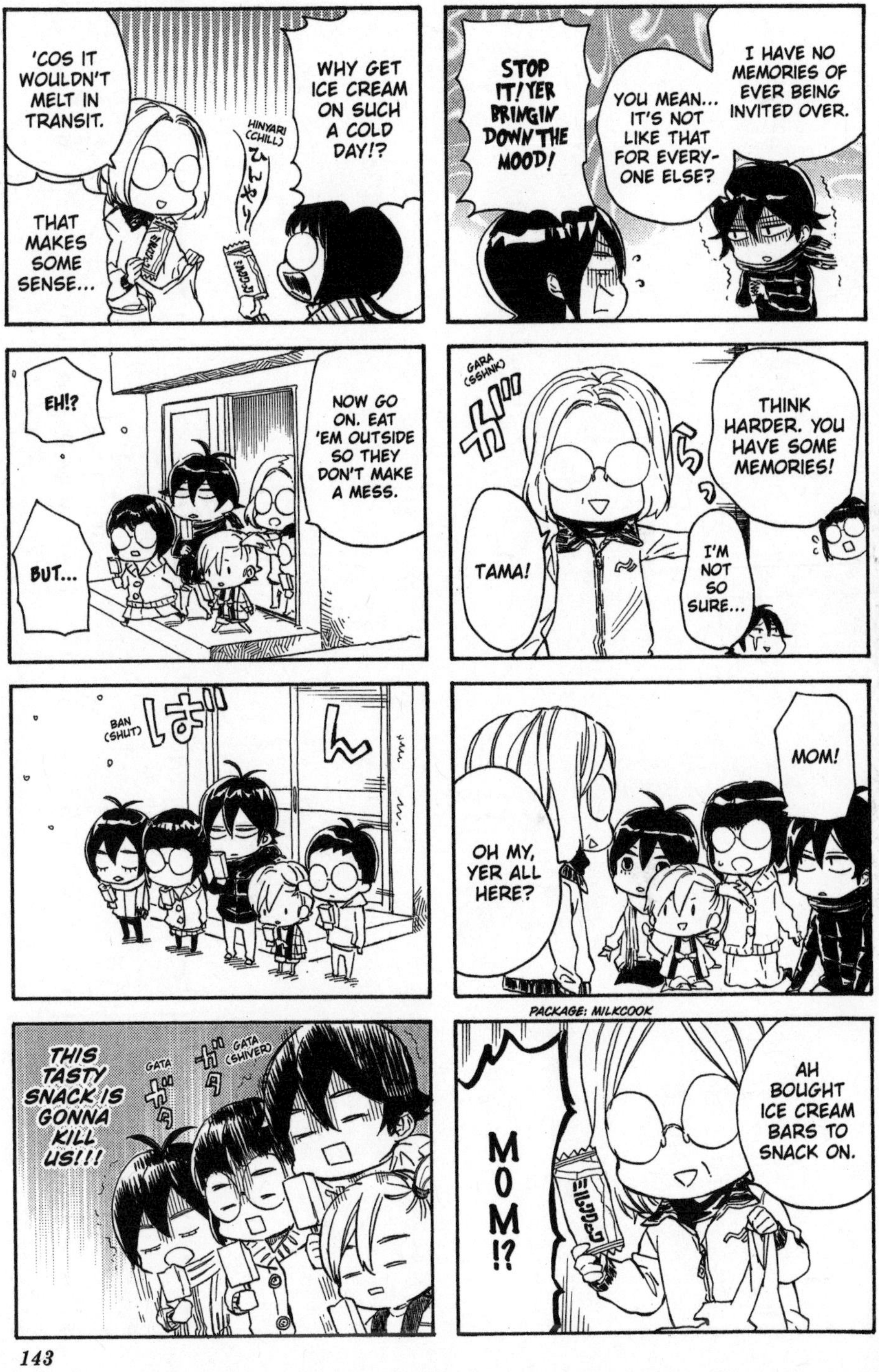
I HAVE NO MEMORIES OF EVER BEING INVITED OVER.
YOU MEAN... IT'S NOT LIKE THAT FOR EVERY-ONE ELSE?
STOP IT! YER BRINGIN' DOWN THE MOOD!
GARA (SSHNK)
THINK HARDER. YOU HAVE SOME MEMORIES!
I'M NOT SO SURE...
TAMA!
MOM!
OH MY, YER ALL HERE?
PACKAGE: MILKCOOK
AH BOUGHT ICE CREAM BARS TO SNACK ON.
MOM!?
WHY GET ICE CREAM ON SUCH A COLD DAY!?
HINYARI (CHILL)
'COS IT WOULDN'T MELT IN TRANSIT.
THAT MAKES SOME SENSE...
NOW GO ON. EAT 'EM OUTSIDE SO THEY DON'T MAKE A MESS.
EH!?
BUT...
BAN (SHUT)
GATA (SHIVER)
GATA
THIS TASTY SNACK IS GONNA KILL US!!!

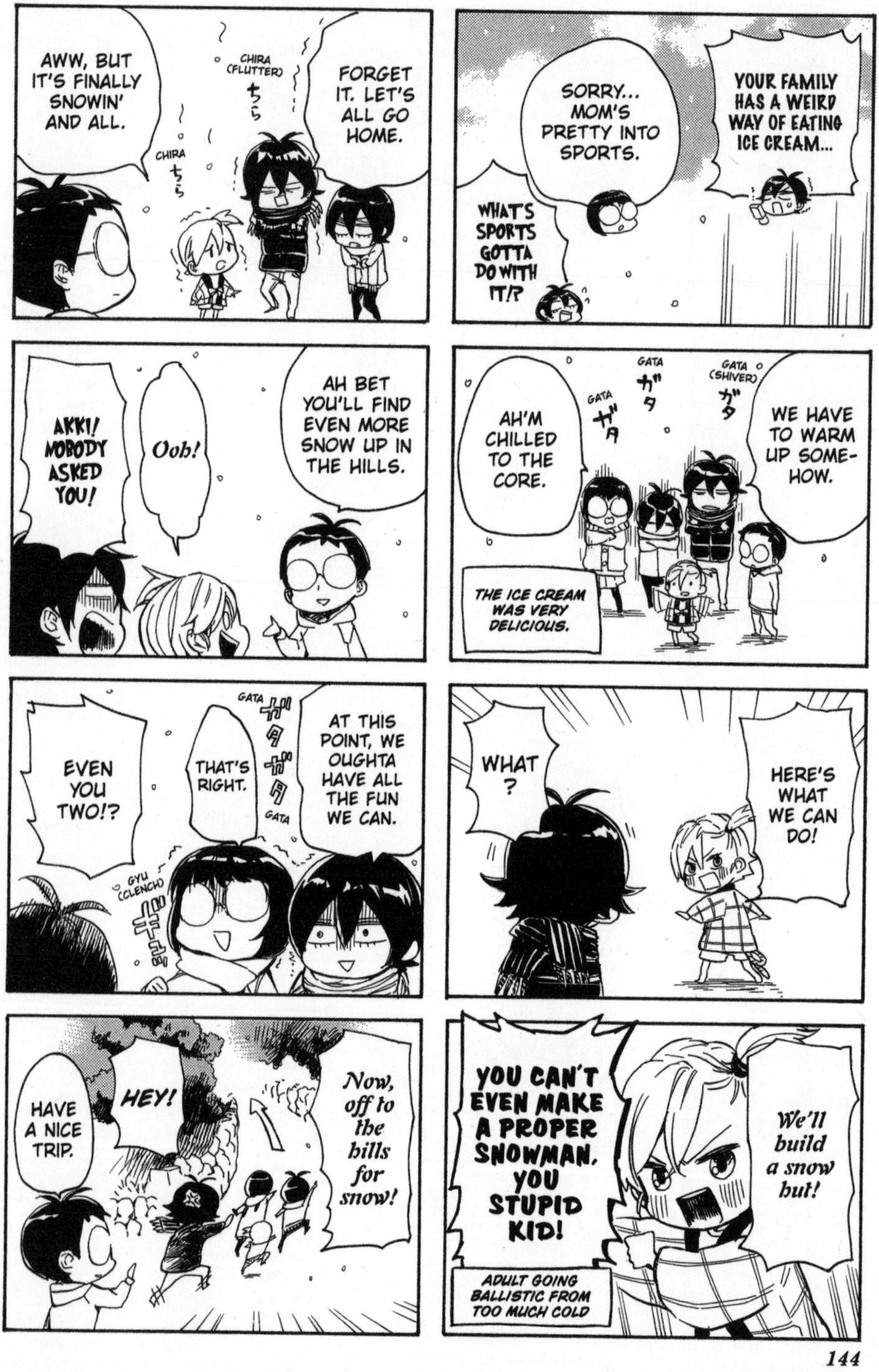
YOUR FAMILY HAS A WEIRD WAY OF EATING ICE CREAM...
SORRY... MOM'S PRETTY INTO SPORTS.
WHAT'S SPORTS GOTTA DO WITH IT!?
GATA (SHIVER) ガタ
GATA ガタ
GATA ガタ
WE HAVE TO WARM UP SOME-HOW.
AH'M CHILLED TO THE CORE.
THE ICE CREAM WAS VERY DELICIOUS.
HERE'S WHAT WE CAN DO!
WHAT?
We'll build a snow hut!
YOU CAN'T EVEN MAKE A PROPER SNOWMAN, YOU STUPID KID!
ADULT GOING BALLISTIC FROM TOO MUCH COLD
FORGET IT. LET'S ALL GO HOME.
CHIRA (FLUTTER) ちら
CHIRA ちら
AWW, BUT IT'S FINALLY SNOWIN' AND ALL.
AH BET YOU'LL FIND EVEN MORE SNOW UP IN THE HILLS.
Ooh!
AKKI! NOBODY ASKED YOU!
AT THIS POINT, WE OUGHTA HAVE ALL THE FUN WE CAN.
GATA ガタ
GATA ガタ
THAT'S RIGHT.
GYU (CLENCH) ギュ
EVEN YOU TWO!?
Now, off to the hills for snow!
HEY!
HAVE A NICE TRIP.

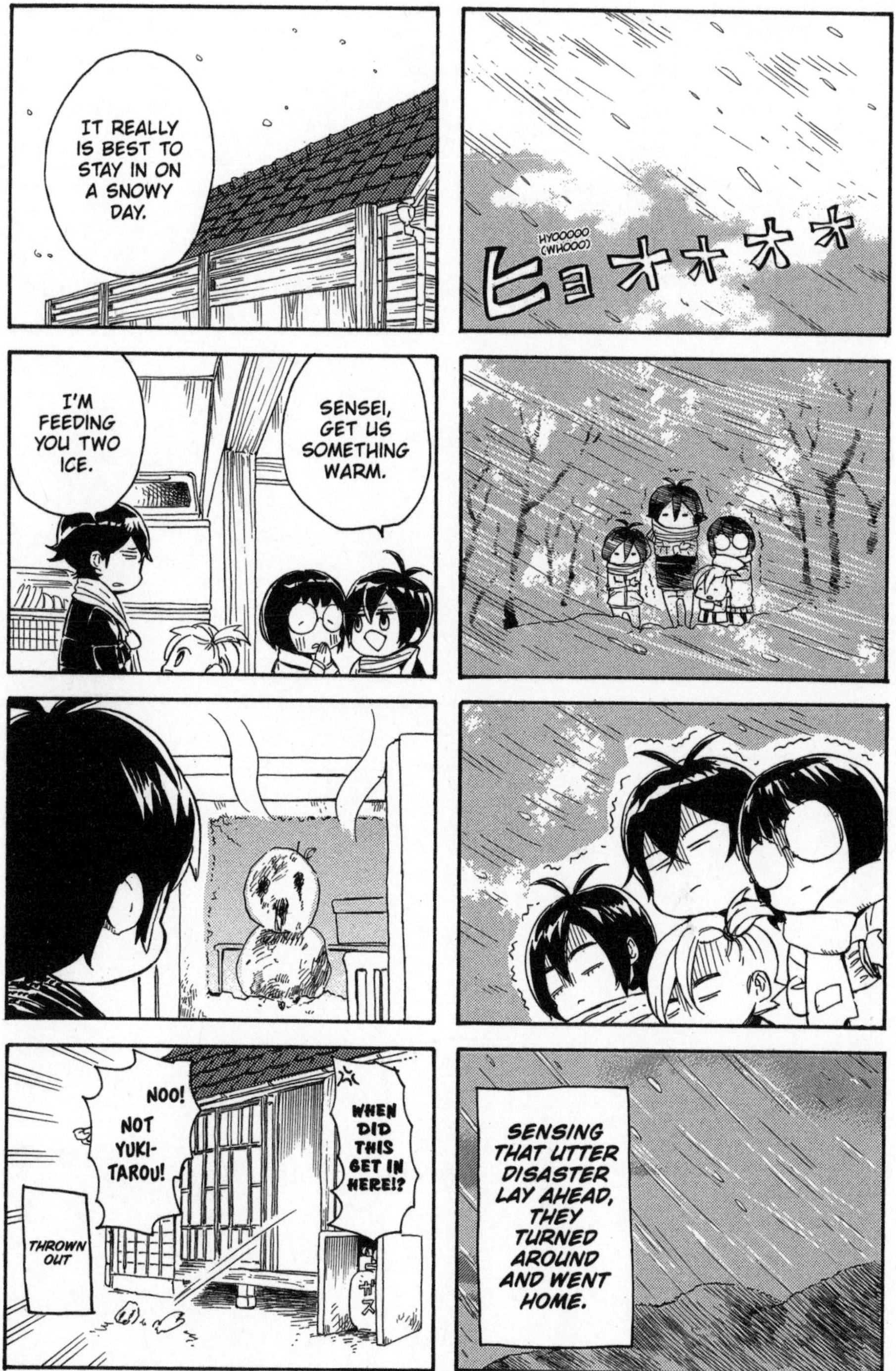
HYOOOOO (WHOOO)
ヒョオォオオ
IT REALLY IS BEST TO STAY IN ON A SNOWY DAY.
SENSEI, GET US SOMETHING WARM.
I'M FEEDING YOU TWO ICE.
SENSING THAT UTTER DISASTER LAY AHEAD, THEY TURNED AROUND AND WENT HOME.
WHEN DID THIS GET IN HERE!?
NOO! NOT YUKI-TAROU!
THROWN OUT
ガス

TANK: GAS

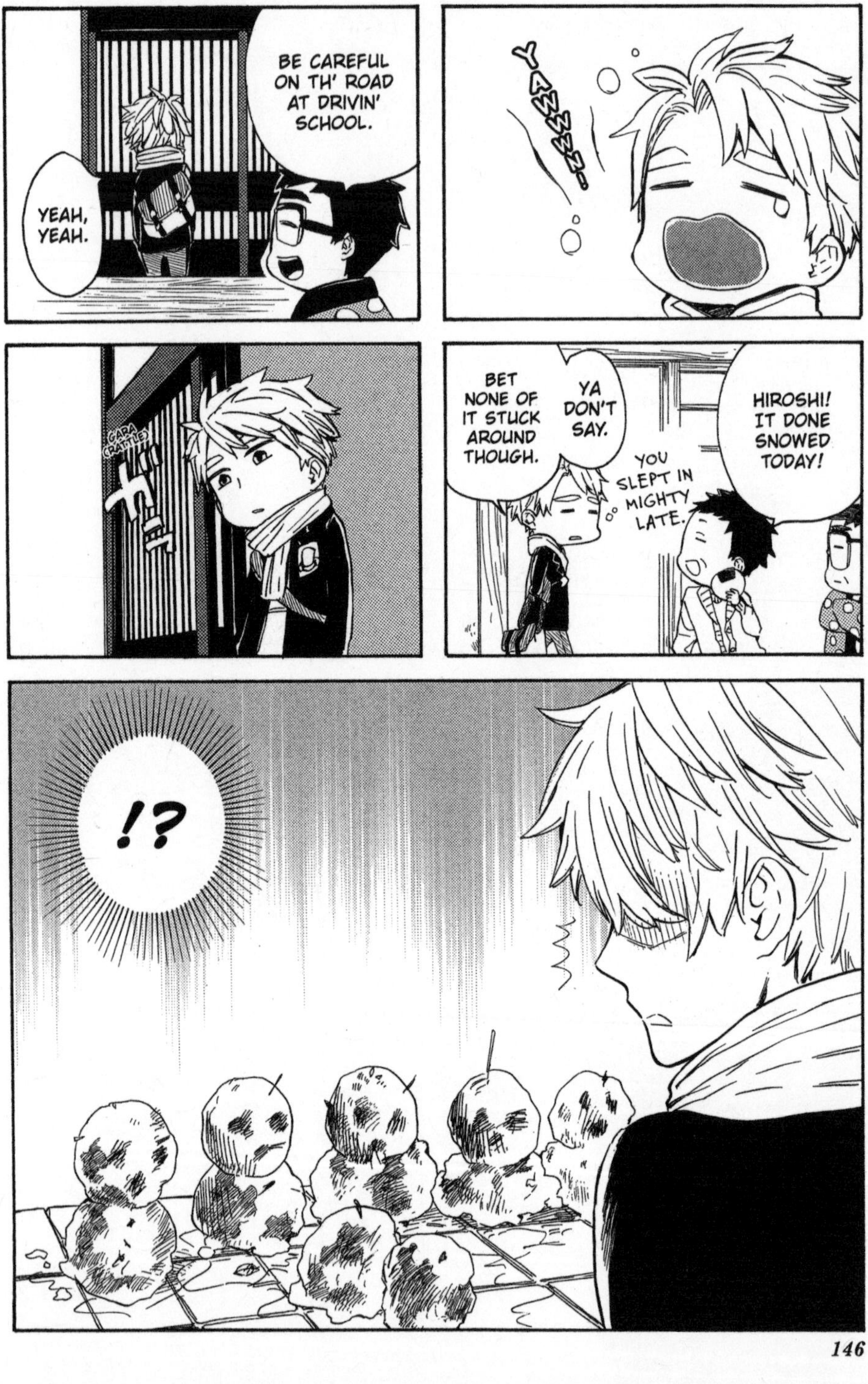
YAWWWN!
BE CAREFUL ON TH' ROAD AT DRIVIN' SCHOOL.
YEAH, YEAH.
HIROSHI! IT DONE SNOWED TODAY!
YOU SLEPT IN MIGHTY LATE.
YA DON'T SAY.
BET NONE OF IT STUCK AROUND THOUGH.
GARA (RATTLE)
!?

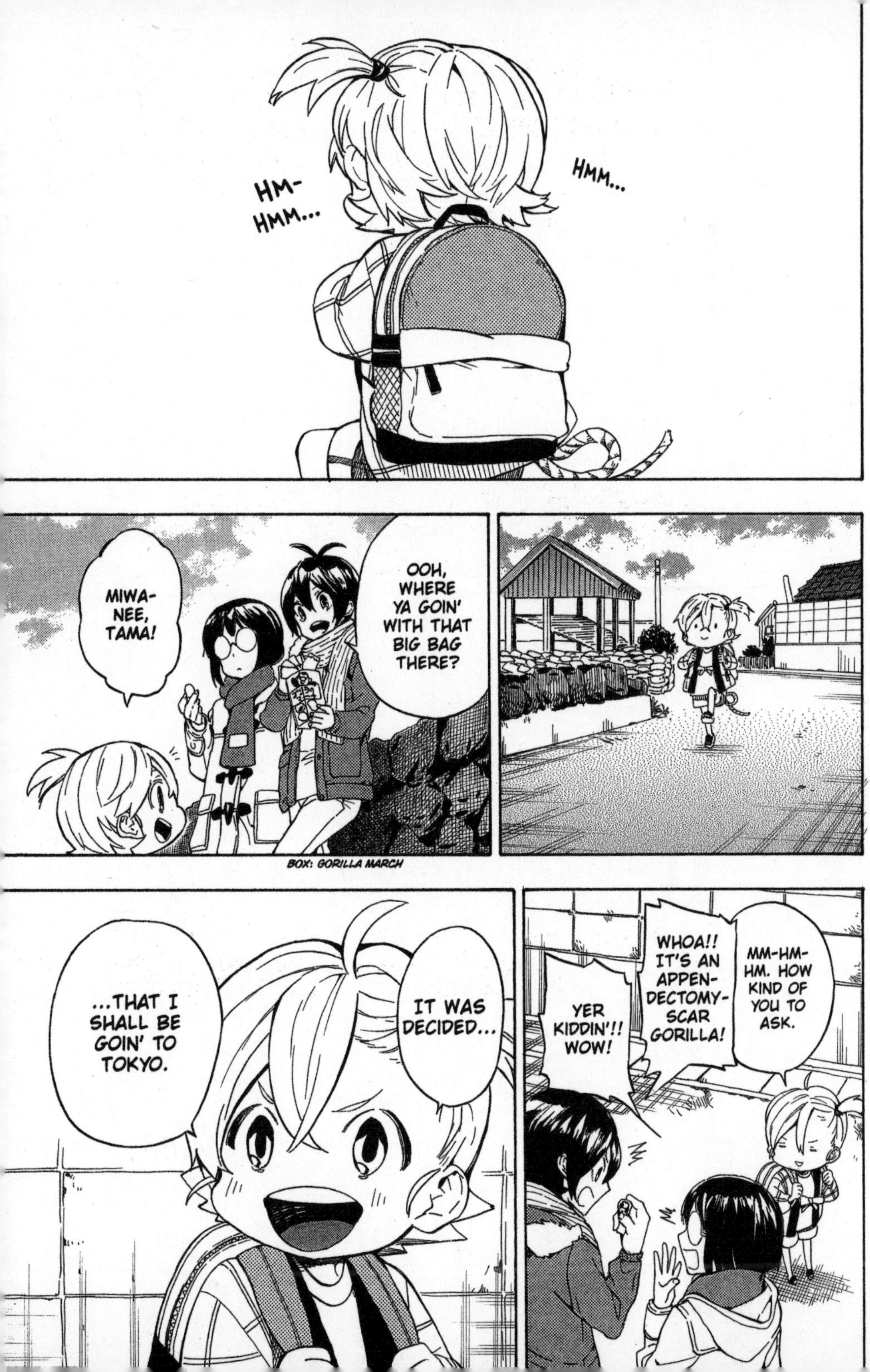
HMM...
HM-HMM...
OOH, WHERE YA GOIN' WITH THAT BIG BAG THERE?
MIWA-NEE, TAMA!
BOX: GORILLA MARCH
MM-HM-HM. HOW KIND OF YOU TO ASK.
WHOA!! IT'S AN APPEN-DECTOMY-SCAR GORILLA!
YER KIDDIN'!! WOW!
IT WAS DECIDED...
...THAT I SHALL BE GOIN' TO TOKYO.

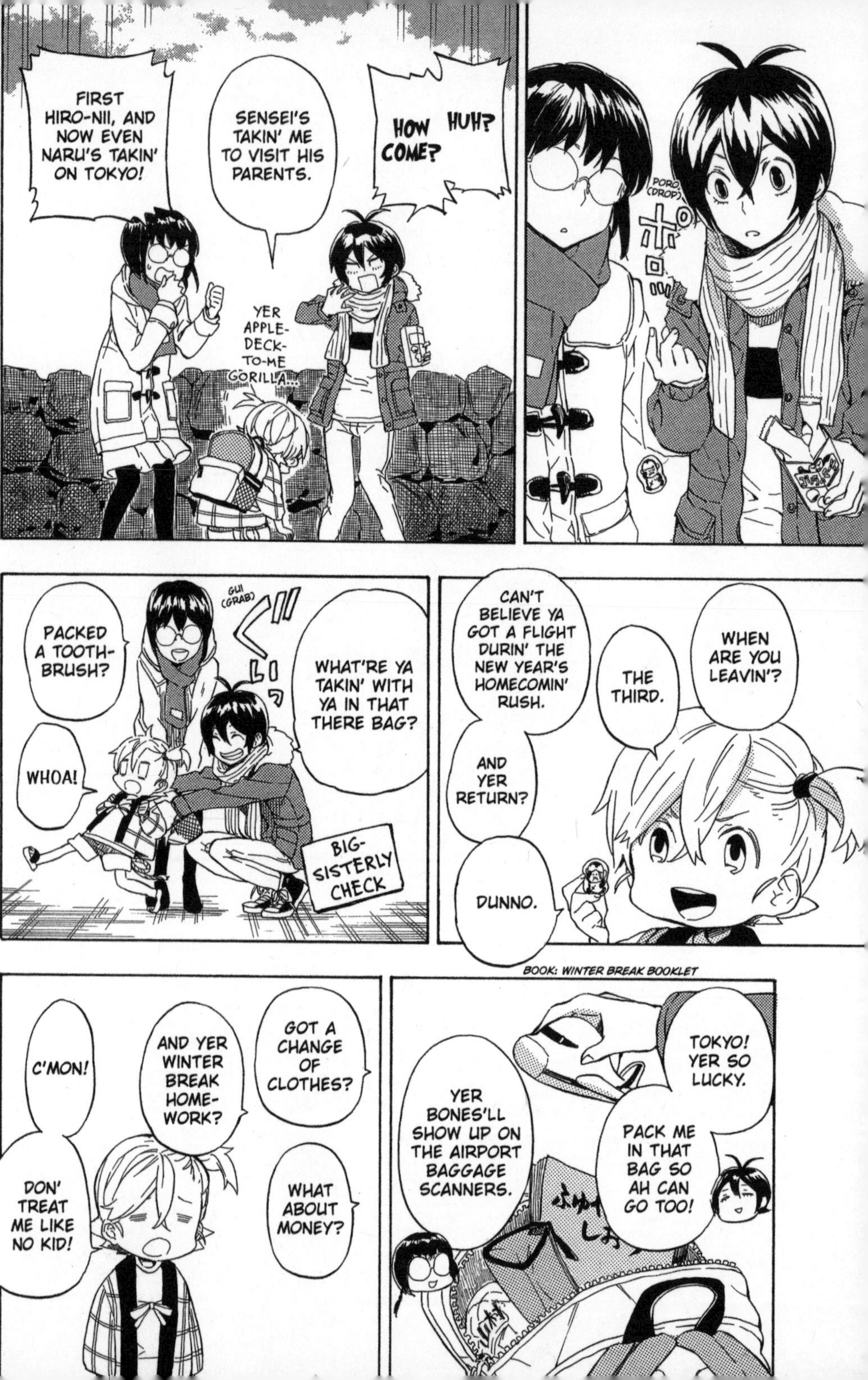
PORO (DROP)
HUH?
HOW COME?
SENSEI'S TAKIN' ME TO VISIT HIS PARENTS.
FIRST HIRO-NII, AND NOW EVEN NARU'S TAKIN' ON TOKYO!
YER APPLE-DECK-TO-ME GORILLA...
WHEN ARE YOU LEAVIN'?
THE THIRD.
CAN'T BELIEVE YA GOT A FLIGHT DURIN' THE NEW YEAR'S HOMECOMIN' RUSH.
AND YER RETURN?
DUNNO.
GUI (GRAB)
WHAT'RE YA TAKIN' WITH YA IN THAT THERE BAG?
PACKED A TOOTH-BRUSH?
WHOA!
BIG-SISTERLY CHECK
BOOK: WINTER BREAK BOOKLET
TOKYO! YER SO LUCKY.
PACK ME IN THAT BAG SO AH CAN GO TOO!
YER BONES'LL SHOW UP ON THE AIRPORT BAGGAGE SCANNERS.
GOT A CHANGE OF CLOTHES?
AND YER WINTER BREAK HOME-WORK?
C'MON!
WHAT ABOUT MONEY?
DON' TREAT ME LIKE NO KID!

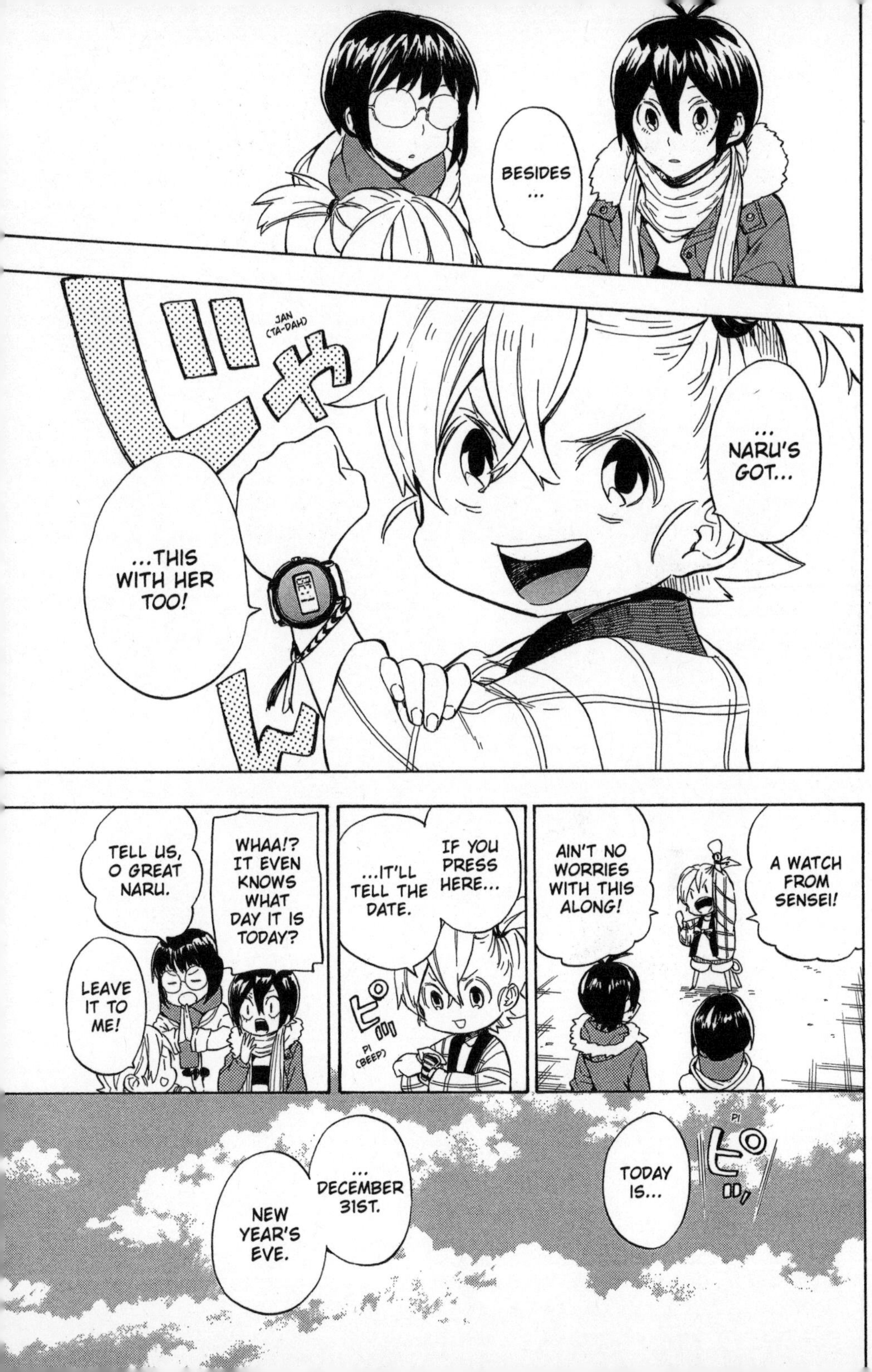
BESIDES ...
... NARU'S GOT...
JAN (TA-DAH)
...THIS WITH HER TOO!
A WATCH FROM SENSEI!
AIN'T NO WORRIES WITH THIS ALONG!
IF YOU PRESS HERE...
...IT'LL TELL THE DATE.
PI (BEEP)
WHAA!? IT EVEN KNOWS WHAT DAY IT IS TODAY?
TELL US, O GREAT NARU.
LEAVE IT TO ME!
PI
TODAY IS...
... DECEMBER 31ST.
NEW YEAR'S EVE.

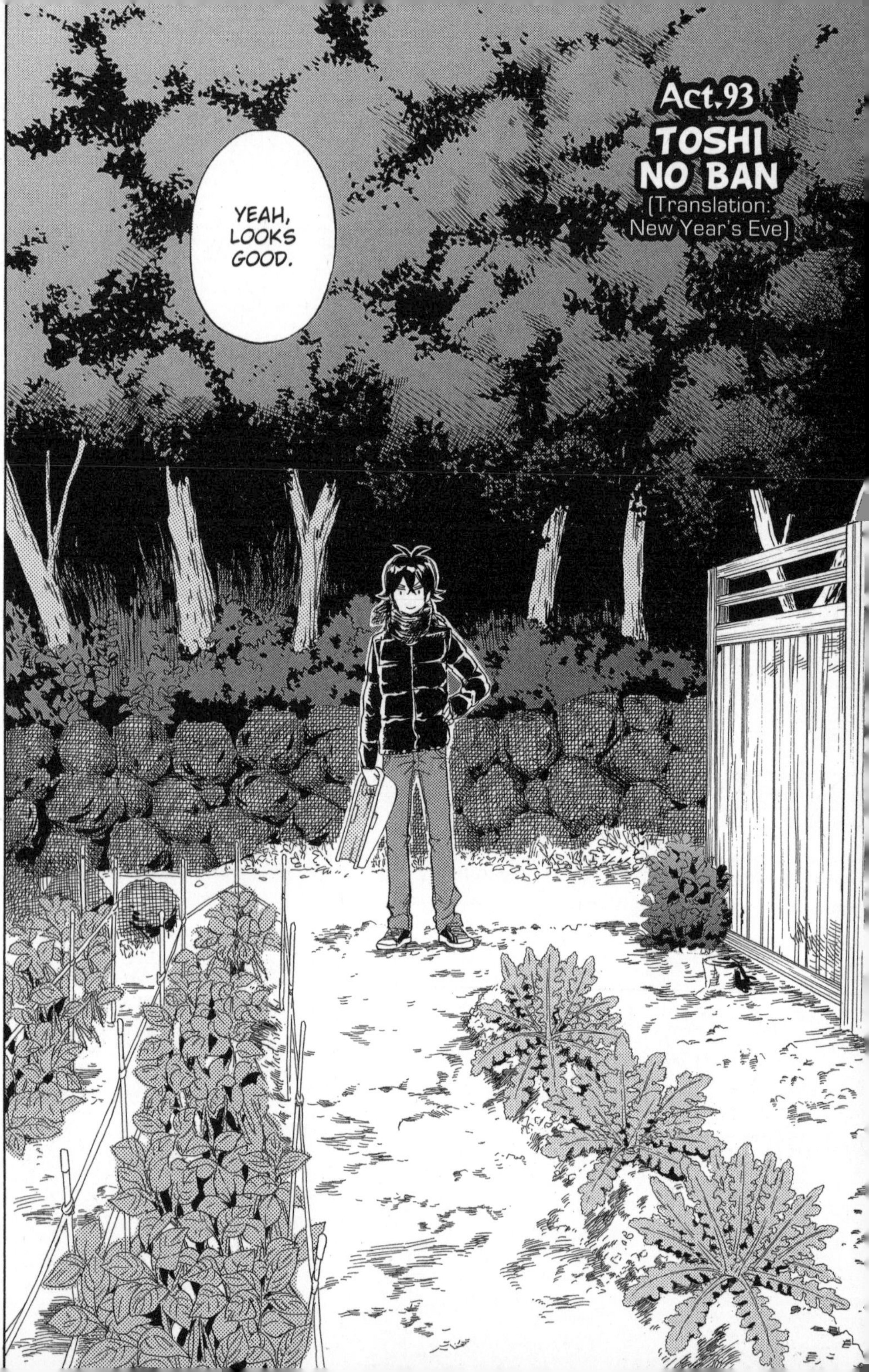

Act.93
TOSHI NO BAN
(Translation: New Year's Eve)
YEAH, LOOKS GOOD.

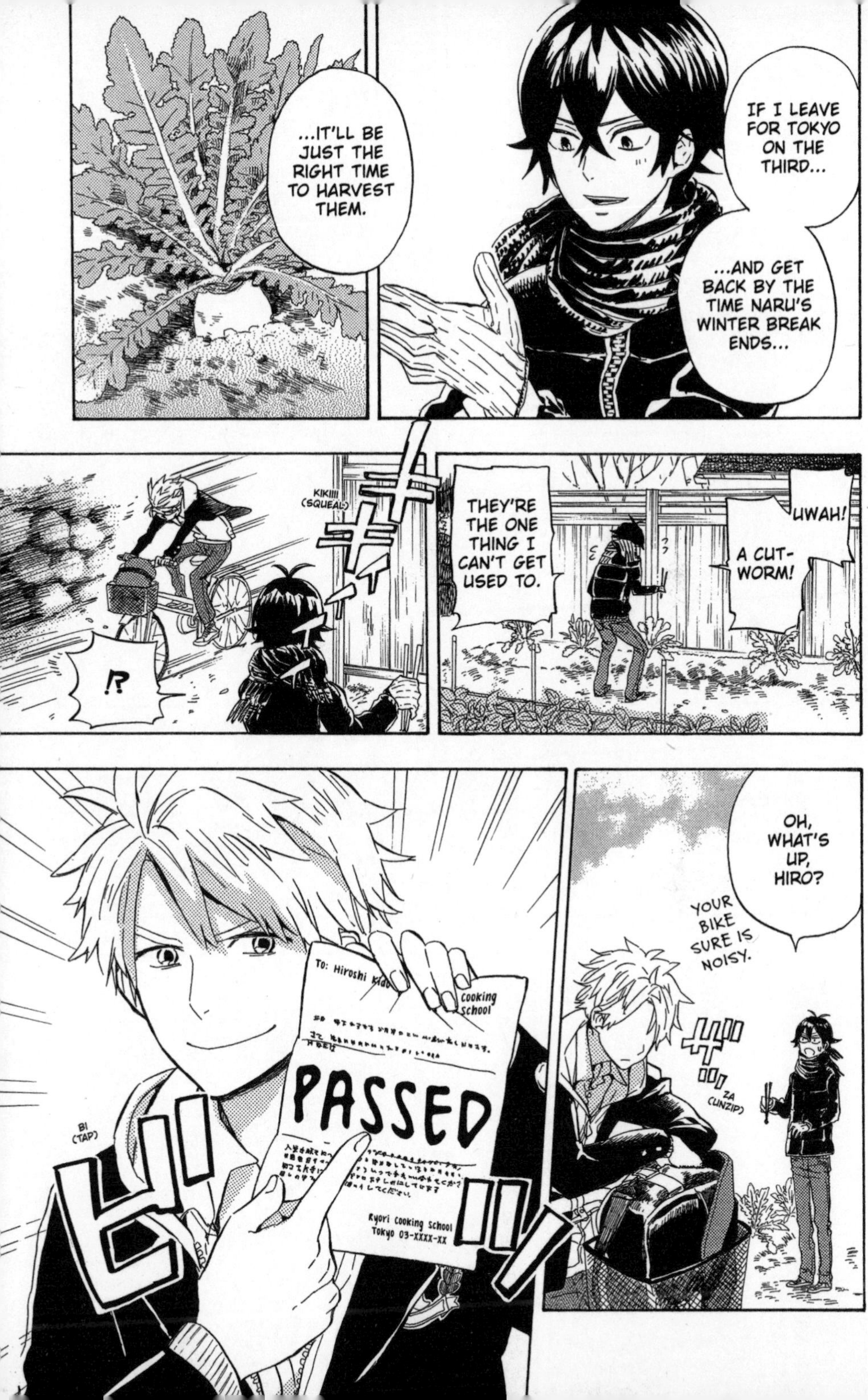
IF I LEAVE FOR TOKYO ON THE THIRD...
...AND GET BACK BY THE TIME NARU'S WINTER BREAK ENDS...
...IT'LL BE JUST THE RIGHT TIME TO HARVEST THEM.
UWAH!
A CUT-WORM!
THEY'RE THE ONE THING I CAN'T GET USED TO.
KIKI!!! (SQUEAL)
!?
OH, WHAT'S UP, HIRO?
YOUR BIKE SURE IS NOISY.
ZA (UNZIP)
BI (TAP)
To: Hiroshi Kido
Cooking School
PASSED
Ryori Cooking School
Tokyo 03-XXXX-XX

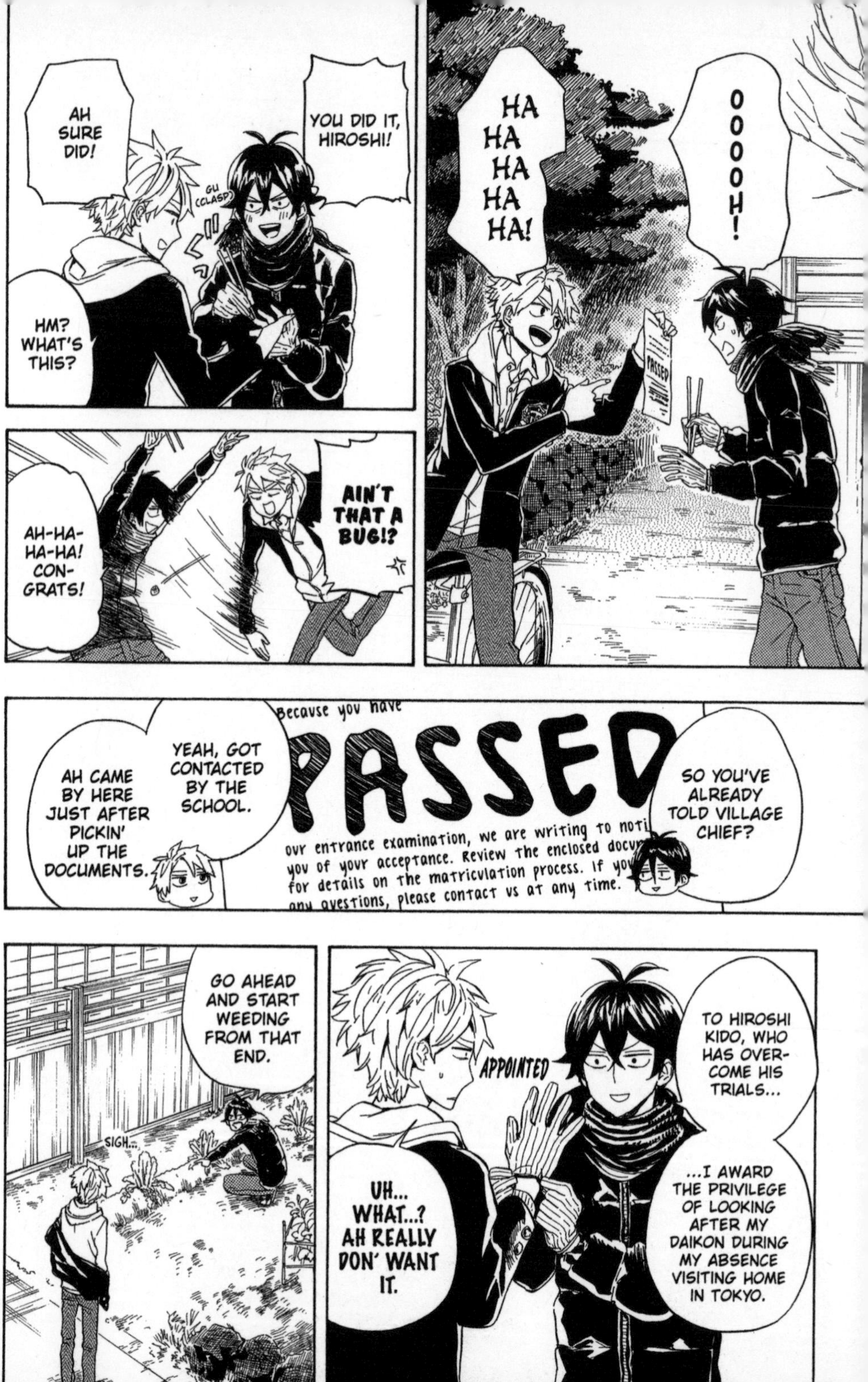
OOOOOH!
HA HA HA HA HA!
PASSED
YOU DID IT, HIROSHI!
AH SURE DID!
GU (CLASP)
HM? WHAT'S THIS?
AIN'T THAT A BUG!?
AH-HA-HA-HA! CON-GRATS!
SO YOU'VE ALREADY TOLD VILLAGE CHIEF?
Because you have
PASSED
our entrance examination, we are writing to noti
you of your acceptance. Review the enclosed docu
for details on the matriculation process. If you
any questions, please contact us at any time.
YEAH, GOT CONTACTED BY THE SCHOOL.
AH CAME BY HERE JUST AFTER PICKIN' UP THE DOCUMENTS.
TO HIROSHI KIDO, WHO HAS OVER-COME HIS TRIALS...
...I AWARD THE PRIVILEGE OF LOOKING AFTER MY DAIKON DURING MY ABSENCE VISITING HOME IN TOKYO.
APPOINTED
UH... WHAT...? AH REALLY DON' WANT IT.
GO AHEAD AND START WEEDING FROM THAT END.
SIGH...

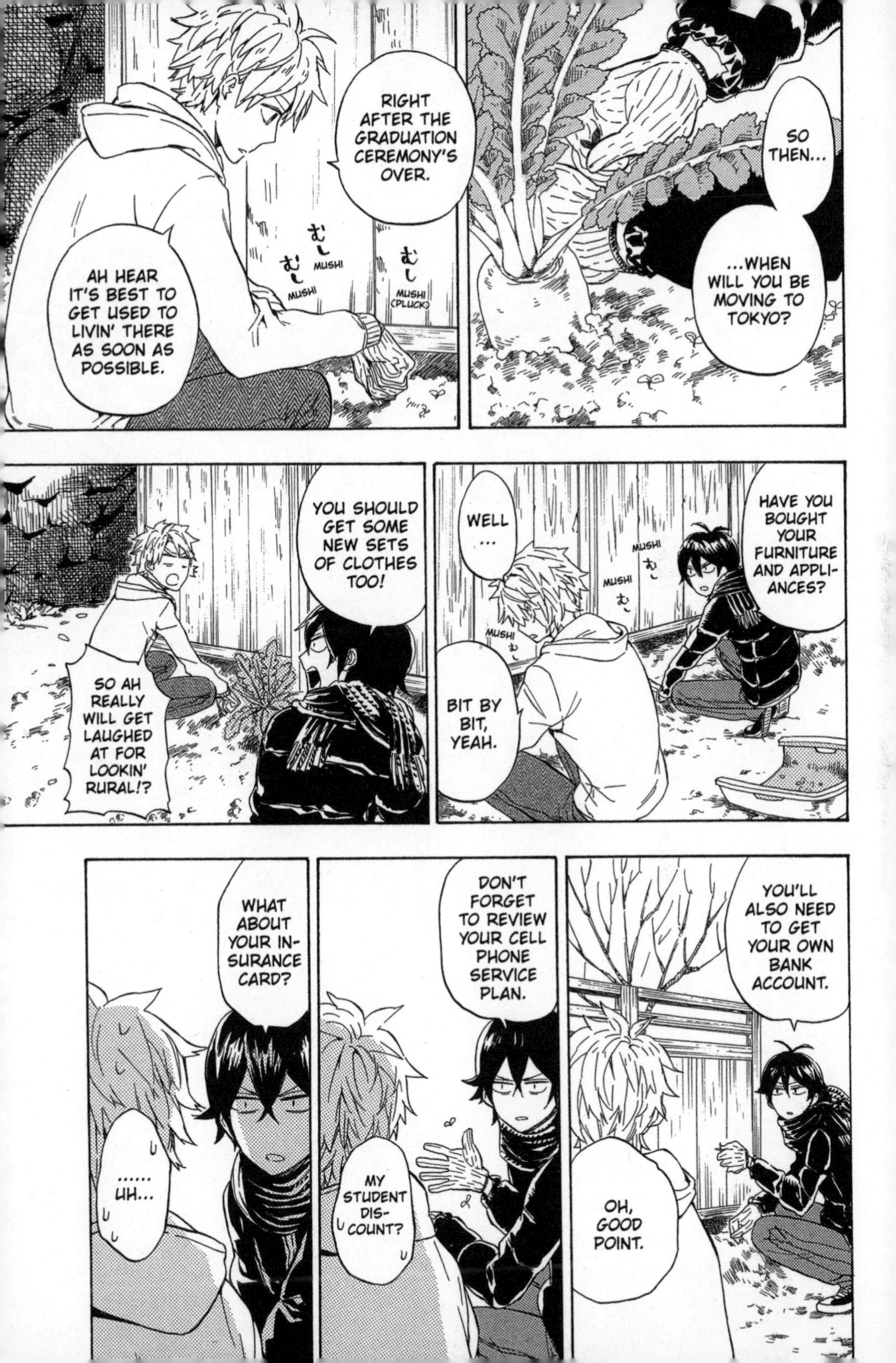
SO THEN...
...WHEN WILL YOU BE MOVING TO TOKYO?
RIGHT AFTER THE GRADUATION CEREMONY'S OVER.
むし MUSHI (PLUCK)
むし MUSHI
むし MUSHI
AH HEAR IT'S BEST TO GET USED TO LIVIN' THERE AS SOON AS POSSIBLE.
HAVE YOU BOUGHT YOUR FURNITURE AND APPLI-ANCES?
MUSHI むし
MUSHI むし
WELL ...
MUSHI むし
BIT BY BIT, YEAH.
YOU SHOULD GET SOME NEW SETS OF CLOTHES TOO!
SO AH REALLY WILL GET LAUGHED AT FOR LOOKIN' RURAL!?
YOU'LL ALSO NEED TO GET YOUR OWN BANK ACCOUNT.
OH, GOOD POINT.
DON'T FORGET TO REVIEW YOUR CELL PHONE SERVICE PLAN.
MY STUDENT DIS-COUNT?
WHAT ABOUT YOUR IN-SURANCE CARD?
...... UH...

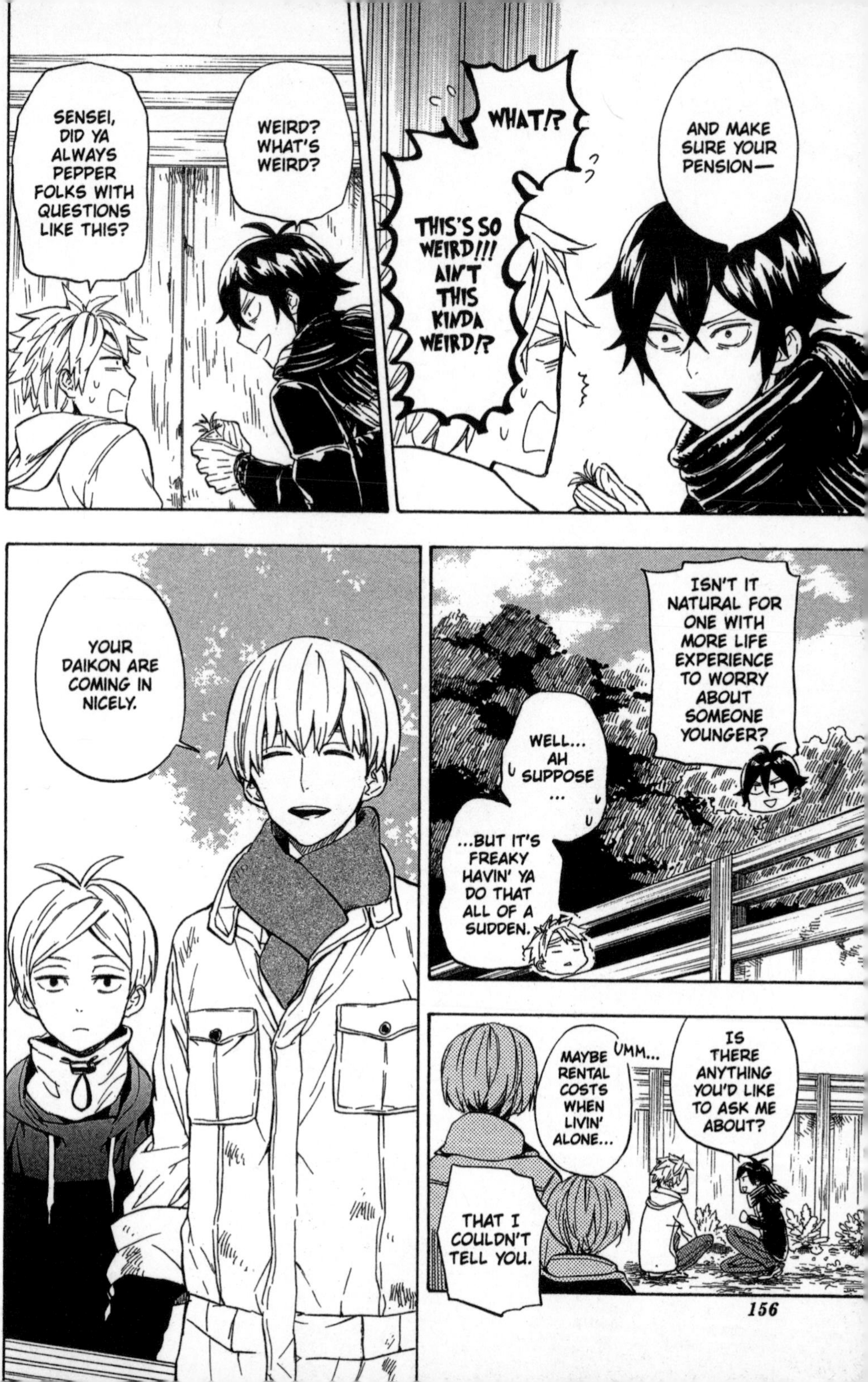
AND MAKE SURE YOUR PENSION—
WHAT!?
THIS'S SO WEIRD!!! AIN'T THIS KINDA WEIRD!?
WEIRD? WHAT'S WEIRD?
SENSEI, DID YA ALWAYS PEPPER FOLKS WITH QUESTIONS LIKE THIS?
ISN'T IT NATURAL FOR ONE WITH MORE LIFE EXPERIENCE TO WORRY ABOUT SOMEONE YOUNGER?
WELL... AH SUPPOSE...
...BUT IT'S FREAKY HAVIN' YA DO THAT ALL OF A SUDDEN.
IS THERE ANYTHING YOU'D LIKE TO ASK ME ABOUT?
UMM...
MAYBE RENTAL COSTS WHEN LIVIN' ALONE...
THAT I COULDN'T TELL YOU.
YOUR DAIKON ARE COMING IN NICELY.

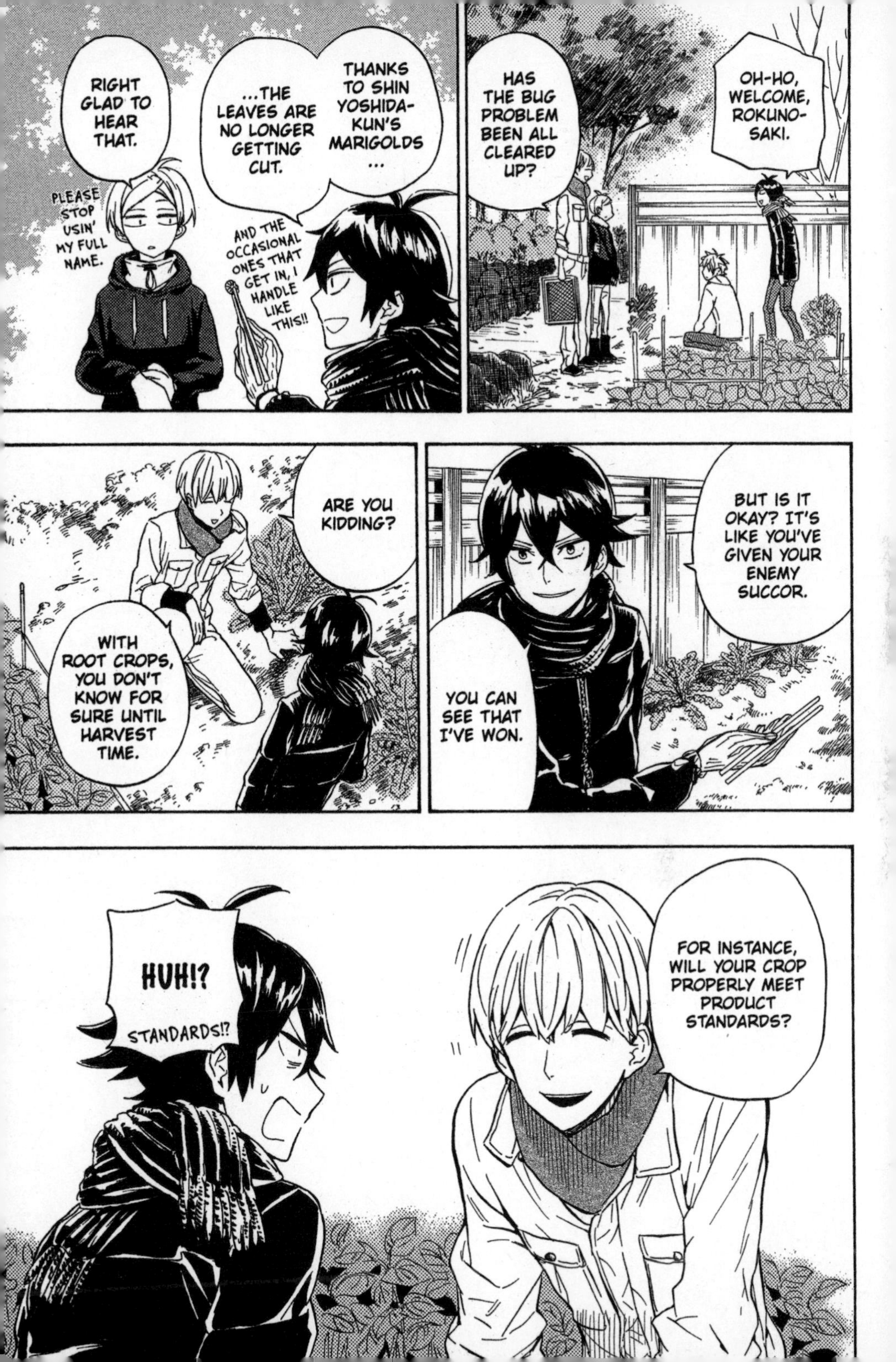
OH-HO, WELCOME, ROKUNO-SAKI.
HAS THE BUG PROBLEM BEEN ALL CLEARED UP?
THANKS TO SHIN YOSHIDA-KUN'S MARIGOLDS ...
...THE LEAVES ARE NO LONGER GETTING CUT.
RIGHT GLAD TO HEAR THAT.
AND THE OCCASIONAL ONES THAT GET IN, I HANDLE LIKE THIS!!
PLEASE STOP USIN' MY FULL NAME.
BUT IS IT OKAY? IT'S LIKE YOU'VE GIVEN YOUR ENEMY SUCCOR.
YOU CAN SEE THAT I'VE WON.
ARE YOU KIDDING?
WITH ROOT CROPS, YOU DON'T KNOW FOR SURE UNTIL HARVEST TIME.
FOR INSTANCE, WILL YOUR CROP PROPERLY MEET PRODUCT STANDARDS?
HUH!?
STANDARDS!?

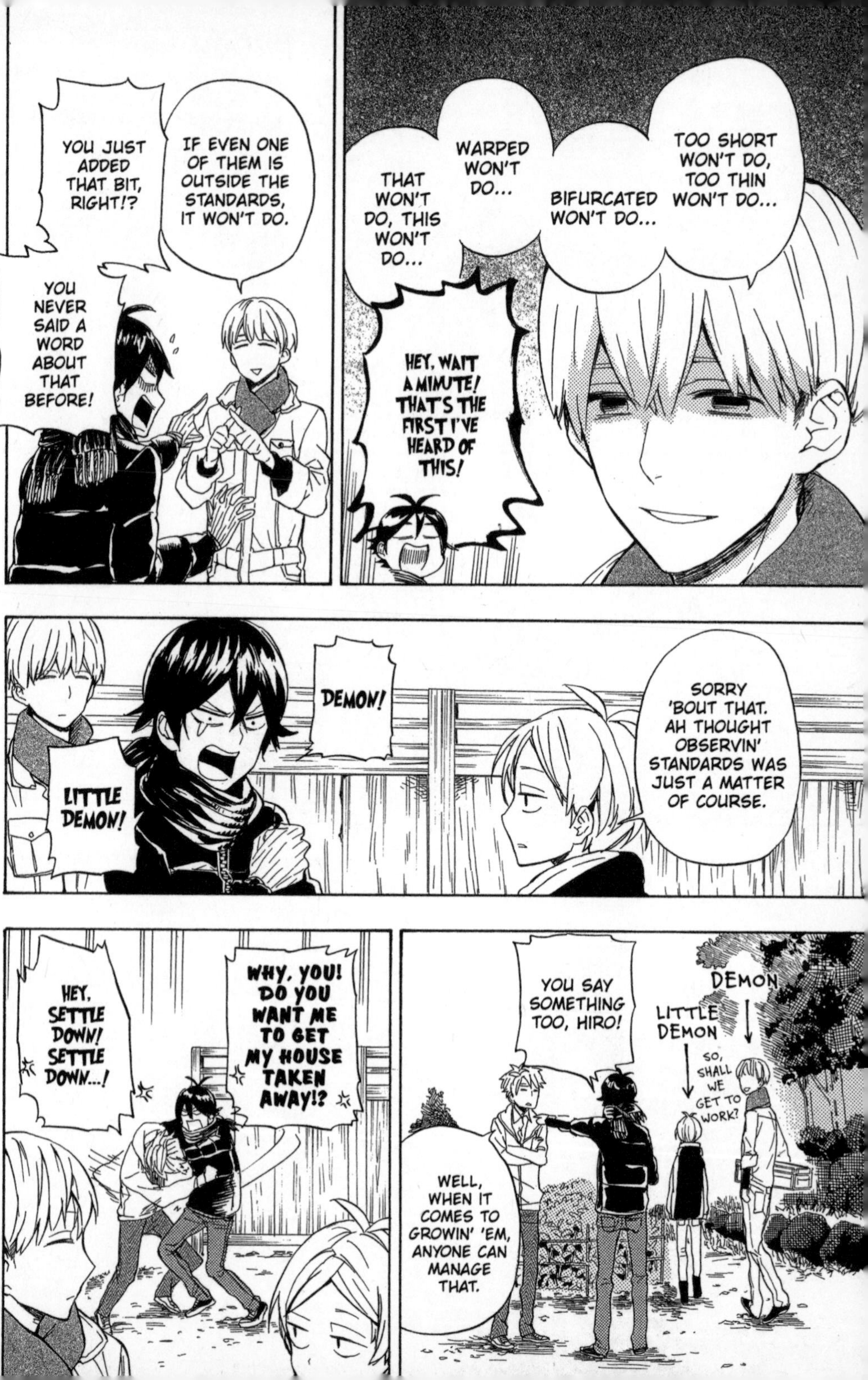
TOO SHORT WON'T DO, TOO THIN WON'T DO...
BIFURCATED WON'T DO...
WARPED WON'T DO...
THAT WON'T DO, THIS WON'T DO...
HEY, WAIT A MINUTE! THAT'S THE FIRST I'VE HEARD OF THIS!
IF EVEN ONE OF THEM IS OUTSIDE THE STANDARDS, IT WON'T DO.
YOU JUST ADDED THAT BIT, RIGHT!?
YOU NEVER SAID A WORD ABOUT THAT BEFORE!
SORRY 'BOUT THAT. AH THOUGHT OBSERVIN' STANDARDS WAS JUST A MATTER OF COURSE.
DEMON!
LITTLE DEMON!
YOU SAY SOMETHING TOO, HIRO!
DEMON
LITTLE DEMON
SO, SHALL WE GET TO WORK?
WELL, WHEN IT COMES TO GROWIN' 'EM, ANYONE CAN MANAGE THAT.
WHY, YOU! DO YOU WANT ME TO GET MY HOUSE TAKEN AWAY!?
HEY, SETTLE DOWN! SETTLE DOWN...!

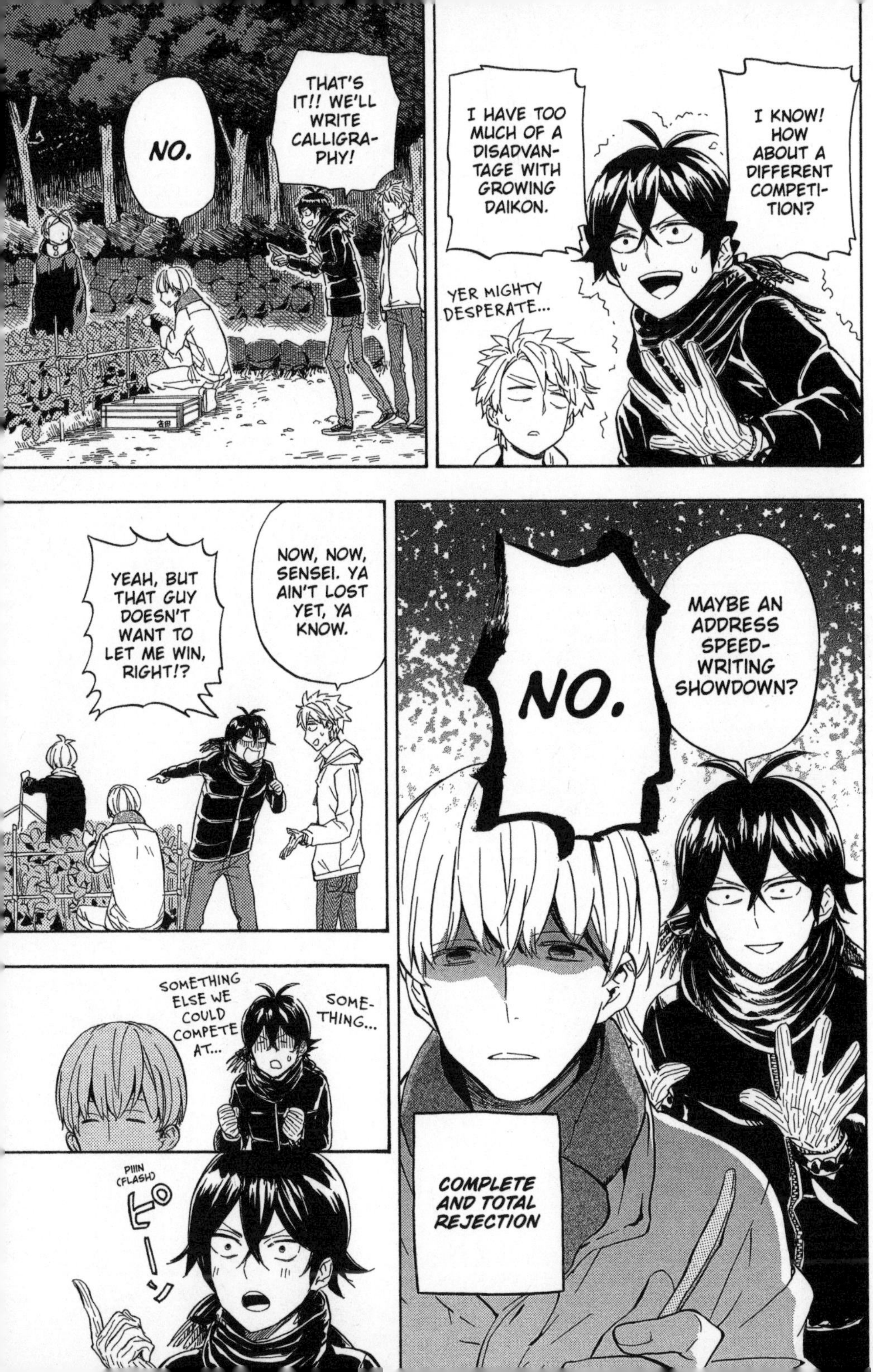
I KNOW! HOW ABOUT A DIFFERENT COMPETITION?
I HAVE TOO MUCH OF A DISADVANTAGE WITH GROWING DAIKON.
YER MIGHTY DESPERATE...
THAT'S IT!! WE'LL WRITE CALLIGRAPHY!
NO.
MAYBE AN ADDRESS SPEED-WRITING SHOWDOWN?
NO.
COMPLETE AND TOTAL REJECTION
NOW, NOW, SENSEI. YA AIN'T LOST YET, YA KNOW.
YEAH, BUT THAT GUY DOESN'T WANT TO LET ME WIN, RIGHT!?
SOMETHING...
SOMETHING ELSE WE COULD COMPETE AT...
PIIIN (FLASH)
ピーン

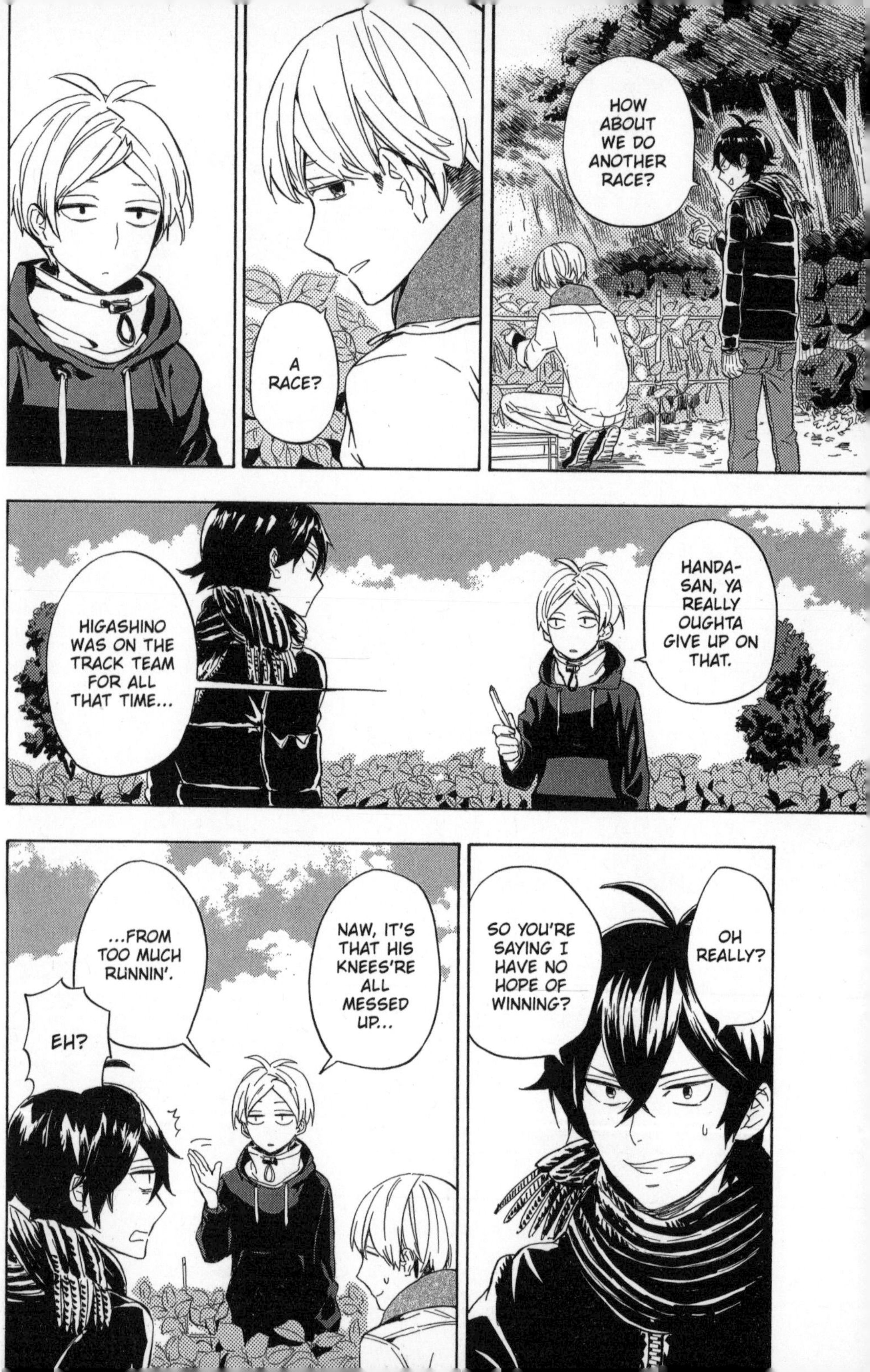
HOW ABOUT WE DO ANOTHER RACE?
A RACE?
HANDA-SAN, YA REALLY OUGHTA GIVE UP ON THAT.
HIGASHINO WAS ON THE TRACK TEAM FOR ALL THAT TIME...
OH REALLY?
SO YOU'RE SAYING I HAVE NO HOPE OF WINNING?
NAW, IT'S THAT HIS KNEES'RE ALL MESSED UP...
...FROM TOO MUCH RUNNIN'.
EH?

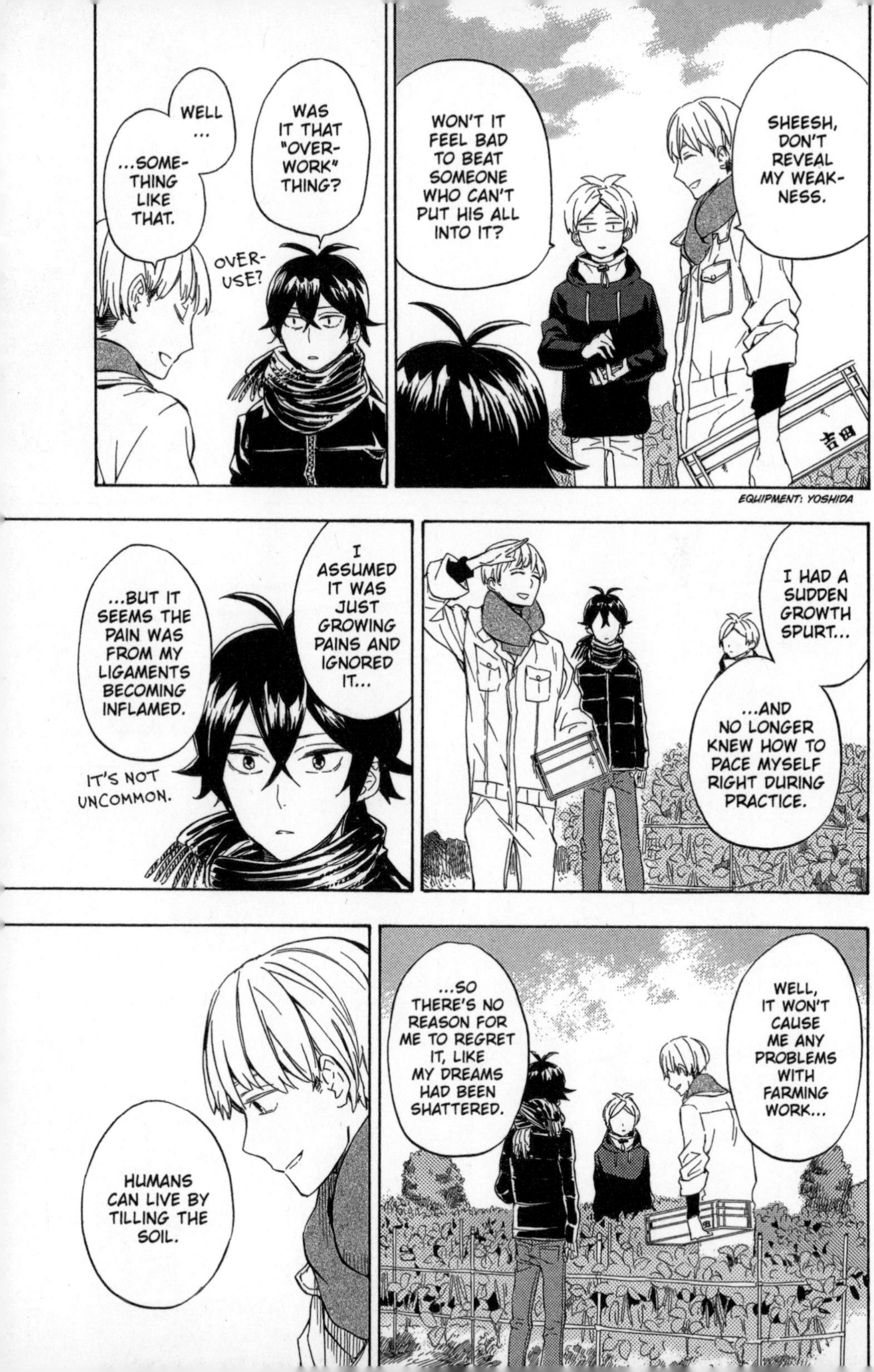
SHEESH, DON'T REVEAL MY WEAKNESS.
WON'T IT FEEL BAD TO BEAT SOMEONE WHO CAN'T PUT HIS ALL INTO IT?
吉田
WAS IT THAT "OVER-WORK" THING?
WELL ...
...SOMETHING LIKE THAT.
OVER-USE?
EQUIPMENT: YOSHIDA
I HAD A SUDDEN GROWTH SPURT...
...AND NO LONGER KNEW HOW TO PACE MYSELF RIGHT DURING PRACTICE.
I ASSUMED IT WAS JUST GROWING PAINS AND IGNORED IT...
...BUT IT SEEMS THE PAIN WAS FROM MY LIGAMENTS BECOMING INFLAMED.
IT'S NOT UNCOMMON.
WELL, IT WON'T CAUSE ME ANY PROBLEMS WITH FARMING WORK...
...SO THERE'S NO REASON FOR ME TO REGRET IT, LIKE MY DREAMS HAD BEEN SHATTERED.
HUMANS CAN LIVE BY TILLING THE SOIL.

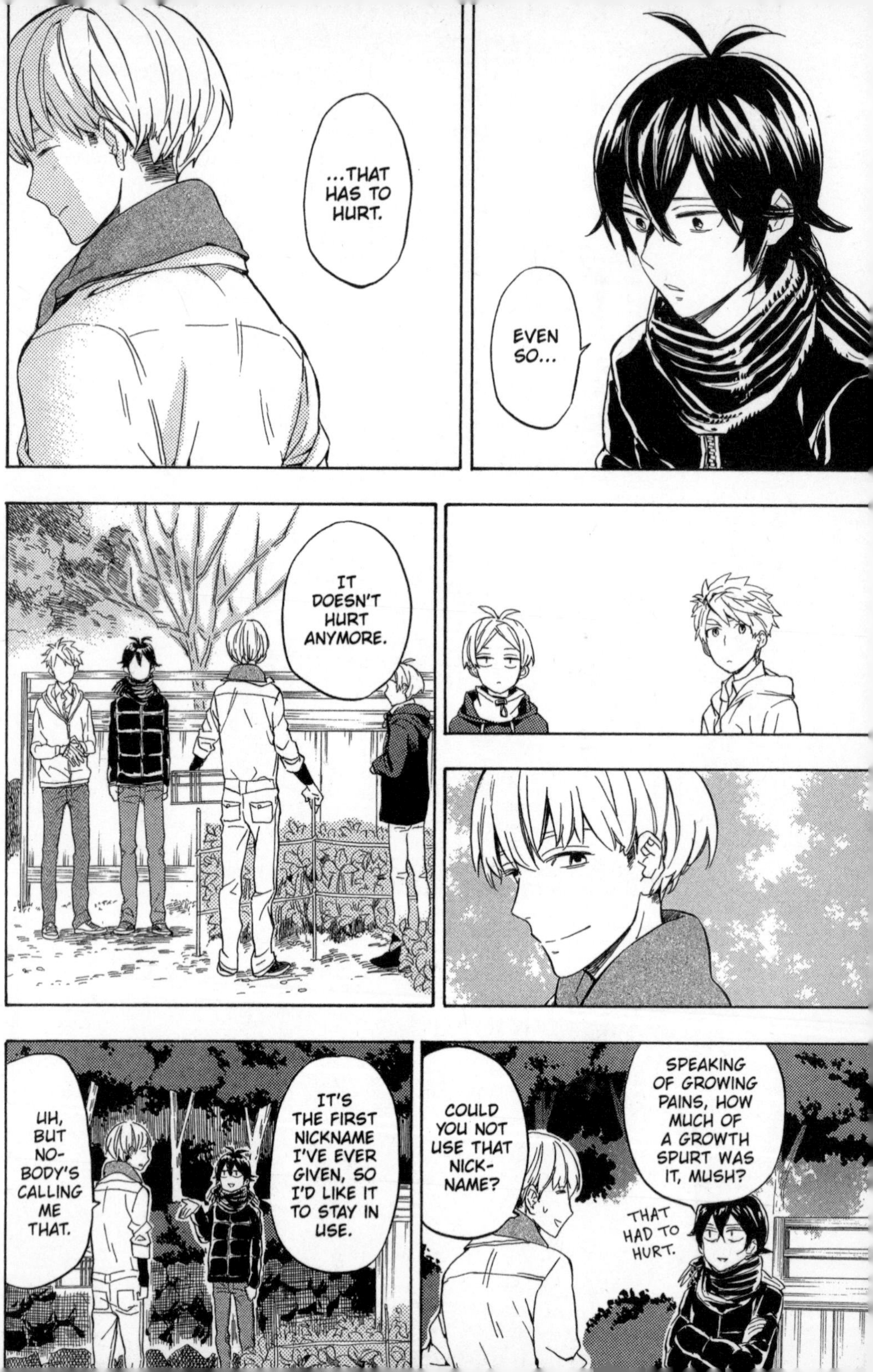
EVEN SO...
...THAT HAS TO HURT.
IT DOESN'T HURT ANYMORE.
SPEAKING OF GROWING PAINS, HOW MUCH OF A GROWTH SPURT WAS IT, MUSH?
THAT HAD TO HURT.
COULD YOU NOT USE THAT NICKNAME?
IT'S THE FIRST NICKNAME I'VE EVER GIVEN, SO I'D LIKE IT TO STAY IN USE.
UH, BUT NOBODY'S CALLING ME THAT.

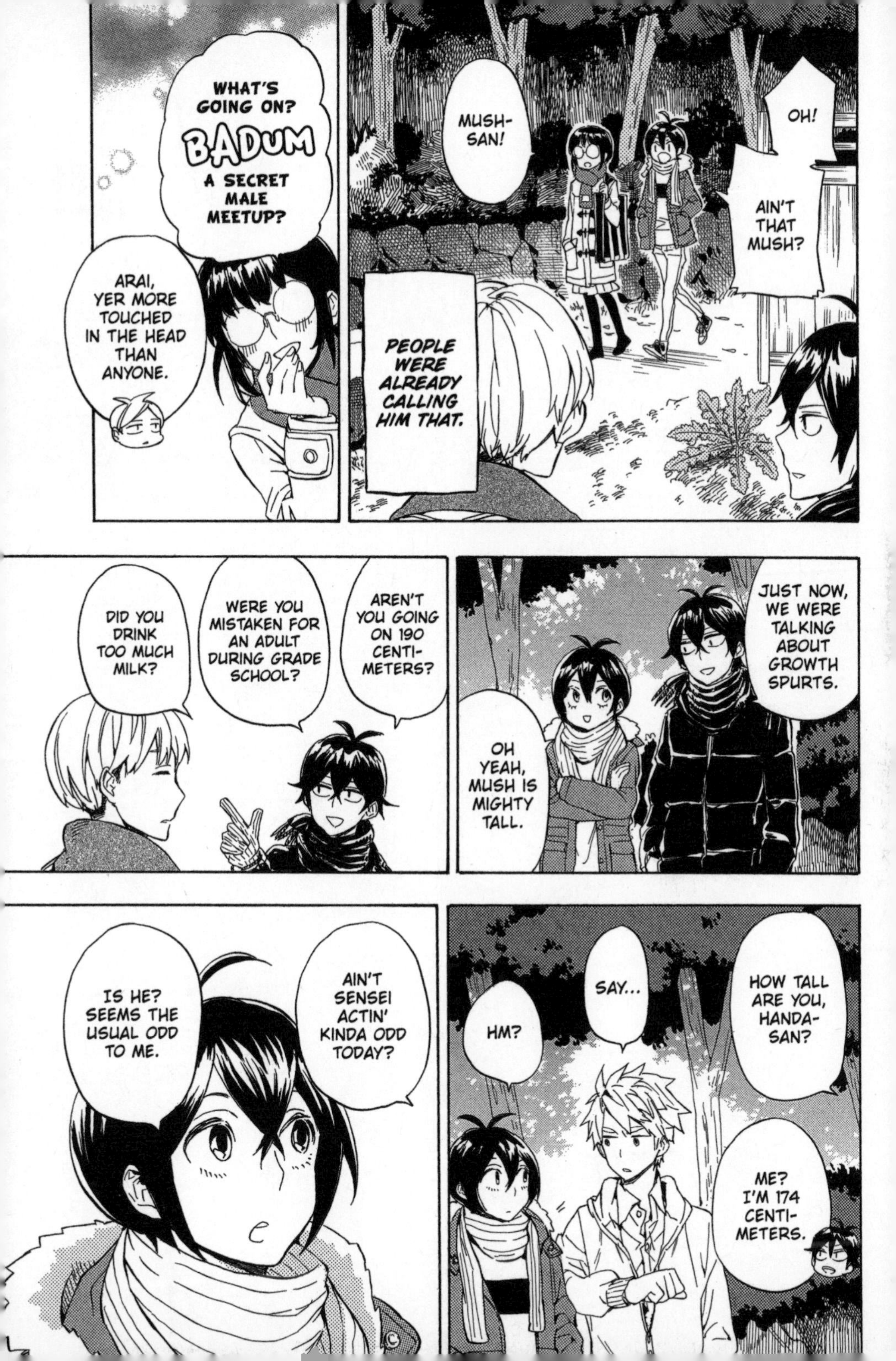
OH!
AIN'T THAT MUSH?
MUSH-SAN!
PEOPLE WERE ALREADY CALLING HIM THAT.
WHAT'S GOING ON?
BADUM
A SECRET MALE MEETUP?
ARAI, YER MORE TOUCHED IN THE HEAD THAN ANYONE.
JUST NOW, WE WERE TALKING ABOUT GROWTH SPURTS.
OH YEAH, MUSH IS MIGHTY TALL.
AREN'T YOU GOING ON 190 CENTI-METERS?
WERE YOU MISTAKEN FOR AN ADULT DURING GRADE SCHOOL?
DID YOU DRINK TOO MUCH MILK?
HOW TALL ARE YOU, HANDA-SAN?
SAY...
HM?
ME? I'M 174 CENTI-METERS.
AIN'T SENSEI ACTIN' KINDA ODD TODAY?
IS HE? SEEMS THE USUAL ODD TO ME.

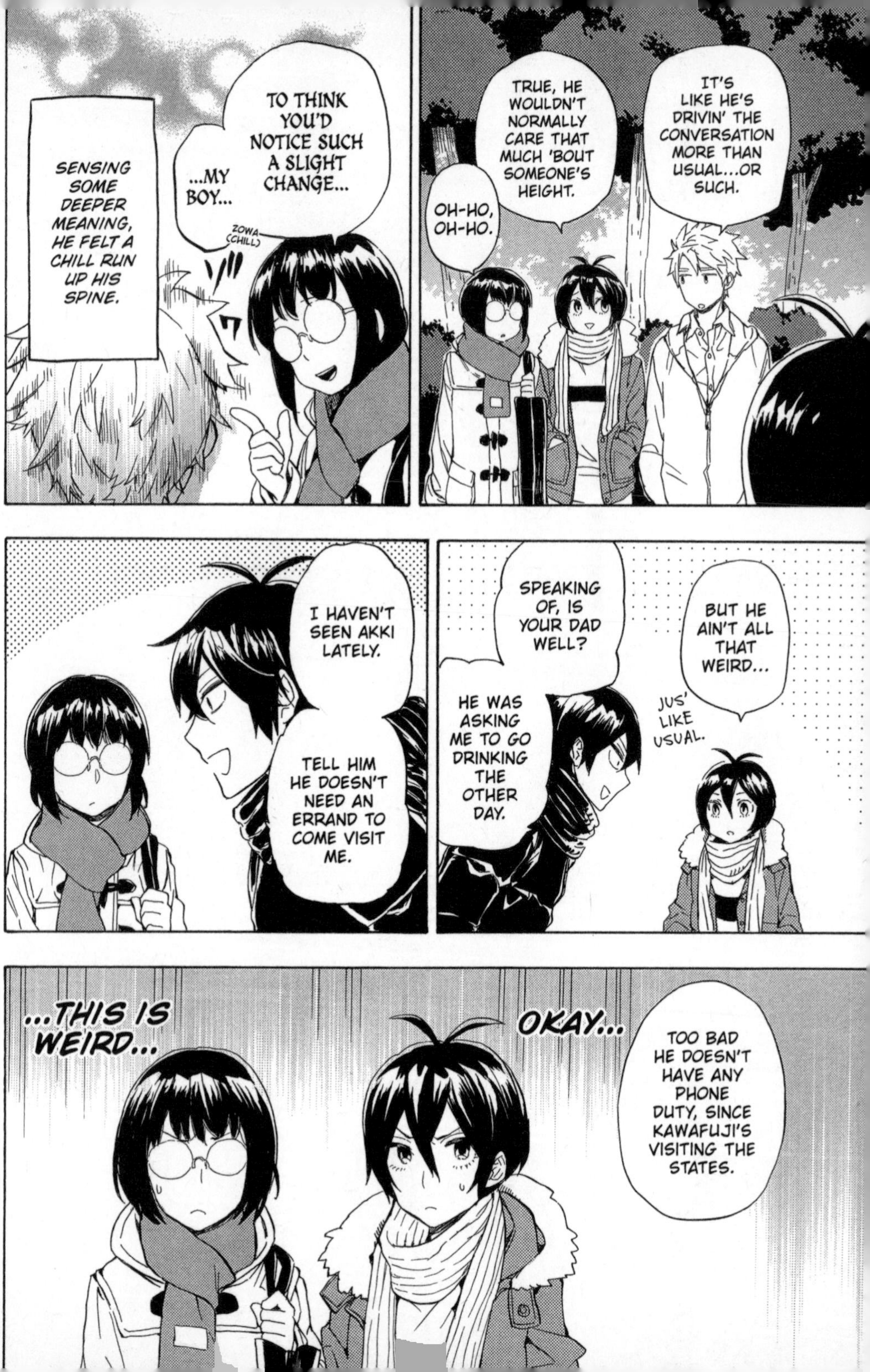
IT'S LIKE HE'S DRIVIN' THE CONVERSATION MORE THAN USUAL...OR SUCH.
TRUE, HE WOULDN'T NORMALLY CARE THAT MUCH 'BOUT SOMEONE'S HEIGHT.
OH-HO, OH-HO.
TO THINK YOU'D NOTICE SUCH A SLIGHT CHANGE...
...MY BOY...
ZOWA (CHILL)
SENSING SOME DEEPER MEANING, HE FELT A CHILL RUN UP HIS SPINE.
BUT HE AIN'T ALL THAT WEIRD...
JUS' LIKE USUAL.
SPEAKING OF, IS YOUR DAD WELL?
HE WAS ASKING ME TO GO DRINKING THE OTHER DAY.
I HAVEN'T SEEN AKKI LATELY.
TELL HIM HE DOESN'T NEED AN ERRAND TO COME VISIT ME.
TOO BAD HE DOESN'T HAVE ANY PHONE DUTY, SINCE KAWAFUJI'S VISITING THE STATES.
OKAY...
...THIS IS WEIRD...

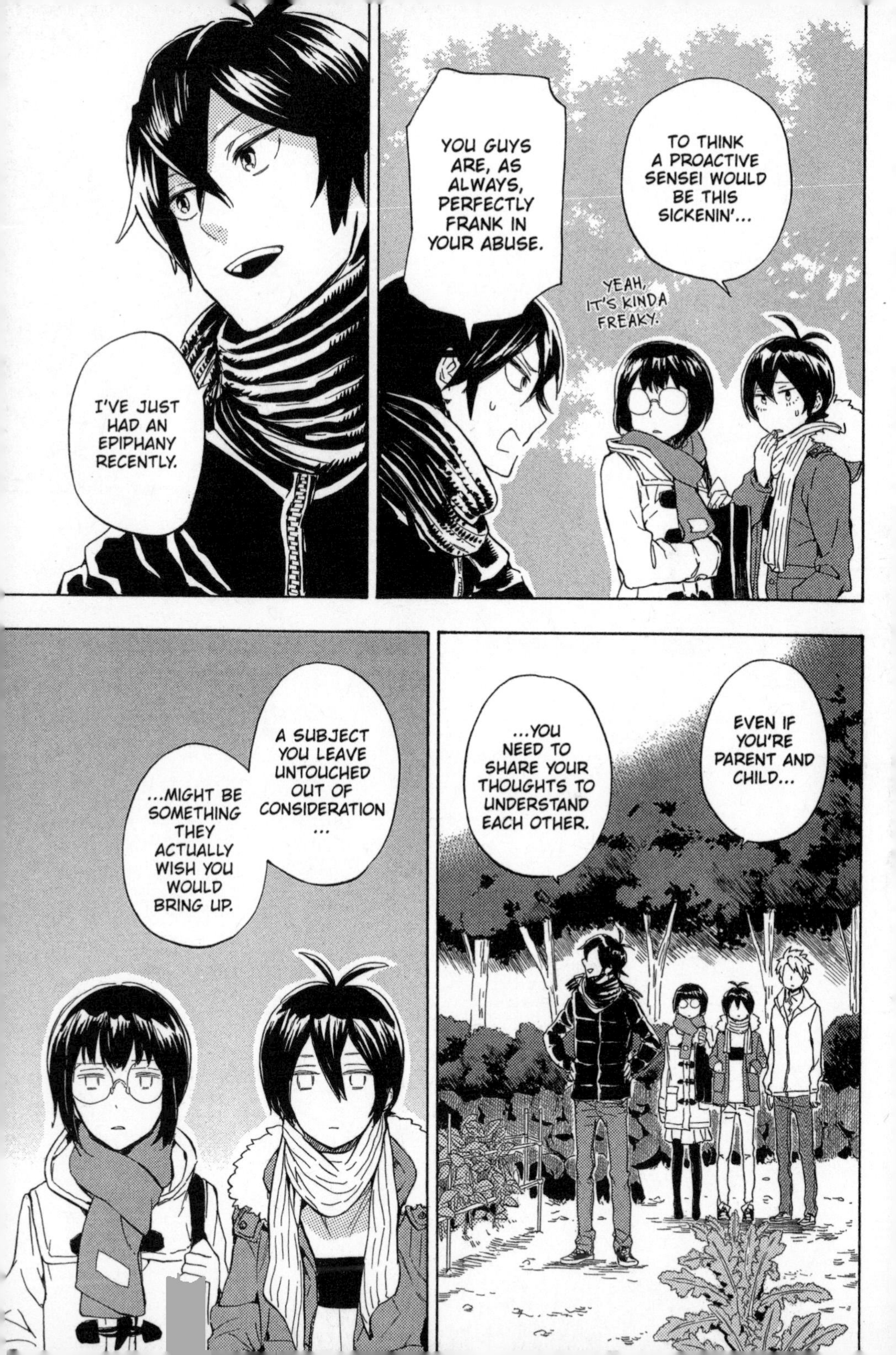
TO THINK A PROACTIVE SENSEI WOULD BE THIS SICKENIN'...
YEAH, IT'S KINDA FREAKY.
YOU GUYS ARE, AS ALWAYS, PERFECTLY FRANK IN YOUR ABUSE.
I'VE JUST HAD AN EPIPHANY RECENTLY.
EVEN IF YOU'RE PARENT AND CHILD...
...YOU NEED TO SHARE YOUR THOUGHTS TO UNDERSTAND EACH OTHER.
A SUBJECT YOU LEAVE UNTOUCHED OUT OF CONSIDERATION...
...MIGHT BE SOMETHING THEY ACTUALLY WISH YOU WOULD BRING UP.

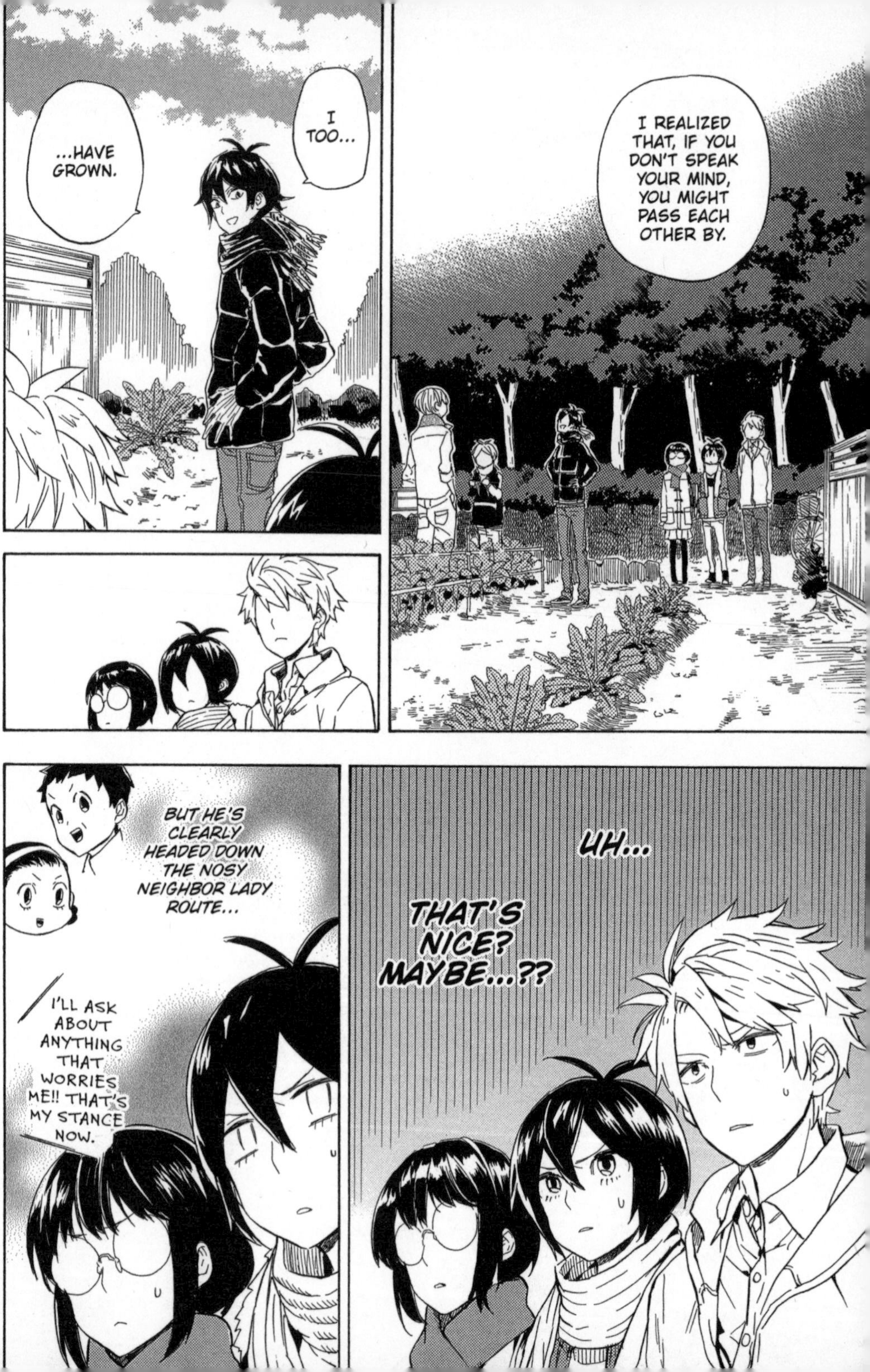
I REALIZED THAT, IF YOU DON'T SPEAK YOUR MIND, YOU MIGHT PASS EACH OTHER BY.
I TOO...
...HAVE GROWN.
UH...
THAT'S NICE? MAYBE...??
BUT HE'S CLEARLY HEADED DOWN THE NOSY NEIGHBOR LADY ROUTE...
I'LL ASK ABOUT ANYTHING THAT WORRIES ME!! THAT'S MY STANCE NOW.

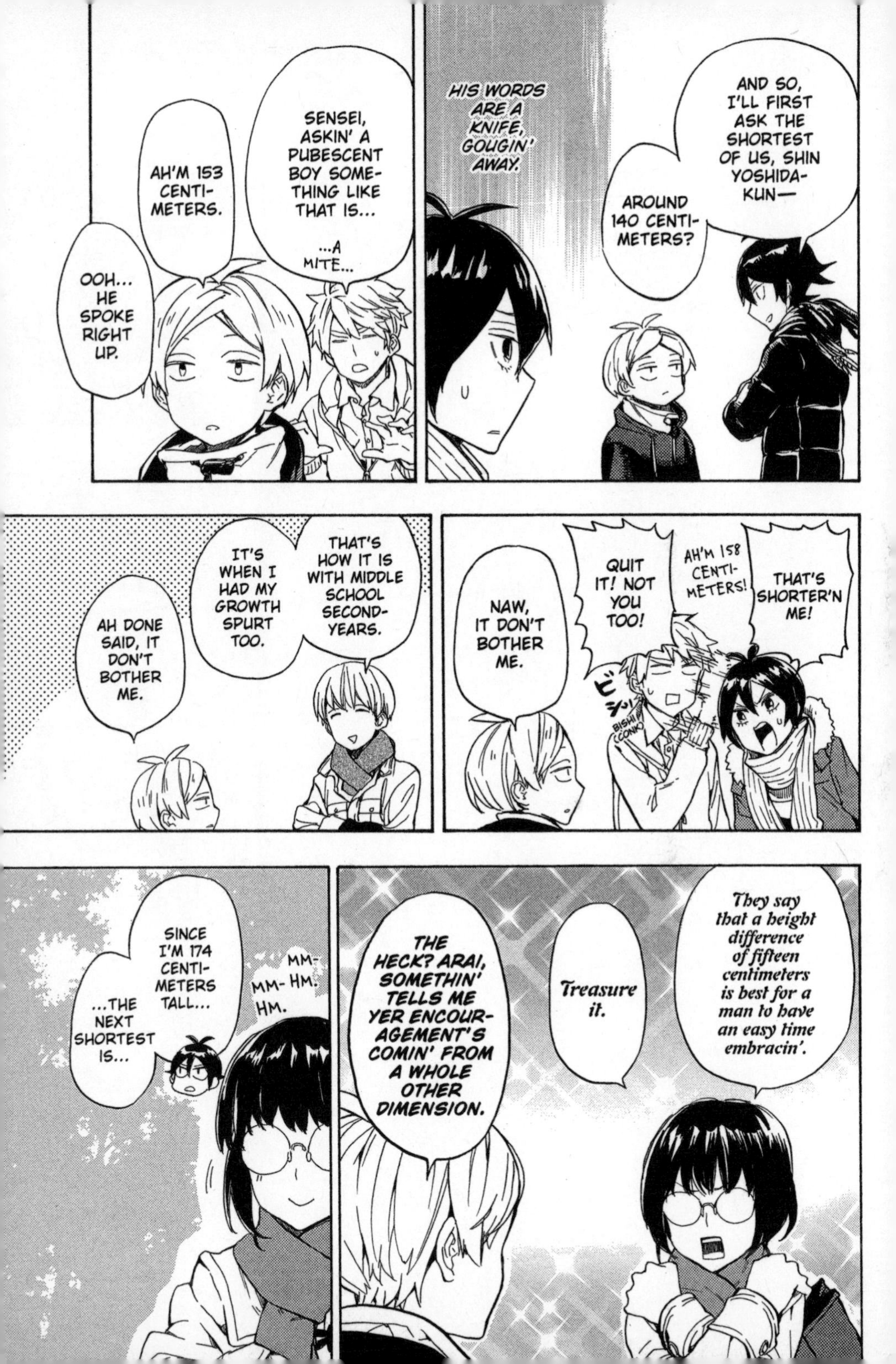
AND SO, I'LL FIRST ASK THE SHORTEST OF US, SHIN YOSHIDA-KUN—
AROUND 140 CENTIMETERS?
HIS WORDS ARE A KNIFE, GOUGIN' AWAY.
SENSEI, ASKIN' A PUBESCENT BOY SOMETHING LIKE THAT IS...
...A MITE...
AH'M 153 CENTIMETERS.
OOH... HE SPOKE RIGHT UP.
THAT'S SHORTER'N ME!
AH'M 158 CENTIMETERS!
QUIT IT! NOT YOU TOO!
BISHI (CONK)
NAW, IT DON'T BOTHER ME.
THAT'S HOW IT IS WITH MIDDLE SCHOOL SECOND-YEARS.
IT'S WHEN I HAD MY GROWTH SPURT TOO.
AH DONE SAID, IT DON'T BOTHER ME.
They say that a height difference of fifteen centimeters is best for a man to have an easy time embracin'.
Treasure it.
THE HECK? ARAI, SOMETHIN' TELLS ME YER ENCOURAGEMENT'S COMIN' FROM A WHOLE OTHER DIMENSION.
MM-HM. MM-HM.
SINCE I'M 174 CENTIMETERS TALL...
...THE NEXT SHORTEST IS...

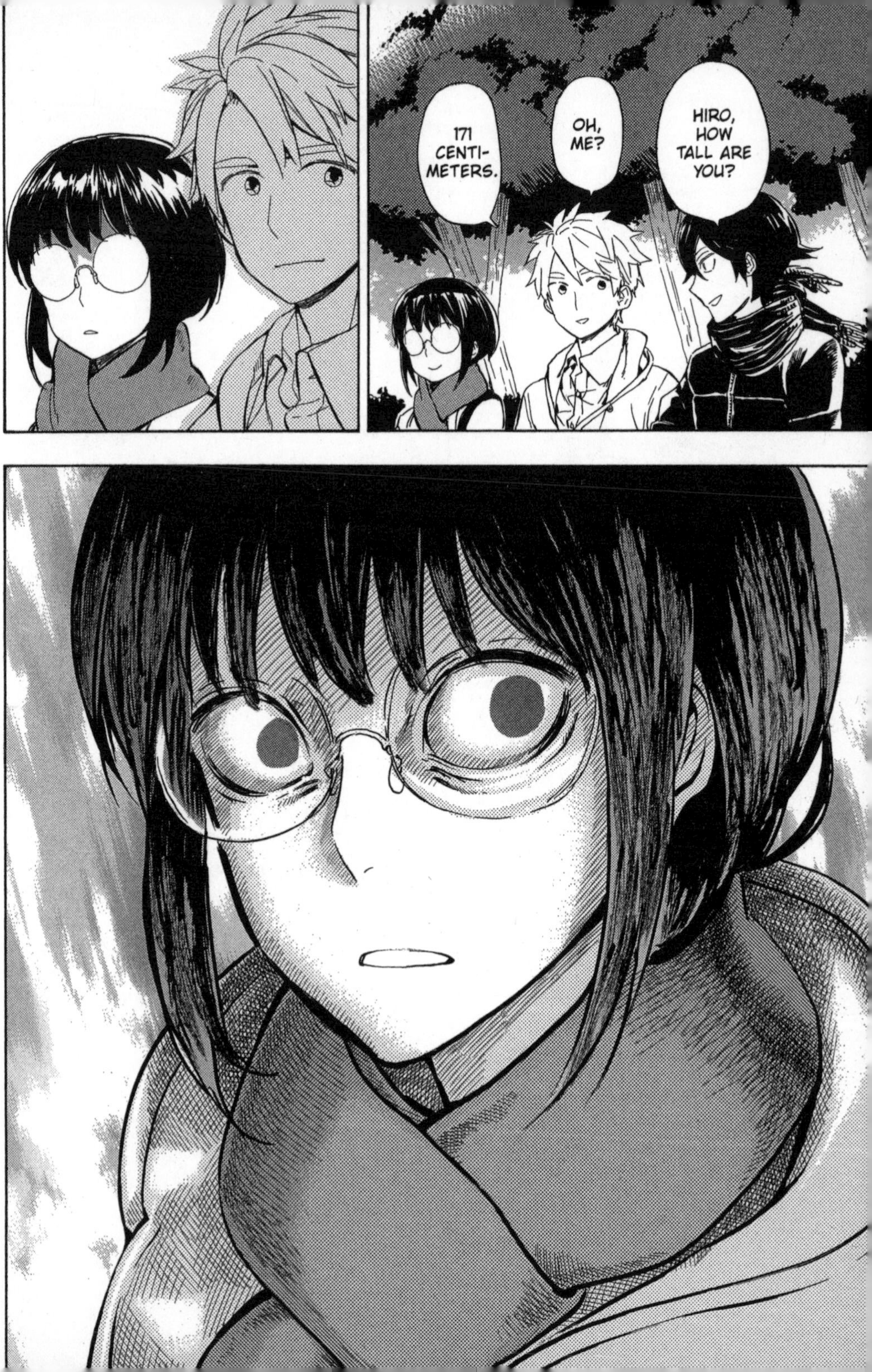
HIRO, HOW TALL ARE YOU?
OH, ME?
171 CENTI-METERS.

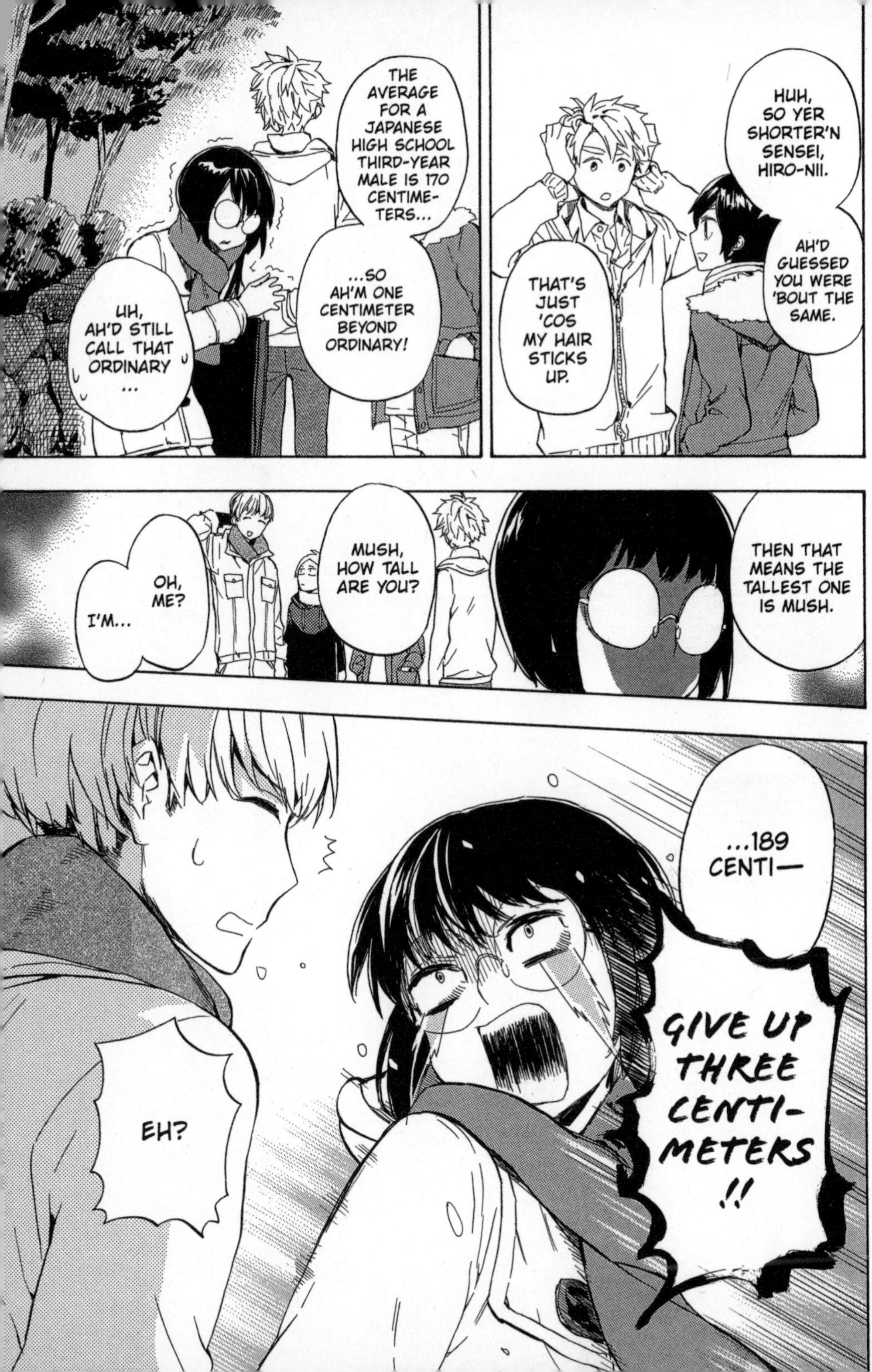
HUH, SO YER SHORTER'N SENSEI, HIRO-NII.
AH'D GUESSED YOU WERE 'BOUT THE SAME.
THAT'S JUST 'COS MY HAIR STICKS UP.
THE AVERAGE FOR A JAPANESE HIGH SCHOOL THIRD-YEAR MALE IS 170 CENTIMETERS...
...SO AH'M ONE CENTIMETER BEYOND ORDINARY!
UH, AH'D STILL CALL THAT ORDINARY ...
THEN THAT MEANS THE TALLEST ONE IS MUSH.
MUSH, HOW TALL ARE YOU?
OH, ME? I'M...
...189 CENTI—
GIVE UP THREE CENTIMETERS !!
EH?

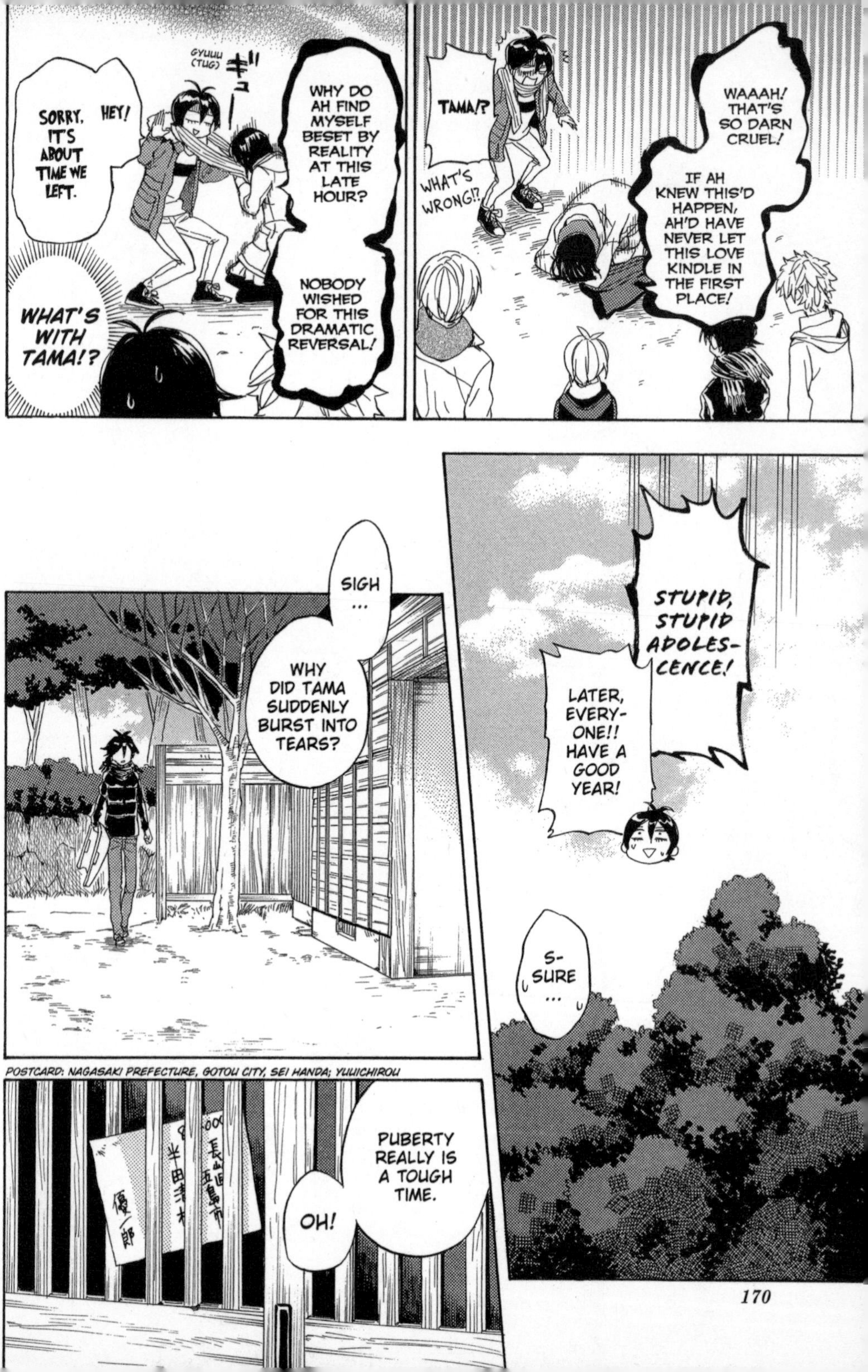
WAAAH! THAT'S SO DARN CRUEL!
IF AH KNEW THIS'D HAPPEN, AH'D HAVE NEVER LET THIS LOVE KINDLE IN THE FIRST PLACE!
TAMA!?
WHAT'S WRONG!?
GYUUU (TUG)
ギュー
WHY DO AH FIND MYSELF BESET BY REALITY AT THIS LATE HOUR?
NOBODY WISHED FOR THIS DRAMATIC REVERSAL!
HEY!
SORRY. IT'S ABOUT TIME WE LEFT.
WHAT'S WITH TAMA!?
STUPID, STUPID ADOLESCENCE!
LATER, EVERYONE!! HAVE A GOOD YEAR!
S-SURE...
SIGH...
WHY DID TAMA SUDDENLY BURST INTO TEARS?
POSTCARD: NAGASAKI PREFECTURE, GOTOU CITY, SEI HANDA; YUUICHIROU
PUBERTY REALLY IS A TOUGH TIME.
OH!

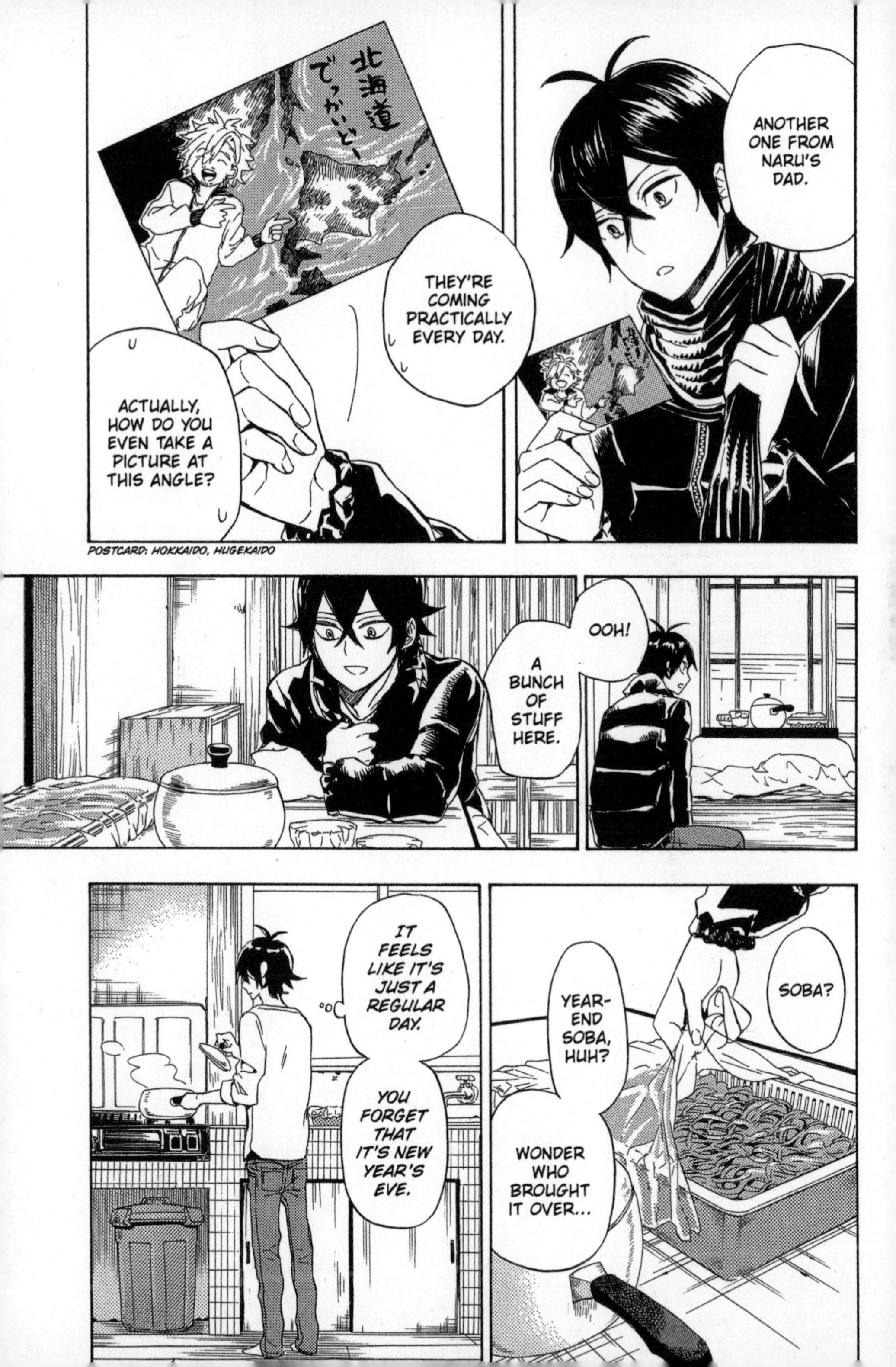
ANOTHER ONE FROM NARU'S DAD.
北海道でっかいどー
THEY'RE COMING PRACTICALLY EVERY DAY.
ACTUALLY, HOW DO YOU EVEN TAKE A PICTURE AT THIS ANGLE?
POSTCARD: HOKKAIDO, HUGEKAIDO
OOH!
A BUNCH OF STUFF HERE.
SOBA?
YEAR-END SOBA, HUH?
WONDER WHO BROUGHT IT OVER...
IT FEELS LIKE IT'S JUST A REGULAR DAY.
YOU FORGET THAT IT'S NEW YEAR'S EVE.

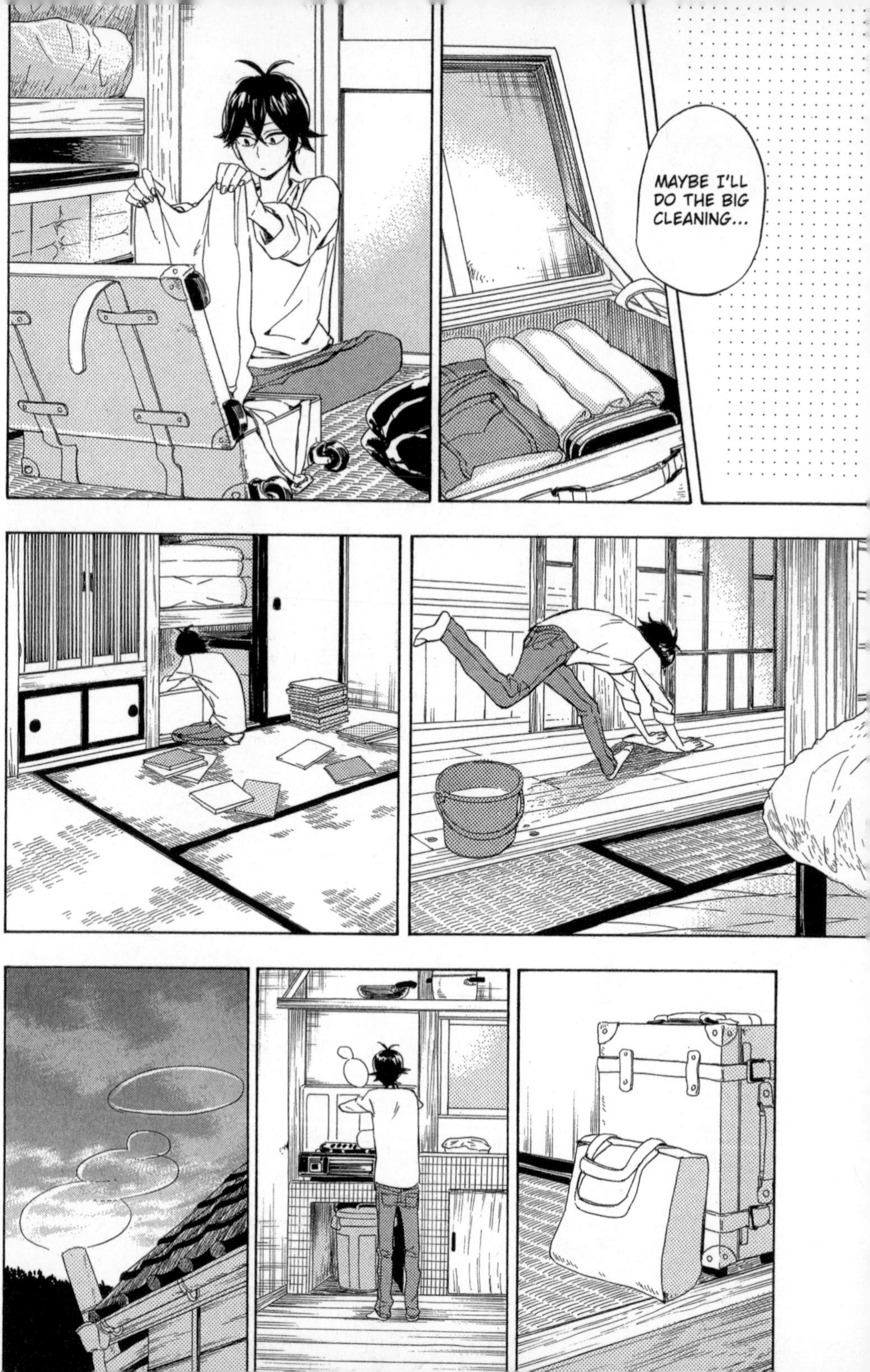
MAYBE I'LL DO THE BIG CLEANING...

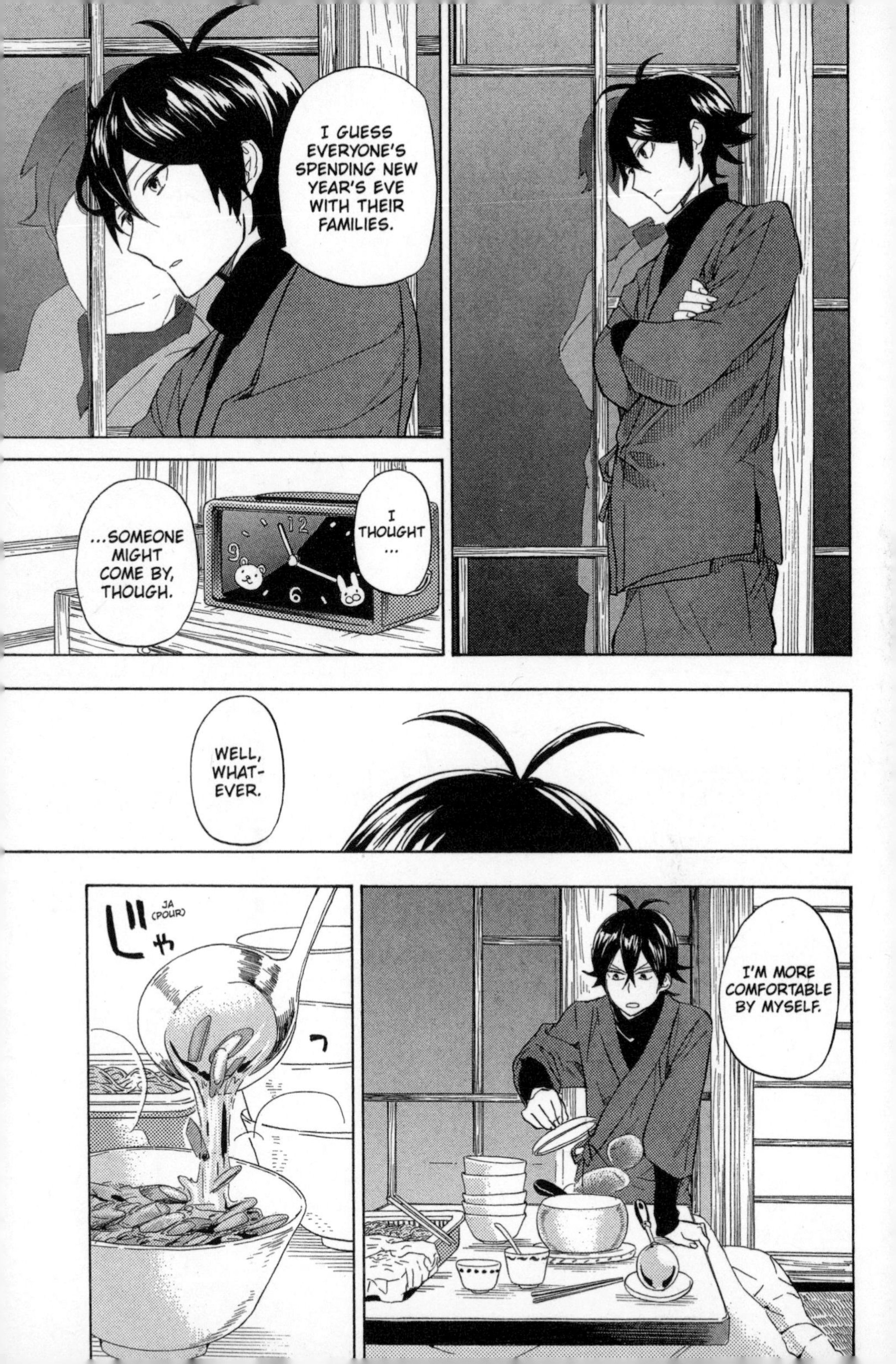
I GUESS EVERYONE'S SPENDING NEW YEAR'S EVE WITH THEIR FAMILIES.
I THOUGHT...
...SOMEONE MIGHT COME BY, THOUGH.
WELL, WHAT-EVER.
I'M MORE COMFORTABLE BY MYSELF.
じゃ
JA (POUR)
つ

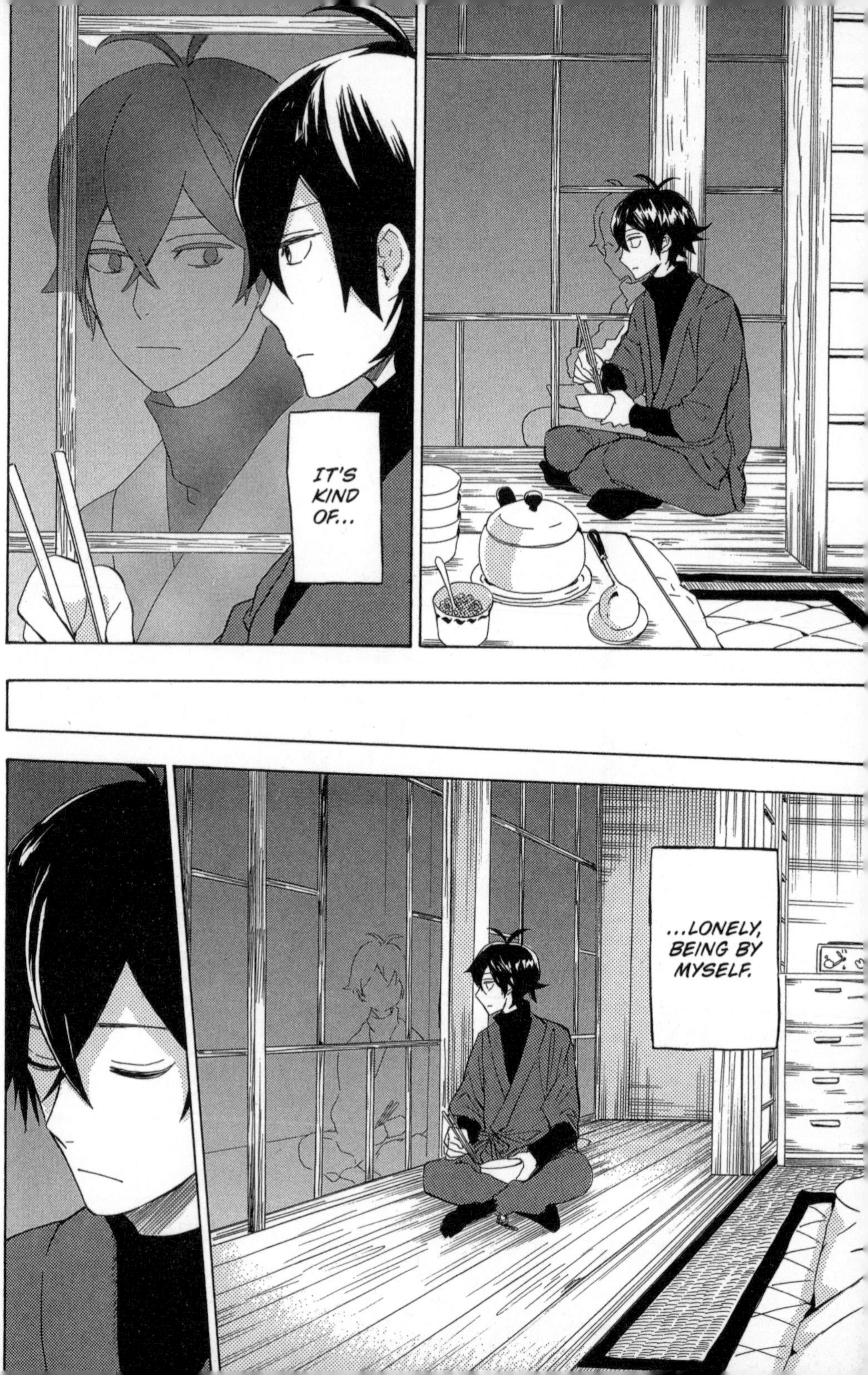
IT'S KIND OF...
...LONELY, BEING BY MYSELF.

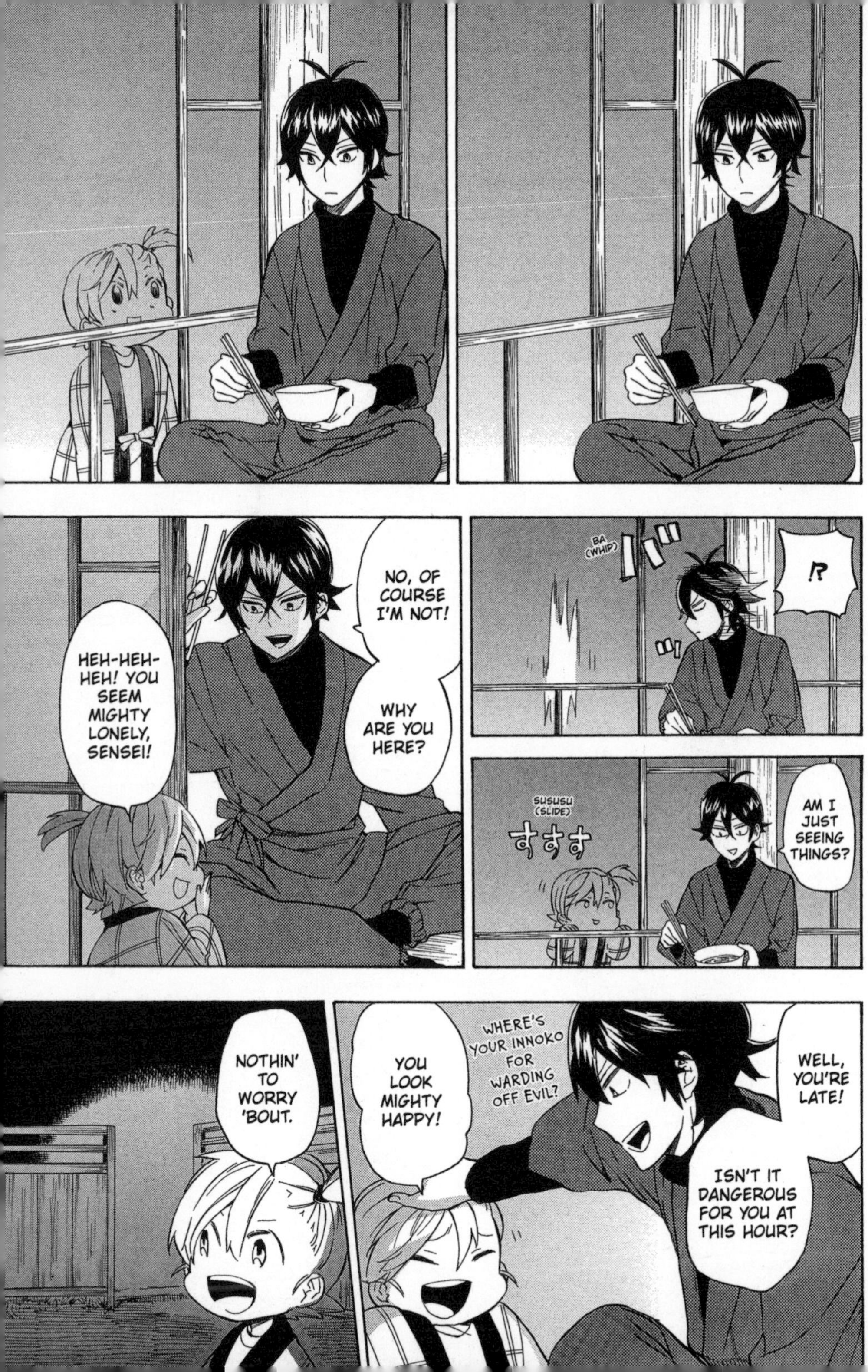
BA (WHIP)
!?
SUSUSU (SLIDE)
すすす
AM I JUST SEEING THINGS?
NO, OF COURSE I'M NOT!
WHY ARE YOU HERE?
HEH-HEH-HEH! YOU SEEM MIGHTY LONELY, SENSEI!
WELL, YOU'RE LATE!
WHERE'S YOUR INNOKO FOR WARDING OFF EVIL?
ISN'T IT DANGEROUS FOR YOU AT THIS HOUR?
YOU LOOK MIGHTY HAPPY!
NOTHIN' TO WORRY 'BOUT.

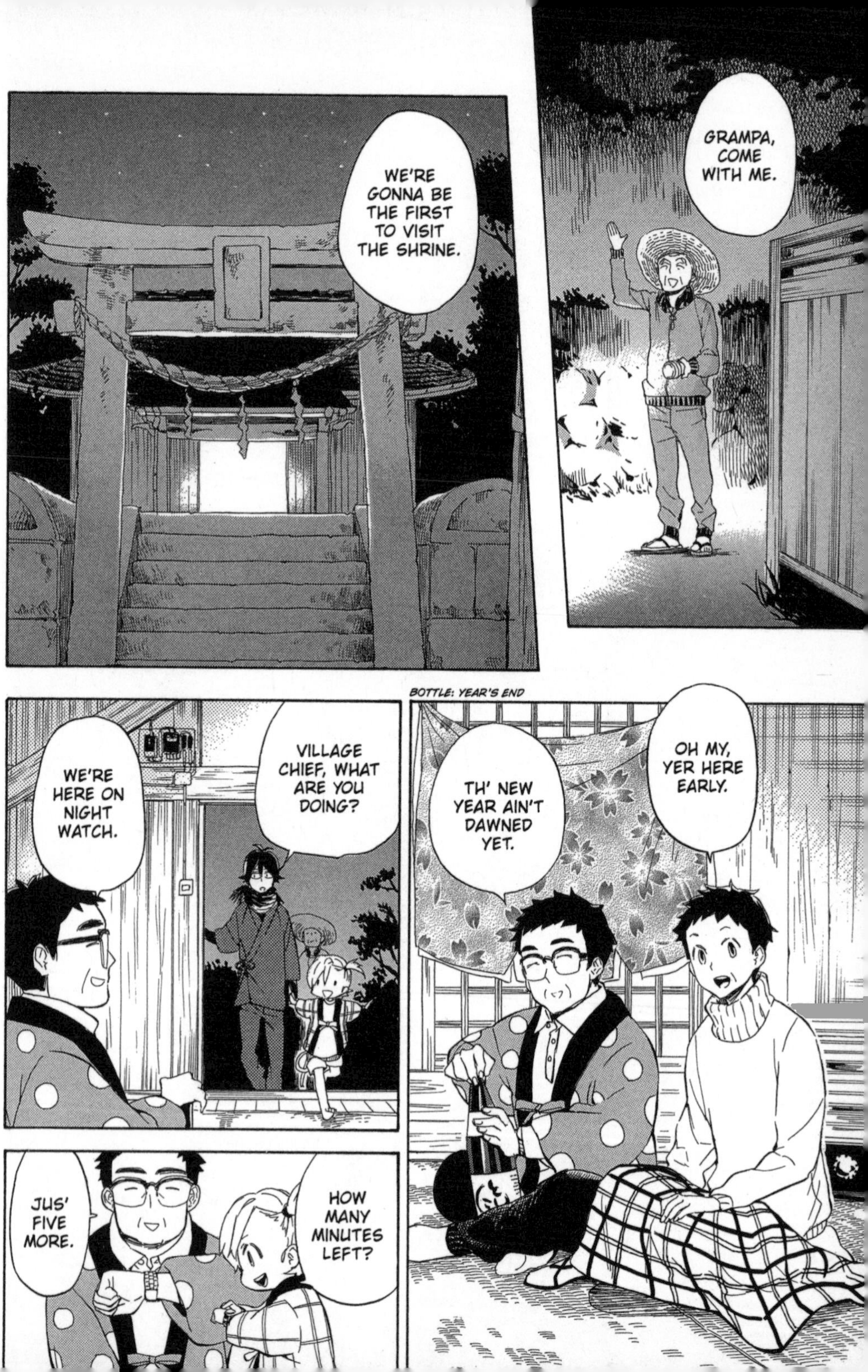
GRAMPA, COME WITH ME.
WE'RE GONNA BE THE FIRST TO VISIT THE SHRINE.
OH MY, YER HERE EARLY.
TH' NEW YEAR AIN'T DAWNED YET.
BOTTLE: YEAR'S END
VILLAGE CHIEF, WHAT ARE YOU DOING?
WE'RE HERE ON NIGHT WATCH.
HOW MANY MINUTES LEFT?
JUS' FIVE MORE.

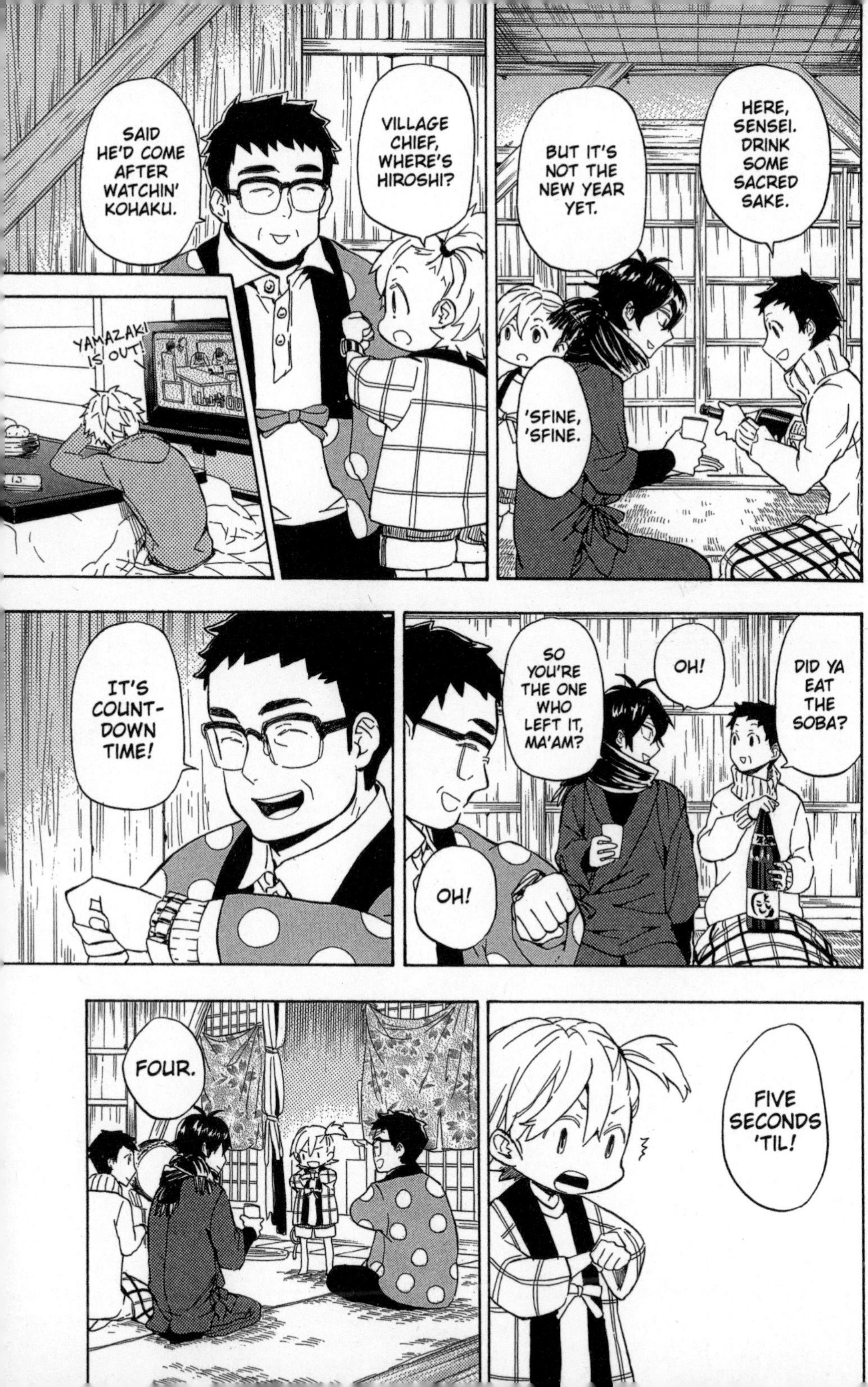
HERE, SENSEI. DRINK SOME SACRED SAKE.
BUT IT'S NOT THE NEW YEAR YET.
'SFINE, 'SFINE.
VILLAGE CHIEF, WHERE'S HIROSHI?
SAID HE'D COME AFTER WATCHIN' KOHAKU.
YAMAZAKI IS OUT!
DID YA EAT THE SOBA?
OH!
SO YOU'RE THE ONE WHO LEFT IT, MA'AM?
OH!
IT'S COUNT-DOWN TIME!
FIVE SECONDS 'TIL!
FOUR.

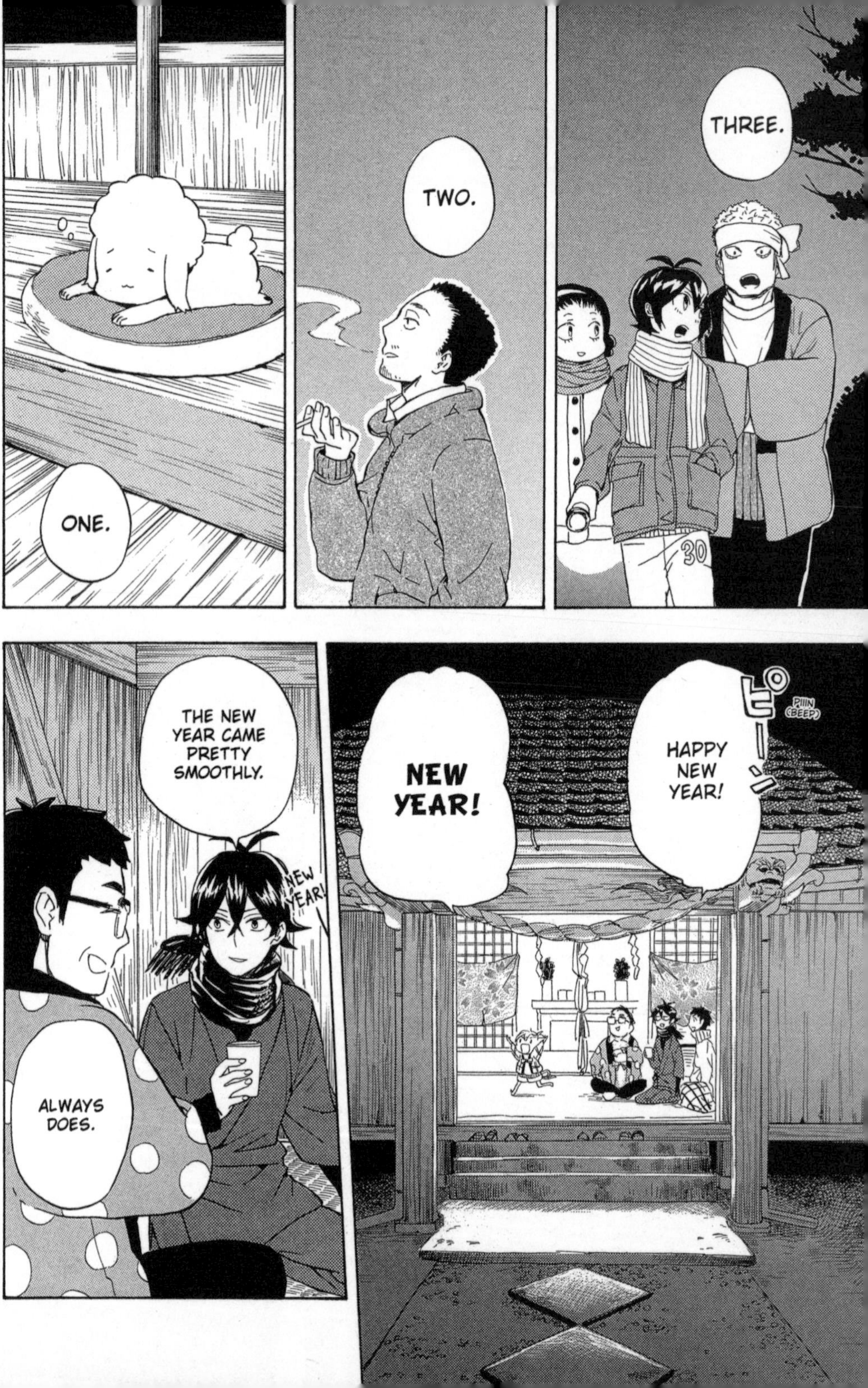
THREE.
TWO.
ONE.
PIIIN (BEEP)
HAPPY NEW YEAR!
NEW YEAR!
THE NEW YEAR CAME PRETTY SMOOTHLY.
NEW YEAR!
ALWAYS DOES.

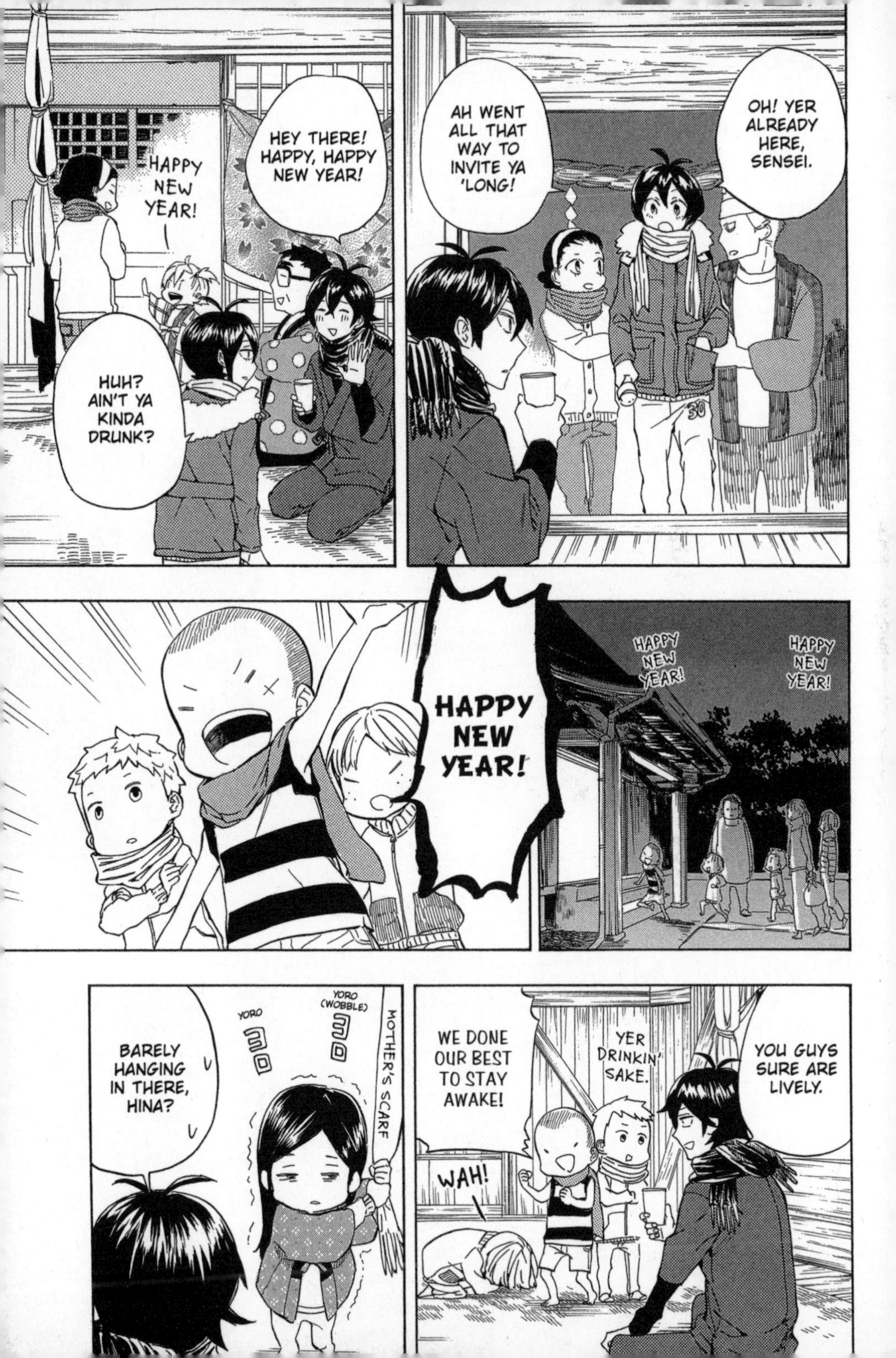
OH! YER ALREADY HERE, SENSEI.
AH WENT ALL THAT WAY TO INVITE YA 'LONG!
HEY THERE! HAPPY, HAPPY NEW YEAR!
HAPPY NEW YEAR!
HUH? AIN'T YA KINDA DRUNK?
HAPPY NEW YEAR!
HAPPY NEW YEAR!
HAPPY NEW YEAR!
YOU GUYS SURE ARE LIVELY.
YER DRINKIN' SAKE.
WE DONE OUR BEST TO STAY AWAKE!
WAH!
MOTHER'S SCARF
YORO (WOBBLE)
YORO
BARELY HANGING IN THERE, HINA?

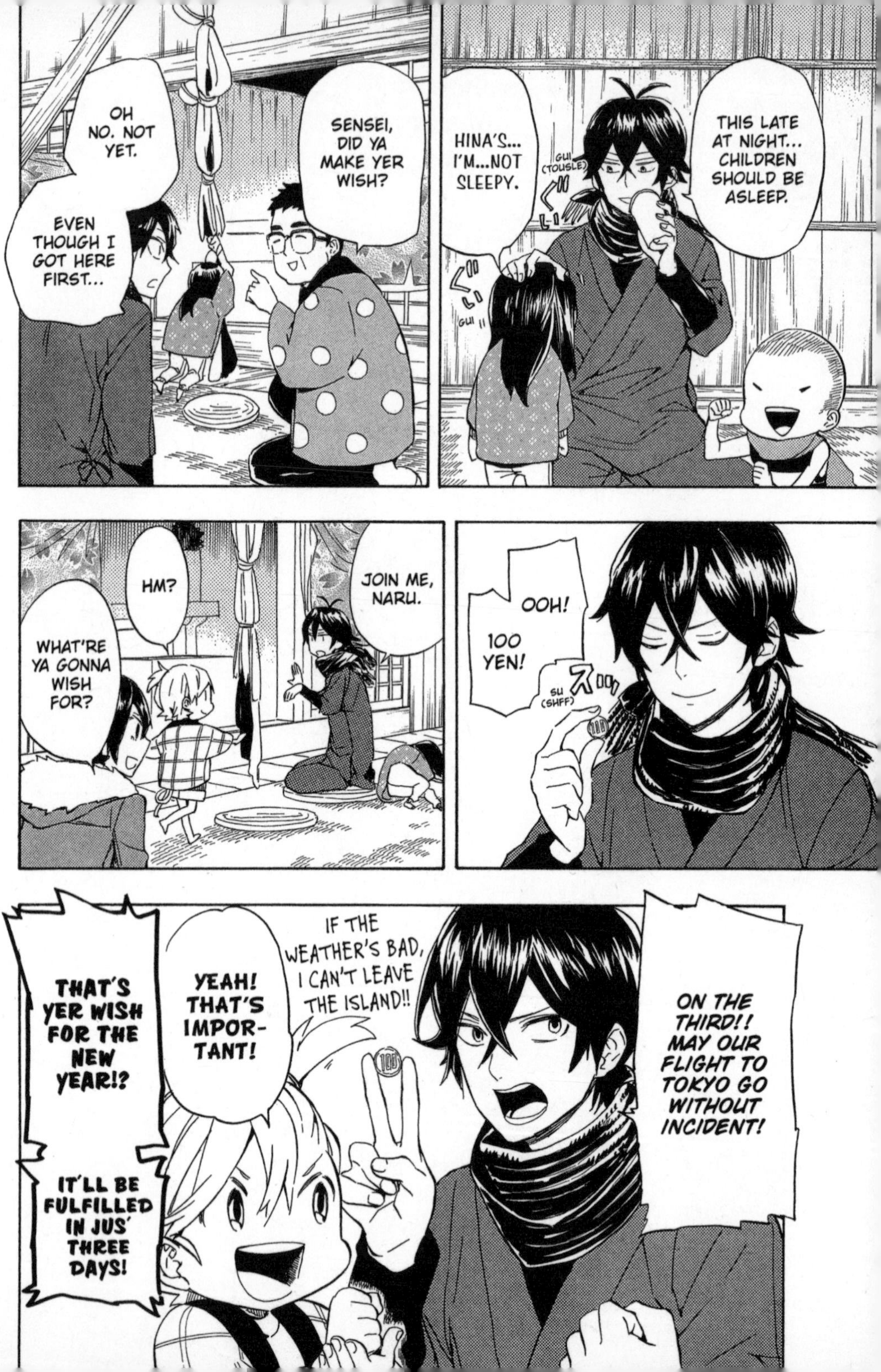
THIS LATE AT NIGHT... CHILDREN SHOULD BE ASLEEP.
GUI (TOUSLE)
GUI
HINA'S... I'M...NOT SLEEPY.
SENSEI, DID YA MAKE YER WISH?
OH NO. NOT YET.
EVEN THOUGH I GOT HERE FIRST...
OOH! 100 YEN!
SU (SHFF)
JOIN ME, NARU.
HM?
WHAT'RE YA GONNA WISH FOR?
ON THE THIRD!! MAY OUR FLIGHT TO TOKYO GO WITHOUT INCIDENT!
IF THE WEATHER'S BAD, I CAN'T LEAVE THE ISLAND!!
YEAH! THAT'S IMPOR-TANT!
THAT'S YER WISH FOR THE NEW YEAR!?
IT'LL BE FULFILLED IN JUS' THREE DAYS!

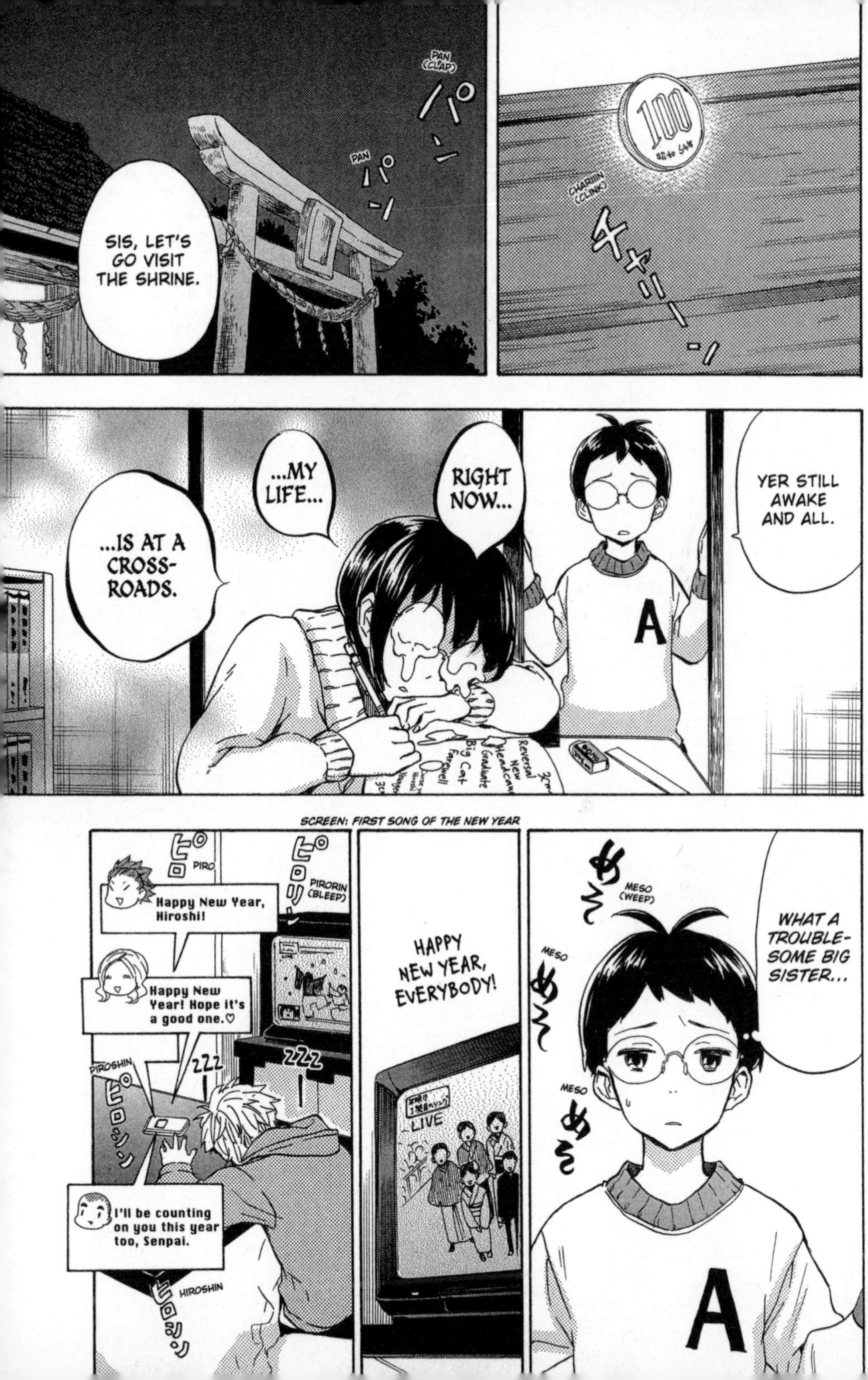
100
CHARIIN (CLINK)
PAN (CLAP)
PAN
SIS, LET'S GO VISIT THE SHRINE.
YER STILL AWAKE AND ALL.
RIGHT NOW...
...MY LIFE...
...IS AT A CROSS-ROADS.
SCREEN: FIRST SONG OF THE NEW YEAR
WHAT A TROUBLE-SOME BIG SISTER...
MESO (WEEP)
MESO
MESO
HAPPY NEW YEAR, EVERYBODY!
LIVE
PIRORIN (BLEEP)
PIRO
Happy New Year, Hiroshi!
Happy New Year! Hope it's a good one.♡
PIROSHIN
ZZZ
ZZZ
I'll be counting on you this year too, Senpai.
HIROSHIN

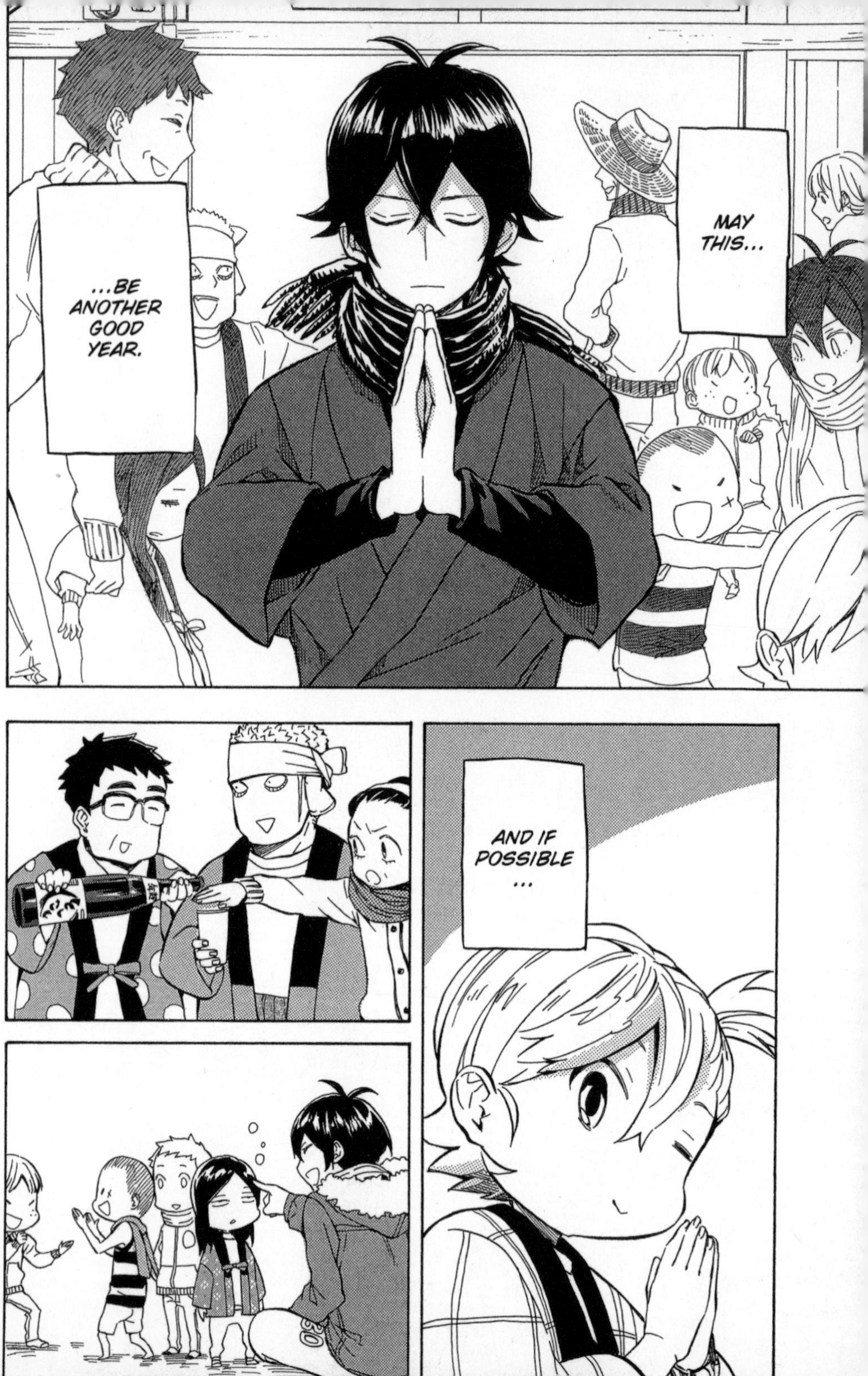
MAY THIS...
...BE ANOTHER GOOD YEAR.
AND IF POSSIBLE ...

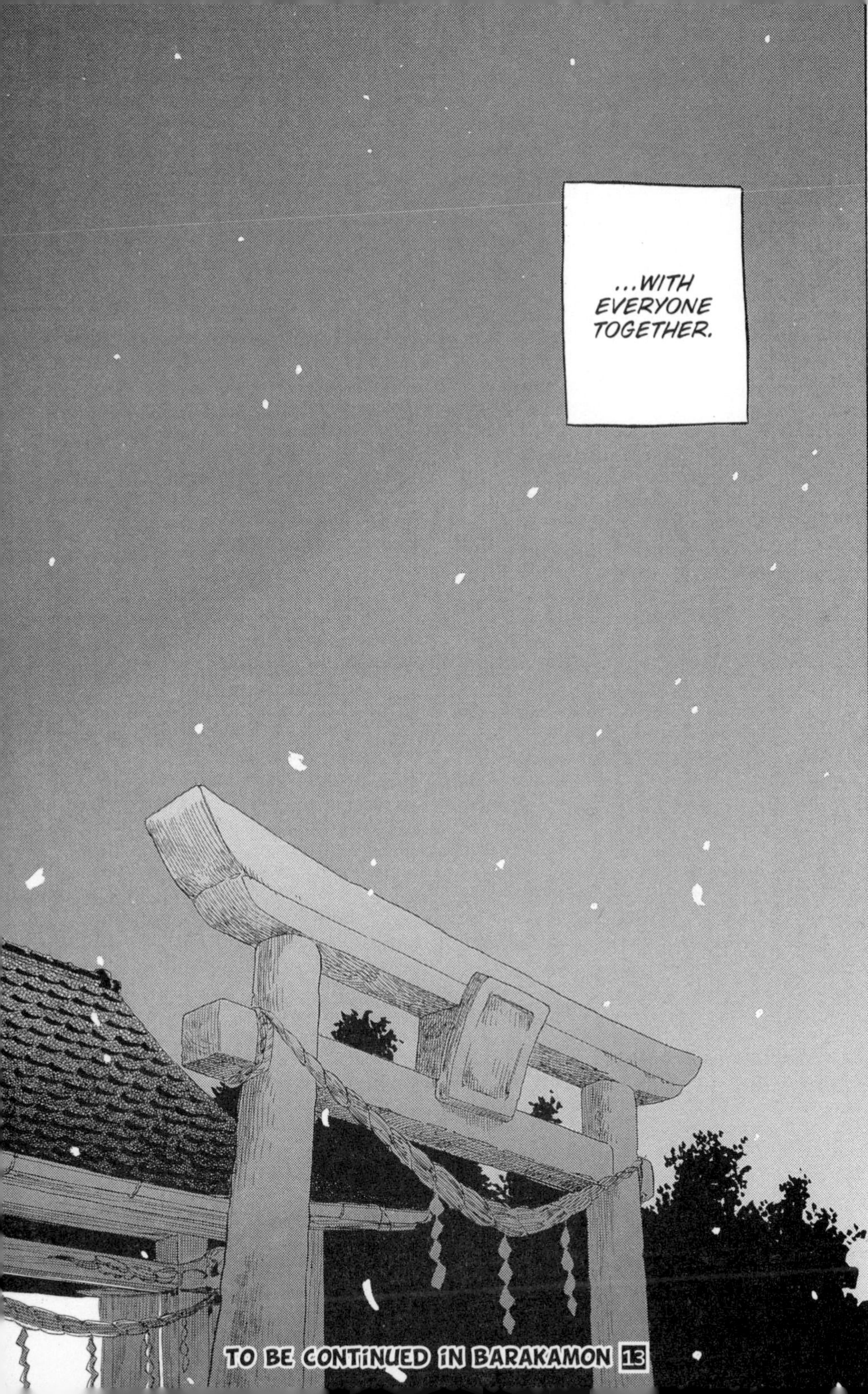
...WITH
EVERYONE
TOGETHER.
TO BE CONTINUED IN BARAKAMON 13

BONUS: DANPO THE 12TH

(Translation: Pond)

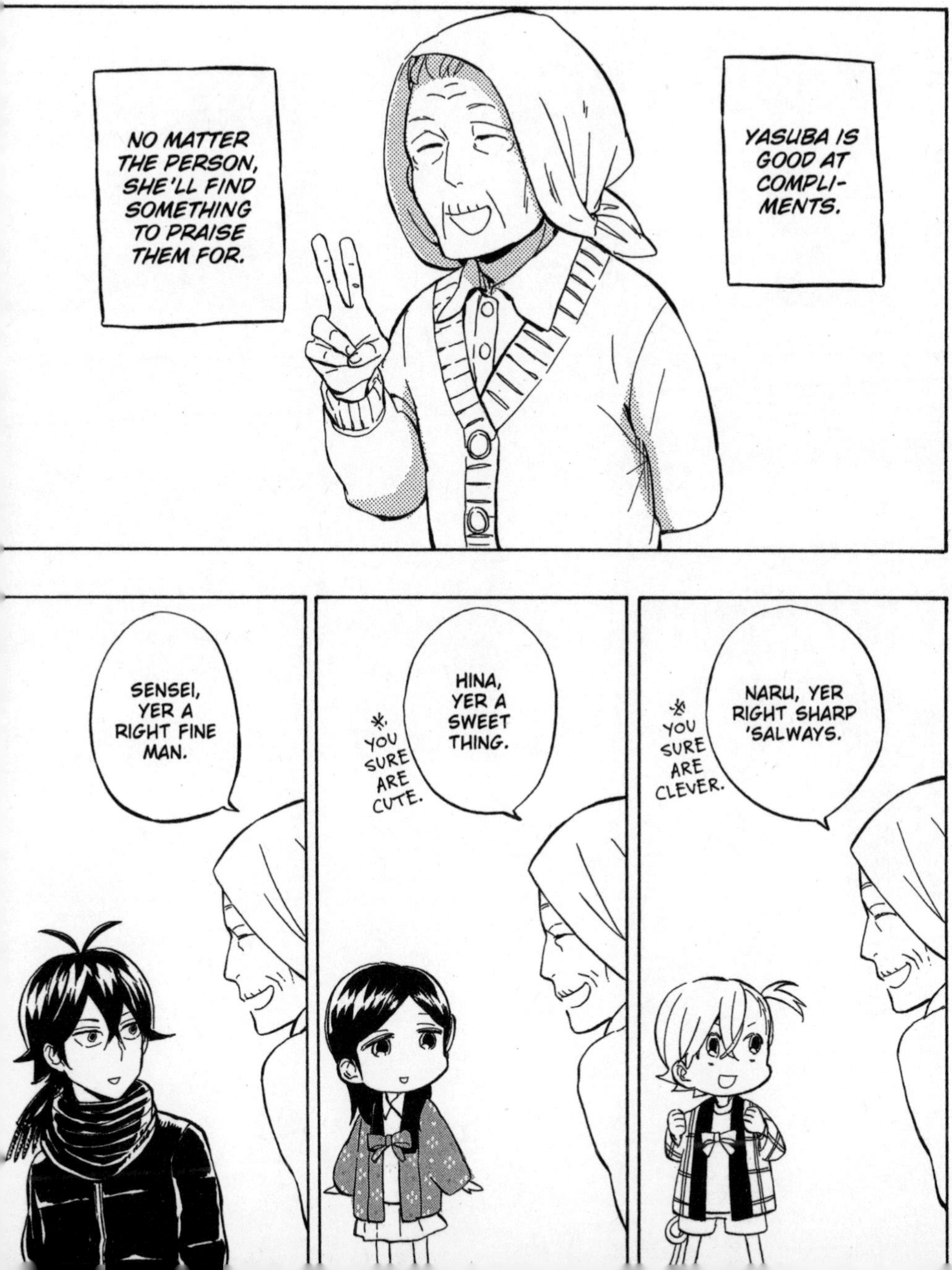

YASUBA IS GOOD AT COMPLI-MENTS.
NO MATTER THE PERSON, SHE'LL FIND SOMETHING TO PRAISE THEM FOR.
NARU, YER RIGHT SHARP 'SALWAYS.
*YOU SURE ARE CLEVER.
HINA, YER A SWEET THING.
*YOU SURE ARE CUTE.
SENSEI, YER A RIGHT FINE MAN.

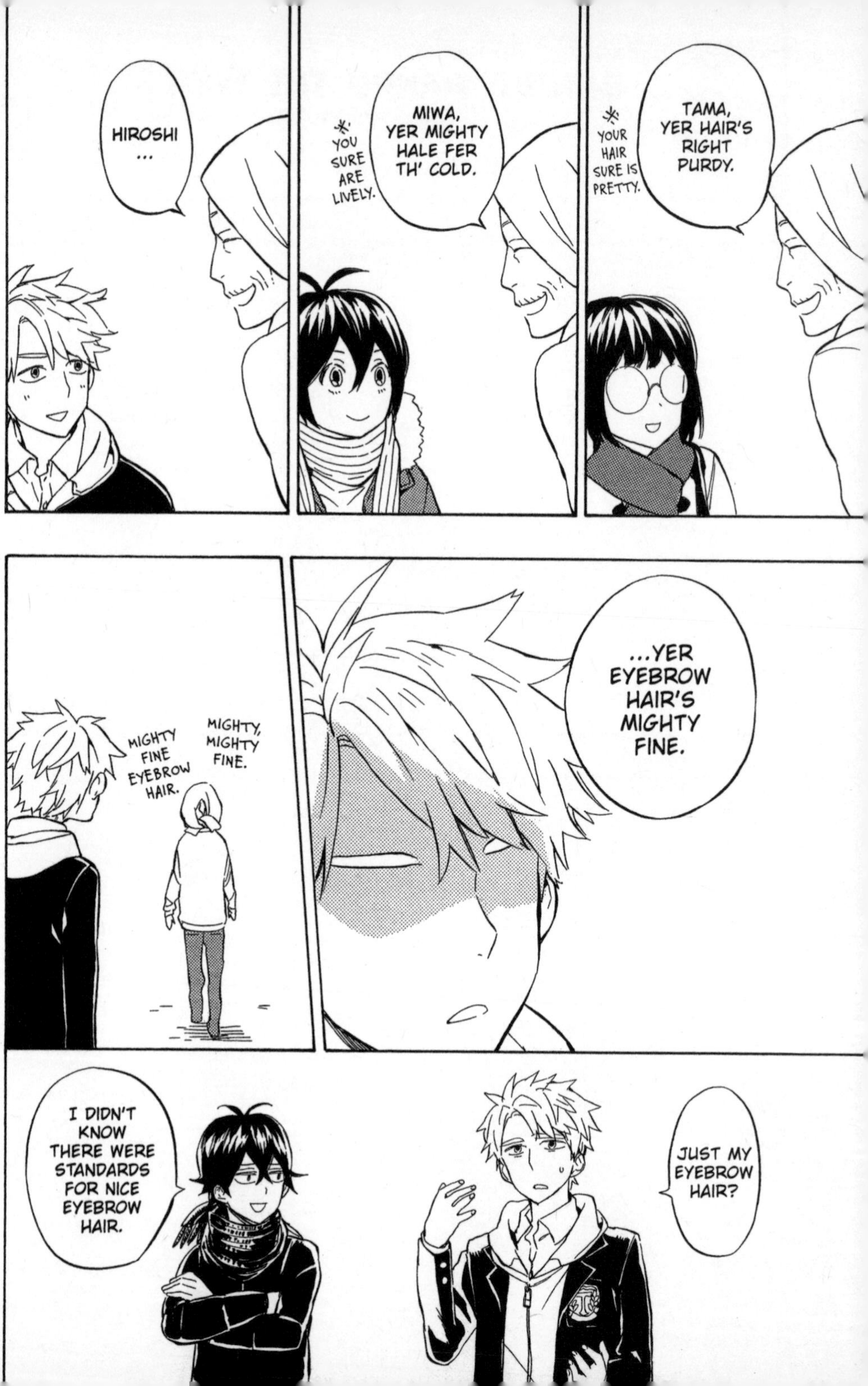
TAMA, YER HAIR'S RIGHT PURDY.
*YOUR HAIR SURE IS PRETTY.
MIWA, YER MIGHTY HALE FER TH' COLD.
*YOU SURE ARE LIVELY.
HIROSHI ...
...YER EYEBROW HAIR'S MIGHTY FINE.
MIGHTY, MIGHTY FINE.
MIGHTY FINE EYEBROW HAIR.
JUST MY EYEBROW HAIR?
I DIDN'T KNOW THERE WERE STANDARDS FOR NICE EYEBROW HAIR.

BONUS: DANPO THE 12TH #2

(Translation: Pond)

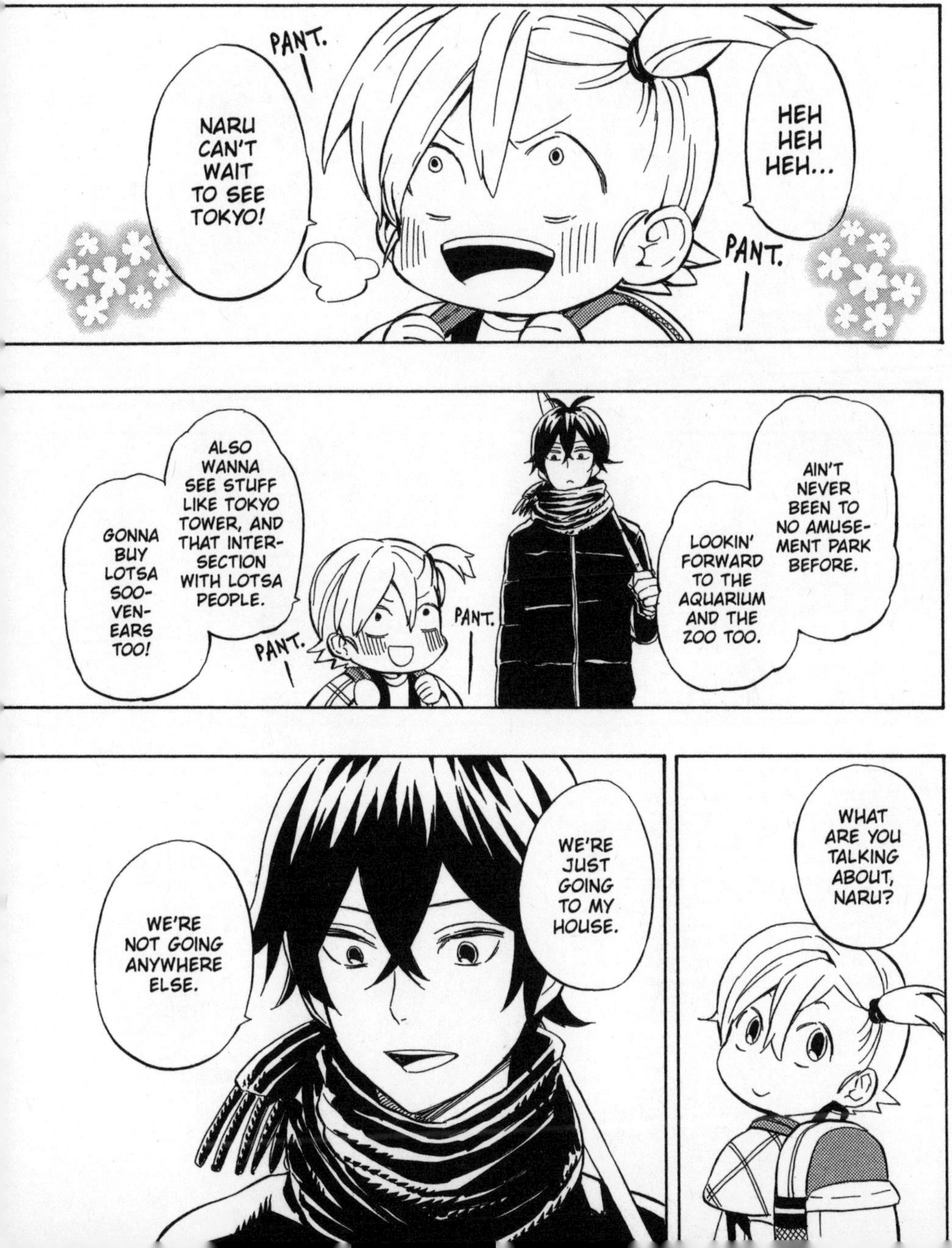
HEH HEH HEH...
PANT.
PANT.
NARU CAN'T WAIT TO SEE TOKYO!
AIN'T NEVER BEEN TO NO AMUSEMENT PARK BEFORE.
LOOKIN' FORWARD TO THE AQUARIUM AND THE ZOO TOO.
PANT.
ALSO WANNA SEE STUFF LIKE TOKYO TOWER, AND THAT INTERSECTION WITH LOTSA PEOPLE.
PANT.
GONNA BUY LOTSA SOOVENEARS TOO!
WHAT ARE YOU TALKING ABOUT, NARU?
WE'RE JUST GOING TO MY HOUSE.
WE'RE NOT GOING ANYWHERE ELSE.

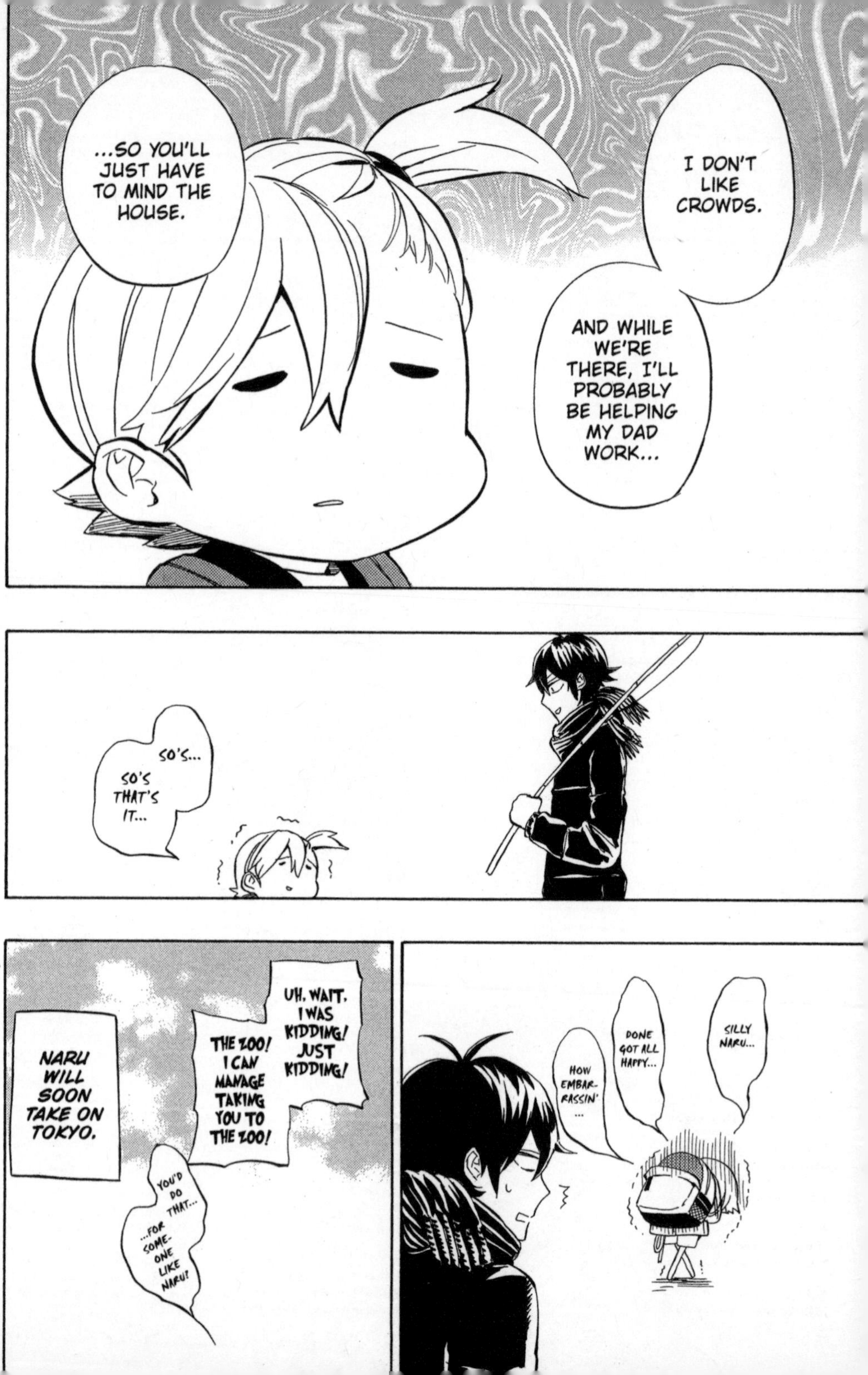
I DON'T LIKE CROWDS.
AND WHILE WE'RE THERE, I'LL PROBABLY BE HELPING MY DAD WORK...
...SO YOU'LL JUST HAVE TO MIND THE HOUSE.
SO'S... SO'S THAT'S IT...
SILLY NARU...
DONE GOT ALL HAPPY...
HOW EMBARRASSIN'...
UH, WAIT, I WAS KIDDING! JUST KIDDING!
THE ZOO! I CAN MANAGE TAKING YOU TO THE ZOO!
NARU WILL SOON TAKE ON TOKYO.
YOU'D DO THAT... ...FOR SOME-ONE LIKE NARU?

TRANSLATION NOTES ·····································

ACT.88

"I" and "me": The focus of this chapter is the first graders using first-person pronouns, instead of calling themselves just by their own names. Japanese has a variety of first-person pronouns, depending mainly on politeness level and gender. What Headmaster writes on the board on page 5 is "*boku*" and "*watashi*"; both are polite ways to say "I," but "boku" is for males while "watashi" is relatively neutral. On page 12, Hina tells Sensei that he should use "boku" instead of the rougher male first-person pronoun "*o-re*."

PAGE 9

kotatsu: A low table with a heating unit underneath it and a curtain around the sides to hold in the heat.

PAGE 15

Hina tricks Sensei: In Japanese, Hina says, "Before all that, I really want to drink *a-re* (that)," then with Sensei primed by the word, she says "café…" and he finishes it with "*o-re* (au lait)"—she got you good, Sensei!

PAGE 28

"As always, we meet at last.": What Miwa said in Japanese was literally, "It's the hundredth year we meet here!" "*Hyakunenme*," which means "hundredth year," is part of the punch line of a *rakugo* traditional story joke that has come to be used as a common phrase meaning "unavoidable fate."

PAGE 32

OTP: A fandom term that stands for "one true pairing," i.e., two characters (or people) that you fervently imagine as having an intimate relationship when they don't.

PAGE 41

fujoshi: You may remember from Volume 2 that a *fujoshi*, or "rotten girl," is a woman who prefers novels and manga that depict male-male romances.

BL: Stands for Boys' Love, a genre of novels, manga, and anime focused on the male-male romances that fujoshi like.

PAGE 46

onisaba sushi: Sushi made using mackerel caught in a particular area of the sea outside Gotou, named after the mountain Onidake found on Fukue Island (the same as the airport).

mijoka: Small Castella wheat cake with a fruit paste filling, a Gotou specialty.

hacchi kankan: Another Gotou specialty, rice cake sprinkled with soy flour, sold in three pieces on a skewer; the name means "Eight Lightning Beasts."

Christmas in Japan: Since less than 1% of the population is Christian, Christmas is a decidedly secular holiday in Japan. Some young children may get presents from Santa Claus, but otherwise, Christmas Eve is more for romantic dates for couples. New Year's Eve is the more important family and religious holiday.

PAGE 59

Funny Faces Game: Fukuwarai is a game commonly played on New Year's Day in Japan, where a blindfolded person puts eyes, nose, mouth, etc., on a face, similar to "Pin the Tail on the Donkey."

PAGE 62

"This ain't for ghost stories.": Naru originally said "That's Junji Inagawa." He's a Japanese radio and TV performer especially known for his radio broadcasts of scary ghost stories. Telling ghost stories is another thing Japanese traditionally do only by candlelight.

"You're doing it wrong too.": Naru's clapping is actually part of the procedure for making wishes at a Shinto shrine.

PAGE 84

UFO: A brand of instant noodles sold in a wide bowl vaguely resembling a flying saucer in shape, with sauce and seasonings to make it taste like *yakisoba* (a stir-fried noodle dish).

PAGE 86

pinkie finger out: Sticking out a pinkie finger and saying "*kore* (this)" is an indirect way for a guy to refer to his girlfriend. Yuuichirou is uncertain about the symbol here, wondering if the index finger should stick out as well.

PAGE 93

"String bean-kun": The Japanese word Yuuichirou used, "*noppo*," means a tall and lanky person, which describes Naru's taller, nameless classmate.

PAGE 131

TOBE: The word on the side of the airplanes means "Fly!"

PAGE 134

teethin' fever: "*Chie-netsu*," the word for "teething fever," literally means "wisdom fever," from the fact that kids get fevers readily around the age when they gain the wisdom to remember things more permanently. The main point is that it's not an actual sickness.

New Year's card: Postcards that practically everyone in Japan sends to let rarely-seen friends and family know how they're doing, much like Christmas cards in the West. They're timed to be delivered right on New Year's Day, making it a heavy work day for the postal service.

PAGE 138

mud:drop ratio: "*Dororitsu*" is a social gaming term for the proportion of rare item or card drops during play; it's likely a pun on "*doro*," short for "*doroppu* (drop)," and "*doro*," the Japanese word for "mud."

PAGE 142

Mangan: Parody name version of *Gangan*, the manga magazine that publishes *Barakamon*.

PAGE 143

Milkcook: The actual ice cream bar brand name is Milcook.

PAGE 144

snow hut: The Japanese word Naru used was "*kamakura*," a type of round igloo-like snow building that's built during snow festivals in parts of northern Japan.

PAGE 146

driving school: Eighteen is the youngest you can get a driver's license in Japan.

PAGE 149

Gorilla March: Parody of Koala March, round, chocolate-filled cookies made to look like koalas engaged in all sorts of activities.

PAGE 150

"Sensei's takin' me to visit his parents.": "*Satogaeri*," the term Naru used, means "returning home" or "visiting parents" but can also refer to a new bride's first visit to her husband's parents.

PAGE 157

given enemy succor: The Japanese phrase Handa used literally means "Send salt to your enemy," a reference to a time during the Warring States period when Kenshin Uesugi sent salt to his longtime rival, Shingen Takeda, whose domain was suffering from lack of salt under an embargo.

PAGE 167-170

centimeter heights: Japan uses the metric system, like most of the world aside from the US. Summary of conversions: 140 cm = 4 ft. 7 in., (Shin) 153 cm = 5 ft., (Miwa) 158 cm = 5 ft. 2 in., 15 cm = 6 in., (Handa) 174 cm = 5 ft. 8.5 in., (Hiroshi) 171 cm = 5 ft. 7 in., 170 cm = 5 ft. 6 in., (Higashino) 189 cm = 6 ft. 2 in., 3 cm = 1 in.

Why is Tama so upset?: Remember, she'd been pairing Hiro and Handa in her mind, with Hiro as the more dominant partner. Now she's found out that the dominant one is actually 3 cm shorter. This requires a complete reevaluation of her pairing scheme! (Just imagine how horrified she'll be once it sinks in that Higashino is exactly 15 cm taller than Handa…)

PAGE 171

Hokkaido Hugekaido: The Japanese pun was *Hokkaido Dekkaido*, from the adjective "*dekai* (huge)."

year-end soba: Soba (buckwheat noodles) are a traditional food to eat on New Year's Eve in Japan.

PAGE 172

big cleaning: *Oosouji* is the major household cleanup done on the final day(s) of the year, a tradition adopted from China.

PAGE 176

shrine visit: One important New Year's Day tradition in Japan is *hatsumode*, paying a visit to a shrine for the first time that year to make an offering and prayer for the New Year.

PAGE 177

Kohaku: One modern Japanese New Year's Eve tradition is watching the Kohaku (Red-White) Song Competition on TV. A variety of singers from different generations sing against each other as two teams, the Red Team and the White Team.

BARAKAMON NEWS

Vol.510

BARAKAMON & *Handa-kun* Deluxe
Acrylic Key-Holder Sets
Send-Away Request Forms Available!!

Choose from two different sets of 4
Specially drawn by Yoshino-sensei!!

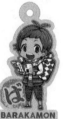

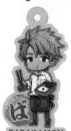

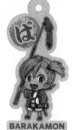

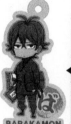

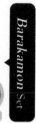

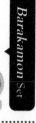

Barakamon Set

ば
BARAKAMON
ば
BARAKAMON
ば
BARAKAMON
ば
BARAKAMON

Handa-kun Set

は
HANDAKUN
は
HANDAKUN
は
HANDAKUN
は
HANDAKUN

Please note that the items on this page were only available in Japan.

Monthly Shonen Gangan October Issue Now on Sale to Popular Acclaim!!

少年
GANGAN
10

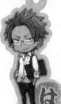

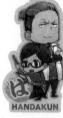

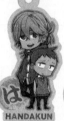

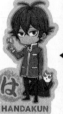

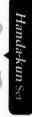

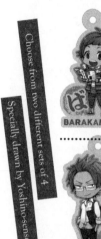

Read about what happens after this volume!!

Two Big Pack-ins

Swap the generations from dads to kids!! A **Book Cover** you can overlay on this volume!!

ばらかもん
12
ヨシノサツキ

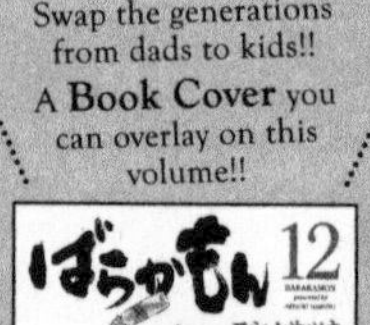

Studying is Fun with Naru!? *Barakamon* Decor **Study Notebook!!**

ばらかもん学習帳
じゆうちょう

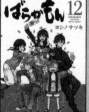

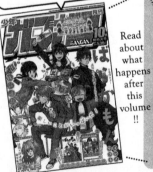

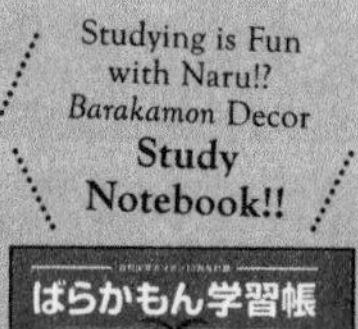

Barakamon Study Notebook, Unlined Pages

The October issue of *Monthly Shonen Gangan*, which goes on sale the same day as this volume, features a *BARAKAMON* cover and opening color pages, double pack-ins and send-away request forms, for a surging wave of *BARAKAMON* variety!! Also of interest is the magazine itself, where you can read about what happens after this volume!! Please be sure to pick up the Oct. issue of *Monthly Shonen Gangan*!

N 12

atsuki Yoshino

WITHDRAWN

Translation/Adaptation: Krista Shipley, Karie Shipley
Lettering: Lys Blakeslee

Barakamon vol. 12 © 2015 Satsuki Yoshino SQUARE ENIX CO., LTD. First published in Japan in 2015 by SQUARE ENIX CO., LTD. English translation rights arranged with SQUARE ENIX CO., LTD. and Yen Press, LLC through Tuttle-Mori Agency, Inc.

English translation © 2016 by SQUARE ENIX CO., LTD.

Yen Press
1290 Avenue of the Americas
New York, NY 10104

Visit us at yenpress.com
facebook.com/yenpress
twitter.com/yenpress
yenpress.tumblr.com
instagram.com/yenpress

First Yen Press Edition: October 2016

Yen Press is an imprint of Yen Press, LLC.
The Yen Press name and logo are trademarks of Yen Press, LLC.

The publisher is not responsible for websites (or their content) that are not owned by the publisher.

Library of Congress Control Number: 2015296448

ISBNs: 978-0-316-54544-0 (paperback)
       978-0-316-46392-8 (ebook)
       978-0-316-46394-2 (app)

10 9 8 7 6 5 4 3 2 1

BVG

Printed in the United States of America